CALIFORNIA
GARDENER'S HANDBOOK

First published in 2013 by Cool Springs Press, an imprint of Quarto Publishing Group USA Inc., 400 First Avenue North, Suite 400, Minneapolis, MN 55401

The information in this book is true and complete to the best of our knowledge. All recommendations are made without any guarantee on the part of the author or Publisher, who also disclaims any liability incurred in connection with the use of this data or specific details.

Cool Springs Press titles are also available at discounts in bulk quantity for industrial or sales-promotional use. For details write to Special Sales Manager at Quarto Publishing Group USA Inc., 400 North First Avenue, Suite 400, Minneapolis, MN 55401 USA. To find out more about our books, visit us online at www.coolspringspress.com.

First published as *California Gardener's Resource*, 2009.

Library of Congress Cataloging-in-Publication Data

Asakawa, Bruce.
  California gardener's handbook : your complete guide : select, plan, plant, maintain, problem-solve / Bruce and Sharon Asakawa.
    p. cm.
  Includes index.
  First published as California gardener's resource, 2009.
  ISBN 978-1-59186-567-4 (softcover)
  1. Gardening--California. I. Asakawa, Sharon. II. Title.

SB453.2.C3A83 2013
635.09794--dc23

2013009475

Acquiring Editor: Billie Brownell
Design Manager: Cindy Samargia Laun
Layout: S. E. Anderson

Printed in China
10 9 8 7 6 5 4 3 2

Photography
William Adams: 20a, 98c, 103a, 107, 140, 142bc, 162b
Bruce Asakawa: 26c, 46a, 47b, 81c, 98b, 105ac, 111, 117b, 119c, 120a, 142a, 161c, 162c, 163c, 165ab, 173b, 178a, 234a, 235bc, 247b, 249c, 250bc, 252b, 253a
John Bagnasco: 198b
Liz Ball: 178b
Liz Ball and Rick Ray: 18a, 25b, 30b, 31b, 41b, 46c, 51a, 85a, 98a, 106b, 174c, 175a, 177c, 179c, 180a, 184, 211ab, 212a, 215c, 217b, 218a, 220, 229a, 230ac, 232ac, 242, 250a, 256a
Courtesy of Phil Bergman, www.junglemusic.com: 158b
Courtesy of The Bovees Nursery: 165c
Karen Bussolini: 29b, 30c
Mike Dirr: 50a
Thomas Eltzroth: 18b, 19ac, 20bc, 21abc, 22ac, 23abc, 24abc, 25a, 26b, 27abc, 28a, 29a, 30a, 37, 42a, 43a, 44ab, 45c, 46b, 48b, 49a, 50bc, 51bc, 58, 60ab, 61b, 62ab, 66, 70c, 74, 80c, 81b, 82b, 84a, 86a, 96b, 97ab, 99bc, 100abc, 101a, 102a, 103b, 104ab, 105b, 106a, 141abc, 158ac, 159b, 160ab, 161a, 163ab, 169, 172, 173a, 174ab, 175b, 176b, 177ab, 178c, 179ab, 180b, 190a, 199, 211c, 212bc, 213b, 214ac, 216bc, 217a, 218c, 223, 226, 227c, 228abc, 229bc, 230b, 231ab, 232b, 233ac, 234b, 235a, 236a, 248a, 251ab, 252ac, 253b, 254ab, 255ab, 256b, 257bc, 261
Lorenzo Gunn: 59b, 61c, 71abc, 79b, 82c, 85b, 96a, 99a, 101c, 102c, 103d, 110, 159ac, 160c, 164a, 213c, 214b, 215b, 216a, 227b, 231c, 233b, 234c, 236bc
Pam Harper: 97c
iStockphoto.com and its artists: 31a, 68, 70b, 80b, 81a, 83ab, 120bc, 122a, 126c, 129bc, 130a, 131b, 137, 164c, 244, 249a

Courtesy of Jackson & Perkins, www.jacksonandperkins.com: 189ab, 190c, 191a, 192abc, 193abc, 194bc, 195ab, 196c, 197abc, 198a, 200, 201, 206
Jupiter Images: 6, 8, 12, 14, 16, 28b, 38, 40, 43c, 57, 60c, 61a, 63, 67, 70a, 72, 76,78, 79a, 80a, 82a, 84bc, 85c, 86bc, 87, 88, 91, 92, 95, 112, 115, 116ab, 117a, 118abc, 119ab, 121, 122b, 123abc, 124abc, 125abc, 126bc, 127ab, 128abc, 130bc, 131a, 133, 136, 138, 152, 153, 154, 157, 162a, 166, 170, 176c, 185, 186, 207, 208, 210, 229, 243
Dency Kane: 105c
Langeveld Bulb Company, courtesy of Armstrong Garden Centers: 41a, 42b, 47a, 48c, 49b, 55
Kirsten Llamas: 43b
Peter Loewer: 117c
Dawn M. Miller, courtesy of Weeks Roses, www.weeksroses.com: 191c
Courtesy of Monrovia, www.monrovia.com: 161b, 213a, 215a, 217c, 218b, 253c
Jerry Pavia: 22b, 25c, 29c, 44a, 45a, 164b, 175c, 224
Photo courtesy of Proven Winners, www.provenwinners.com: 19b, 26a, 28c, 246, 247a, 248bc, 251c, 254c, 255c, 256c
Photo by Gene Sasse, courtesy of Weeks Roses, www.weeksroses. com: 191b, 196ab
Courtesy of Star® Roses, www.starroses.com: 194a, 195c
Nan Sterman: 257a
Mike Tomlinson, courtesy of Dave Wilson Nursery: 83c
UC Botanical Garden: 42c
Courtesy of Van Bourgondien, www.dutchbulbs.com: 45b, 49c
André Viette: 48a, 52, 102b
W. Atlee Burpee & Co.: 127c, 129a

CALIFORNIA
GARDENER'S HANDBOOK

YOUR COMPLETE GUIDE:
SELECT • PLAN • PLANT • MAINTAIN • PROBLEM-SOLVE

BRUCE AND SHARON ASAKAWA

COOL
SPRINGS
PRESS
Home and Garden Experts™
MINNEAPOLIS, MINNESOTA

CONTENTS

WELCOME to GARDENING
in California

One would have to travel through several nations to find the enormous variety of plants, climate and topography that exist in our state. To begin gardening here, gardeners who have moved from another part of the United States or from another country must learn about the different microclimates, soil conditions and plant materials of their areas.

Not only do growing conditions change dramatically from region to region, but they also change within these regions. The United States Department of Agriculture (USDA) cold-hardiness zone map on page 10 shows the approximate zones of average minimum temperatures. A zone assigned to an individual plant indicates the lowest temperature at which the plant can be expected to survive. California has eight of the twelve cold-hardiness zones (4 to 11) across its 160,000 square miles—more than any other state!

The preferred zone range assigned to each plant in this book is based partly on the USDA data, but also on our many years of experience, taking into account factors such as humidity, wind conditions, soil conditions, and salt tolerance. They represent the area in which a plant will grow best, not the only area in which the plant can grow (under certain conditions, one could grow a lemon tree in the mountains even though it would not be the plant's preferred area, although it would involve extra maintenance and care).

Also, in the central and northern regions of the state, seasonal events occur a few weeks later in the year than they do in the southern region.

In addition to these climate zones, every landscape has microclimates that will enhance or diminish a plant's ability to grow—sunny walls, established trees, high and low spots in the garden, etc. We recommend that gardeners record the temperature variations in their yards in order to help them make the best plant selections. So as you read about the time for soil amending and planting, for example, tomatoes, controlling insects and diseases, adjust in your mind the time frame, your microclimate and local variations that might affect the seasonal guidelines.

LAND OF TREMENDOUS DIVERSITY

California is 770 miles long and 250 miles wide. The state lies between 32° 30' and 42° north latitude. These latitudes north or south of the equator include the cities of Haifa, Casablanca, Kyoto, Sydney, Santiago and Cape Town. They represent regions of the world that have similar climate and growing conditions as California. The 163,707 square miles of land that forms our Golden State provides its own set of native plants that can be combined with imported (exotic) plants from all these regions. This means that California is blessed with diversity—diversity in its people, diversity in its geography and diversity in its plants.

California is also a land of astonishing geologic formations. It is a geologic area formed by the north-south peninsular mountain ranges to the east and the east-west Transverse Mountain ranges to the north, offering a Mediterranean climate with subtropical temperatures and lavish vegetation. The Pacific Ocean also moderates potential temperature extremes, resulting in an ideal environment for growing both native and imported plants.

The world's tallest trees, the majestic coastal redwoods, live on a thin veneer of soil along California's northwest coast, capturing water through fog drip, a process where coastal moisture condenses on the trees, accumulates and rains to the ground, creating a moist home for native plants. On the western slope of the Sierra Nevada, the world's supply of straight, dense and aromatic wood for pencils is harvested from California's incense cedar. Its young branches and foliage are also woven into decorative cedar roping for the holidays. The sole species of palm tree endemic to California is the California fan palm, found near the extreme western end of the Sonoran Desert in Riverside and Imperial Valley. Travel north of the Peninsular ranges, across the Transverse ranges, and you enter the Mojave Desert, known as the "high desert," home of the unique Joshua trees, the creosote bush (one of the oldest living plants), and the California Poppy Reserve. The area is subject to severe temperature fluctuations, freezing in the winter and broiling in the summer.

The Coastal Mountain range extends northward from the western end of the Transverse ranges and parallel to the Pacific Ocean. This is where stands of California Live Oaks and Monterey Pines anchor the sky to the earth. Continuing northward along the coast to the San Francisco Bay area, the influence of the Pacific pushes farther inland as the ocean moisture moves through the delta regions and moderates the extreme temperatures of the vineyard-filled Napa Valley. As you move further inland toward Redding, on the eastern side of the Coastal range of the mountains the geography is dominated by the southern end of the Cascade Mountains, where soils are of volcanic origin.

The Great Central Valley, which includes Sacramento and the San Joaquin Valleys, is one of the most intense agricultural growing regions in the world, with alluvial soils that make it the most fertile land in California. The Central Valley is bounded on the east by the Sierra Nevada, and on the west by Coastal Mountain ranges.

Weather is another important influence in the seasonal variations of California. The weather emanating in the Pacific Northwest surges southward through Oregon's southern Cascades before entering California's northern tier of counties. Late in summer and in early fall, northerly winds storm through the communities of Red Bluff, Weed and Redding into the northern Sacramento Valley. When there is a high-pressure cell over Utah and Nevada's Great Basin, the air heats up, rises, loses its moisture and accelerates as it descends in a southwesterly direction. This weather phenomenon is similar to the Foehn of Switzerland, the Mistrals of France and the Chinooks of the eastern Rockies. Unless watered thoroughly before the winds arrive, these hot, dry winds desiccate plants.

CALIFORNIA GARDENING: REWARDS

A tremendous reward of gardening throughout most of California is the year-long growing season. The nursery industry does not shut down in the fall as it does in other states. This year-long growing season coupled with the continuously growing

population, has allowed California to become one of the world's leaders in the nursery industry.

The chapters on annuals, bulbs, citrus and nut trees and fruits, groundcovers and vines, lawns, palms and tropical plants, perennials, roses, shrubs, trees and waterwise plants all include indigenous plants as well as many others from around the world that thrive in California. Our state may be known for its native plant diversity, but we estimate that at least ninety percent of the plant material used for landscaping comes from other parts of the world. Some of the exotic plants have actually displaced many of California's native plants. You might see a hibiscus from China, a bird of paradise from South Africa, an amaryllis (actually a *Hippeastrum*) from South America and a Persian buttercup from Europe, all coexisting in the same landscape.

At the end of each chapter, there are brief month-by-month planting, care and maintenance guidelines to insure that your plants—whether native or non-native—will thrive in the landscape. Bruce and I have taken horticultural trips all over the world to view a large number of our plant

POPPY

entries in their native habitats, and we will share this information with our readers.

CALIFORNIA GARDENING: CHALLENGES

The countless variations in California's climates and soils bring their share of challenges. There are periods of drought, dry winds and a scarcity of chill hours in the coastal climates, all conditions that could limit the varieties that can be grown in certain areas.

Californians are also facing harsher economic realities, limited or diminishing natural resources—especially water—overpopulation, pollution consequences and recycling issues. Housing density shrinks the space available for gardening, and the scale of gardening may become smaller. Consulting these pages will help answer the questions: How does a gardener deal with California's horticultural diversity, and how do we responsibly address all the gardening challenges in the present and in the future?

THE CONCEPT OF A SUSTAINABLE LANDSCAPE

This book also embraces the concept of sustainable landscapes. From an ecological and practical standpoint, it is important to plan for and incorporate this practice rather than the traditional design of expansive lawns and water-thirsty plant selections. The main emphasis is to select plants that should be able to sustain themselves for two or three growing seasons without supplemental irrigation. Their survival would rely solely on seasonal rainfall.

Two considerations are needed to develop a sustainable garden. The first is to select the right combination of plants, those that fill the functional and cultural needs of your garden design. The second is to position the plants where they can optimize their growth. In short, it is the right plant in the right place. These two considerations include the steps necessary to establish the right plant and to select a location that optimizes the plant's potential. Once the right plants are selected, positioned and established, they fend for themselves during adverse conditions, such as periods of drought, desiccating winds and searing heat, freezing cold or torrential rains. In the case of drought, they might not look their best after a prolonged period of dryness, but they should be resilient and flourish once more when water is available.

The concept of a sustainable landscape is to group the plants that need the least amount of water in the most strategic locations. These plants, including trees, are the first-tier plants and the most important groupings. Once first-tier plants become established, they remain viable through one or two seasons of drought. They might not look good, they might even defoliate, but if they are the right plants in the right places, they will resume their growth when conditions become more supportive. Second-tier plants sustain growth with deep irrigation once a month during the growing season and third-tier plants perish if they are not irrigated once a week.

To make appropriate decisions about first-, second- and third-tier plants, survey your neighborhood for plants that have been growing for at least ten years.

USE THIS BOOK AS A GUIDELINE

Since most California seasons are never as defined as the specific days or months of a calendar, it is important to use the information in this book as a guideline. If there is one reality we have learned during the past fifty years talking on the radio to gardening aficionados and visiting many wonderful gardens of the world, it is that there is never just one way to be successful at gardening, but if you care for your plants based primarily on your observations and experience, chances are your garden will flourish.

USDA COLD-HARDINESS ZONES

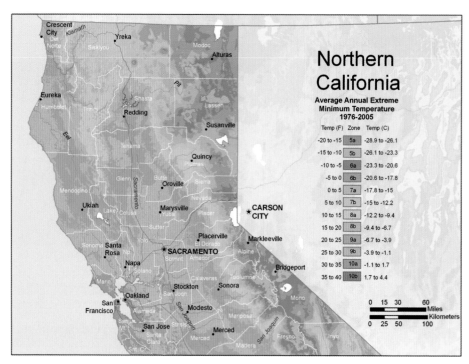

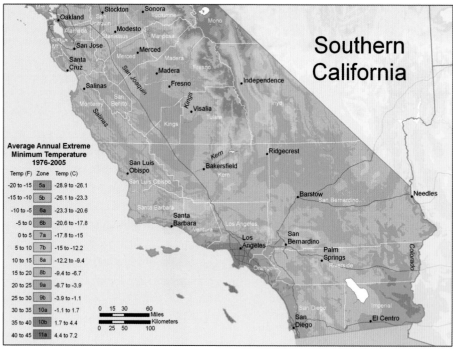

PREFERRED ZONES—Cold-hardiness zone designations were developed by the United States Department of Agriculture (USDA) to indicate the minimum average temperature for an area. A zone assigned to an individual plant indicates the lowest temperature at which the plant can be expected to survive over the winter. California has an extremely wide zone range, from zone 4 to zone 11. The preferred zone range assigned to each plant in this book is based partly on the USDA cold-hardiness zone range, but mostly on our many years of experience. Our preferred zone recommendations take into account factors such as humidity, wind conditions, soil conditions, and salt tolerance. They represent the area in which a plant will grow best, not the only area in which the plant can grow.

ANNUAL PRECIPITATION

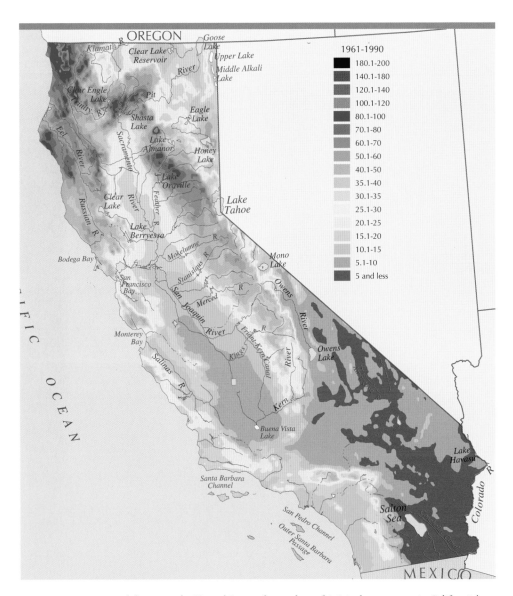

Precipitation varies widely across the United States, from a low of 2.3 inches per year in California's Death Valley, to a high of 460 inches on Hawaii's Mount Waialeale. Nevada ranks as the driest state, with an average annual precipitation of 9.5 inches, and Hawaii is the wettest at 70.3 inches. The average annual precipitation for California is 21.44 inches.

Above: This information was provided courtesy www.nationalatlas.com.

Opposite: USDA Plant Hardiness Zone Maps, 2012. Agricultural Research Service, U.S. Department of Agriculture. Accessed from http://planthardiness.ars.usda.gov.

JOSHUA TREE

HOW TO USE THE CALIFORNIA GARDENER'S HANDBOOK

Each entry in this book includes specific information about each plant, including its botanical and common name, when it blooms and how large it gets, and so on. I've included information about the best time to plant and the best spot for each plant, along with its long-term care, watering, pruning, fertilizing, and the pests you are most likely to encounter. Each entry suggest ways to use the plan in your garden, as well as a description of varieties that may be different sizes or bloom in different colors or in different seasons.

Be sure to watch for the icons that tell you how much sun and water each plant needs, as well as some of its other interesting characteristics such as whether it is edible, attracts butterflies, works along the coast, and more.

SUN PREFERENCES

Full sun is six hours or more of direct sun per day. Part sun is four to six hours of direct sun, preferably in the morning with protection from hot afternoon sun. Part shade is two to four hours of direct sun per day, primarily in the morning, or all day bright indirect light. Shade means all indirect light or dappled shade.

Full Sun   Part Sun   Part Shade   Shade

WATER USAGE REQUIREMENTS

High-water plants do best in soils that are consistently damp but not saturated. Medium-water plants need water when the soil is dry 3 to 6 inches down from the surface. Low-water plants need very little water once they are established.

High   Medium   Low

LANDSCAPING TIPS & IDEAS

In this section, I make suggestions about ways to incorporate each plant into your garden's design to create a beautiful garden bed, a lovely composition of potted plants, or solve a common gardening problem. I also suggest plant combinations based on similarity of cultural needs and the aesthetics of their combinations. You will find wonderful varieties of each plant, or a related plant, or even an alternate plant to serve the same purpose in the garden. A note about using these plants: There simply is not enough room to include every variety, so use these lists as starting points. There are countless more species and varieties that will perform beautifully in your garden. Don't be afraid to experiment.

ADDITIONAL BENEFITS

Many plants offer benefits that further enhance their appeal. The following symbols indicate some of the more interesting benefits:

 Attracts butterflies and/or moths

 Attracts hummingbirds

 Some or all parts of this plant are edible

 Leaves or flowers are fragrant

 Plants make attractive fruits

 Flowers, leaves, branches, and/or fruits are suitable for bouquets or cut flower arrangements

 Long blooming

 California native

 Supports bees

 Provides food or shelter for wildlife (including birds other than hummingbirds)

 Has colorful foliage

 Drought tolerant

 Grows well in a container

 Grows well in Mediterranean climate conditions

 Adds a tropical look to the garden

 Tolerates beach conditions (bright sun, wind, and/or salt spray)

ANNUALS
for California

Annuals bring serendipitous bursts of color to permanent plantings. A mixture of annuals with perennials, shrubs, groundcovers and even fruits and vegetables creates an interplay of texture and color, a living orchestra. Permanent plants may require far less care than annuals and they may flower quite heavily during certain seasons, but most annuals "bloom their heads off" over a very long period of time.

THE MERITS OF ANNUALS

With their vividly painted faces and interesting shapes, sizes and scents, they attract pollinating birds, bees and other insects. While there are differences in growth, bloom and seed cycles, most annuals have evolved to survive during the brief growing season from the time the snow pack melts until summer or autumn winds dry out the landscape. Yet, in mild-winter areas, many act like perennials.

Annuals more than compensate for their short lifespan by helping define the rhythms of the seasonal garden. Cool-weather annuals, such as Iceland Poppy, Pansy, Wood Violets, and Phlox, grow and blossom during winter and spring. When planted in warmer regions in the fall, many cool-weather annuals continue to bloom until the heat and humidity of summer peaks. When they fade, you can replace them with hot-weather lovers such as Cosmos, Ageratum and Alyssum. Many are already in flower when you plant them in early spring and they continue to bloom until the first frost in fall. Some, such as Coleus, may even last through winter if protected from the cold.

Some annuals, like California Poppies and Nasturtiums, are excellent when planted en masse for spectacular splashes of garden color. Others, like Alyssum, Ageratum, and Pansies are well suited for borders and low edging around beds and walkways. Climbing Sweet Peas can be used as quick-growing screens. Many annuals are sources of cut, dried or edible flowers.

Less expensive and less permanent than shrubs, trees and perennials, annuals allow for greater experimentation and frivolous fun. Use them to brighten a shady area, fill in a blank space or cover a spent bulb bed.

If flower color is the fortissimo in your garden symphony, the diminuendo is the muted qualities of annual foliage. The fresh, green, rounded leaves of Nasturtiums and the foliage of some California Poppies make beautiful ornamentals by themselves.

WHEN AND HOW TO PLANT ANNUALS

Annuals can be started by seed or from containers. The most economical way is to start from seeds, and it can be very rewarding to see those tiny leaves popping up in flats. Seeds sown indoors are safe from being washed out by torrential rains, eaten by birds, nipped in the bud by frost, or choked to death by weeds.

As a general rule, delay sowing seeds outdoors or setting out starter plants until the soil warms to about 60 degrees Fahrenheit—although Phlox, Poppies, Alyssum, and Sweet Pea may be set out sooner. Start seed indoors about eight weeks prior to the last frost in your area, or anytime if winters are mild. By setting starter plants in your garden, you can get a jump-start on flowers, which will appear several weeks earlier than if you sow seeds directly in the beds.

For the highest rate of germination for annuals sown from seed, use a starter flat indoors or cold frame outdoors and create half-inch furrows filled with potting soil. Sprinkle with water, make another shallow furrow in the soil, place the seed in this furrow, cover the seed with another layer of potting soil, and water thoroughly with a fine mist. Consult the directions on seed packets for planting depth, spacing, and thinning recommendations.

INSTANT COLOR VS. A LONGER SEASON

To add instant color with bedding plants, you can buy them in containers or flats already in flower. If you need a finished-looking garden immediately, buy the plants in flower; but for a longer blooming performance, look for smaller plants that have not yet formed flower buds. Since annuals grow fast, buying them small allows the plants to adapt to

LARKSPUR

your garden conditions more easily before expending energy on flowers. You can also start fertilizing earlier, the plants are less likely to be root bound (which stunts growth), and you can pinch back earlier to promote branching and compact growth.

DO A LITTLE EXPLORING

To determine what annuals are doing well in your region and which are most attractive to you, visit public and private gardens in your area, consult your local nursery, or your University of California Cooperative Extension office. There is also nothing wrong with the learn-by-doing method, especially with annuals, since they are relatively easy to grow, inexpensive, and can be replaced two or three times a year. As in life, there are no mistakes in gardening, only learning experiences.

With so many annual varieties, there is bound to be a suitable choice for any purpose—whether to brighten an area around the dark foliage of background shrubs, to fill in flower beds, to overplant bulb beds for color after spring-flowering bulbs are spent, or to bring the outdoors indoors with vases of cut-flower bouquets. With just a little effort and planning, you can have your symphony of color from spring through fall, even all year-round in mild-winter regions, amidst your stalwart trees, shrubs, perennials, groundcovers, and edible crops. The addition of annuals brings music to all your senses.

IMPORTANT TO READ THE SEED PACKET INFORMATION

The information listed on seed packets is important, especially when the seeds should be started before planting them outdoors. While six to eight weeks in the usual time for many annuals such as Ageratum and Dusty Miller, Impatiens and Snapdragons need about ten weeks before outdoor life. Early germinators including Cosmos and Marigold, only need about four weeks. Also, some specialty hybrids may take more or less time than their generic cousins.

To take the guesswork out of when to sow seeds indoors, count back from the last average frost date in your area and chart the start dates of your selected seeds. If you sow them before that charted date, you may end up with leggy and weak seedlings because they have grown too long indoors. Allow an additional two weeks to "harden" your tender seedlings by taking them outdoors for longer and longer periods during the day and increasing the sun exposure before transplanting them. Near the end of the second week, they should be acclimated enough to stay outdoors overnight.

Double-check for any special requirements. Some seeds, such as Morning Glory and Sweet Peas, require scarifying (scratching or nicking the seed with a file or sand paper to help germination). Others, such as varieties of wildflowers, need stratifying (the process to overcome dormancy by cold treatment, usually wrapping seeds in a moistened paper towel, placing them in a re-sealable plastic bag, and setting in a refrigerator's vegetable bin for about a month).

Seed packets also tell you everything you should know about planting depth, amount of light, and whether or not the variety needs light or darkness for germination. Some annual seeds prefer light, such as Four o' Clocks and Sunflowers, while others grow in darkness, like Celosia.

Just as on milk cartons, look for a seed packet's expiration date. Last year's date may affect the seed's viability. To determine their viability place 10 seeds on a moistened paper towel, fold the towel in half, and put it in a sealed plastic bag. Set the bag in a warm location such as on top of the refrigerator. Check periodically up to fifteen days. Determine the germination percentage by counting the number of sprouted seeds. For example, if five or seven seeds sprouted, then that rate is 50 to 70 percent. If this is the case, sow the seeds more thickly than recommended to compensate for the lower germination percentage. Discard the seeds into a compost pile when germination is less than 50 percent, unless you don't mind the extra work.

SUPPLIES FOR SEED PROPAGATION

Germinating seeds indoors makes it easier to maintain a suggested average air temperature between 65 and 70 degrees Fahrenheit. You need:

- Well-draining, organic potting soil or a soil-less mix for starting seeds.
- Heating mat to keep the soil temperature at 65 to 70 degrees Fahrenheit.
  (Follow the temperature recommendations on the seed packet).
- 2-inch-diameter peat pots or expandable peat pellets, known as Jiffy 7's, which contain starter nutrients and a fungicide to control pathogens, such as damping off. (Since peat pots or peat pellets degrade readily, they can be planted directly into the ground without taking the seedlings out and possibly damaging their tender roots).
- Cart or shelving with grow lights if there is insufficient natural light indoors.
- Nurseries commonly sell their starter plants in six- or eight-cell plastic containers. After the plants have been removed, they can be reused instead of thrown away. Simply sterilize in a solution of one part bleach to ten parts water to prevent a spread of fungal or bacterial disease.

AGERATUM
Ageratum houstonianum

Hardiness—All zones

Color(s)—Blue, lavender, lilac, mauve, pink, and white flowers

Bloom Period—Spring through autumn

Mature Size (H & W)—6 to 8 in. x 8 to 10 in.

Water Needs—Water once or twice a week during hot, dry weather.

Planting/Care—Plant from seed or from color packs in spring after the last frost, spacing them 8 in. apart. Ageratums prefer a rich, moist, loam soil with a pH of 6.7 to 7.0. Fertilize in spring and summer and deadhead regularly to prolong the blooming season.

Pests/Diseases—Low-growing Ageratum is a haven for slugs and snails. Control with a molluscicide such as iron phosphate. Also watch out for sow bugs and earwigs.

Landscaping Tips & Ideas—Ideal for mixed flower beds, as edging along borders or towards the front of containers. Phlox, Shasta Daisy and Daylily are ideal companion plants. For a taller variety select 'Blue Horizon' but for a low grower choose 'Blue Danube'.

ALYSSUM
Lobularia maritima / Alyssum maritimum

Hardiness—All zones

Color(s)—White, pink, rose-red, violet, and lilac

Bloom Period—Spring through fall

Mature Size (H & W)—4 in. x 6 to 12 in.

Water Needs—Once or twice a week depending on weather/ growth conditions.

Planting/Care—Plant in spring, spacing 6 to 8 in. apart. Prefers well-drained, moist loam soil with a pH of 6.8-7.0. Fertilize every 4-6 weeks with an organic fertilizer. Clip the plant back 50% after the first flush of blossoms to prolong the flowering season.

Pests/Diseases—Not susceptible to many diseases or pests, but inspect foliage and flowers regularly for chewing insects.

Landscaping Tips & Ideas—Use Alyssum in rock gardens or as a ground cover in mixed flower beds or as an edging in containers. Sweet Alyssum grows well with Shore Juniper, Daylily, Lily of the Nile and Wallflower.

ANGELONIA
Angelonia augustifolia

Hardiness—All zones

Color(s)—Rose, plum, blue, lavender, white and combination stripes, and bicolors

Bloom Period—Spring to autumn

Mature Size (H & W)—18 to 36 in. x 18 in.

Water Needs—Once or twice a week depending on soil and weather conditions.

Planting/Care—Needs well-draining, loam soil with a pH of 6.8-7.0 and space them 6-8 in. apart. Fertilize with a slow-release or organic food every 4-6 weeks during growth and bloom periods. Deadhead regularly to prolong blooming.

Pests/Diseases—If chewing insect or snail and slug damage is extensive, use Spinosad to control chewing insects and an iron phosphate molluscicide for snails and slugs.

Landscaping Tips/Ideas—With their miniature orchid-like clusters of flowers, the Angelface® hybrids are perfect in mixed borders or in containers and they love the heat.

BACOPA/SUTERA
Sutera hybrids

Hardiness—All zones

Color(s)—Blue, white, pink and lavender

Bloom Period—Spring through fall

Mature Size (H & W)—3 to 5 in. x 3 to 5 in.

Water Needs—Water every 5-7 days.

Planting/Care—Prefers slightly acid, well-draining, loam soils and may also need supplemental iron and cottonseed meal fertilizer during growth and bloom cycles.

Pests/Diseases—Fairly disease and insect resistant

Landscaping Tips & Ideas—Unlike most plants, Sutera will not wilt when drought stressed, but will drop its flowers and buds and take about two weeks for the plant to return into bloom. Snowstorm® 'Giant Snowflake' is more mounded and upright than trailing varieties and fills in bare spots in the garden or mixed containers. Good companion plants are Verbena, Coleus and Petunias.

CALENDULA
Calendula officinalis

Hardiness—All zones

Color(s)—Yellow, orange and cream

Bloom Period—Spring through fall or until first frost

Mature Size (H & W)—12 to 30 in. x 12-30 in.

Water Needs—Water every 7 to 10 days, more frequently during warmer weather.

Planting/Care—Available as color packs or as seeds. Needs only average, but well-drained soil and regular feedings during growth and bloom cycles. During hot summer months, cut back and they will bloom again in the fall.

Pests/Diseases—Resistant to most pests and diseases except powdery mildew, which can be controlled with horticultural oil or an organic fungicide.

Landscaping Tips & Ideas—Use with Snapdragons and Pansies in flower beds, borders or containers or vegetable beds. It is also known as Pot Marigold because the outer flower petals are used in cooking as a flavoring and to add color to soups, salads and stews.

CALIBRACHOA
Calibrachoa hybrids

Hardiness—All zones

Color(s)—Yellow, orange, red, pink, purple, and white

Bloom Period—Spring through fall.

Mature Size (H & W)—6 to 12 in. x 6 to 12 in. depending on variety.

Water Needs—Water every 7-10 days or 5-7 days if in containers

Planting/Care—Space plants about 8-12 inches apart and use a well-draining soil. Keep the soil on the acidic side by fertilizing with cottonseed meal and supplement with a foliar feed.

Pests/Diseases—Few diseases and pests. except aphids and chewing insects; wash off aphids with a strong stream of water, and spray with Spinosad for chewing insect control.

Landscaping Tips & Ideas—Superbells® are fast-growing, disease and heat-resistant and produce hundreds of small petunia-like blooms. They are self-cleaning, water-thrifty and cascade over hanging baskets, containers. Million Bells® are more upright and flower even during short days.

CALIFORNIA POPPY
Eschscholzia californica

Hardiness—All zones

Color(s)—Orange or yellow, but hybrids come in creamy white, scarlet, copper, or pinkish-red

Bloom Period—Spring

Mature Size (H & W)—8 to 12 in. x 8 to 12 in.

Water Needs—Water as needed every 1-2 weeks

Planting/Care—Plant from color packs in spring or broadcast seed before fall rains. California poppies prefer sandy loam soil. Fertilize with an organic fertilizer during the growing season once every 4-6 weeks. Leave the spent flowers alone for seed production and dispersal. Keep the area free of weeds for best growing conditions.

Pests/Diseases—Unless damage is extensive, handpick and squash snails and slugs.

Landscaping Tips & Ideas—Grow en masse in expansive areas near edges of lawns, on sunny slopes or naturalized in rock gardens. Plant with other California natives or water-thrifty plants or Bird of Paradise, Shore Juniper and Silverberry.

CANDYTUFT
Iberis umbellata

Hardiness—All zones

Color(s)—White, lilac, pink, and red

Bloom Period—Spring until first frost

Mature Size (H & W)—12 to 18 in. x 12 to 18 in.

Water Needs—Water every 7-10 days

Planting/Care—Plant in early spring from color packs or seeds. Space plants in well-draining soil 6-12 inches apart and set in full sun. Seeds germinate quickly and easily when sown directly outdoors. Remove faded flowers to prolong bloom.

Pests/Diseases—Candytuft is susceptible to root rot, so allow to dry out slightly between watering.

Landscaping Tips & Ideas—Taller and less compact than its perennial cousin, it is just as beautiful when planted en masse in flower beds, borders, rock gardens or containers. 'Giant Hyacinth Flowered' is a British florist's type of Candytuft with 15-inch stems and large, white Hyacinth-like blooms that are great for cut flowers and in the garden.

CAPE MALLOW
Anisodontea hybrids

Hardiness—All zones

Color(s)—Rose, pastel pink and cranberry red

Bloom Period—Spring to fall, all year in warm areas

Mature Size (H & W)—24 to 36 in. x 24 to 36 in.

Water Needs—Water regularly every 7-10 days until established.

Planting/Care—Plant in full sun except where summers are very hot, plant in part shade. Cape Mallows need well-draining, fairly rich soils and frequent watering, but once established become water-thrifty. Fertilize during growth and bloom cycles.

Diseases—Watch out for spider mites, white fly and aphids and if spraying with a strong stream of water does not control them, use a systemic miticide or horticultural oil.

Landscaping Tips & Ideas—Recent hybrids such as 'Barely Boysenberry' are heat lovers and have upright habits. These hybrids have a more compact form and behave well in a mixed planting bed towards the middle or back or in a container.

COCKSCOMB
Celosia spp.

Hardiness—All zones

Color(s)—Orange, red, gold, pink, yellow, and purple

Bloom Period—Summer to fall

Mature Size (H & W)—12 to 36 in. x 6 to 18 in.

Water Needs—Water every 5-7 days.

Planting/Care—Cockscombs need average but well-drained soil planted by seed or color packs in spring. Use a slow-release or organic fertilizer every 4-6 weeks.

Pests/Diseases—Stem rot can be a problem in soggy soils, so amend the soil very well for good drainage. Control spider mite infestations with a miticide.

Landscaping Tips & Ideas—Flowers can resemble feathery plumes (*C.* 'Plumosa'), cockscombs or fans (*C.* 'Cristata') that grow 2-3 ft. tall or dwarf-sized at 10-12 in. They make bright, exotic accents in beds, borders and containers. Take advantage of their many dramatic forms in cut or dried flower arrangements.

COSMOS
Cosmos bipinnatus

Hardiness—All zones

Color(s)—Orange or yellow, but hybrids come in creamy white, scarlet, copper, or pinkish-red

Bloom Period—Spring

Mature Size (H & W)—8 to 12 in. x 8 to 12 in.

Water Needs—Water as needed every 1-2 weeks

Planting/Care—Plant from color packs in spring or broadcast seed before fall rains. Fertilize with an organic fertilizer during the growing season once every 4-6 weeks. Leave the spent flowers alone for seed production and dispersal. Keep the area free of weeds for best growing conditions.

Pests/Diseases—Unless damage is extensive, handpick and squash snails and slugs.

Landscaping Tips & Ideas—Grow en masse in expansive areas near edges of lawns, on sunny slopes or naturalized in rock gardens. Plant with other California natives or water-thrifty plants or Bird of Paradise, Shore Juniper and Silverberry.

DUSTY MILLER
Senecio cineraria

Hardiness—All zones

Color(s)—Silver white foliage, yellow flowers

Bloom Period—Not significant

Mature Size (H & W)—8 to 16 in. x 8 to 12 in.

Water Needs—Water every 7-10 days once plant is established.

Planting/Care—Start from plants, cuttings or seeds and plant outdoors when the evening temperatures are in the 50s F. To promote foliar growth, deadhead the flowers.

Pests/Diseases—Foliage is deer resistant. Avoid root rot by allowing soil to dry out between watering.

Landscaping Tips & Ideas—Dusty Miller's silver-grey foliage is a dramatic contrast to more colorful plants and looks great in the front of borders or in mixed containers and window boxes as well as highlighting the evening garden. For a different flower arrangement, use the foliage with red roses or other colorful flowers.

FLOWERING TOBACCO (NICOTIANA)
Nicotiana alata

Hardiness—All zones

Color(s)—Lime green, white, pink, and red

Bloom Period—Summer to fall

Mature Size (H & W)—12 to 48 in. x 12 in.

Water Needs—Water about once a week.

Planting/Care—Needs full sun in cool-summer areas, but for warmer regions, provide partial shade. Plant from color packs or seeds in spring after the last day of frost and space about 12 in. apart.

Pests/Diseases—Leafminer larva produce distinctive tunnels in the leaf. Cut off damaged leaves or if infestation is extensive, spray with Spinosad.

Landscaping Tips & Ideas—Deer-resistant but since all parts of plant are toxic, including the seed, keep away from small children and pets. 'Lime Green' bears distinctive fresh lime flowers and contrasts beautifully with Impatiens, Salvias and Lobelias. For an intensely perfumed stalk of white flowers, plant *N.* 'Grandiflora'. It's wonderful in containers, mixed flower beds or naturalized.

FOUR O'CLOCK
Mirabilis jurapa

Hardiness—All zones

Color(s)—Red, pink, yellow and white

Bloom Period—Summer to fall

Mature Size (H & W)—18 to 36 in. x 18 to 24 in.

Water Needs—Water every 5-7 days.

Planting/Care—Commonly grown from seeds sown directly into the garden just after the last frost date. Thin seedlings to 24 inches. Prefers full sun, but tolerate part shade. Plant in compost-rich well-draining soil and feed with an organic fertilizer every 4 weeks and supplement with liquid kelp during growth and bloom periods.

Pests/Diseases—Pests and diseases are few, but if problems persist, treat with organic repellents and fungicides.

Landscaping Tips & Ideas—Fragrant Four o' Clock flowers should be planted where people will notice them in the early evening hours because they stay open at night. They are also perfect in borders and as hedging. All parts are toxic, so keep away from children and pets.

HOLLYHOCK
Alcea rosea

Hardiness—All zones

Color(s)—Pink, red, white, yellow, peach, and black

Bloom Period—Late spring or early summer

Mature Size (H & W)—2 to 9 ft. x 18 to 24 in.

Water Needs—Water every 5-7 days.

Planting/Care—Plant in humus-rich, well-draining soil in full sun with good air circulation, but avoid areas of heavy wind. If planting from seed, buy cultivars that are listed as annuals to get flowers the first year.

Pests/Diseases—Prone to rust caused by wet, humid weather. Avoid watering overhead, cut off and dispose of diseased leaves, and if the problem persists, spray with a horticultural oil or systemic fungicide. Pick off caterpillars by hand.

Landscaping Tips & Ideas—Hollyhocks are must-haves in cottage style gardens, along a fence, as a focal point in large containers and towards the back of planting beds. For eye-popping drama, plant 'Double Apricot' and 'Black' varieties.

ICELAND POPPY
Papaver nudicaule

Hardiness—All zones

Color(s)—White, yellow, orange or red flowers

Bloom Period—Spring to summer

Mature Size (H & W)—8 to 12 in. x 10 in.

Water Needs—Water every 7-10 days as needed.

Planting/Care—Grow best where the nights are cool and the days are warm. Plant in fall in well-draining soil with a pH of 6.89-7.0. To extend the bloom season, deadhead regularly.

Pests/Diseases—There are few disease or insect problems, but Spinosad and horticultural oil are effective controls of chewing insects and many fungal diseases.

Landscaping Tips & Ideas—Use as an ornamental in mixed flower beds, as a border plant and in containers. They grow well with Pansies and Rock Rose. For cut flowers, immerse the ends in boiling water, then set in cold water for a couple of hours before arranging (to prevent the loss of latex and avoid flower wilt).

JOHNNY-JUMP-UP
Viola cornuta

Hardiness—All zones

Color(s)—Blue, yellow, purple, white, and bicolors

Bloom Period—Early spring, fall, winter

Mature Size (H & W)—6 to 10 in. x 3 to 6 in.

Water Needs—Once or twice a week

Planting/Care—Available in color packs or seed. Plant after the last frost date and space 6 inches apart. Will do best in full sun, but in warmer areas, provide partial shade. Plant in well-draining soil to avoid root rot problems. Add an organic fertilizer about once a month during growth and bloom cycles. Deadhead to extend bloom season, but heat will shorten its life.

Pests/Diseases—Control snails and slugs with iron phosphate.

Landscaping Tips & Ideas—Johnny-Jump-Ups have smaller, but more numerous blossoms compared to Pansies and are ideal for hanging baskets and containers. They can also be used in mass plantings for a cool season groundcover over bulbs.

LARKSPUR
Consolida ajacis (Delphinium ambiguum)

Hardiness—All zones

Color(s)—Blue, lavender, white, rose, pink, blue and white bicolors

Bloom Period—Early spring through early summer

Mature Size (H & W)—12 to 36 in. x 12 to 18 in.

Water Needs—Water every 5 to 7 days.

Planting/Care—Available in color packs or seeds. Larkspur does best in cool weather, so plant in fall or early spring. Protect from strong winds, stake if needed and use an organic fertilizer. Since all parts of Larkspur are toxic, even the seed, keep away from children and pets.

Pests/Diseases—Avoid root rot by making sure the soil drains well and not soggy. Overcrowding and moisture on the foliage can cause powdery mildew.

Landscaping Tips & Ideas—Larkspur is popular in cottage gardens. 'Chorus Violet' and Imperial 'Allouette' stand on tiptoes at 4 feet and combine beautifully with Poppies, Roses, Lavender, Geraniums, and Phlox.

LOBELIA
Lobelia erinus

Hardiness—All zones

Color(s)—Blue, pink, purple, and white

Bloom Period—Summer to first frost

Mature Size (H & W)—3 to 6 in. x 5 to 18 in. wide, depending on variety

Water Needs—Water every 5-7 days depending on weather and bloom cycles.

Planting/Care—Available as color packs and seeds. Plant after the last frost date or in mild-winter areas, in the fall. Lobelias prefer full sun or partial shade (in hot summer regions), rich, well-amended soil.

Pests/Diseases—If pervasive, control spider mites with a miticide and thrips with Spinosad. Botrytis is a fungal disease that occurs during cool, wet spring months. Pull out infected plants and dispose in the trash.

Landscaping Tips & Ideas—Compact forms such as 'Fountain Blue' or 'Crystal Palace' are used for border edging and trailing varieties like the Cascade series in containers or hanging baskets.

MARIGOLD
Tagetes spp.

Hardiness—All zones

Color(s)—Orange, yellow, reddish-brown, and white

Bloom Period—June until frost

Mature Size (H & W)—6 to 36 in. x 6 to 36 in. depending on species/variety

Water Needs—Water every 5-7 days during warm weather.

Planting/Care—Plant from color pack or seeds and space 10-30 inches apart depending on cultivar in richly amended soil after the last frost date in well-draining soil and full sun. Deadhead regularly.

Pests/Diseases—Control powdery mildew with an organic fungicide or horticultural oil. Avoid damping off by making sure the soil drains well.

Landscaping Tips & Ideas—*T. erecta* and *T. lucida* have open and upright growth, while *T. patula* and *T. signata* tend to be more compact and spreading. *T.* 'Cempoalxochitl' grows into a giant 3-6 ft. tall, stand alone focal plant, but *T. patula* 'Bonanza' is perfect for edging borders or in mixed containers.

MORNING GLORY
Ipomoea spp.

Hardiness—All zones

Color(s)—Lavender, blue, red, pink, white, or bicolors

Bloom Period—Summer to fall

Mature Size (H & W)—10 to 15 ft. x 12 in. vine

Water Needs—Water every 5-7 days.

Planting/Care—Morning Glory needs a sturdy support such as a trellis, rust-proof wire or existing structure (fence, wall). Thrives in full sun, in average soil with adequate moisture. For abundant flowers, avoid chemical fertilizers. Propagates easily from cuttings or seeds planted in spring.

Pests/Diseases—For chewing insects, hand pick and squash or spray with Spinosad.

Landscaping Tips & Ideas—Morning Glories (*I. nil*, *I. tricolor*) add a colorful vertical interest to the garden, cascading over walls and fences or containers and combine beautifully with other cottage garden flowers. Most cultivars open in the morning and close in the afternoon. *I. tricolor* 'Heavenly Blue' is one of the most popular bearing large 5 in. flowers.

MOSS ROSE
Portulaca grandiflora

Hardiness—All zones

Color(s)—Red, pink, orange, yellow, and white

Bloom Period—Summer to fall

Mature Size (H & W)—6 in. x 18 in.

Water Needs—Water sparingly, likes to dry out between waterings.

Planting/Care—Moss Rose does best in hot, dry conditions and needs excellent drainage. Sandy soils and slopes are ideal places to plant. Provide at least 6 to 8 hours of full sun and fertilize 1 to 2 times in summer with a slow-release or organic food. Seeds are very tiny, so mix with sand and scatter outdoors in spring.

Pests/Diseases—Few diseases or pests, but if aphids appear, wash them off with a strong stream of water.

Landscaping Tips & Ideas—This succulent is ideal for hot, sunny spots such as rock gardens, in clay pots or hanging baskets. More recent varieties like 'Afternoon Delight' boast flowers that remain open longer in the afternoon.

NASTURTIUM
Tropaeolum majus

Hardiness—All zones

Color(s)—Yellow, orange, scarlet, pink, white with green and variegated foliage

Bloom Period—Spring through summer

Mature Size (H & W)—4 to 10 in. x 4 to 6 ft.

Water Needs—Water every 7-10 days depending on weather conditions.

Planting/Care—Plant year-round in frost-free zones or after the last freeze in colder areas. Nick seeds with a file and soak overnight to speed germination. Plant ½-in. deep and space 4-6 in. for bush varieties, 8-10 in. for vine varieties. Prefers well-draining, loose-textured soils with a pH of 7.0.

Pests/Diseases—Control snails and slugs with an iron phosphate molluscicide. Spray with a horticultural oil or Spinosad for sucking, rasping and chewing insects.

Landscaping Tips & Ideas—'Amazon Jewel' has variegated leaves and camouflages spent bulb beds. Plant on slopes or with California Lilacs, Roses, Geraniums, Shasta Daisies and under trees or spilling over containers.

NEMESIA
Nemesia hybrids

Hardiness—All zones

Color(s)—Yellow, red, pink, purple, blue, white, lavender, and bicolors.

Bloom Period—Spring through fall

Mature Size (H & W)—6 to 14 in. x 6 to 12 in.

Water Needs—Water every 7-10 days.

Planting/Care—Thrives in full sun, cooler summers and well-drained soils. Use an organic fertilizer in spring and if flower production declines, cut back as much as 50% to encourage new growth and increased blooms.

Pests/Diseases—Susceptible to root rot if soil is too soggy.

Landscaping Tips & Ideas—Puffy, miniature snapdragon-like flowers are perfect accents towards the front of mixed flower beds or in hanging baskets. The Sunsatia® series are self-cleaning, heat-tolerant and tolerate dry conditions and the Innocence® series are known for their fragrance. Plant with Petunias, Calibrachoas and Johnny-Jump-Ups.

ORNAMENTAL KALE
Brassica oleracea

Hardiness—All zones

Color(s)—Pink, rose, creamy yellow, magenta, and white foliage

Bloom Period—Not applicable

Mature Size (H & W)—12 to 24 in. x 12 to 24 in.

Water Needs—Water every 7 to 10 days.

Planting/Care—Available as color packs or seeds. Plant outdoors in spring or late summer/early fall in rich amended soil in full sun, and fertilize every 4 weeks with liquid kelp or fish emulsion.

Pests/Diseases—Ornamental Kale has fewer pest and disease problems than other cruciferous vegetables. Handpick and squash caterpillars, snails and slugs and spray with an organic fungicide such as Serenade for powdery or downy mildews.

Landscaping Tips & Ideas—For fall and winter color, Ornamental Kale is beautiful as edging in mixed flower beds, as a focal point in containers, in rock gardens or combined with Alyssum and Lobelia. They are also stunning in cut flower arrangements.

PALUDOSUM DAISY
Chrysanthemum paludosum
(Mauranthemum paludosum)

Hardiness—All zones

Color(s)—White or yellow

Bloom Period—Summer to fall

Mature Size (H & W)—6 to 12 in. x 6 to 12 in.

Water Needs—Water every 7-10 days.

Planting/Care—Paludosum Daisy tolerates sand and clayey soils with a wide pH range from 4.5 to 8, but amend with humus or compost. Provide full sun to part sun and fertilize every 4 weeks with an organic food and supplement during the bloom cycle with a liquid kelp or fish emulsion. Sow seeds directly outdoors or transplant in early spring.

Pests/Diseases—Few disease or insect problems

Landscaping Tips & Ideas—'White Buttons' produces masses of petite, yellow-centered white daisies and like other Paludosum Daisies look perfect in window boxes, containers and flower beds. Use as a long-lasting filler in cut flower arrangements, but to prolong the bloom cycle, deadhead spent flowers.

PANSY
Viola x wittrockiana

Hardiness—All zones

Color(s)—Violet, lavender, blue, purple, yellow, orange, and bi-colors

Bloom Period—Spring, fall and winter

Mature Size (H & W)—8 to 10 in. x 6 to 10 in.

Water Needs—Water once a week depending on weather conditions.

Planting/Care—Plant in early autumn or plant from seed in mid-summer in mild climates, but in hot-summer areas, wait until fall. Pansies prefer a well-composted soil with a pH of 6.7-7.0. Fertilize with a slow-release or organic fertilizer during the growing and blooming cycles.

Pests/Diseases—Damping-off occurs when the main stems deteriorate at ground level, eventually falling over. Remove the diseased plants, solarize the soil and start afresh with new plants planted in fresh soil.

Landscaping Tips & Ideas—The very large, tricolored 'Majestic' or 'Matrix Morpheus' and the ruffled 'Fizzy Lemon-berry' are fantastic in containers or mixed bedding areas. Combine with Wallflower, Candytuft, Ageratum, Alyssum, and Phlox.

PETUNIA
Petunia hybrids

Hardiness—All zones

Color(s)—Multitude of colors, picotee and bicolors.

Bloom Period—Spring through fall

Mature Size (H & W)—6 to 20 in. x 6 to 20 in. depending on cultivar

Water Needs—Water every 5-7 days.

Planting/Care—Plant from color packs in humus-rich soil with 6.0-6.8 pH. Single-flowered types tolerate alkaline soil if well-draining. Fertilize every 2 to 4 weeks with liquid kelp or fish emulsion. Cut back rangy growth by 50% to renew growth.

Pests/Diseases—Botrytis can be a problem in humid climates, so select more resistant varieties. Control Geranium budworm (tattered flowers or fail to open) with Spinosad.

Landscaping Tips & Ideas—The spreading habit of Supertunia® 'Vista Bubblegum' makes a fantastic ground-cover smothered in pink flowers. For large, ruffled, fragrant flowers in hanging baskets, try the Doubles series. In hot, humid areas plant Surfinia® hybrids because they are more resistant to botrytis.

PHLOX
Phlox drummondii

Hardiness—All zones

Color(s)—Red, pink, white, and purple

Bloom Period—Early spring through fall

Mature Size (H & W)—8 to 12 in. x 8 to 12 in.

Water Needs—Water every 7-10 days.

Planting/Care—Plant from early spring through fall from color packs. For mild winter areas, sow seeds in fall for early spring bloom or sow after the last frost date. In cool-summer areas, plant seeds every 4-6 weeks to lengthen the flowering season.

Pests/Diseases—Horticultural oil or an organic fungicide controls mildew and mites. For caterpillars use Spinosad and handpick snails and slugs, or use an organic molluscicide.

Landscaping Tips & Ideas—Although Phlox is a traditional cool-weather plant, recent hybrids are water-thrifty as well as heat- and humidity-tolerant. Phlox are stunning in hanging baskets, containers and as a mid-border addition. Lily of the Nile and Candytuft are ideal companion plants.

PINCUSHION FLOWER

Scabiosa atropurpurea (S. grandiflora)

Hardiness—All zones

Color(s)—Deep maroon, salmon pink, purple, rose, and white

Bloom Period—June to fall

Mature Size (H & W)—18 to 36 in. x 12 in.

Water Needs—Water every 5 to 7 days.

Planting/Care—Plant in spring from color packs or seed directly in the garden. Needs humus or compost-amended soil with a slightly alkaline pH. Feed every 4 to 6 weeks with an organic fertilizer. Deadhead the spent flowers. Flowers are sensitive to water, so do not water overhead.

Pests/Diseases—Few insect problems, but mildew may appear if there is poor air circulation.

Landscaping Tips & Ideas—A must-have in cottage or cut flower gardens, in borders and in the middle of mixed beds or containers. For a beautiful contrast, plant near Zinnias, Paludosum Daisies and Phlox. Plant 'Ace of Spades', 'Scarlet' or 'Florist's Blue' for long-lasting cut flowers.

PRIMROSE
Primula vulgaris

Hardiness—All zones

Color(s)—Pink, purple, yellow, orange, red, bronze, wine, picotee, and bicolors

Bloom Period—Spring to fall

Mature Size (H & W)—6 to 12 in. x 12 to 18 in.

Water Needs—Water every 5-7 days.

Planting/Care—Grows best in cool, moist weather planted in humus-rich, well-draining soil with a slightly acidic pH. In cool-summers with overcast or foggy conditions, plants can be in full sun, but where summers are hot, place them in part shade.

Pests/Diseases—Control snails and slugs with iron phosphate or in Southern California use decollate snails.

Landscaping Tips & Ideas—Although Primrose are technically perennials, they are often used as annuals in hot, dry summer conditions. Underplant with other acid-lovers like Camellias and Azaleas, spring-blooming trees and bulbs. There are also double primroses like the Belarina® series that are very fragrant and make the prettiest container plants.

SKULLCAPS
Scutellaria hybrids

Hardiness—All zones

Color(s)—Red, orange, pink, white, scarlet, and bicolors

Bloom Period—Spring to fall

Mature Size (H & W)—10 to 16 in. x 12 in.

Water Needs—Water every 7-10 days.

Planting/Care—Plant in rich, amended soil with a pH of 6.5. For cool summer areas plant in full sun, but in hot, dry summer regions, plant in part sun. Deadhead spent flowers to prolong bloom cycle and fertilize with a slow-release or organic food every 4-6 weeks. If brought indoors in autumn with bright indirect light, the plants may last longer.

Pests/Diseases—Deer and rabbit resistant. For aphids wash them off with a strong stream of water.

Landscaping Tips & Ideas—*Scutellaria* bear upright clusters of tubular flowers and should be planted in the middle of containers or flower beds for an eye-catching display. Combine with Pincushion Flowers, Cleomes and Phlox.

SNAPDRAGON
Antirrhinum majus

Hardiness—All zones

Color(s)—Many colors and bicolors

Bloom Period—Winter to spring

Mature Size (H & W)—10 to 24 in. x 6 to 12 in.

Water Needs—Water once a week or more during dry periods.

Planting/Care—Snapdragons thrive in well-drained soil with a neutral pH. Plant seedlings and color packs outdoors in the fall for winter and spring blooms. Deadhead to prolong the flowering period. If stem tips are pinched off when the plants are 2-4 in., it can produce 7-8 blossom spikes in a season.

Pests/Diseases—Rust can be a problem.

Landscaping Tips & Ideas—Snapdragons are beautiful in cut flower gardens, borders, large containers as vertical accents and dwarf selections are perfect in rock gardens and pots. For fragrance and statuesque beauty (3 ft.), 'Double Azalea Apricot' takes the grand prize of all snapdragons. Ideal companions are Baby's Breath and Larkspur.

SPIDER FLOWER
Cleome hassleriana

Hardiness—All zones

Color(s)—Rose, pink, burgundy, violet, and white

Bloom Period—Early summer to mid-fall

Mature Size (H & W)—24 to 30 in. x 24 in.

Water Needs—Water every 5-10 days depending on weather conditions and bloom cycle.

Planting/Care—Provide well-draining soil and plant 12-36 inches apart in full sun, but in hot, dry regions set in partial shade. It prefers a pH of 7.0. Do not allow soil to dry out completely before watering again, and protect against strong winds. Staking is not necessary.

Pests/Diseases—Aphids and whitefly can affect Cleomes, but they can be controlled with a strong stream of water. For heavier infestations, a horticultural oil or systemic control may be needed.

Landscaping Tips & Ideas—Delicate, feather-like flowers add movement and beauty when planted near the back of flower beds or in containers, and they also blend well with shrubs and perennials.

SPURRED SNAPDRAGON
(TOADFLAX)
Linaria reticulata

Hardiness—All zones

Color(s)—Bicolors in maroon and yellow or magenta and red or in single colors of red, white, pink, or purple

Bloom Period—Spring through autumn

Mature Size (H & W)—18 to 30 in. x 12 in.

Water Needs—Once established, it is drought-tolerant.

Planting/Care—Adaptable to most soil types but does best in rich, well-draining soil. An organic or slow-release fertilizer is best during growth and bloom seasons. Deadhead regularly to prolong bloom cycles.

Pests/Diseases—Deer and snail resistant

Landscaping Tips/Ideas—For eye-popping color use 'Flamenco' or 'Velvet Red' in planting beds, mixed borders or containers. A pot filled with either of these two varieties is a bold and colorful statement. Good summer companions include dwarf Sunflowers, Zinnias, Nemesia, and Cleomes.

STOCK
Matthiola incana

Hardiness—Preferred zones 7-11

Color(s)—Pink, red, purple, lavender, blue, yellow, cream and white

Bloom Period—Winter to spring

Mature Size (H & W)—12 to 36 in. x 10 to 16 in.

Water Needs—Water every 7 to 10 days.

Planting/Care—Plant in well-amended soil with good drainage. For mild winter areas, plant from seed or color packs in early fall but for cold winters, plant in early spring. Stock stops blooming in hot weather.

Pests/Diseases—Deer-resistant and few insect problems, but if fungal leaf spot is pervasive, pull out infected plants.

Landscaping Tips & Ideas—Ideal for the cottage and cut flower garden. Plant near walkways, window boxes and towards the front of borders, so their spicy perfume can be appreciated. *M. bicornis* is especially fragrant at night and should be planted under a window, and the Legacy series bears double flowers. Combine with Nemesia, Pansies and Sweet Peas.

SUNFLOWER
Helianthus annuus

Hardiness—All zones

Color(s)—Yellow, cream, red, orange, and bicolors

Bloom Period—Late spring to fall

Mature Size (H & W)—2 to 16 ft. x 2 ft.

Water Needs—Water about once a week.

Planting/Care—Dig up and amend the soil thoroughly and add a slow-release or organic fertilizer. Supplement every 1-2 weeks with a liquid kelp or fish emulsion. Sow seeds directly in the garden when day/night temperatures are 50°+F.

Pests/Diseases—Prevent snails and slugs with iron phosphate. Loosely cover seedlings with netting to protect against birds.

Landscaping Tips & Ideas—Use as a temporary "living fence" or plant smaller cultivars for a stunning cut flower garden. Cut off the seed head when the back is brown, and dry in an airy place. Scrape off seeds when the head is dry. 'Velvet Queen' does not shed indoors, and 'Sunzilla' is one of the tallest at 12 to 16 ft.

SWEET PEAS
Lathyrus odoratus

Hardiness—All zones

Color(s)—Blue, pink, white, red, purple, orange, and bicolors

Bloom Period—Spring

Mature Size (H & W)—8 to 10 in. x 8 to 10 in.

Water Needs—Water every 7-10 days.

Planting/Care—Nick seeds with a file and soak overnight to speed germination. Sow 1 in. deep in rows in early spring and space 2 in. apart. In mild-winter areas, sow directly in the ground in late summer for late-winter blooms. Anchor the trellis for support and plant in a humus-rich, loam soil.

Pests/Diseases—Use netting to protect from birds and iron phosphate to control snails and slugs.

Landscaping Tips & Ideas—To prolong its life cycle, deadhead before the spent flowers go to seed. 'Saltwater Taffy Swirls' has very long stems in pastel colors, but for beds and borders, the knee-high 'Explorer', at 2½ ft. tall, needs no support.

SWEET WILLIAM
Dianthus barbatus

Hardiness—All zones

Color(s)—White, pink, red, purple, and bicolors

Bloom Period—Spring through fall

Mature Size (H & W)—6 to 24 in. x 6 to 12 in.

Water Needs—Water every 5-7 days.

Planting/Care—Best grown in organically amended, well-draining soil in full sun, except provide afternoon shade in hot summer areas. Plant by seed in spring for bloom the following year or by color packs for same-year bloom.

Pests/Diseases—In poor-draining soils, crown rot or rust may be a problem. Hand pick and squish snails and slugs, or use an organic iron phosphate molluscicide. It is rabbit resistant.

Landscaping Tips & Ideas—Excellent for cut-flower, cottage or rock gardens, in containers or edging borders. 'Sooty' flowers are deep-maroon with an irresistible chocolate fragrance. 'Lace Mantle' offers a variety of pastel colors with a sweet clove perfume. Combine with Nemesia, Snapdragons and Paludosum Daisies.

ZINNIA
Zinnia elegans

Hardiness—All zones

Color(s)—Purple, pink, red, yellow, orange, and white

Bloom Period—Summer to fall

Mature Size (H & W)—12 to 48 in. x 12 to 24 in.

Water Needs—Water every 5-7 days.

Planting/Care—Sow from seed directly in the garden, or plant in late spring for summer blooms. Needs humus-rich, well-draining soil. Feed regularly with an organic liquid fertilizer about every two weeks.

Pests/Diseases—In foggy, overcast regions, mildew may be a problem. Avoid overhead watering and spray with a horticultural oil or organic fungicide.

Landscaping Tips & Ideas—Zinnias come in fantastic colors and flower forms—double, cactus and crested—and should be included in any summer garden. Select taller varieties (3-4 ft.) like 'Big Red Hybrid' for the cut flower garden or the dwarf (under 1 ft.) 'Thumbelina' for containers and unique bicolors in the Swizzle series or the lime-green 'Envy'.

ANNUALS TO PLANT IN SPRING

PLANT NAME	START FROM
Alyssum	seeds or pony packs
Baby's Breath	seeds or 4-inch pot size plants
Calibrachoa	color packs or 4-inch pot size plants
Candytuft	seeds, pony packs, or color packs
Celosia	pony packs or color packs
Cosmos	seeds, pony packs, or color packs
Four o'Clock	seeds or pony packs
Globe Amaranth	seeds or pony packs
Iceland Poppy	color packs or 4-inch pot size plants
Impatiens	seeds, pony packs, or color packs
Indian Pea	seeds
Lobelia	seeds or pony packs
Marigold	seeds or pony packs
Moss Rose	seeds or pony packs
Nasturtium	seeds
Nemesia	color packs or 4-inch pot size plants
Pansy	4-inch pot size plants
Petunia	seeds, pony packs, color packs, or 4-inch pot size plants
Phlox	seeds, pony packs, or color packs
Primrose	4-inch pot size plants
Snapdragon	seeds, pony packs, or color packs
Spurred Snapdragon	seeds or 4-inch pot size plants
Sunflower	seeds or 1-gallon size pots
Sweetpea	seeds or pony packs
Viola	pony packs or color packs
Zinnia	seeds or pony packs

ANNUALS TO PLANT IN SUMMER

PLANT NAME	START FROM
African Daisy	color packs, 4-or 6-inch pots, or 1-gallon size plants
Ageratum	pony packs, color packs, or 4-inch pot size plants
Alyssum	seeds, pony packs, or color packs
Amaranthus	color packs or 4-inch pot size plants
Angelonia	color packs or 4- or 6-inch pot size plants
Baby's Breath	4-inch pots or 1-gallon size plants
Calibrachoa	pony packs or 4-inch pots
Cockscomb	color packs or 4-inch pot size plants
Coleus	color packs or 4- or 6-inch pot size plants
Cosmos	color packs or 4-inch pot size plants
Dianthus	pony packs, color packs, or 4-inch pot size plants
Dusty Miller	pony packs, color packs, or 4- or 6-inch pot size plants
Four o'Clock	seeds, pony packs, or color packs

Impatiens	color packs or 4- or 6-inch pot size plants
Lisianthus	color packs or 4- or 6-inch pot size plants
Lobelia	seeds or pony packs
Marigold	pony packs, color packs, or 4-inch pot size plants
Morning Glory	seeds or pony packs
Petunia	pony packs
Phlox	pony packs or 4-inch pot size plants
Pinks	pony packs, color packs, or 1-gallon size plants
Sunflower	color packs, 4-or 6-inch pots, or 1-gallon size plants
Verbena	color packs
Wax Begonia	4- or 6-inch pot size plants
Zinnia	pony packs or color packs

ANNUALS TO PLANT IN AUTUMN

PLANT NAME	START FROM
Alyssum	seeds or pony packs
Annual African Daisy	4- or 6-inch pot size plants
Annual Phlox	color packs
Baby's Breath	4-inch pot size plants or 1-gallon size plants
Calendula	pony packs
Cineraria	color packs or 4- or 6-inch pot size plants
Columbine	4- or 6-inch pot size plants or 1-gallon size plants
Dianthus	color packs
Foxglove	4- or 6-inch pot size plants or 1 gallon size plants
Hollyhock	6-inch pot size plants or 1-gallon size plants
Iceland Poppy	pony packs or 4-inch pot size plants
Johnny-jump-up	pony packs or color packs
Larkspur	4- or 6-inch pot size plants
Lobelia	pony packs or color packs
Nasturtium	seeds
Nemesia	4-inch pot size plants
Ornamental Kale	4- or 6-inch pot size plants or 1-gallon size plants
Ornamental Pepper	color packs or 1-gallon size plants
Paludosum Daisy	4- or 6-inch pot size plants
Pansy	seeds, pony packs, or 4-inch pot size plants
Primrose	4-inch pot size plants
Snapdragon	pony packs
Stock	pony packs or color packs
Sweetpea	seeds, pony packs, or color packs
Sweet William	color packs
Viola	seeds, pony packs, or color packs

ANNUALS TO PLANT FROM SEED IN LATE WINTER

Ageratum	Bachelor Button	Bells of Ireland	Candytuft	Clarkia
Forget-me-not	Impatiens	Linaria	Lobelia	Nicotiana
Petunia	Phlox	Statice	Stock	Verbena

HEAT-TOLERANT ANNUALS

Baby's Breath	Cockscomb	Coreopsis	Cosmos	Four o' Clock
Globe Amaranth	Gloriosa Daisy	Lobelia	Marigold	Morning Glory
Moss Rose	Ornamental Pepper	Petunia	Pincushion Flower	Strawflower
Sunflower	Sweet Alyssum	Zinnia		

COOL-SEASON ANNUALS

Calendula	California Poppy	Clarkia	Cornflower	Iceland Poppy
Larkspur	Nasturtium	Nemesia	Pansy	Pink
Snapdragon	Stock	Sweet Pea	Toadflax (Linaria)	Viola
Wallflower				

DROUGHT-TOLERANT ANNUALS

African Daisy	California Poppy	Dusty Miller	Gazania	Globe Amaranth
Moss Rose	Sea Pink	Statice	Sweet Alyssum	

ANNUALS FOR SHADE

Cineraria	Flowering Tobacco	Impatiens	Monkey Flower	Primrose

JANUARY

- Visit online websites for annuals such as www.all-americaselections.org, and order seed catalogues to try some different varieties.

- Set out a rain gauge and high-low thermometer to record rainfall and temperatures in your journal.

- If you haven't done so already, plant cool-season Alyssum, Dianthus, Dusty Miller, Iceland Poppy, Johnny-Jump-Up, Larkspur, Lobelia, Nemesia, Ornamental Kale, Paludosum Daisy, Candytuft, Pansy, Phlox, Primrose, Snapdragon, Stock, and Sweet William in frost-free areas.

- Redirect more energy into root development and develop more blooming stems by pinching off flower buds and tip growth.

- To speed seedling growth, cover annual beds with a row cover like Reemay® or Agrofabric that let in the sun and rain, but trap the heat.

- A pre-emergent weed killer will prevent weeds in flower beds for 4-6 months (don't apply if planting seeds).

FEBRUARY

- Winter rains soften soils and gophers become more active. Before they destroy flower beds and borders, set out manual traps or use baits.

- Move container plants away from cold winds into more protected areas such as covered patios, but remember to water if they are out of the rain.

- Get a jump-start on spring annuals by starting from seed and plant in expandable peat pellets or seed trays.

- Feed annuals with organic fertilizers. The organic nutrients will become available as soil temperatures warm up. For indoor seedlings, use an organic water-soluble fertilizer after they have a second set of true leaves (the first two leaves that appear are cotyledons and the true leaves appear above them).

- Young seedlings, Pansies and Violas are susceptible to damping off, a fungal disease that causes them to collapse suddenly. Pull out and dispose in trash.

MARCH

- Recycle spent winter annuals and old leaves by putting them through a shredder or chopping them up with clippers and putting them in a compost bin to protect against overwintering disease.

- Transplanting solutions with indolebutyric acid and an organic humate product encourage the development of plant root systems.

- Purchase cold-tolerant annuals such as Alyssum, Cornflowers, Cosmos, Dianthus, Four o' Clocks, Pansies, Stock and Violas over the more frost-tender Celosia, Marigolds and Zinnias until warm temperatures are here to stay.

- Transplant seedlings outdoors after the last possibility of frost has passed. For the interior and mountainous regions it may be as late as April. Acclimate outdoors when they are 4 inches or if there are 2 to 4 pairs of true leaves, for longer and longer periods during the day in a protected location and bring them indoors at night. After 2 weeks, they should be able to stay outdoors all night.

APRIL

- To plant seeds directly outdoors, prepare and amend the flower beds so that the soil is loam or sandy loam, and follow the seed packet's depth and planting directions.

- Stop weeds in beds with a pre-emergent that will not hurt existing plants. Avoid using if planting seeds (it will keep all seeds from germinating).

- Purchase beneficial insects such as ladybugs, lacewings, praying mantis, predatory mites and wasps to control harmful insects.

- Protect bedding plants from slugs and snails with an organic molluscicide that contains iron phosphate. It is not harmful to pets or children and degrades into fertilizer for the annuals.

- Re-apply a mulch to keep the layer at 2-3 inches over flower beds, containers and borders to conserve moisture, to keep out weeds and to protect plant roots from temperature fluctuations.

- Tuck warm season annuals among trees, shrubs and bulb beds or snuggle them in the lawn area.

MAY

- Purchase summer annuals now and avoid root-bound plants (with roots growing out of the drainage holes). Pinch back the tips to stimulate root growth.

- Petunias and Calibrachoa are water-thirsty annuals, while others such as Celosia, Cosmos, Moss Rose, and Spurred Snapdragons tolerate drier conditions once established.

- Toward the end of spring cool-season seed heads form. Collect heirloom seeds for next year's supply of fall-winter annuals. Collect when the seed heads feel dry to the touch and store in airtight jars. Don't collect seeds from hybrids because their seeds do not replicate true to form. It is not necessary to collect self-sowing Alyssum, Nasturtiums and California Poppies.

- If not saving seeds deadhead faded flowers weekly to extend the bloom cycle or plant self-cleaning varieties such as Four o' Clocks, Calibrachoa and Petunias.

- Thrill children with 'Sunzillas' because these sunflowers are giant 16-footers. Watch them grow practically every day. Water and fertilize regularly to keep them growing strong.

JUNE

- Plants in terracotta containers dry out more quickly than plastic, which retains moisture better. Coat the inside of clay pots with an asphalt emulsion or sealer.

- Annuals live their life in one season so they are perfect for a child to observe the complete cycle in just a few weeks. Plant a child-friendly butterfly and hummingbird garden (Marigolds and Zinnias) or a scented garden (Four o' Clocks, Phlox, Chocolate Cosmos).

- Remove cool season annuals and fill in the spaces with hot-weather color.

- Plant taller annuals like Cosmos, Zinnias and Sunflowers towards the back or center of flower beds or pots; followed by Phlox or Paludosum Daisies; lastly, add low-growing or cascading varieties around the edge like Calibrachoa.

- Fertilize bedding annuals from early summer at least once a month with a liquid organic kelp or fish emulsion or hand broadcast a complete, granular, organic fertilizer onto the ground. In containers, fertilize every two weeks with a liquid food.

JULY

- Deeply water all your summer annuals because summer heat can wilt them, but don't overwater native or drought-tolerant selections.

- Fill in bare spaces with summer-through-fall flowers including Alyssum, Celosia, Cosmos, Petunia, Portulaca and Zinnia. For shady spots, plant Coleus and Impatiens.

- If you spot holes in foliage and flowers, budworm and caterpillars could be the culprits. For severe infestation, spray with Spinosad. It comes from a chemical produced bacteria and is effective against most chewing insects, but safe for beneficial insects and predatory wasps. Spray in the late afternoon or early evening after bees have returned to their hives.

- Continue to plant summer-loving annuals from color packs because many tender seedlings are usually no match for intense heat or dry winds.

- Seedlings that are more robust such as Sunflowers, Marigolds and Zinnias can be sown outdoors because they germinate quickly and grow like weeds.

AUGUST

- Use seed-starting flats or peat pots to plant fall annuals from seed like Dianthus, Iceland Poppies, Pansies, Snapdragons, Stock and Violas and they will be ready to transplant by mid-fall.

- Control leggy growth on annuals by cutting them back at least one-third or more to encourage fall re-blooming of Zinnias, Cosmos and Marigolds.

- Watch out for whiteflies during hot temperatures. Apply a 1-inch layer of worm castings around the affected plant and spray with a rose and flower insect killer. Worm castings contain chitinase which dissolves the exoskeletons of many harmful insects including whiteflies.

- Spruce up the summer garden with hanging baskets. Line wire baskets with sphagnum moss, fill with an organic, well-draining potting soil, add coconut coir to help retain moisture and plant cascading Petunias, Alyssum and Angelonia for spots of color.

- Replace summer annuals that are losing their growth and blooming momentum and replace them with cool-season annuals.

SEPTEMBER

- Santa Ana winds and high temperatures can occur but as the fall season progresses, days shorten and temperatures drop. Adjust irrigation timers and systems for the decrease in water needs.

- Renovate the soil by turning it over, blending in an organic, granular food or a preplant fertilizer at a rate of 2 pounds per hundred square feet and humus mulch at a rate of 2 cubic feet per hundred square feet and worm castings at the bag's recommended rate.

- During hot summer months, mulch decomposes rapidly; replenish the mulch to 2-3 in. in planting beds and containers.

- For fall and holiday color, plant Calendula, Pansies, Iceland Poppy, Primrose and Snapdragons. Wait until October for hot, dry inland areas.

- In mild-winter areas, sow Sweet Pea seeds directly in the garden from now to November to give their roots a good head start for a late winter or early spring bloom.

OCTOBER

- Apply a humic acid product to the entire garden. It will help feed the beneficial soil microbes and in turn, fortify plants for cooler weather.

- Even in fall there are lots of annuals to plant: Alyssum, Dianthus, Dusty Miller, Iceland Poppy, Johnny-Jump-Up, Larkspur, Lobelia, Nemesia, Ornamental Kale, Paludosum Daisy, Candytuft, Pansy, Phlox, Primrose, Snapdragon, Stock and Sweet William.

- Scatter wildflower seeds in autumn. Tiny seeds like California Poppies and other Violas are very tiny. For easier planting, mix seeds with ¼ cup of fine sand (available at your nursery) in a plastic bag, shake thoroughly and then broadcast the seeds outdoors or in a pot filled with potting soil.

- Don't forget that autumn or winter annuals are effective when planted in hanging baskets and pots.

- Keep old cotton sheets handy in case there is a forecast of early frost. Cover loosely in the early evening and remove during the day when the temperatures have warmed up.

NOVEMBER

- California's rainy season begins from November to the middle of March, but supplemental watering of annuals may be necessary. If fungal diseases such as rust and mildew are a problem, water in the early morning so the plant has time to dry out during the day.

- Pests and disease may remain a problem. Spray with Spinosad for the chewing pests and use a horticultural oil for mildew, black spot and scale.

- Collect heirloom seeds (hybrid varieties will not come true to the parent) for next year's supply of summer annuals before digging the plants up.

- To continue planting annuals in beds, despite frosty weather, lay down an agricultural blanket such as Reemay®. It allows light and moisture, but provides an extra 3-4 degrees protection.

- For next year, design a raised bed for a cut-flower garden. Raised beds are easier to control weeds and if designed with a maximum width of 4 feet, easy to tend.

DECEMBER

- Keep a journal to record temperatures, rainfall and a list of your favorite annuals.

- Check old seed packets' expiration dates. Test seed viability by placing 10 on a moistened paper towel, fold in half and seal in a baggie. Set the bag in a warm place. If after 15 days, less than five have germinated, discard.

- A good rule of thumb for planting seeds: the smaller the seed, the shallower the planting depth (depth of one to three times the seed diameter). After planting, moisten with a gentle spray to keep seeds from washing away, cover with a plastic lid, set where there is bright indirect light and provide warmth (between 68-75 degrees).

- Plant winter annuals in containers if the outdoor soil is too saturated. Candytuft, Ornamental Kale, Iceland Poppies, Johnny-Jump-Up, Pansies, Primroses, Snapdragons and Stock are ideal for containers.

- Turn off irrigation systems and drain the lines and valves where freezing weather is common.

HOLLYHOCK

BULBS, CORMS, RHIZOMES & TUBERS
for California

When we kneel down in the cool soil, scoop out holes, and plant our brown parchment—wrapped bulbs, we are acting on a fundamentally optimistic gardening belief that from such plain, often ugly vessels will emerge breathtaking blossoms of every shape, size, form, color, and fragrance, transforming our garden into a shimmering tapestry of seasonal magic.

PLAN YOUR BULB SHOWCASE

Plan your design on paper and keep it simple, especially if you are a novice. Use two or three colors, or select just a few varieties of bulbs, picking out at least twelve of each kind, and group them in clusters or scatter in drifts.

One of the most important considerations when developing a bulb showcase is knowledge of heights and bloom times of the plants. Place the taller plants at the back or center of the bed and plant the shorter ones in the middle and front. For maximum visual impact, select bulbs that bloom at the same time. If early-, mid-, and late-flowering varieties are mixed together, the look will be less dramatic, but the succession of blooms will make the season last longer. Daffodils come in a range of early- to mid- to late-season varieties; Persian Buttercups flower later than Daffodils and extend the bloom time after the others fade. Once the spring buds peak out, begin planting clusters of Lilies, Dahlias, Gladioli, and Tuberoses in anticipation of the warm summer months.

Don't forget that the adage about nice things coming in small packages applies to bulbs like Grape Hyacinth and miniature forms of Daffodils.

NOT ALL BULBOUS PLANTS ARE TRUE BULBS

The term "bulb" is often used loosely, as many bulbous plants are technically not true bulbs. True bulbs have pointed tops, short underground stems on basal plates, and new growths, called bulblets, that form from offshoots of the parent bulbs. Amaryllis, Grape Hyacinth, and Daffodils are considered true bulbs because they grow from enlarged buds with modified leaves called scales.

Included in the family of "bulbous plants that are not true bulbs" are those produced from corms, rhizomes, and tubers. Corms are similar to bulbs, except that each summer a new corm grows on top of the original one. As the parent corm disappears, the roots of the new corm grow downward into the hole left by the decayed corm. Gladioli and Freesias grow from corms that divide by growing small corms, called cormels, around the base of the parent bulb.

Unlike corms, which grow upward, rhizomes are specialized stems that spread horizontally, underground, or on the surface with adventitious roots, and they sprout stems, leaves, and flowers from the rhizomes' upper sections. Peruvian Lilies and Tuberoses grow from rhizomes and are propagated by cutting out a section of their spreading layers.

Dahlias and Ranunculus grow from tubers, which are swollen rhizomes that produce pulpy, instead of scaly, stems. Tubers normally grow just below the surface of the soil and, like bulbs, store food for the plants. The buds on tubers become stems, leaves, and flowers, and clusters of roots form at the base. They multiply by division, and as they divide, the parent tuber deteriorates.

Whether bulbous plants derive from a true bulb, corm, rhizome, or tuber, there is a flowering bulb to suit every taste and to serve every garden purpose. And when it comes time to do the actual planting, choose the biggest, plumpest bulbs that are clean, solid, and free from scars. With faith in the magic of nature, bulbs bring forth spring and summer jewel-like colors in mixed borders, rock gardens, and random drifts in lawns or along slopes.

FORCING BULBS INDOORS

IN POTS

If bulbs such as Paperwhites, Daffodils, Crocus, Dutch Tulips or Hyacinths have been planted by October 1, most will be ready to move into the house by Christmas. Remember to refrigerate (do not freeze) Dutch Tulips and Hyacinths in paper bags 8-10 weeks prior to planting them in pots. It

TULIP

is not necessary to pre-chill Daffodils, Paperwhites and Crocus. Use a light, organic potting soil, partially fill, and plant the bulbs so their "noses" are barely covered with the remaining mix and water thoroughly. Plant pots at weekly intervals for a continuous supply of spring flowers indoors even though it is still winter. Since forcing depletes the resources of most bulbs (with the exception of *Hippeastrum*) and are unlikely to flower vigorously again, it is best to throw them away after the flowers are spent and look forward to next year's forcing.

IN WATER

Set Paperwhites (*Narcissus*), Crocus, Amaryllis (actually *Hippeastrum*) and Hyacinths in water-filled vases designed for these varieties. Place in a cool, dark room (50°F. or less) for 4-8 weeks until the root system is established and there is tip bulb growth. Move to a room where there is bright, indirect light and the plant will bloom. If Paperwhites become leggy, tie up the foliage and if Amaryllis gets top heavy, provide stake support. Another option to anchor the bulbs more securely is to

place them in tall clear glass containers (fish bowls or cylinders), add ⅓ decorative stones, fill with water barely covering the surface of the rocks (so the water barely reaches the bulb base) and place the bulbs in the container. Whether in vases, bowls or cylinders, replenish water up to the original levels as needed.

CUT FLOWER TIPS

- Wear gloves when handling flowers, especially for those with sensitive skin.
- Harvest flowers for indoor arrangements in the early morning when plant moisture levels are at their peak.
- If flowers have multiple buds, cut when the first buds open and the majority of the buds are showing color.
- For single flowers cut when the bud is showing color, but Dahlias need to be cut when fully open because their buds will not open once cut.
- Once inside, re-cut the stems at an angle (so the cut ends have as much surface area exposed to water) and under water (to avoid air bubbles forming in the stems).
- Trim off any foliage that falls below the water line.
- For the longest lasting cut flowers, add a commercial floral preservative because it contains the correct amount of biocides and nutrients.
- Some bulb flowers exude gooey latex when cut that is harmful to other blossoms. Narcissus and Amaryllis in particular need to have their cut stems washed off, add a drop of bleach to the vase water and allow them to stand in it separately for at least 24 hours before combining them with other flowers.
- Keep cut flowers away from heating/air-conditioning vents and sources of ethylene gas such as fruits, especially apples.
- For dried flowers or seed heads (Sicilian Honey Lily have beautiful seed heads), harvest just before they are fully open and hang them upside-down in a dark, dry area with good air circulation such as a closet or garage.

AFRICAN CORN LILY
Ixia hybrids

Hardiness—Preferred zones 7-11

Color(s)—Yellow, cream, red, orange and pink

Bloom Period—Late spring

Mature Size (H & W)—18 to 20 in. x 12 to 18 in.

Water Needs—Water every 7-10 days during growth and bloom cycles and stop watering during dormancy.

Planting/Care—Plant corms in autumn in well-draining soil 3-4 in. deep and 3 in. apart. Where winter freezes are common, dig up in the fall and re-plant after the last frost date, but in mild winter regions, keep in the ground.

Pests/Diseases—Few disease or pest problems except watch for gophers and moles. Control with manual traps.

Landscaping Tips & Ideas—South African native with star-shaped floral clusters are showy in cut flower or rock gardens, in borders and beds and in containers. As a cut flower, it lasts about 2 weeks. 'Emperor Red' and 'Emperor Pink' are colorful additions to any garden.

AMARYLLIS
Hippeastrum hybrids

Hardiness—Preferred zones 10-11

Color(s)—Rainbow of colors, picotee, and bicolors

Bloom Period—Spring, but can be forced for winter blooms

Mature Size (H & W)—7-24 in. x 7-24 in.

Water Needs—Water once a week during growth and bloom periods.

Planting/Care—Plant in well-draining soil in full sun, protect from frost and space 18 inches apart. Keep the top 25% of the bulb above soil level, water once then wait until green growth appears. For winter holiday forcing in pots, use potting soil. Fertilize once a week when growing and blooming.

Pests/Diseases—Remove damaged foliage if leaves have yellow or white spots caused by spotted wilt.

Landscaping Tips & Ideas—Among many to consider: 'Merry Christmas' for huge, Christmas red singles; 'Elvas' for double-flowered, pink-white and raspberry streaks and the miniature 'Papilio Improved' with flowers of cream, burgundy and bronze. Bulbs are toxic if ingested so plant away from children and pets.

ANEMONE
Anemone hybrid

Hardiness—Preferred zones 5-10

Color(s)—Pink, blue, purple, red and white

Bloom Period—Spring

Mature Size (H & W)—6 to 18 in. x 6 to 12 in.

Water Needs—Water every 5-7 days during growth and bloom cycles, but stop watering after leaves yellow in summer.

Planting/Care—Soak tubers 2-4 hours before planting (scarred side up) in fall or in spring after the last frost. Plant 1-2 in. deep and 8-12 in. apart in rich amended soil with excellent drainage.

Pests/Diseases—Protect tender and young plants from birds. Control snails and slugs by hand-picking or use an organic iron phosphate molluscicide.

Landscaping Tips & Ideas—With 1-2½ in. large flowers, Anemones are ideal when planted en masse in borders, rock or cut flower gardens, or in containers. Treat as an annual where summers are rainy or warm-winter regions. All parts are toxic when ingested so keep away from children and pets.

AZTEC LILY
Sprekelia formosissima

Hardiness—Preferred zones 8-11

Color(s)—Red

Bloom Period—Early summer

Mature Size (H & W)—12 in. x 12 in.

Water Needs—Water every 5-7 days during growth and bloom seasons.

Planting/Care—Plant in fall, 3 to 4 in. deep and 8 in. apart in humus or mulch-amended, well-draining soil. Where winters freeze, plant in spring and dig out in fall, but where winters are mild, leave in place to naturalize.

Pests/Diseases—Bulbs are prone to rotting if planted in poor draining soil or wet winters during dormancy.

Landscaping Tips & Ideas—A bright addition to the early summer border with its 6 in. orchid-like blooms. It will re-bloom in mild climates several times a year if given a dry period after flowering then resume watering to trigger new growth. In containers re-pot every 3 to 4 years.

BABIANA
(BABOON FLOWER)
Babiana ringens

Hardiness—Preferred zones 8-10

Color(s)—Magenta-red with yellow throat

Bloom Period—Mid- to late-spring

Mature Size (H & W)—6 to 12 in. x 6 to 12 in.

Water Needs—Water every 7-10 days during growth and bloom cycles, stop watering during summer dormancy.

Planting/Care—Plant this South African native in well-draining, sandy loam soil, 4 in. deep and 4-6 in. apart. Naturalize in mild winter areas but where winters are cold, dig up and store in a dry place. Use an organic, not chemical fertilizer when growing and blooming.

Pests/Diseases—Few pests or diseases except snail and slugs. Hand-pick or control with an iron phosphate molluscicide.

Landscaping Tips & Ideas—Showy flowers grow from the sides of the plant and its main stalk is sterile, but is used for a perch for pollinating sunbirds. Plant along the edge of a border or path, in a rock garden or in pots.

BEARDED IRIS

Iris germanica hybrid

Hardiness—Preferred zones 3-10

Color(s)—A rainbow of hues and bicolors

Bloom Period—Late spring to summer

Mature Size (H & W)—8 to 36 in. x 18 to 20 in.

Water Needs—Water when first planting, but decrease watering until new growth appears. Then water every 7-14 days until fall rains.

Planting/Care—Plant from July to fall. Requires good drainage and full sun except in hot climates, provide afternoon shade. Space 12 to 24 in. apart with tops just below the surface. Fertilize with an organic food when growth begins and again after the bloom season. Divide every 3-4 years.

Pests/Diseases—Rhizome rot is caused by poor-draining soil.

Landscaping Tips & Ideas—Another outstanding plant in borders, containers, cut flower or cottage gardens. Remontant varieties bloom in the spring and re-bloom in the fall such as 'Immortality' and 'Beverly Sills.'

BLOOD LILY
(PAINTBRUSH LILY)

Haemanthus spp.

Hardiness—Preferred zones 10-11

Color(s)—White, red, orange, and pink

Bloom Period—Blooms repeatedly

Mature Size (H & W)—12 to 18 in. x 12 to 18 in.

Water Needs—Water every 7 to 10 days.

Planting/Care—Plant in slightly acid, well-draining soil in partial to full shade. Feed with an organic, not chemical, fertilizer. Propagate by divisions or by seed. Clusters of berry-like seeds form after the flowers are spent. Remove outer coating and plant directly outdoors 2 in. deep. For sensitive skin, wear gloves when handling seeds.

Pests/Diseases—Few pests or diseases except protect from snail and slug damage by hand-picking or an organic molluscicide.

Landscaping Tips & Ideas—Bright flowers ranging from creamy white with gold stamens, pink with yellow tipped stamens and brilliant orange with bright yellow stamens. Their splashes of color are perfect in shady spots under trees, in rock gardens and in containers.

CALLA LILY

Zantedeschia aethiopica

Hardiness—Preferred zones 8-10

Color(s)—White and cream

Bloom Period—Spring-summer

Mature Size (H & W)—2 to 4 ft. x 2 to 4 ft.

Water Needs—Water every 5-7 days depending on weather and growth conditions.

Planting/Care—Endemic to boggy areas in South Africa, plant rhizomes fall-spring, 4 in. deep and 1 ft. apart in full sun for mild-winter areas, but in part shade for hot summer regions. Provide rich amended, slightly acid evenly moist soil and feed with cottonseed meal every 4-6 weeks. Rhizomes toxic when ingested.

Pests/Diseases—Control snails and slugs with iron phosphate, an organic molluscicide.

Landscaping Tips & Ideas—For Mediterranean climates, plant near ponds or in cut flower gardens. 'Green Goddess' spathes are green with white throats, 'White Giant' grows 6 ft. and 'Childsiana' varieties remain at 12 in. Where freezes are common, plant in pots and protect during winter.

CYCLAMEN
Cyclamen persicum

Hardiness—Preferred zones 8-11

Color(s)—Red, white, pink or purple

Bloom Period—Winter-spring and fall

Mature Size (H & W)—8-12 in. x 10 in.

Water Needs—Water every 7-10 days during growth cycle.

Planting/Care—Plant in shade or dappled light in well-drained, slightly alkaline soils. Fertilize twice a month with an organic, water-soluble food. Water around the edges of the tuber, not overhead. Reduce watering when growth cycle ends and extend the dry period for 2-3 months. Then re-start watering schedule again.

Pests/Diseases—Snails, slugs and Cyclamen mites can be problems. If damage is extensive, use an iron phosphate snail bait or hand-pick and squish and use horticultural oil for mites.

Landscaping Tips & Ideas—Plant underneath with other shade-lovers: Camellias, Azaleas, Clivias and Impatiens. To extend the bloom season, remove the spent flowers, stem and all. Plant in the ground in frost-free areas, but in colder areas plant in containers.

DAFFODILS
Narcissus hybrid

Hardiness—Preferred zones 7-11

Color(s)—Orange, yellow, white, and bicolors

Bloom Period—Late winter, spring

Mature Size (H & W)—1 to 2 ft. x 1 to 2 ft.

Water Needs—Water every 5-7 days during spring, decrease frequency in fall and winter and discontinue in the summer.

Planting/Care—Plant in fall or spring after the last frost, spacing 4 to 8 in. apart at a depth of 1 to 1½ ft. Provide full or part sun and excellent drainage. Fertilize monthly during growth and blooms seasons.

Pests/Diseases—Repels deer and gophers because of its toxic alkaloids.

Landscaping Tips & Ideas—Plant Daffodils en masse to naturalize in grasslands or woodlands or scatter the bulbs and plant in a freeform pattern under deciduous trees. In containers or in flowerbeds, overplant Daffodils with Violas, Pansies, Nemesia and Freesia. For a long bloom season, plant a mixture of early-mid-late blooming types.

DAHLIA
Dahlia hybrids

Hardiness—Preferred zones 10-11

Color(s)—Red, orange, yellow, pink, white, and bicolors

Bloom Period—Summer-fall

Mature Size (H & W)—2 to 7 ft. x 2 to 4 ft.

Water Needs—Water 1-2 times a week during growth and bloom seasons.

Planting/Care—Plant in full sun in spring from tubers in amended, well-draining soils. Leave tubers in the ground, except where it freezes, dig up in the fall, store in a dry place and replant in the spring.

Pests/Diseases—For mildew, spider mites and rust spray with a horticultural oil.

Landscaping Tips & Ideas—Ideal companion plants are: Foxglove, Delphinium and Lavender. When new growth is 4 inches, thin out leaving only the three strongest stems. Repeat throughout the growth cycle. Disbud again when the first flower buds appear, keeping only the central bud. Disbudding is not necessary for dwarf or short varieties.

DUTCH IRIS
Iris x hollandica

Hardiness—Preferred zones 5-8

Color(s)—Blue, purple, yellow, bronze, white, orange, and bicolors

Bloom Period—Early to late spring

Mature Size (H & W)—18 to 22 in. x 18 to 22 in.

Water Needs—Water every 5-7 days during growth.

Planting/Care—Plant 4-6 in. deep and space 4-6 in. apart in autumn in full sun. Where summers are dry, allow to naturalize, but for wet summers, dig up after foliage yellows, store and replant after 2 months.

Pests/Diseases—Control moles and gophers with physical traps and avoid fungal diseases by planting in well-draining soil and allowing the soil to dry out slightly between waterings.

Landscaping Tips & Ideas—If left in the ground, plant with Daffodils and other spring bloomers and combine with later blooming annuals like Hollyhocks to camouflage the Dutch Iris' yellowing foliage. 'Eye of the Tiger', 'Telstar', and 'Oriental Beauty' are just a few of the stunning bicolored selections.

FALLING STARS
(COPPERTIP, CROCOSMIA)
Crocosmia hybrids (formerly *Tritonia*)

Hardiness—Preferred zones 8-10

Color(s)—Red, orange, yellow

Bloom Period—Spring or summer

Mature Size (H & W)—2 to 4 ft. x 2 to 4 ft.

Water Needs—Water every 10 days during growth period.

Planting/Care—Provide excellent drainage and amended soil to prevent corms from rotting. Space 3 in. apart and plant 2 in. deep. Needs full sun but where summers are hot, provide afternoon shade. Dig up corms and store until spring during winter freezes. Reduce watering to every 2-3 weeks after growth and bloom cycle.

Pests/Diseases—Control spider mites and thrips with Spinosad, an organic control for chewing insects.

Landscaping Tips & Ideas—Naturalize on slopes or plant in cut flower or rock gardens. 'Lucifer' bears bright red flowers on 4 ft. tall plants, 'Babylon' is 2-3 ft. with orange and scarlet blossoms and 'Citronella' bears pale yellow flowers with dark eyes.

FREESIA
Freesia hybrid

Hardiness—Preferred Zones 9-11

Color(s)—Red, orange, yellow, pink, purple, and white

Bloom Period—Spring

Mature Size (H & W)—1 to 1½ ft. x 1 to 1½ ft.

Water Needs—Water every 5 to 7 days during growth and bloom. Stop when foliage is completely yellow.

Planting/Care—Plant in fall in frost-free regions and in spring after last frost in colder climates. Needs full sun in well-draining, amended soil. Plant pointed ends up, 2 to 3 in. deep, 3 in. apart. In winter frosts, dig up after foliage is yellow and store in a dry place and replant in spring.

Pests/Diseases—Fungal and insect problems are minimal.

Landscaping Tips & Ideas—'Striped Jewel' has white flowers with purple venation and 'Antique Freesia' is very fragrant and naturalizes in Mediterranean climates. Mass in rock gardens, along borders and in containers or overplant with Candytuft, Wallflower or other annuals.

GIANT SQUILL
(SEA ONION)
Urginea maritima

Hardiness—Preferred zones 10-11

Color(s)—White

Bloom Period—Late summer, early fall

Mature Size (H & W)—4 to 6 ft. x 1½ to 2 ft.

Water Needs—Water sparingly until fall.

Planting/Care—Native to Greece, the Giant Squill thrives in Southern California's dry summers and wet winters. Plant the giant bulb with its growing tip slightly above the soil level. Needs full sun with well-draining soil. Once established, do not fertilize or provide supplemental water. Foliage appears after flowering spikes in autumn. Cut off yellow foliage in spring.

Pests/Diseases—Resistant to gophers due to its high alkaloid content. Hand-pick and squash snails and slugs.

Landscaping Tips & Ideas—Giant Squill is ideal in Mediterranean and water- thrifty landscapes. The flowering spikes create a stunning vertical element and are even more dramatic with backlighting at night. Cut Squill flowers will continue to grow and last for 2 weeks.

GLADIOLUS
Gladiolus hybrid

Hardiness—Preferred zones 9-11

Color(s)—Red, orange, yellow, pink, white, and bicolors

Bloom Period—Late spring-summer

Mature Size (H & W)—1 to 4 ft. x 1 to 3 ft.

Water Needs—Water every 5-7 days during growth and bloom cycles.

Planting/Care—Plant in evenly moist, well-drained soil in full sun. Where winters are mild, plant the corms in fall or spring after the last frost. Space 6-8 in. apart and 2-4 in. deep. Fertilize monthly during growth and bloom periods.

Pests/Diseases—Deformed and discolored flowers are often caused by thrips. Use a systemic or an organic Spinosad to control.

Landscaping Tips & Ideas—Every 2-3 weeks from the first planting until July, plant Gladiolus bulbs successively for flowers until early fall. Perfect in cottage gardens, try the species 'Byzantine Gladiolus' for bold magenta color and sturdy 2-3 ft. growth. Good companions include Dahlias and other summer bloomers.

GRAPE HYACINTH
Muscari neglectum

Hardiness—Preferred zones 7-11

Color(s)—Blue or dark-blue

Bloom Period—Late winter, early spring

Mature Size (H & W)—4 to 6 in. x 4 to 6 in.

Water Needs—Water once a week during growth and bloom seasons.

Planting/Care—Plant in early fall, in well-amended and good draining soil with a pH of 6.0-6.5. Needs full or part sun, plant 4 in. deep and 3 in. apart. Fertilize once a month after growth appears with an organic water-soluble food.

Pests/Diseases—Deer-resistant. Control snails and slugs by hand-picking or use an iron phosphate molluscicide.

Landscaping Tips & Ideas—Plant underneath Azaleas or Magnolias or in low bowls with other bulbs such as Freesias and Cyclamen. They naturalize well with Daffodils in rock gardens or in drifts.

HARLEQUIN FLOWER
Sparaxis tricolor

Hardiness—Preferred zones 10-11

Color(s)—White, yellow, red, and orange with yellow centers edged in black

Bloom Period—April-May

Mature Size (H & W)—12 to 18 in. x 5 in.

Water Needs—Water during growth and bloom cycles, decrease during summer dormancy.

Planting/Care—South African native is easy to grow in compost-amended, well-draining soil and thrives in Mediterranean climates. Plant in full sun in early fall, 2 in. deep and space 4 in. apart. Fertilize with an organic water soluble food during growth and bloom seasons. Dig up and store corms in cold winter regions before frost.

Pests/Diseases—Few pests or disease except protect from gophers by planting corms in wire cages or containers.

Landscaping Tips & Ideas—Bright, star-shaped flowers show off the best when grouped in clumps in rock gardens or mixed flower beds, along borders and containers. Combine with annuals and other bulbs like Sicilian Honey Lily and Saffron Crocus.

MARSH LILY (CRINUM)
Crinum spp.

Hardiness—Preferred zones 8-11

Color(s)—White, pink

Bloom Period—Spring-summer

Mature Size (H & W)—4 ft. or taller x 4 ft.

Water Needs—Water year-round every 7-10 days during growth and bloom cycles.

Planting/Care—Plant in spring or fall in humus-amended soil with bulb tops at soil level and space 2-4 ft. apart. In Mediterranean regions, it remains evergreen, but where winter freezes are common, mulch heavily. All parts are toxic if ingested so keep away from small children and pets.

Pests/Diseases—Due to its toxic alkaloids, it has few pests, except caterpillars, slugs and snails.

Landscaping Tips & Ideas—Plant under palm trees, near water features or combine with Beach Strawberry or Trailing African Daisy to highlight the Crinums. Consider among the many species: 'Queen Emma' grows up to 6 ft. tall with huge clusters of light pink flowers or 'Ellen Bosanquet' with fragrant, rose-colored flowers.

NAKED LADY
(BELLADONA LILY)
Amaryllis belladonna

Hardiness—Preferred zones 8-10

Color(s)—Rosy pink

Bloom Period—Late summer to fall

Mature Size (H & W)—2 to 3 ft. x 2 ft.

Water Needs—Water after initial planting.

Planting/Care—Thrives in warm, dry summer regions. Flower stalks appear before foliage with clusters of fragrant, trumpet-shaped blossoms. Plant in well-draining soil, 12 in. apart with bulb tops at or a bit above soil level. Provide full sun and leave it alone for a long-lived bulb. Cut off yellow foliage when dormant in early summer.

Pests/Diseases—Gopher and deer-resistant. Bulbs will rot if planted in clay or soggy soils.

Landscaping Tips & Ideas—Plant with other water-thrifty South African or Mediterranean natives such as Ixia, Giant Squill and Gladiolus in cut flower or rock gardens, toward the back of flower beds or borders. All parts are toxic if ingested, so keep away from children or pets.

ORIENTAL LILY AND ORIENPETS

Lilium hybrids

Hardiness—Preferred zones 5-10

Color(s)—White, pink, yellow, red

Bloom Period—Midsummer to fall.

Mature Size (H & W)—3 to 5 ft. x 1 to 3 ft.

Water Needs—Needs water year-round, decrease water after leaves yellow, but don't allow roots to dry completely.

Planting/Care—Plant 2½ times as deep as bulb's diameter and space 1 ft. apart in full sun except where over 90°F, provide afternoon shade. Needs well-drained and amended soil. Use an organic fertilizer when growth occurs and when budded flowers are showing color.

Pests/Diseases—Protect from gophers by planting in wire baskets.

Landscaping Tips & Ideas—With large perfumed blooms, plant close to pathways for all to enjoy. 'Casablanca' and 'Stargazer' are magnificent Oriental Lilies. Orienpets (crosses between Oriental and Trumpet Lilies) are more heat-tolerant. 'Vice Versa' is fragrant with hints of citrus, and its coral red brightens the summer garden.

PERUVIAN LILY

Alstroemeria aurantiaca

Hardiness—Preferred zones 9-11

Color(s)—Pink, lavender, yellow, orange, and bicolors

Bloom Period—Spring-summer

Mature Size (H & W)—2 to 4 ft. x 2 to 4 ft.

Water Needs—Water every 5-7 days during growth and bloom cycles.

Planting/Care—Plant in spring after the last frost from seed or rhizomes in full sun (for hot climates afternoon shade) and rich, well-drained sandy soil with a neutral pH of 7.0. When plants go dormant after bloom, do not water unless there are no winter rains. Fertilize once a month during the growing and blooming seasons.

Pests/Diseases—Thrips can distort and discolor flowers. Spray with an organic Spinosad or a systemic listed to control thrips.

Landscaping Tips & Ideas—*Alstroemeria* are lovely in cut-flower gardens or in the middle of borders and mixed beds. Combine with Tuberose, Shasta Daisies and Paludosum Daisies. To encourage repeat blooming, yank out flowering stems from the base.

PERUVIAN SCILLA

Scilla peruviana

Hardiness—Preferred zones 8-10

Color(s)—Lavender-blue or white

Bloom Period—Late spring, early summer

Mature Size (H & W)—8 to 12 in. x 8 to 12 in.

Water Needs—Water every 7-10 days, reduce water after foliage yellows.

Planting/Care—In autumn, plant bulbs in humus-rich, well-drained soil with the top of the bulb at or slightly above soil level, 6 in. apart. Needs full sun and an organic fertilizer during growth and bloom periods. Plant in containers for cold-winter regions and take indoors prior to first frost and bring them outside when danger of frost is over.

Pests/Diseases—Deer-resistant. Bulbs prone to rot or sooty mold if planted where poor air circulation or poor-draining soil.

Landscaping Tips & Ideas—Fantastic 6 in. globe-shaped flower head with over 100 lavender, blue florets shows off in containers, along pathways, as edging in mixed borders and in rock gardens.

RANUNCULUS
(PERSIAN BUTTERCUP)
Ranunculus asiaticus

Hardiness—Preferred zones 8-11

Color(s)—A rainbow of colors, plus picotee and bicolors

Bloom Period—Late winter, spring or summer

Mature Size (H & W)—12 to 24 in. x 12 to 24 in.

Water Needs—Soak after planting, resume watering when new leaves appear and continue until foliage yellows.

Planting/Care—Plant tubers in fall where winters are mild or spring after the last frost. Needs rich, fast-draining soil. Bury tubers "toes down" spacing 4 to 6 in. apart, 2 in. deep in full sun.

Pests/Diseases—While leaves are still immature, protect from birds with netting or chicken wire. Keep away from children and pets because all parts are toxic.

Landscaping Tips & Ideas—Fabulous in borders or containers in a solid mass or mixed with Iceland Poppies, Alyssum, Pansies, Shasta Daisies and Narcissus. Try 'Tecolote' for huge, colorful, cabbage-rose-like flowers on 18-24 in. stems.

SAFFRON CROCUS
Crocus sativus

Hardiness—Preferred zones 6-9

Color(s)—Purple

Bloom Period—Fall

Mature Size (H & W)—2½ in. x 2½ in.

Water Needs—Water every 7-10 days during growth and bloom cycles. Stop watering when dormant.

Planting/Care—Plant corms in humus-amended, well-draining soil, 2-3 in. deep and 3-4 in. apart. Where summers are hot, plant in part sun, but provide full sun in mild summer regions. Apply an organic, water-soluble fertilizer after flowers are spent. Divide corms after leaves brown and replant in newly amended soil, but Saffron will not naturalize where winters are warm.

Pests/Diseases—Protect from gophers by planting in wire baskets.

Landscaping Tips & Ideas—Lovely additions in rock gardens, containers and in the front of borders. For culinary use, remove the reddish-orange stigmas as soon as the blooms open, dry and store in airtight container. Stigmas from a dozen flowers should be enough for a paella.

SICILIAN HONEY LILY
(ORNAMENTAL ONION)
Nectaroscordum siculum
(Allium bulgaricum)

Hardiness—Preferred zones 6-10

Color(s)—White with purplish center

Bloom Period—May-June

Mature Size (H & W)—2 to 4 ft. x 1½ to 2 ft.

Water Needs—Water every 7-10 days during growth and bloom seasons, water infrequently during summer months.

Planting/Care—A Mediterranean native, plant this sun-loving ornamental Allium bulb in autumn in well-drained soil 2 in. deep and 18 in. apart. Feed with an organic fertilizer in spring and again in fall.

Pests/Diseases—Deer and rodent resistant. If aphids are a problem wash off with a strong stream of water.

Landscaping Tips & Ideas—With clusters of up to 30 nodding, bell-shaped, florets, it is an elegant and colorful addition to a water-thrifty garden or in containers. Plant with other Mediterranean and South African bulbs such as *Hippeastrum*, *Babiana* and Giant Squill. After flowers are spent, the seedheads are excellent for dried arrangements.

SPRING STARFLOWER
Ipheion uniflorum

Hardiness—Preferred zones 6-9

Color(s)—White, blue

Bloom Period—Late winter-spring

Mature Size (H & W)—4 to 6 in. x 4 to 6 in.

Water Needs—Water once a week but discontinue during summer dormancy.

Planting/Care—Plant bulbs in humus or compost amended, well-draining soil 2 in. deep and 2 in. apart. Needs full or part sun and feed with a water-soluble organic fertilizer during growth and bloom cycles. During summer dormancy, avoid watering. Divide infrequently and allow to multiply for a better floral display,

Pests/Diseases—Few pests or diseases as long as soil drains well. Control aphids with a horticultural oil.

Landscaping Tips & Ideas—Use as edging, tuck between steppingstones, plant under deciduous shrubs or naturalize among low grasses or woodlands. Star-shaped, scented flowers are dark blue ('Wisley Blue'), periwinkle blue ('Rolf Fiedler') and white ('White Star') provide a beautiful contrast to Daffodils, tulips and other spring-flowering bulbs.

SPIDER LILY
Hymenocallis spp.

Hardiness—Preferred zones 8-10

Color(s)—White, yellow and bicolors

Bloom Period—Late spring-summer

Mature Size (H & W)—12 to 24 in. x 12 to 18 in.

Water Needs—Water every 7-10 days during growth and keep roots moist during dormancy, but water less.

Planting/Care—Plant in fall with humus-amended, excellent draining soil in full sun. Wait until spring where winters are cold. Cover the bulb tips 1 in. below the soil and space 6 in. apart. Where frost is common, dig up when bulbs are dormant and store; otherwise leave in ground.

Pests/Diseases—Fungal diseases are usually caused by poor-draining soil or poor air circulation.

Landscaping Tips & Ideas—Fragrant flowers resemble Daffodils with spidery petals and need to be planted along pathways or in containers to enjoy their perfume. 'Exotica' bears large white flowers with a lemony perfume and 'Sulfur Queen' has 6 in., pale yellow with green striped blossoms.

TUBEROSE
Polianthes tuberosa

Hardiness—Preferred zones 10-11

Color(s)—Creamy-white

Bloom Period—Summer or fall

Mature Size (H & W)—2 to 3 ft. x 2 to 3 ft.

Water Needs—Water 5-7 days during growth and bloom periods.

Planting/Care—Plant after the last frost date from rhizomes in the ground (2 in. deep and 5 in. apart) or containers. Needs richly amended, well-draining soil with a pH of 6.7. Once a rhizome has flowered, it will not re-flower, but the "baby" rhizomes develop around the "mother" and will bloom within 4 years. Provide part or full shade in hot climates and full sun in mild climates. Fertilize during growth and bloom periods with cottonseed meal and stop watering after foliage yellows.

Pests/Diseases—Few insect or disease problems but all parts are toxic so keep away from children and pets.

Landscaping Tips & Ideas—Ideal in a cut flower garden or mixed flower beds with Gladiolus, Delphinium, Foxglove, Daylily, and Roses.

TUBEROUS BEGONIA
Begonia hybrid

Hardiness—Preferred zones 9-11

Color(s)—Every color except blue; picotee, and bicolors

Bloom Period—Summer-fall

Mature Size (H & W)—12 to 18 in. x 12 to 18 in.

Water Needs—Water once a week or more during growth and bloom cycles.

Planting/Care—Prefers cool, coastal conditions. Plant from tubers during winter. Provide rich, humus-amended soil and cover tuber with about 25% of the mix. Keep soil moist while rooting and set in indirect light where temperatures are above 65°F. When two leaves appear, and when temperature is 50°F plus, move outdoors. Keep soil moist. Reduce watering in fall after leaves yellow. Fertilize regularly with water-soluble food until tuber goes dormant.

Pests/Diseases—Powdery mildew can be controlled with a horticultural oil or organic fungicide.

Landscaping Tips & Ideas—Plant in hanging baskets to better appreciate saucer-sized blooms with frilly, double and tight-centered forms that resemble giant Carnations, Camellias and Roses.

TULIP
Tulipa spp.

Hardiness—Preferred Zones 3-10 depending on species

Color(s)—Pink, orange, yellow, red, and bicolors

Bloom Period—Early spring

Mature Size (H & W)—8 to 10 in. x 6 to 10 in.

Water Needs—Water every 5-7 days during growth, but stop during dormancy.

Planting/Care—Plant in well-draining, humus-amended soil in full sun. In hot climates, plant bulbs 2 inches deeper than package recommendations.

Pests/Diseases—Protect from gophers by planting in wire cages or containers. For aphids, wash off with a strong stream of water.

Landscaping Tips & Ideas—Species tulips are smaller than Dutch hybrids, but naturalize in many California regions and are charming nestled amidst winter annuals or planted in drifts and in rock gardens. *T. chrysantha* (8-10 in., yellow with red reverse, USDA Zones 3-9) *T. clusiana* ('Lady Jane' candy-cane red and white, 12 in., Zones 4-8) and *T. saxatilis* (6 in. rose lilac with yellow eye Zones 5-10).

WATSONIA
Watsonia spp.

Hardiness—Preferred zones 9-11

Color(s)—Red, pink, purple, orange, white

Bloom Period—Spring-summer depending on species

Mature Size (H & W)—3-5 ft.

Water Needs—Water every 7-10 days during growth and bloom, but discontinue when plants go dormant.

Planting/Care—Needs well-draining amended soils and full sun. Plant corms in fall, 4 in. deep and space 6 in. apart. Allow to naturalize except where winters are cold, dig up after foliage dies back, store and re-plant in spring.

Pests/Diseases—Root rot develops when there is poor soil drainage. Control thrips with an organic insecticide such as Spinosad or a systemic.

Landscaping Tips & Ideas—This South African native resembles Gladiolus, except floral spikes have more petite, trumpet-shaped and fragrant flowers. Use effectively in cut flower and rock gardens, toward the back of mixed perennial borders or containers. Stunning with Lily of the Nile or other South African bulbs.

MORE RECOMMENDATIONS

- CLUSTER LILY *Brodiaea* USDA Zones 7-10. Native to Pacific Coast. Purple, blue, yellow, white flowers in spring-summer. Ideal for water-thrifty gardens. Naturally found in clay soils where there are winter rains but completely dry in summer.

- DUTCH TULIP *Tulipa* hybrids USDA Zones 3-7. For zones 8 or warmer, it will be necessary to chill bulbs for 8-12 weeks in the refrigerator (not the freezer) at 35-45° F. Some nurseries and mail-order companies sell chilled tulips. Once blooms are spent in zones 8 or above, it is best to treat as annuals.

- FANCY-LEAFED CALADIUM *Caladium bicolor* USDA Zones 9-11. Tropical tuber prized for large, multi-colored foliage in hues of green, white, red, pink, silver, and bronze. They are 2-to-4-ft. tall and as wide. Does best in shade. Plant in spring, dig up and store after leaves die back in fall, and replant after the last day of frost.

- FAWN LILY (DOG'S TOOTH VIOLET, TROUT LILY) *Erythronium californicum* USDA Zones 3-9. Bears lily-like, cream or yellow flowers on 6-10 in. stems. Water during growth and bloom periods, but withhold water during dormancy. Use in rock gardens and water-thrifty landscapes.

- GLORY LILY *Gloriosa superba* 'Rothschildiana' USDA Zones 8-11. Can climb up to 6 ft. Bears nodding, bright-yellow and orange lily flowers. Stop watering when dormant in winter.

- GUERNSEY LILY (SPIDER LILY) *Nerine bowdenii* USDA Zones 7-10. Pink, white and red spider lilies bloom in late summer or fall on leafless stems. Water this South African native only during growth and bloom cycles.

- HYACINTH *Hyacinthus orientalis* hybrids USDA Zones 4-8. Chill bulbs like Tulips for zones higher than 8. Intoxicating fragrance with large floral spikes. Keep in well-draining soil. Deer resistant.

- LEOPARD LILY *Lilium pardalinum* USDA Zones 5-9. California native that thrives wherever it is not too hot. Bright reddish-orange petals freckled with gold and brown spots on 4-6 ft. tall plants. Blooms in late spring or early summer. Keep dry when leaves yellow completely.

- MARIPOSA LILY (MARIPOSA TULIP) *Calochortas* USDA Zones 7-9. Common California native. 12-24 in. tall. Cup-shaped yellow, purple, red, pink, or white blossoms with brush marks in contrasting browns and yellows. Wonderful in rock gardens or can be naturalized as long as they are kept dry in summer.

ORIENTAL LILY

- ORNAMENTAL ALLIUM *Allium* USDA Zones 4-10 depending on the species. Related to the edible onion. Size ranging from 6 in. to over 5 ft. Bears red, pink, violet, blue, yellow, burgundy, or white small flowers clustered in a ball-shape on bare stems. Use in fresh or dried arrangements and mixed flower beds.

- PINEAPPLE FLOWER *Eucomis* spp. USDA Zones 7-11. Native to tropical South Africa bearing spikes of compact clusters of green edged in purple or greenish-white, ½ in. blossoms with leaf-like bracts on top of the spikes that look like the tops of pineapples. Plant in fall for summer blooms. Excellent cut flower and shows off well in containers.

- TIGER FLOWER (MEXICAN SHELL FLOWER) *Tigridia pavonia* USDA Zones 8-11. Native to Mexico with vibrant, three outer-petaled flowers in red, yellow, orange, pink, and white. Plant in spring, water during growth period, withhold water after leaves yellow. Grow in containers or in water-thrifty landscapes.

JANUARY

- Brighten rainy days by browsing through catalogues and websites to order spring- and summer-blooming bulbs.

- Edelweissperennials.com, oldhousegardens.com and telosrarebulbs.com offer selections of bulbs that are good choices for the West Coast climate.

- Garden centers offer spring bulbs for sale.

- Inspect stored bulbs, corms, rhizomes and tubers and throw away if rotten or shriveled.

- *Hippeastrum* (marketed as Amaryllis) forced indoors during the winter will re-bloom if planted outdoors. Cut off the spent flower head after the petals have dropped encouraging all the energy to return to the bulb. Plant outdoors with the top 25% above the soil level. It will re-bloom the following spring (not the current spring). Other forced bulbs such as Narcissus, Hyacinth and Crocus are unlikely to re-bloom outdoors, and it is best to throw the spent plants away.

- Replenish bulb beds with mulch or compost (25%), and dig it in to about 12 in. deep.

FEBRUARY

- Pre-chilled pips of Lily-of-the-Valley are available for indoor pleasure.

- In warm-winter regions, plant bulbs for spring and summer blooms: Tuberous Begonia, Caladium, Calla, Dahlia, Gladiolus, Gloriosa Lily, Pineapple Lily, Tigridia, and Tuberose. For areas where frost is common, wait another month or two until the danger of frost has passed.

- Apply a pre-emergent to existing bulb and new bulb beds to prevent weeds for up to 6 months.

- Do not hoe around Lilies because their roots may be damaged. Hand-weed and avoid any pre-emergent, because it hinders Lily root development.

- Critters will be digging up, burrowing and browsing tender bulb growth except bulbs with high alkaloid content, such as Narcissus. Prevent digging up just-planted bulbs by pegging down plastic netting or wire mesh until the tempting odor of freshly turned earth has dissipated. Discourage burrowers by planting in buried pots or wire baskets. Protect from browsers with chicken wire barriers or olfactory deterrents.

MARCH

- Give all spring bulbs a generous dose of organic liquid fertilizer about 3 times every two weeks and snip off developing seed heads to boost next year's display.

- Control mildew with a horticultural oil or an organic fungicide.

- When chewing insects become a problem, use an organic control such as Spinosad. It is safe for most beneficial insects, but to protect bees, spray in the late afternoon or early evening when they have returned to their hives.

- Southern Californians are allowed to use decollate snails to control juvenile snails, but in Northern California use an iron phosphate snail and slug killer because it is safe for children, pets and wildlife.

- Label any clumps of spring-flowering bulbs that naturalize such as Daffodils or rhizomes such as Bearded Iris that have not flowered as vigorously as in years past. Feed them every 2 weeks with an organic liquid feed until their foliage begins to yellow.

APRIL

- If soil is clayey, incorporate lots of humus or compost to improve drainage and prevent bulb rot.

- When spring bulbs have bloomed out, continue to water and care for the plants until the foliage has yellowed completely. Nutrients need to be returned to the bulb so that it can bear again next spring. Interplant with taller spring annuals or perennials to camouflage the bulb's yellowing foliage.

- Release beneficial insects such as lacewings, ladybugs, predatory wasps, and mites and praying mantis to control unwanted bugs.

- Plant Dahlias and other cold-sensitive tubers and bulbs after the last day of frost for summer-fall color. Dahlias forms range from huge dinner-plate, cactus and semi-cactus, decorative formal or informal, waterlily to the petite pompom.

- For a long flowering season, plant Gladiolus corms in succession now through May. Choose a range of varieties with different heights and colors.

- Continue to deadhead spring blooming bulbs such as Daffodils to extend the bloom season.

MAY

- Stake Gladiolus, Watsonia and other bulb plants that bear long spikes of flowers or plant shrubs and other perennials that will support the top-heavy blossoms.

- Plant a selection of summer and fall bulbs in pots to fill in gaps in your beds and to take center stage on patios, decks, and near water features. *Eucomis*, Dahlias and Callas are great choices.

- There are many different species of Lilies with varying shapes, colors as well as fragrance, making them great choices for the summer garden. Remember that most Lilies prefer their faces in the sun and toes in the shade, with loose, rich, evenly moist, well-drained soils. Select Asiatic Lilies for early blooms; Oriental Lilies for taller and later flowers and Orienpets for voluptuous, fragrant and colorful crosses of Oriental and Trumpet Lilies.

- For more fragrance in the summer garden, select Tuberoses. Mexican Single Tuberose white flowers bloom on 3-4 ft. spikes; 'Pearl' is a shorter, later-bloomer with double flowers.

JUNE

- Watch out for thrips on Gladiolus, Watsonia and other summer bloomers. Spray with Spinosad or use a thrips-specific systemic.

- Deeply water summer bulbs and continue to water late-spring bulbs until dormancy. Summer heat can dry out the garden quickly, but do not overwater drought-resistant plants, such as South African, Mediterranean and California natives.

- Inspect container plants for root-bound conditions and re-pot with a good organic potting mix.

- Remove bulbs' foliage after they are completely yellow and dry.

- Snip off spent summer blooming bulb flowers such as Lilies as soon as their flower petals have fallen, but leave the stems and foliage. This prevents plants from wasting energy by producing seeds and encourages them to continue building up the nutrient reserves in the bulbs for next year.

- If plants produce attractive seed heads they should be allowed to form. Cut, dry and use in "everlasting" flower arrangements like the Sicilian Honey Lily.

JULY

- Caterpillars and whiteflies proliferate during hot weather. Apply a 1-in. layer of worm castings around bulb plants. Spray with Spinosad every 7-10 days to control the chewing insect population.

- Continue to stake and tie Dahlia stems and other large-flowering summer bulb plants so the wind won't topple them.

- Pick off small lily bulbils from stems and plant in pots filled with ¾ organic potting soil and ¼ perlite. It takes about 3 years to reach flowering size.

- As soon as the Giant Squill's flowers begin to open on its stalk, cut it down at the base and use for an amazing and dramatic cut flower. If in water, the stem continues to grow taller, the flowers continue to open all the way to the top and the stalks will twist and curve as it grows. As a cut flower, it lasts for about two weeks.

AUGUST

- A good organic liquid fertilizer is kelp extract because it contains plant growth hormones, gibberellins and cytokinins. Apply about three times during a bulb plant's growth and bloom periods.

- Lift bulb clumps that you labeled in spring as not blooming as vigorously as in years past, divide and replant into freshly prepared soil. Be sure to plant at the same level and space apart as you would new bulbs, rhizomes, corms, etc.

- Unless saving seeds, remove spent summer bulb flowers, but continue to water and care for them until the leaves have completely yellowed.

- Plant or move Bearded Iris rhizomes. Iris planted in summer are more likely to bloom next spring. Give it full sun, at least half day. In hot inland regions, barely cover the rhizome tops with soil to prevent sun scald, but closer to coastal areas, allow the tops to peak slightly above the soil. Divide Bearded iris about every three years.

SEPTEMBER

- Get bulb beds ready to plant spring bulbs. Make sure there is at least 25% volume of humus or compost dug in to a depth of 12 inches. Also add a product with humic acids to revitalize the soil.

- Most nurseries have spring-flowering bulbs such as Daffodils, Dutch Iris, *Muscari* and Ranunculus for sale now that can be planted in the fall in mild-winter regions. Where winter frosts are common, wait until spring.

- Bearded Iris rhizomes are also available now for fall planting. Remember to plant the rhizomes a bit above the soil level where summers are mild, but inland and desert regions should cover with a thin layer of soil to prevent sunburn.

- Plant winter Cyclamen for blooms by November or December.

- Plant Mediterranean, South African and native bulbs now for spring color such as: Babiana, Freesia, Sparaxis, Tritonia and Watsonia. Wait until late winter for Tulips, Hyacinths and Crocus.

OCTOBER

- Fall is a good time to divide and transplant overgrown clumps of South African bulbs such as Freesia, African Corn Lily (*Ixia*), Harlequin Flower (*Sparaxis*) and Watsonia. Transplant as you would new bulbs in well-amended, good-draining soil.

- Hyacinths, Dutch tulips and other bulbs needing cold snaps should be stored in paper bags (never plastic) and refrigerated (not in the freezer) for 8-10 weeks prior to planting outdoors in mild-winter regions.

- Plant up some Daffodil bulbs in pots to use for filling up bare spaces in borders. They will flower in late winter or early spring. Always use commercial potting soil for containers. Garden soil compacts in containers.

- In frost-prone climates, lift cold-sensitive bulbs such as Watsonia, Dahlias, etc. and store in a cool, dry, protected area such as the garage.

- If spring and summer bulb seeds have germinated and developed into seedlings, you can leave them in place or transplant elsewhere.

NOVEMBER

- Still time to plant all types of bulbs except those requiring winter chilling. Include an organic pre-plant or bulb fertilizer during planting time.

- Purchase bulbs for indoor enjoyment from Thanksgiving through the New Year. Force *Hippeastrum* (sold as Amaryllis during the holidays) and *Narcissus* in vases and bowls filled with water or decorative rock to enjoy or give as gifts during the winter holidays such as Amaryllis, Crocus, Freesias, Paperwhites, and Tulips.

- Feed winter-blooming bulbs, corms and rhizomes such as Cyclamen with an organic fertilizer.

- Bait flower beds with an organic iron phosphate to control slugs and snails that will come out in the wet season.

- Plant native bulbs from Mariposa and Globe Tulips (*Calochortus* spp.) to *Brodiaea* and *Tritelia*.

- If soil is not well-drained or in frost-prone areas, wait until tender bulbs/corms/rhizomes such as Dahlia, Begonia, Canna and Caladium go dormant before digging up and storing in a cool, dry place.

DECEMBER

- Check potted bulbs, especially under covered patios or eaves, to make sure they are being watered sufficiently.

- If winter rains do not arrive, water newly planted bulbs every 7-10 days during growth and bloom periods.

- For warm-winter areas, plant Crocus, Hyacinth and Dutch Tulips that have been in the refrigerator for 8-10 weeks in full or part sun. Planting depth should be about twice the diameter of the bulb. Plant winter-annuals above spring and summer bulbs for long-lasting color such as Pansies, Primrose, Viola, Stock, and Iceland Poppy.

- Hyacinths, Crocus, Paperwhites, and Amaryllis that have been forced indoors do best in a cool room with bright, filtered light. Keep them away from heater vents and bowls of fresh fruit (fruit are notorious sources of ethylene gas that accelerate the decline of indoor plants).

- Check for mealybugs and scale insects on indoor bulb foliage. Wash off with water or use a Q-tip saturated with alcohol.

- To divide Dahlia tubers in mild winter areas, sever the tuber from the plant cluster and include a section of the crown with one or two eyes, store and plant in spring.

SAFFRON CROCUS

CITRUS
for California

Citrus are plant nomads that have been brought from Southern China, Southeast Asia and other parts of the world in the form of hundreds of varieties and subspecies. They have taken root and made themselves at home in the sunny warmth of our Golden State.

THE VIRTUES OF CITRUS

Citrus trees are handsome throughout the year and are ideal additions to orchards and mild-climate gardens. They are quite ornamental with their lustrous-green foliage, large clusters of intensely perfumed, creamy or purplish blossoms, immature green fruits, and mature bright nuggets of sunshine. The crops of tasty fruits are a bonus, particularly in winter when other trees are dormant.

Although citrus plants belong to either the *Citrus*, *Microcitrus* or *Fortunella* genus and have been hybridized to create one of the most complex fruits on earth, they share many common characteristics. They are evergreen with fragrant flowers that are mostly creamy-white, often tinged with pink or purple. The fruits have leathery rinds and fleshy interiors that are divided into sections and separated by parchment-like membranes. Many varieties are available both as standard 20-foot and dwarf six- to ten-foot trees. Standard trees provide a shaded respite from the sun, and dwarf varieties make wonderful hedges, espaliers or container plants. Most citrus trees sold at nurseries are composite trees, meaning their rootstocks differ from their tops, which are called scions. The rootstocks have been genetically developed to resist pests, diseases, or less-than-optimum soil conditions and are grafted on to compatible scions that have superior fruit quality.

SELECT A HEALTHY TREE

Select well-grown one- or two-year-old trees that are between one-half to one inch in diameter when measured one inch above the graft union. Older trees tend to be root bound and do not establish as quickly when they are planted. A healthy, vigorous tree should have large leaves all along the length of its trunk with a uniform green color, free from pest damage. The branching should be symmetrical, and the bark should be bright and clean with a healed graft union that is six inches above the ground.

GROW A VARIETY FOR YOUR CLIMATE

Growing tasty fruit begins with selecting a variety that suits your climate. Some citrus do not produce sweet fruit near the coast where temperatures are cool. Lemons and Limes require less heat and they do produce good fruit near the coast. The Valencia Orange produces good fruit from the coast to the desert. Navel Oranges, Mandarins and Tangelos require more heat and do best in inland valleys. Grapefruit need prolonged periods of high heat to develop peak flavor and they grow best in the desert, although recent hybrids such as the 'Oroblanco' have a lower heat requirement.

Resistance to cold weather is variable, with the Satsuma Mandarin and Nagami Kumquat being the most tolerant, Sweet Oranges, Grapefruits, Tangelos, and other Mandarins intermediate, Lemons less tolerant, and Limes the least tolerant. Unlike other fruits, citrus do not contain much starch, so they do not sweeten once plucked from the tree; thus, they should be picked only when fully ripe.

PROVIDE PROPER CARE

In addition to a suitable climate, successful citrus cultivation depends on year-round care. Proper irrigation is very important. All citrus need well-drained soils—if allowed to stand in water, the roots will be damaged and leaf drop will result. To resolve drainage problems, plant citrus in raised beds filled with potting soil and mulch. Do not plant shallow-rooted plants that need frequent watering (like lawns, ground covers, annuals) beneath citrus trees, or the soil will be too moist for the trees.

Add three to four inches of mulch under the tree to conserve water, prevent weeds, and absorb damaging salts from the water. Fertilize with a complete citrus food in late winter after the fruit has set and grown one-half inch in diameter, and again in early summer. Follow the directions on package labels because different manufacturers formulate different ingredients and percentages. If new leaves are turning yellow, iron deficiency may be the problem. Iron chelate is an appropriate remedy for iron chlorosis. Zinc deficiency causes yellow mottling or blotching of the green leaves and can be remedied with chelated zinc as a foliar spray or as a soil application.

KEEP PRUNING TO A MINIMUM

Prune citrus after fruiting is completed during spring and summer but keep pruning to a minimum, just for shape and to remove dead wood, broken or damaged limbs, water sprouts, and suckers. Protect the inner branches from exposure to the sun's intense rays by painting with whitewash or latex paint.

"June drop" and insect infestations are some common citrus maladies. "June drop" is the sudden shedding of immature fruit, which is nature's way of adjusting the crop size to the tree's capability to produce good fruit. If the weather is unusually hot or dry, the drop may be sizable. The fruit may also split and drop off if there is too much water. If it becomes necessary to control aphids, scale, mealybugs, thrips, mites and leaf rollers, select methods that are appropriate for the particular pest and locality.

MORE THAN FRUIT FACTORIES

Whether displayed as an ornamental or grown in an orchard, citrus trees are more than fruit factories: they are handsome shade, hedge, container, and specimen trees. In California, Citrus fruits represent the sweetness in life.

LIME

AUSTRALIAN FINGER LIME
Microcitrus australasica

Hardiness—Preferred Zones 10 and above

Color(s)—White flowers

Flower Period—May to July

Fruit Period—November to December

Mature Size (H & W)—4-9 ft. x 4-6 ft.

Water Needs—Deep, regular water every 10-14 days

Planting/Care—Native to Queensland as an understory plant, plant in full sun in mild-winter or coastal areas but further inland, where it is very hot, provide afternoon shade. Does not tolerate frost. Provide richly amended, well-draining soil and fertilize with an organic citrus food twice a year (late winter and early summer).

Pests/Diseases—Control scale with an organic canola oil-based product. To prevent fungal rot, keep mulch 2-4 in. away from the base of the tree.

Landscaping Tips & Ideas—Plant in a container or directly in the ground in frost-free regions. Chefs prize the 3-7-in. tapered fruits because its juice vesicles burst out when they are sliced and resemble caviar. The tangy, refreshing lime-tasting fruits are used as garnish, in salads, soups, jams, sauces and Thai curries.

CALAMONDIN
Citrofortunella microcarpa

Hardiness—Preferred Zones 10-11

Color(s)—White flowers

Bloom Period—Year-round

Fruit Period—Winter-fall in N. California; winter-midsummer in S. California; early winter to early spring in desert.

Mature Size (H & W)—6 to 10 ft. x 6 to 8 ft.

Water Needs—Water deeply and regularly every 10-14 days depending on growth and weather conditions.

Planting/Care—Plant in spring after the last frost date and space 12 ft. apart. Construct a 6-10 ft. diameter watering basin and cover with 3 in. of mulch or compost. See page 87.

Pests/Diseases—Wrap copper bands around the trunk to keep snails out of the tree's canopy. Spray aphids and mites with an organic canola-based oil.

Landscaping Tips & Ideas—Makes a wonderful ornamental background or shade tree in the landscape and an ideal indoor or outdoor container. It is a bit more cold-tolerant than many other citrus.

KUMQUAT
Fortunella japonica

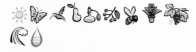

Hardiness—Preferred Zones 9-11

Color(s)—White flowers

Bloom Period—Spring to midsummer

Fruit Period—Late winter or early spring.

Mature Size (H & W)—8 ft. x 6 ft.

Water Needs—Water regularly and deeply every 10-14 days depending on growth, fruit and weather conditions.

Planting/Care—Plant in spring, spacing about 10 ft. apart in full sun. Needs rich, well-drained soil with a pH of 6.7-7.0. Fertilize in late winter and early summer with a granular organic citrus food.

Kumquats thrive in hot, humid summers, but can also adapt to cooler conditions.

Pests/Diseases—Control Citrus red or brown scale with an organic canola based or Neem oil.

Landscaping Tips & Ideas—With their golden orange-colored fruits, Kumquats are prized as ornamentals and make good foundation shrubs and plants for terrace, patio and bonsai containers. The fruits are small but can be eaten whole, peel and pulp. Chefs use them in sauces, marmalade, garnishes and piquant preserves.

GRAPEFRUIT
Citrus paradisi

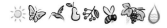

Hardiness—Preferred Zones 10-11

Color(s)—Creamy-white flowers

Bloom Period—March-April

Fruit Period—Ripens every 12-14 mo. in low deserts; every 18 months on coast.

Mature Size (H & W)—10 to 15 ft. x 15 ft.

Water Needs—Every 10-14 days depending on growth and weather.

Planting/Care—Plant in spring spacing about 15 ft. apart and build a watering basin outlined on page 87. Grapefruit have the highest heat requirement of all citrus and most varieties require a long, hot growing season.

Pests/Diseases—Control giant whitefly and mites with an organic canola-based or Neem oil.

Landscaping Tips & Ideas—Ideal as background, ornamental or shade trees in the landscape. Bears attractive large yellow or pink-blushed fruits. Two types: seeded tends to be more flavorful and separates into segments easily and seedless varieties. For coastal or mild-summer regions, consider 'Oroblanco' a sweet, white grapefruit that thrives in cooler climates.

LEMON
Citrus limon

Hardiness—Preferred Zones 9-11

Color(s)—White flowers

Bloom Period—Almost year-round in coastal areas, spring in interior regions.

Mature Size (H & W)—10 to 15 ft. x 12 to 15 ft.

Water Needs—Water deeply every 10-14 days depending on growth, fruit and weather conditions.

Planting/Care—Requires full sun in loam-textured, well-drained soil with 6.7-7.0 pH. See page 87 for more information. Does not need too much heat to ripen, but it is frost-sensitive and may suffer damage when temperatures dip below 30°F.

Pests/Diseases—Control mite infestations with an organic canola based or Neem oil. Mites cause russeting or silvering of the rind.

Landscaping Tips & Ideas—Lemon trees can be pruned into espaliers or planted as ornamental or background trees. They are also desirable in containers for terraces and patios. Culinary uses include: juices, sauces, pie fillings, sorbets, puddings and preserves. 'Meyer' Lemon is one of the sweetest lemons and prized by cooks.

LIME
Citrus aurantifolia

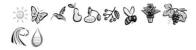

Hardiness—Preferred Zones 10-11

Color(s)—White flowers

Bloom Period—Spring-summer

Fruit Period—All year, but primarily in winter

Mature Size (H & W)—8 to 12 ft. x 10 ft.

Water Needs—Water deeply every 10-14 days depending on growth, fruit and weather conditions.

Planting/Care—Plant in spring spacing 10-15 ft apart in full sun. Provide well-drained, loam soil and build a watering basin. See page 87. Fruit flavor develops best where summers are hot and humid.

Pests/Diseases—If damage from mites and snails is extensive, apply an organic canola based or Neem oil for insects and an iron phosphate molluscicide for snails.

Landscaping Tips & Ideas—Use a Lime tree in containers or as a foundation plant. Mexican Key Lime is popular for drinks, but Persian or Tahiti Lime is a more attractive ornamental and bears larger fruits that are about as juicy and flavorful as the Mexican Lime.

MANDARIN
Citrus reticulata

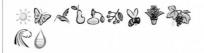

Hardiness—Preferred Zones 10-11

Color(s)—White flowers

Bloom Period—Spring-fall

Fruit Period—December-January

Mature Size (H & W)—10 to 15 ft. x 12 to 15 ft.

Water Needs—Water deeply every 10-14 days depending on growth, fruit and weather conditions.

Planting/Care—Prefers full sun in well-drained soils. Plant in spring, spacing 10-15 ft. apart. Most are frost-hardy, tolerating short dips in temperatures as low as 28°F; fruit cannot survive frost.

Pests/Diseases—Thinning the tree's interior will help prevent pest and disease infestations by promoting good air circulation.

Landscaping Tips & Ideas—Most Mandarins are alternate bearing which means they yield a large crop of small fruit one year, followed by a less prolific crop of large fruit the next year. To increase fruit production, plant a different Mandarin or Tangelo type for cross-pollination. Wonderful in the garden and in containers.

PUMMELO
Citrus grandis

Hardiness—Preferred Zones 10-11

Color(s)—White flowers

Bloom Period—Depends on variety

Fruit Period—April-June except inland December-April and in desert December-February

Mature Size (H & W)—10 to 25 ft. x 15 to 20 ft

Water Needs—Water deeply every 10-14 days and allow soil to dry out slightly before watering.

Planting/Care—Plant in spring and space 15-20 ft. apart in full sun and rich, well-drained soil. See page 87. Fertilize twice a year in late winter and early summer. Thrives in warm areas close to the sea.

Pests/Diseases—Control scale or citrus wooly whitefly with an organic canola-based or Neem oil.

Landscaping Tips & Ideas—Produces the largest citrus fruits often weighing several pounds. Sweeter than most grapefruits, 'Chandler' produces pink-fleshed fruit on a large, spreading tree and is excellent for the home gardener. Makes a perfect background plant.

SWEET ORANGE
Citrus sinensis

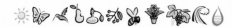

Hardiness—Preferred Zones 10-11

Color(s)—White flowers

Bloom Period—Depends on variety

Fruit Period—'Washington Navel' early to midwinter; 'Valencia' spring-summer

Mature Size (H & W)—10 to 15 ft. x 12 ft.

Water Needs—Water deeply every 10-14 days.

Planting/Care—Plant in spring in full sun and space about 10-15 ft. apart. Provide rich-amended and well-draining soil with a pH of 6.7-7.0. Build a watering basin. See page 87.

Pests/Diseases—Protect from ants by using ant baits, where ants take it to the next nest, destroying the population.

Landscaping Tips & Ideas—If there is space and in a frost-free area, plant a 'Washington Navel' and a 'Valencia' for fresh oranges about ten months out of the year. 'Washington' and 'Valencia' are available as standards and dwarfs and can be used as background trees or in large containers. 'Cara Cara' is a navel with reddish-pink flesh and a rich, sweet taste.

TANGELO
Citrus x tangelo

Hardiness—Preferred Zones 10-11

Color(s)—White flowers; fruit colors range from pale-yellow to deep-orange

Bloom Period—Spring

Fruit Period—Late fall to mid-late winter depending on variety.

Mature Size (H & W)—10 to 15 ft. x 12 ft.

Water Needs—Soak deeply every 10-14 days depending on growth, fruit and weather conditions.

Planting/Care—Plant in spring and space about 15 ft. apart. Build a watering basin. See page 87.

Pests/Diseases—Keep snails away from canopies by wrapping the trunk with copper bands available at retail nurseries.

Landscaping Tips & Ideas—Tangelos are hybrids of Mandarins crossed with Grapefruits or Pummelos. For a more prolific crop, cross-pollinate with a Mandarin. It is a good orchard or foundation tree. 'Minneola' produces orange-red fruit that tastes like Mandarin. 'Wekiwa' resembles a small grapefruit, but tastes like a mandarin and 'Orlando' bears slightly flat, orange fruits with a sweet-tangy taste.

MORE RECOMMENDATIONS

- BLOOD ORANGE *Citrus sinensis* Zones 10-11. Known for deep-red flesh and juice. Excellent flavor with hints of raspberry. 'Moro' bears from early winter-spring.

- CITRON *Citrus medica* Zones 10-11. Has one of the longest histories of cultivation dating back to hundreds of years before Christ. Grows sour fruit similar to lemon practically all year long with highly fragrant rinds, but little juice. Thorny and scraggly plant, but fruits from 'Buddha's Hand' (shaped like fingers) and 'Ertog' (used during the Jewish Feast of the Tabernacles) are used to perfume rooms.

- KUMQUAT *Fortunella japonica* Zones 9-11. 'Nagami' is the most common, but 'Meiwa' rind and flesh is sweeter.

- SOUR ORANGE *Citrus aurantium* Zones 9-11. Very ornamental 8-10 ft. shrub or tree with heavily perfumed flowers such as 'Bouquet de Fleurs'. Great for hedging or planted near a sunny walkway, but fruits are small and bitter.

- MANDARIN (TANGERINE) *Citrus reticulata* Zones 10-11. 'Gold Nugget'(ripens late winter-spring, seedless), 'Honey' (ripens late winter-spring, seedless), 'Page' (smaller fruit, but very juicy fruits fall-winter), 'Pixie' (excellent flavor bears mid-late season) and 'Owari Satsuma' (very sweet flavor, ripens earliest of the Mandarin from early fall to December) are favorites for flavor, juiciness, easy peeling, and sweetness.

- SUDACHI *Citrus sudachi* Zones 10-11. A delicacy from Tokushima prefecture in Shikoku, Japan. Small, round green citrus fruits ripen in the fall, flowers in the spring. Zestier and more fragrant than lemon or lime with a higher calcium and vitamin C content than lemon.

- YUZU *Citrus ichangensis* x *C. reticulata* Zones 9-11. Native to China, Tibet and highlands of Japan, it is one of the most cold-tolerant citrus down to 10°F. Bears flowers in the spring and yellow fruits in the fall. Juice is prized in Asian sauces, beverages and marinades.

ORANGE BLOSSOM

JANUARY

- Protect citrus from frost by spraying with an anti-transpirant such as Cloud Cover or Wilt-Pruf or if in containers, move to a more protected area. Using Christmas tree lights is another decorative, but effective way to provide an extra couple degrees protection.

- Rain gauges are important to monitor and record rainfall for your journal. With a record over several years, this should give you a better idea regarding water frequency for your citrus.

- During blustery rainy days, catch up on your reading about new and interesting citrus via catalogues and websites.

- Do not prune citrus trees in winter because it might stimulate frost-tender growth.

- If there are two crops of citrus on the tree at the same time, remove the latest crop before the tree blossoms and sets its next crop.

- Mandarins are ready to harvest during winter when they are heavy with juice, but avoid puffy, lightweight fruits that have soft spots.

FEBRUARY

- For coastal Southern California, fertilize now. For inland areas, wait until the end of February and for mountain regions wait until freezing temperatures end. Nutrients will become available as soil temperatures rise.

- Broadcast the citrus food (granular, organic) about 2 ft. away from the trunk out to the drip line and water in thoroughly.

- Set gopher and rat traps near citrus before they become a problem. Roof rats eat the innards, leaving an empty sack of rind with a symmetrical entrance hole.

- Spray with an organic canola oil based control for over-wintering scale or mites.

- Prepare planting pits as soon as the soil is workable for new citrus plants. See page 82 for more information. If soil drains slowly, plant in raised beds or on a soil mound, but if drainage is average add a 4-6 in. layer of humus mulch or compost to a depth of 1 ft.

MARCH

- Warm, moist weather encourages snail and slug populations. Use 2-in.-wide copper bands around the base of trees to keep them out of the canopies. Copper gives the slime crawlers an electrical shock. To control them on the ground, use decollate snails in Southern California or an iron phosphate molluscicide elsewhere.

- Spring is the best time to plant citrus, but for frost-prone regions, wait until the danger of frost has passed. Citrus are available as standard (20-30 ft. tall) or dwarf (5-15 ft.). Plant in free-draining soil, with at least 8 hours of sun and protected from wind.

- When to water? Water newly planted trees twice weekly by summer and possibly even more during dry, hot weather. Make sure the soil is moist but not soggy.

- For interior and mountain regions, continue to protect tender citrus.

- Leaf drop on orange trees is a normal occurrence in spring, particularly Washington navels and Valencia.

APRIL

- Wait until frost-damaged trees begin growing again before removing any damaged or dead branches. Also prune for shape, cut off interfering branches, control height for easy harvest and remove suckers growing from below the graft. In frost-prone areas wait until late spring or early summer to prune.

- Use a product containing humic acids to revitalize the soil.

- Apply worm castings around citrus for extra nutrients and to help resist pests.

- Where frost is common, select more cold-tolerant citrus such as Kumquats, Satsuma Mandarins, Sour Orange, Yuzu, and Calamondin. Another option is to plant dwarf citrus in containers that can be easily moved and protected during freezes.

- As the rainy season ends, supplemental irrigation is necessary. If the soil is sandy loam, supply 4-6 in. of water to the watering basin every 7-14 days.

- Fertilize citrus again after the tree blooms and the fruits develop to ½-in. diameter.

MAY

- To control unwanted insects release beneficial ladybugs, lacewings, predatory mites, wasps and praying mantis. Also spray with organic Spinosad every 7-10 days, but make sure bees have returned to their hives in the late afternoon or early evening. Spinosad does not harm beneficial insects once it is dry,

- Plant African Blue Basil, Hall's Honeysuckle and Red Apple groundcover to attract bees and birds to pollinate the citrus blossoms.

- If space is limited, plant three varieties of dwarf citrus in a single planting pit (space 3-4 ft. on center) or choose a salad citrus with multiple varieties grafted or budded onto a single rootstock. If one grafted variety becomes more vigorous than the others, prune to keep growth proportional.

- Harvest Valencia in spring-summer. Produces excellent fruit for juicing oranges, especially where summers are hot.

- Since many citrus have sharp thorns, wear gloves and a long-sleeved shirt when harvesting or pruning.

JUNE

- Pocket gophers are active during warmer months and can destroy tree roots. Get rid of them without using toxic baits by setting manual traps. Cats are good hunters as well as gopher or king snakes.

- Clean up fallen citrus fruit and debris to prevent pests such as borers and other larvae.

- For citrus in containers re-pot if root-bound or freshen up the soil with a humic acid product, worm castings and organic potting soil.

- Citrus leafminers in the larval stage tunnel inside foliage, leaving unsightly patterns and leaf curl. They will not seriously harm established citrus trees, but if damage is extensive control with organic Spinosad. It is safe to use on plants with edible crops and will not harm beneficial insects once dried.

- Huanglongbing bacterial disease is vectored by the citrus Asian psyllid causing fruits to not ripen, become inedible and eventually killing the tree. Contact your local UC Cooperative Extension office for confirmation.

JULY

- For hot inland and desert regions, protect the bark of citrus trees from the scorching summer sun by planting citrus with an eastern exposure, painting the trunks with a water-soluble latex white paint from the root flare to the first or second scaffold or using a tree wrap available at retail nurseries.

- Don't compound the possibility of sunburn with chemical fertilizers. Use organic or slow-release fertilizers that only make nutrients available as the trees need them, rather than promoting tender, foliar growth that are prone to sun scald.

- If sharp citrus thorns are a problem, prune them off where practical.

- In coastal areas of California, there is still time to plant citrus but protect newly planted trees from transplant shock and heat fluctuations by spraying the foliage with an antitranspirant and apply a root stimulator with indolebutyric acid 3 times at two-week intervals.

- Fertilize again with an organic granular citrus food in early summer.

AUGUST

- Re-greening is a citrus response to warm summer weather (particularly Valencia oranges) and does not harm the fruit, but the fruit will not regain its orange coloration.

- Control ants in citrus trees with baits that they take to the nest destroying the queen and colony. Also get rid of aphids because ants farm aphids and other "honeydew" secreting insects on trees. Spray with a canola-based horticultural oil.

- Keep containers moist with the addition of coir (coconut fiber) or corn-based polymer.

- Give citrus trees an occasional hosing down from top to bottom to wash off dust and pests.

- Remove all mummified fruit (shriveled, hard, moldy fruit) from the tree's canopies and pick up and discard any fruit on the ground.

- Squirrels are active in the garden storing fruits for winter. If they are a problem, live trap them and relocate away from the garden, but check first with the county Wildlife Service for local regulations.

SEPTEMBER

- Replenish mulches because hot temperatures decompose them quickly. A 3- to 4-in. layer of mulch effectively protects citrus against temperature extremes, keeps weeds from germinating and conserves water.

- Continue to clean up old and rotted fruit around citrus to prevent habitats for disease and pests.

- As the weather cools many citrus begin to ripen. Periodically taste-test Mandarin, Navel, Kumquat and Blood Oranges one or two at a time before harvesting too many because they do not ripen off the tree.

- If normally sweet-tasting citrus tastes sour, it may be the result of low temperatures, overcast days or nutrient deficiency. Fertilize about 4 times a year and supplement with an organic foliar feed.

- When hot, dry winds from the Great Basin or from the Cascades are predicted, irrigate citrus trees a day or two before their predicted arrival.

- If winds are prevalent, build a wind deflector constructed of three 8-ft. posts with plastic sheeting attached.

OCTOBER

- If in a frost-free zone with mild winters, autumn is still a good time to plant citrus.

- Fall is the best time for the final application of a product that contains humic acids to keep the soil alive and to protect tender growth from freezing.

- Cool autumns trigger the orange coloration of citrus fruit.

- Moist, cool weather marks the return of snails and slugs. Use copper bands around the citrus tree trunks to keep them from tree canopies and broadcast a safe, organic iron phosphate to control them on the ground.

MANDARIN

- Where winter freezes are common, move container citrus to covered, protected areas such as a greenhouse or patio and spray with a canola-based oil to control scale or mites that might have established themselves during their stay out on summer patios.

- Shore up the watering basins to prepare for the rainy season. Read the Watering Basin, page 87.

NOVEMBER

- Adjust irrigation clock to keep the soil in the root zone moist. If there is a sufficient rainfall to wet the soil to a depth of 2 ft., turn off the irrigation, but during drought, monitor the soil with a tensiometer or soil probe and water when it indicates that the first 12 inches is dry.

- When applying mulch around citrus trees, allow a 4- 6-in. space around the trunk to prevent brown rot gummosis, an oozing wound in decaying bark. Treat brown rot by keeping the trunk base dry, removing the infected bark and painting with Bordeaux paste (a mixture of copper sulfate and hydrated lime).

- Stop weeds before they germinate with a pre-emergent herbicide.

- The season for many citrus varieties to ripen is late fall through winter, but most can hold their fruit for quite some time without losing their quality.

- Fertilize fall-planted citrus with an organic citrus food in frost-free regions

DECEMBER

- Remember to water citrus in containers that might be under the eaves of houses or covered patios. If allowed to dry out, they are more susceptible to cold damage. Container citrus also need a 3-in. protective layer of mulch.

- Protect citrus from frost damage by wrapping trunks in tree wrap available at nurseries and covering foliage overnight with cotton sheets.

- Safeguard roots from root-rot. Do not overwater during winter months.

- Citrus trees are still available at retail nurseries, especially dwarf varieties with fruit and make thoughtful gifts. Provide a redwood tub or half-barrel, drill eight, 1-in.-diameter drainage holes, install casters under the container and plant with an organic, well-draining potting soil.

- Use chelated micronutrients if foliage is chlorotic with green veins and yellow interveins. General fertilizing is not necessary during winter months.

- Harvest time for Lemons and Lime is heaviest in winter-spring although they will bear year-round where winters and summers are mild.

NUT TREES
for California

Nut trees are among the most romantic reminders of seasonal changes. In late winter or early spring, pink Almond blossoms hurriedly flower ahead of their more reticent leaves. In late spring, clusters of green, hard-shelled Macadamia nuts hang from their branches like oversized grapes. And similar to the sound of raindrops, Chestnuts plop, plop, plop to the ground from spreading branches in fall. By late autumn or early winter, the fiery golden hues of Pecan leaves blaze.

NUT TREES AND THE HOME GARDENER

During winter, we appreciate the tree's silhouette, roughly textured bark and outstretched branches, still regal in its barren simplicity. With the exception of Almonds, nut trees can grow into very large specimens and create wonderful shade wherever they plant their feet. Unfortunately, most are ill-suited for small yards, but if there is plenty of elbow room they bring beauty, stature, and crops to the landscape. As long as the climate is suitable, even exotic Macadamias and Pistachios can be yours for the picking, almost as easily as from the grocery store.

Unless you are a stickler for maximum fruit production, the home gardener can harvest a decent-sized crop with some basic planting and maintenance schedules. Think of nut trees as beautiful shade habitats for people and for wildlife that can also reward you with a harvest.

SELECT THE RIGHT TREE FOR THE RIGHT SITE

All nut trees prefer deep, fertile soil with good drainage and an even supply of water. When planted in full sun, some trees, such as the Chestnut and Pecan, can become arboreal skyscrapers, while the comparatively diminutive Almond can mature on its tiptoes to twenty feet. It is important that you choose the right tree for the right site. Many nut trees, including Pecans and most Almonds are not self-fruitful and need one or two compatible cultivars planted within a hundred feet of each other for successful cross-pollination. Pistachio trees are dioecious, and they need one male tree for up to ten female trees in order to bear properly. Where there is adequate summer rainfall, little irrigation is required, but where the climates are hot and dry, they need occasional and deep irrigation.

The deep taproots of Almond and Walnut trees make them difficult to transplant. Plant them in permanent spots in holes deep enough to accommodate their entire taproots without bending them.

Some of the best trees for cold climates are the Chestnut, Walnut or Almond, but for milder climates consider Pistachios, Pecans, and Macadamias. Keep in mind that nut crops drop so plant them where falling fruits are not a problem.

NUT TREES AND WILDLIFE

Most nut trees are viewed as tasty buffets for wildlife. Assorted olfactory repellents or visual deterrents can discourage unwanted wildlife, but if they are hungry enough be prepared to do battle or plant enough trees so there will be plenty for all to share. The English Walnut has its own protective system. It manufactures a chemical compound called juglone. This compound deters many species of plants, including Tomatoes, from growing too close to it. Interestingly enough, it has no effect on brambles, such as Blackberries. Perhaps allowing thorny brambles on the tree's trunk is a way to discourage foraging squirrels, rats, and raccoons.

THE ODDS ARE GETTING BETTER

Odds are in your favor for successful cultivation of nut trees. As long as you learn about your site, choose suitable varieties, and give them proper care and attention, your nut-bearing trees will provide edible fruits, natural beauty, shade, and wildlife shelter for years to come.

ALMOND
Prunus dulcis (Rosaceae)

Hardiness—Zones 7-10

Color—Pink/white flowers

Bloom Period—Winter-early spring

Fruit Period—Autumn

Mature Size (H & W)—15-30 ft. x 20 ft.

Water Needs—Deep soak to saturate the entire root zone (2 ft. depth). When soil dries down to 12 inches, water again.

Planting/Care—Plant in winter from bare-root stock or plant from containers in spring or summer, spacing 20 ft. apart. Build a watering basin. See "The Planting Pit, Backfill and Watering Basin" on page 87. Needs long, hot, dry summers for good harvests.

Pests/Diseases—Control peach leaf curl by applying dormant spray, three times: in autumn when the leave fall, December and just before the buds swell and show color.

Landscaping Tips & Ideas—Most almonds are not self-fertile and need a cross-pollinator. Almonds produce from 5-7 years of age. Use as shade accents among shrubs and borders. Refer to page 72 for varietal recommendations.

CHESTNUT
Castanea hybrids

Hardiness—Zones 5-9

Color—Inconspicuous

Bloom Period—June

Fruit Period—Mid-September-November

Mature Size (H & W)—70+ ft. and as wide

Water Needs—For sandy loam soil, irrigate every 2-3 weeks to a depth of 3-4 ft. from May-September.

Planting/Care—Provide well-drained, sandy loam soil or plant on a slope if site is clayey. Requires slightly acid soil and will not tolerate alkaline soil. Space trees 40 ft. apart and fertilize once in spring with an organic, granular food containing micronutrients.

Pests/Diseases—Poor soil drainage causes phytophthera (root and crown rot). Control adult chestnut weevils with an organic insecticide such as Spinosad. Destroy larvae and eggs in nuts with hot water for 20 minutes.

Landscaping Tips & Ideas—Plant a 'Nevada' or a seedling Colossal to cross-pollinate. Make sure the pollenizer is no farther than 100 ft. The trees are majestic if you have the space.

ENGLISH WALNUT
Juglans regia

Hardiness—Zones 5-9

Color—Inconspicuous

Bloom Period—Spring

Fruit Period—September-October

Mature Size (H & W)—30 to 50+ ft. x 30 ft.

Water Needs—Water deeply during the growing season, but keep away from the trunk by building a double watering basin (inner ring would have a 4-ft.-diameter "dry zone"). See page 87. Withhold water when dormant.

Planting/Care—Plant in winter from bare-root or in spring from containers, spacing 40-50 ft. apart. Fertilize twice at year: in spring and again in fall with an organic granular food.

Pests/Diseases—Controls for aphids, codling moth and walnut husk fly are difficult for a mature tree. Contact a licensed pest control advisor for appropriate insecticidal remedies.

Landscaping Tips & Ideas—Excellent ornamental tree for an expansive garden, but it is incompatible with lawns because excess moisture might cause water molds and crown rot.

MACADAMIA NUT
Macadamia tetraphylla

Hardiness—Zones 10-11

Color—Pinkish-white flowers

Bloom Period—Late winter or early spring

Fruit Period—Late fall-early winter

Mature Size (H & W)—15 to 30 ft. x 20 ft.

Water Needs—Water 2-3 times a week when immature and water once a week during growing season.

Planting/Care—Plant in spring from containers, spacing 20 ft. apart. Construct a 10 ft. watering basin. See page 87. Soils needs to be humus or mulch amended, well-draining and provide full sun.

Pests/Diseases—Control mealybugs, aphids, ants, thrips and scale with a canola-based horticultural oil.

Landscaping Tips & Ideas—Prune to develop a central leader with strong lateral branches that begin 3-4 ft. above the ground. Makes a handsome shade tree and does best 1-10 miles from coastal areas, in frost-free, mile climates. Once established, Macadamias survive high heat.

PECANS
Carya illinoinensis (Juglandaceae)

Hardiness—Zones 5-9

Color—Pale green

Bloom Period—Spring

Fruit Period—Autumn

Mature Size (H & W)—30 to 60+ft. x as wide

Water Needs—From April-October, water slowly down to the feeder roots 12-24 in. deep out to the drip line, but away from the trunk. No supplemental water during dormancy.

Planting/Care—Plant in winter from bare-root or in spring from containers spacing 50 ft. apart. Build a 10 ft. watering basin. See page 87. Needs full sun in well-drained loam soil (tolerates alkaline soils). Does best where summers are long and hot but will produce in mild-summer climates.

Pests/Diseases—For squirrels use live traps to relocate (check with wildlife agency for regulations) and for birds try visual deterrents or share the bounty with your resident wildlife.

Landscaping Tips & Ideas—Pecans make lovely shade trees for large gardens, birdlife havens and in winter, their barren simplicity is regal.

PISTACHIO
Pistacia vera 'Kerman'

Hardiness—Zones 10-11

Color—Red or white flowers

Bloom Period—Early spring

Fruit Period—Mid-summer to October

Mature Size (H & W)—15 to 30 ft. x 15 to 20 ft

Water Needs—Water during nut development (June-August), but stop in mid-August to promote ripening, resume watering after the harvest and withhold when dormant. Drought-tolerant once established.

Planting/Care—Plant in winter in spring from containers, spacing 15-20 ft. apart. Build a watering basin. See page 87. Needs full sun, well-draining soil and at least one male pollinator tree for up to 10 female trees.

Pests/Diseases—Avoid root rot by making sure the tree is not in standing water and wash off sucking insects with a strong stream of water.

Landscaping Tips & Ideas—Pistachio trees are alternate bearing (bear heavily one year and little the next). They mature at 8 years and can bear for 600+ years if given proper care.

MORE RECOMMENDATIONS

ALMOND

- 'All-in-one' One of the best varieties for the home orchard, semi-dwarf, self-fruitful, 500 chill hours. Soft-shelled, ripens in late September to early October.

- Garden Prince' is the top variety for the home gardener, genetic dwarf that grows 8-12 ft., self-fruitful, soft-shelled and ripens late September-early October. '

- Nonpareil' Most popular commercial Almond, thin-shelled, heavy bearing, needs a pollinizer, 400 hours chill hours, blooms midseason, and ripens in September.

- 'Texas' ('Mission'), semi–self-fruitful, 500 chill hours, ripens in October, has a hard shell, and pollinates 'Nonpareil'.

ENGLISH WALNUT

- 'Carmelo' bears very large walnuts, in late September, 700 chill hours, late-blooming and leafing, self-fruitful.

- 'Carpathian' ('Mesa') bears in early October, 700 chill hours, late blooming, self-fruitful.

- 'Chandler' bears excellent quality nuts in mid-September, smaller tree and good choice for home gardener, 700 chill hours, self-fruitful.

- 'Pedro' is another smallish (up to 30 ft.), self-fertile, 400 chill hours, bears sweet-tasting nuts in September and produces well in milder climates of Southern California.

MACADAMIA

- 'Beaumont' is a cultivar recommended for home gardens, introduced by the California Macadamia Society.

- *M. tetraphylla* 'Cate' originated in Malibu, California, thin shell, good quality nut, ripens in late October-November.

- *M. integrifolia* 'James' originate in La Habra Heights, California, produces after 2-3 years, yields more per acre than any other California cultivar.

PECAN

- 'Choctaw' bears excellent flavor, thin-shell nuts, 250 chill hours, pollinated by 'Western Schley'.

- 'Mohawk bears large, thin-shell nuts, great choice for home gardens, 250 chill hours, self-fruitful.

- 'Western Schley' bears large, soft-shell flavorful nuts, 250 chill hours, ripens in November, excellent for California deserts and higher altitudes.

PISTACHIO

- 'Peters' is a male variety that pollinizes 'Kerman and also pollinizes 'Bronte', 'Trabonella', and 'Red Aleppo', does not bear fruit, 800 chill hours, drought resistant once established.

ALMOND

JANUARY

- Plant Almond, Chestnut, Walnut and Pecans from bare-root stock. Make sure the growing requirements match your garden conditions and plant them just above the graft union.

- Most nut trees need plenty of space away from structures, deep, well-amended, well-drained soil, and while growing and fruiting, a regular supply of water.

- Where frosts are common select late-blooming varieties.

- Soak trees deeply after planting. Water three times the first week and adjust frequency and amount to climatic, soil and growth conditions.

- English Walnuts are ideally suited for large landscapes where they can be planted without other plants close to their drip lines. Do not plant if allergic to pollen.

- Withhold water completely while nut trees are dormant or water just enough to keep roots moist during a period of drought.

- Apply dormant oil for insect control to all deciduous nut trees. Use copper fungicide or lime-sulfur to control fungal diseases and canola-based oil to smother over-wintering insects.

FEBRUARY

- Clear out old leaves and debris around nut trees to get rid of habitats for pests.

- Softer soils encourage gopher and mole activity. Set manual traps rather than toxic baits to prevent damage to tree root systems and to protect against secondary kill. If setting traps is too intimidating, try olfactory repellents that have been specifically created to repel herbivorous gophers and insectivorous moles.

- Keep snails out of tree canopies by wrapping a 4-in. copper barrier around the trunks. Periodically check and re-wrap to accommodate trunk growth. For slugs, use an organic iron phosphate molluscicide.

- Bare-root nut trees are still available, but avoid those that have been stored indoors with dried out stems.

- Prune Almond branches in late winter before new growth emerges. Cut out dead or interfering branches or prune to control growth.

- When planting new trees, use a root stimulator with indolebutyric acid to encourage the development of feeder roots. Apply three times, two weeks apart.

MARCH

- An application of pre-emergent weed control in spring keeps weeds from germinating for about 4 months around nut trees. Apply two more times in the summer and in late autumn.

- Cut unwanted suckers at soil level or spray with a sucker-stopping product when they are about 6-12 inches tall.

- Watch for ants, especially in Almond tree because they penetrate the husks and ruin the nuts. Wrap the trunk with wide electrical tape and apply an ant sticky barrier on the tape. When the sticky barrier dries, replace the tape and re-apply.

- Prune young English Walnut trees in early spring, right after the buds swell and fertilize mature Walnuts with a complete, organic granular food (they should be fertilized one more time in fall). Make sure the fertilizer does not make contact with the tree trunk.

- Deer begin to munch on new, tender growth. Keep them away with olfactory repellents, motion-activated sprinklers or lights.

APRIL

- Plant Macadamia, Pistachio and other nut trees in spring from containers after danger of frost has passed. Plant so that the tree is at the same level as its original container.

- Soak trees deeply after planting. Water three times the first week and maintain a watering regimen that keeps the roots moist, but not soggy.

- For Pistachio, develop 3-5 main limbs at one-foot intervals, with the first limb at least 3-4 ft. above the ground.

- Macadamia are evergreens that thrive in frost-free climates with regular irrigation throughout the year and are suitable in containers with proper pruning. Fertilize mature Macadamia twice a year with an organic Citrus food at a rate of 5 pounds per application.

- Prune Macadamia trees while still young to develop a central leader with strong lateral branches that begin 3-4 ft. above the ground.

- Fertilize Chestnuts once in spring with 1 pound of cottonseed meal per 1-in. of trunk's diameter.

MAY

- Prune and remove frost-damaged branches after new growth emerges. Apply a humic acid product and worm castings to help the damaged trees to recover.

- Look out for nesting birds and try not to disturb them when pruning your trees or better yet, delay the pruning until the young have flown away.

- Hang pheromone traps in your trees to prevent codling moth larvae tunneling into the nuts. The pheremone acts as an attractant for male moths and lures them to a sticky death. Replace every month while moths are active.

- When watering Walnut trees, make sure that water does not reach within 4 ft. of the trunk because of susceptibility to water mold or crown rot.

ENGLISH WALNUT

- Although mature Chestnuts are drought resistant, it is best to irrigate deeply from May through early fall, (if in sandy loam soil) every 2-3 weeks to a depth a 3-4 ft. for good nut production.

JUNE

- Deep water all nut trees especially during growth and nut production seasons. Summer heat can stress many of them.

- Make sure mulch is at least 2-inches around the nut trees, but keep away from their trunks.

- A 1-in. layer of worm castings helps to protect against insect infestations.

- Remedy micronutrient deficiency with an application of chelated iron.

- From late June through fall, Walnut husk flies overwinter as pupae in the soil and emerge as adults from late June-fall. The female lays eggs below the surface of Walnut husks decaying the nuts, shriveling the meat, increasing mold growth and staining the shell. Maggots hatch, drop to the ground and pupate until winter. Consult with a local UC Cooperative Extension for monitoring and precise timing of control because timing is not the same in every garden or orchard.

- Keep Pistachios away from carriers of Verticillium wilt such as Strawberries, Melons and Squash.

JULY

- Spinosad is an organic control derived from bacteria and is effective against chewing insects but does not harm edible crops or most beneficial insects. Protect bees by spraying when the bees have returned to their hives, during the late afternoon or early evening.

- Hose down trees thoroughly to wash off dust and pests such as aphids and whiteflies, but be careful not to knock off developing nuts.

- Attach a 3-ft.-wide ring of aluminum flashing around the trunk to keep hungry squirrels out. It is effective when the tree is away from wires and other plants that agile squirrels might be able to use to get to the nuts. Loosen ring as the tree grows.

- Summer is the best time to lightly prune Chestnuts for interfering growth, dead or damaged branches.

- Although established nut trees survive short periods of drought, especially Pistachio and Walnuts, they produce best with regular irrigation.

AUGUST

- Ants will continue to be a problem in winter unless controlled now. Use baits that are taken back to the nest to destroy the queen and the entire colony.

- Make sure nut trees planted in the last two years do not dry out. Mature trees are more drought tolerant, but young trees need regular water.

- Chestnut weevils lay eggs in ripening nuts. The eggs hatch when the nuts fall and the larva burrow into the ground and emerge as adults to start the egg laying cycle again. Control adults with an organic insecticide such as Spinosad, but once the eggs have been laid in the nuts, it is more practical to parboil the nuts and store in the freezer to break the cycle. Also chickens and Guinea Fowl are excellent predators for larvae and pupae.

- Fertilize Walnuts one more time with a complete organic granular food just before the fall harvest, but keep away from the trunk.

SEPTEMBER

- Re-build mulch around trees to a depth of 2 inches, but keep away from the trunks.

- Stop fall weeds from germinating around nut trees out to their drip lines, until they are at least 3-4 years old. Use a pre-emergent weed killer for a 4-month control.

- Walnuts ripen from mid-September to October. Remove any husks and dry in shaded area with good air circulation until kernels are brittle. They are completely dry when the papery dividers (pellicles) between the nutmeat halves, snap rather than bend.

- From mid-September to October, Pistachio nuts can be shaken from their branches. Remove the hulls within 24 hours to prevent stained shells, then dry in the sun until their chartreuse or hollow kernels are crisp.

- Between mid-September to November Chestnuts are ready to harvest. They shed their prickly burr jackets when ready to fall to the ground. Best to lay a tarp around the tree to catch the falling Chestnuts.

OCTOBER

- Reduce water for deciduous nut trees as they begin to go dormant, but during hot, dry Santa Ana conditions, water nut trees in the morning or evening to mitigate against evaporation and to keep roots moist.

- In frost-free climates, fall is still a good time to plant nut trees while the soils are still warm.

- Fertilize mature Macadamias with one more application of organic, granular fertilizer.

- Shake off almonds after hulls have cracked and slightly dry. If you wait for them to drop, many may rot. Make sure hulls are dry enough by shaking them to hear a rattling sound. Remove hulls and spread nuts out to dry in full sun for 24-48 hours.

- Harvest Pecans from mid-October through November just as the hulls lose color or splits by shaking or knocking them down. Hull and dry in a protected, airy location before storing in airtight containers in the freezer.

NOVEMBER

- All nut trees benefit from an autumn application of worm castings and a humic acid product. This feeds the beneficial microbes and helps prepare the trees for cooler weather.

- Clean up old or rotted nuts and fallen leaves around the trees to help prevent disease and insect infestations next year.

- Rake and compost leaves, except dispose of Walnut leaves in the trash because they contain juglone, a plant growth inhibitor for apples, potatoes, tomatoes and other plants.

- Macadamia nuts drop to the ground from late fall to spring depending on variety. Lay a tarp down to harvest. Crack the husks with pliers, spread out in shade with good air circulation and dry for two weeks. Then oven bake at the lowest temperature (100°F) for about 12 hours, stirring periodically. Store in a heavy plastic bag in a cool, dry place. Remove the shells with a nutcracker that has been designed to crack through hard shells.

DECEMBER

- Where soil is workable, prepare planting pits for future bare-root nut trees. Dig a hole 2-3 times and as wide as the tree's root ball.

- Protect tender, young nut trees from frost with Christmas lights, spraying with an antitranspirant such as Wilt-Pruf or Cloud Cover or if small enough, covering with a cotton sheet overnight and removing during daytime. Fortunately most mature trees are more tolerant of frosts.

- During dormant season prune older trees to thin out crowded or crossing branches or to remove any damaged or dead wood or limbs that are too close to the ground, especially Walnuts.

- For Almonds, cut off oldest fruiting wood (about 20%) for new spur development.

- Most deciduous nut trees do not need supplemental watering during winter dormancy including Almond, Walnut, Chestnut, Pecan and Pistachio.

- Fertilize Macadamias, Pecans and Pistachio in late winter with a complete, organic granular food to supply the nutrients necessary for early spring's blooms.

FRUITS &
BERRIES
for California

There is something magical about trees that bear flowers and edible fruit. With their fresh spring blossoms, summer and fall bounty, and blaze of autumn color, they transform a bland landscape into a Garden of Eden. Exquisite pink and white clouds of perfumed Apricot, Nectarine, and Plum blossoms fall in a blizzard of floral snowflakes to make way for their sun-warmed fruits. Plucking a crisp, crunchy red Apple or a golden-orange Persimmon from your own tree is a particular delight.

EVEN IN WINTER

Even in their winter guise, these trees continue to have an allure. The winter-slanting sun's rays highlight the sweeping branches of a Fig tree and gild the bark of the Sweet Cherry with the rich color of chestnut brown. Winter also brings unexpected color in the form of Pomegranates, dangling red baubles that add a festive holiday flair to bare limbs.

ORCHARD OR EDIBLE LANDSCAPE

Many people think fruit trees should be grown in an orchard setting, planted in militarily precise rows apart from everything else. The advantage of this agricultural style is convenience, especially if you grow several standard fruit trees over a large area; the disadvantage is that it is not aesthetically pleasing and tends to interfere with the harmony of the landscape.

If space is limited or your preference is toward a blended design, without fruit trees set apart, then an edible landscape is a wonderful alternative. You double your pleasure by growing fruit trees not only for their crops, but for their ornamental value. If your yard is small, plant dwarf varieties or espalier to make a decorative screen, or to camouflage a sterile wall.

THREE STEPS TO A THRIVING FRUIT TREE

Whether your intent is to create an orchard or an edible landscape, the first step to having a thriving fruit tree is to select a suitable site. Most fruit trees need a sunny location where fragile blossoms and pollinating bees, butterflies, and birds are sheltered from blustery, prevailing winds. All fruit trees do best in well-drained soils, but if the soil is not well-drained, it is still possible to grow dwarf fruit trees in raised beds or containers. Consider dwarf rather than standard varieties for small spaces—not only do they take up less room, but they bear normal-sized fruit, and most produce about as much fruit as a standard tree.

The second step is to select plants adapted to your climate. You should consider the chilling requirement, which is defined as the number of cool-temperature hours below 45 degrees Fahrenheit that a particular plant needs during winter before it breaks out of dormancy and starts growing again. Some trees need a higher number of winter-chill hours than others. Another important consideration is a plant's cold-hardiness, which reflects the lowest temperature it can tolerate and survive during winter dormancy. For fruit trees to flourish, there needs to be a balance between winter-chill hours and cold-hardiness. In cold regions, you can select high-chill cultivars, which remain dormant until dangers of frost have passed—in mild-winter areas, their long dormancy would probably produce weak shoots, and they might not bloom at all. Further complicating proper selection is the fact that temperatures vary in specific regions depending on elevation, and they may vary even in your own garden. We have several different microclimates in our yard. Our low-elevation areas are frost pockets, and the middle and top of our slopes are much warmer. If you keep all of these variables in mind, you can select the right tree for the right spot.

The third step is to determine how your tree of choice is pollinated, and whether or not it is self-fruitful. Many Apples, Sweet Cherries, Pears, and Plums are not self-fruitful and need at least one or two compatible cultivars planted within 100 feet of each other in order to bear fruit.

Consult your local nursery, University of California Extension fruit specialist, or talk to your neighbors about the kinds of fruits and

WHITE GRAPE

specific cultivars that thrive where you live, as well as pest and disease problems you may encounter and how to manage them.

AN ODE TO NATURE

There is nothing quite like eating Figs, Nectarines, or Cherries picked fresh from your own trees and preserving them in jams, stuffing them in pies, baking them in breads, or freezing them for summer reminders in winter. While harvesting the edible bounty is the most obvious reward, there are other lessons to be learned. Whenever we look at our fruit trees, Vivaldi's symphonic ode to nature, "The Four Seasons," comes to mind. Each tree's leaves, flowers, fruits, and branching silhouette are magical metaphors for the circle of life.

APPLE
Malus sylvestris

Hardiness—Zones 4-10

Color—Pale pink

Bloom Period/Fruit Period—Spring/Late summer-fall

Mature Size (H & W)—6 to 40 ft. x 10 to 30 ft.

Water Needs—Soak newly planted tree deeply. Water thereafter once a week and mature trees every 1-3 weeks depending on soil, climatic and growth conditions.

Planting/Care—Plant in late winter from bare-root or in spring from containers. Space 20 ft. apart if dwarf or semi-dwarf, 35-40 ft. if standard.

Pests/Diseases—Scab, fire blight, mites, aphids and codling moths may cause problems. Month by Month covers controls.

Landscaping Tips & Ideas—Use in containers, as hedges and espaliers. For mild winters 'Anna' is self-fruitful and for optimum production plant with another self-fruitful, 'Dorsett Golden'. ' Garden Delicious' (600 chill hours) is 8-10 ft. or smaller with pruning. 'Fuji' and 'Red Delicious' (Brisbee Spur) are best for 600-700 chill hours area.

APRICOT
Prunus armeniaca

Hardiness—Zones 5-10

Color—Pink,white

Bloom Period/Fruit Period—Spring/Spring-early summer

Mature Size (H & W)—10 to 15 ft. and as wide

Water Needs—Soak deeply after planting then water once a week and for mature trees water weekly from bloom to fruiting time and decrease or withhold during winter dormancy.

Planting/Care—Plant in late winter from bare-root or in spring from containers. Space dwarf or semi-dwarf plants 10-15 ft. apart and 20 ft. apart if standard.

Pests/Diseases—To control overwintering insects, apply a dormant oil in fall when the leaves drop, at the end of December and before the buds swell and show color.

Landscaping Tips & Ideas—Apricots make wonderful shade trees and espaliers. Self-fruitful varieties include 'Goldkist' and 'Katy' (300 chill hours) for warm winter areas, Royal Blenheim' (400 chill hours) and 'Moorpark' (600 chill hours) for chillier climates.

AVOCADO
Persea americana

Hardiness—Zones 10-11

Color—Cream

Bloom Period/Fruit Period—Winter-spring, depending on variety/Winter to fall or fall to winter, depending on variety

Mature Size (H & W)—10 to 30+ ft. and as wide

Water Needs—Keep soil evenly moist and occasionally deep water to wash out accumulated salts.

Planting/Care—Needs excellent-draining soil and full sun. Poor drainage can lead to phytophthora root rot, often fatal to Avocado trees.

Pests/Diseases—Control persea mite (causes yellowish and black spots on leaves and leaf drop) with predatory mites available at insectories.

Landscaping Tips & Ideas—Plant a type A ('Haas')and type B ('Fuerte') avocado for best production. 'Holiday' is ideal for containers because it is 10-12 ft. and provides fruit from Labor Day to New Year's. 'Don Gillogly' is a seedling from Haas that is hardy to 27°F.

BANANA
Musa acuminita

Hardiness—Zones 10-11

Color—Purple bud and white flowers with mature fruits of red, yellow, or brown

Bloom Period/Fruit Period—Summer-spring, depending on the cultivar

Mature Size (H & W)—Dwarf 7 to 15 ft.

Water Needs—Needs plenty of water

Planting/Care—Grows best in hot-wet tropical climates protected from the wind or plant in containers and move during cold temperatures. For most home gardens, select dwarf varieties. Plant in spring in deep, humus-amended, well-draining and acidic soil. Provide full sun and allow to high soil moisture. Hold off on fertilizing for 2-3 months after planting.

Pests/Diseases—Ants "farm" scale and aphids for their honeydew (excretions) and the honeydew in turn causes sooty mold. Apply sticky barriers around the base of the plant or use ant baits.

Landscaping Tips & Ideas—Attractive in tropical landscapes, along pools or ponds, in containers. 'Ice Cream' fruit looks like its namesake, tastes like vanilla custard and grows to 12-15 ft.

BLACKBERRY
Rubus fruticosas

Hardiness—Zones 5-11

Color—Pink, white flowers

Bloom Period/Fruit Period—Spring/Summer

Mature Size (H & W)—6 to 15 ft. long

Water Needs—Water regularly during growth and fruit cycles. Decrease or withhold in fall and winter months.

Planting/Care—Plant in late winter from bare-root, space 6-8 ft. apart. Since berries bear on second-year canes, train first-year laterals on a sturdy support such as a trellis and prune only weak or diseased canes. Fertilize in spring with a complete, organic granular food.

Pests/Diseases—Spray with a canola-based oil for fungus rot and organic Spinosad for chewing insects.

Landscaping Tips & Ideas—Trailing Western type of Blackberries grow primarily in mild, coastal areas of California where their vigorous, trailing, thorny habits are easiest to cultivate. 'Marion', 'Olallie' are popular choices, but 'Navajo' is the choice for thornless stems.

BOYSENBERRY
Rubus x loganobaccus 'Boysen'

Hardiness—Zones 6-11

Color—White flowers

Bloom Period/Fruit Period—Early spring/Late spring-summer

Mature Size (H & W)—8 to 15 ft. long

Water Needs—Water deeply after planting and then weekly until established. Decrease water during fall and winter months.

Planting/Care—Plant in late winter from bare-root or in spring from containers Space 8-12 ft apart. Fertilize in early spring with an organic granular food. Does best in mild winter areas, but can grow in cooler areas as well.

Pests/Diseases—To help disease prevention, do not water overhead and spray with an organic Spinosad if chewing insects become a problem.

Landscaping Tips & Ideas—Start trellising as soon as the canes grow, prune after harvest removing canes that produced the current crop and tip this year's growth to encourage laterals for next season's fruit. 'Logan' bear large berries with thornless canes..

DRAGON FRUIT
(PITAHAYA, STRAWBERRY PEAR)
Hylocereus and *Selenicereus* spp.

Hardiness—Zones 10-11

Color—Creamy-white

Bloom Period/Fruit Period—Summer/Early fall-winter

Mature Size (H & W)—8 ft. x spreading

Water Needs—Water from April-fall every 7-14 days for growth and fruiting.

Planting/Care—Plant in black, plastic 15-gallon containers filled with cactus mix. Add 10% worm castings. Provide sturdy support and protect from winds.

Pests/Diseases—Keep ants away by using baits. Sunburn or cold, wet winters create cork-like spotting on stems. Provide partial shade in the afternoon and spray with a kelp solution.

Landscaping Tips & Ideas—Climbing cactus provides a beautiful display of fragrant, bell-shaped, nocturnal flowers. The aerial root system is best supported on trellises, tree stumps or sturdy stakes. The magenta-red Pitahaya has sweet red or white flesh speckled with black sesame-like seeds and the yellow cultivars have very sweet white flesh. Fruits range in size from ½ to 3 pounds.

FIG
Ficus carica

Hardiness—Zones 9-11

Color—Not applicable

Bloom Period/Fruit Period—The fruit is actually the flower./Once or twice, early summer and late summer to fall.

Mature Size (H & W)—15 to 25 ft. and as wide

Water Needs—Drought tolerant except when fruiting, then water regularly every 10-14 days.

Planting/Care—Plant in late winter from bare-root or from containers in spring or fall and space 35-feet apart. Place where fruit drop and aggressive root systems are not problems. Fertilize in late winter with a complete, organic granular food.

Pests/Diseases—Protect against gophers by planting in wire baskets.

Landscaping Tips & Ideas—Use as shade tree, but can prune into a shrub or an espalier. 'Brown Turkey' and 'Mission' bear purplish-brown fruit and light strawberry flesh. For few seeds 'White Genoa' bears yellowish-green fruit or 'White Kadota' has lemon yellow fruit with amber flesh.

GOJI BERRY
(WOLFBERRY)
Lycium barbarum

Hardiness—Zones 5-15

Color—Lavender and white flowers

Bloom Period/Fruit Period—Early summer/Autumn

Mature Size (H & W)—8-10 ft. x as wide

Water Needs—Drought tolerant but for optimum growth and fruiting, water from spring-autumn every 7-14 days. Decrease or withhold during winter months.

Planting/Care—Plant in full sun from containers anytime from spring-fall in well-draining soil. Can survive temperatures between -15°F to over 100°F. Prune for shape after harvest.

Pests/Diseases—Few disease or pest problems except protect berries from birds and squirrels. Set traps if gophers are present.

Landscaping Tips & Ideas—Plant where there is enough space for it to grow. Recent research indicates that the orange-red berry's antioxidant level is much higher than blueberries. Its flavor is similar to a combination of Cranberry, Cherry and Raspberry and is also a source of protein, amino acids, beta-carotene and vitamins B and C.

GRAPES
Vitis vinifera hybrids

Hardiness—Zones 10-11

Color—Pale green

Bloom Period/Fruit Period—Spring/Late summer-fall

Mature Size (H & W)—8 ft. and spreading

Water Needs—Drip irrigation is most efficient for Grapes. Provide supplemental water during growth and fruiting cycles, and decrease in winter.

Planting/Care—Plant in draining, sandy loam soil. Provide full sun on a slope for good air circulation. Year-old bare-root vines are available in winter. Space 6-8 ft. apart. Provide vertical and horizontal supports.

Pests/Diseases—Pierce's bacterial disease is vectored by the sharpshooter insect and causes vines to die. Contact the local Cooperative Extension Office for control suggestions. Control powdery mildew with a canola-based horticultural oil.

Landscaping Tips & Ideas—Seedless, self-fruitful European Grape 'Flame' needs hot summers, but 'Perlette' tolerates milder summers. For coastal and inland valleys, select self-fruitful wine cultivars 'Cabernet Sauvignon' (warm summers) but where summers are cool, try 'Chardonnay'.

GUAVA
Psidium guajava

Hardiness—Zones 10-11

Color—Greenish-white flowers

Bloom Period/Fruit Period—Spring/Summer

Mature Size (H & W)—6-25 ft. x as wide

Water Needs—Deep water during growth and fruiting, but allow the soil to dry before watering again.

Planting/Care—Plant from containers in spring after the danger of frost has passed. Although high temperatures and drought conditions are tolerated, Guavas grow best in warm, frost-free locations. Plant in full sun in well-draining, richly amended, free-draining soil.

Pests/Diseases—Control whiteflies and thrips with an organic Spinosad and spray with a canola-based horticultural oil for aphids, scale and mealybugs.

Landscaping Tips & Ideas—Common Guavas are self-fruitful, need room to spread out and make lovely shade trees. For colder climates down to zone 9 and in a smaller space, plant a Strawberry Guava (*P. cattleianum*) because it remains a shrub or a multi-trunked 10-15 ft. tree.

JAPANESE PLUM
Prunus salicina

Hardiness—Zones 7-10

Color—White

Bloom Period/Fruit Period—Spring/Summer

Mature Size (H & W)—5 to 25 ft. x 10 to 15 ft.

Water Needs—Regular deep watering is important especially during summer.

Planting/Care—Plant in late winter from bare-root or in spring from containers. Space dwarf or semi-dwarf 6 to 10 ft. and 10-15 ft. for standards.

Pests/Diseases—Control Plum sawfly and mites with organic Spinosad and rust with a canola-based horticultural oil. Do not spray with oil when temperatures exceed 85°F.

Landscaping Tips & Ideas—Japanese Plum trees fruit on year-old shoots and older spurs, so prune selectively each year during dormancy. 'Santa Rosa' is the most popular commercial and home selection and is an excellent pollinizer for Satsuma'. Aprium 'Cot-N-Candy'and Nectaplum 'Spice Zee' are hybrids of Apricot, Plum or Nectarine and have amazing sweet flavor.

KIWI FRUIT
(CHINESE GOOSEBERRY)
Actinidia spp.

Hardiness—Zones 8-11

Color—Creamy white

Bloom Period/Fruit Period—Late spring/ Autumn

Mature Size (H & W)—25 ft. long

Water Needs—Water regularly during the growing season because Kiwis have shallow root systems.

Planting/Care—Plant in spring from containers, space 15 ft. apart and provide sturdy support structures. Train vines to grow with a single trunk and a single strong leader along an overhead wire.

Pests/Diseases—Spray with an organic Spinosad to control leaf rollers, beetles and caterpillars. Botrytis may result from poor-draining soil.

Landscaping Tips & Ideas—Known for fuzzy brown fruits with green flesh, the deciduous vines also provide seasonal shade on pergolas or trellises. For cool climates (800 chill hours), plant 'All Purpose Male Kiwi' to pollinize 'Hayward Female Kiwi' or a self-fruitful 'Issai' bearing fuzz-less fruits (800 hours). For mild southern California areas, plant 'Tomuri Male Kiwi' to pollinate 'Vincent Female Kiwi'.

LYCHEE
Litchi chinensis

Hardiness—Zones 10-11

Color—Chartreuse-yellow

Bloom Period/Fruit Period—Late spring/ Late summer-fall

Mature Size (H & W)—15 to 35 ft. and as wide

Water Needs—Water regularly from fruit set until late summer to fall, but reduce for a few months prior to lowering.

Planting/Care—Provide a cool, dry, frost-free autumn and winter to induce flowering with warm, humid spring and summer temperatures. Avoid windy sites.

Pests/Diseases—Ants harvest pollen compromising fruiting. Use ant baits that are taken back to the nest to destroy the queen and the colony. Also apply a sticky barrier around the trunk. Control scale with a canola-based oil.

Landscaping Tips & Ideas—The 7-year wait for fruit production is well worth the wait. Raspberry-red clusters of up to forty, rough-skinned fruits are ready to pick when they are soft to the touch. The taste is very sweet and juicy. A beautiful tree in the landscape and fruits that are prized for their exquisite taste.

MULBERRY
Morus spp.

Hardiness—Zones 5-11

Color—Insignificant

Bloom Period—Spring

Mature Size (H & W)—30 ft. x 50 ft.

Water Needs—Relatively drought-resistant once established, but supplemental watering during dry periods is necessary for good fruit productions. Decrease or withhold during winter dormancy.

Planting/Care—Plant from bare-root in late winter or in spring from containers. Needs full sun and well-drained, loam soil.

Pests/Diseases—Few disease or pest problems except birds love the fruit, but there is usually plenty to share.

Landscaping Tips & Ideas—Allow plenty of space for this stately, deciduous tree and keep away from driveways or sidewalks because most fruits stain. *Morus alba* 'White' bears sweet white fruit shaped like blackberries and 'Pakistan' bears 2-5 in.-long, blackish-red, blackberry-like fruits that are sweet and non-staining. It is also disease resistant and ideal for mild climates.

NECTARINE
Prunus persica nucipersica

Hardiness—Zones 5-10

Color—Pink

Bloom Period/Fruit Period—Spring/
Late summer

Mature Size (H & W)—12 to 20 ft. x
10 to 15 ft.

Water Needs—Water regularly and deeply
once a week during growth, bloom and
fruiting cycles, but decrease during winter
months. Keep soil moist but not soggy.

Planting/Care—Plant in late winter from
bare-root or in spring from containers
and space dwarfs or semi-dwarfs 6-10 ft.
apart, 8-20 ft. apart for standards. Provide
full sun and well-draining soil.

Pests/Diseases—To control brown rot,
use a dormant spray when the tree is
dormant according to the label.

Landscaping Tips & Ideas—Since
Nectarines are self-fruitful, you can plant
just one in the orchard or landscape, or
use as a patio container or espalier.
'Goldmine' and 'Snow Queen' are
freestone with white-fleshed sweet fruit
and 'Garden Delight' and 'Necta Zee'
grow to just 5-6 ft.

PEACH
Prunus persica

Hardiness—Zones 5-10

Color—Rose

Bloom Period/Fruit Period—Early spring/
Summer

Mature Size (H & W)—8 to 15 ft. and
as wide

Water Needs—Supply 2 inches of water
per week for mature trees, decrease during
fall and winter.

Planting/Care—Plant in late winter from
bare-root or in spring from containers and
space dwarf or semi-dwarf 6-10 ft. apart
and 12-20 ft. apart for standards. Provide
full sun and well-draining soil.

Pests/Diseases—Treat Peach leaf curl
with a dormant spray and control peach
tree borer with a parasitic nematode in a
squeeze bottle applicator.

Landscaping Tips & Ideas—Standards
are lovely in the landscape and dwarf trees
make ideal patio containers. 'Snow Beauty'
(750 chill hours) and 'Donut' (400 hours)
are white-fleshed fruits and 'Saturn' (250
chill hours) is not only tasty, but its
double-pink blossoms are spectacular
in spring.

PEAR
Pyrus communis

Hardiness—Zones 6-9

Color—Cream

Bloom Period/Fruit Period—Spring/
Early-late summer

Mature Size (H & W)—20-30 ft. x as wide

Water Needs—Water regularly during
growth, bloom and fruit cycles, decrease
in fall and winter.

Planting/Care—Plant in winter from
bare-root or in spring from containers and
space 6-8 ft. apart for dwarf, 10-15 ft. for
semi-dwarf and 20 ft. for standard.

Pests/Diseases—Fireblight browns new
growth. Prune diseased branch 6 in.
beyond the infection and sterilize pruner
with a horticultural disinfectant or plant
disease-resistant cultivars.

Landscaping Tips & Ideas—Espalier dwarf
varieties, hedgerow them (space 8-14 ft.
apart) or plant as accent trees. Fireblight
resistant Pears include: 'Hood' (100 chill
hours) is interfruitful with 'Flordahome';
'Harrow Delight' (700 hours) is interfruitful
with 'Bartlett', 'Bosc' or 'D'Anjou' and
'California' is self-fruitful (700 hours) for
hot inland climates.

PERSIMMON
Diospyros kaki

Hardiness—Zones 8-10

Color—White

Bloom Period/Fruit Period—Spring/ Early-late fall

Mature Size (H & W)—15 to 20 ft. x as wide

Water Needs—Water about once a week after planting, water from fruit set to harvest for established trees and decrease or withhold during dormancy.

Planting/Care—Plant in full sun with well-draining sandy loam soil. For large fruits, prune to train a central leader with well-spaced laterals.

Pests/Diseases—Keep birds away from fruit with bird netting and use a canola-based horticultural oil if mealybugs or scale infestations are extensive.

Landscaping Tips & Ideas—Ornamental tree ideal in the landscape or as an espalier in container. Self-fruitful 'Fuyu', 'Izu' and 'Coffee Cake' are the non-astringent, flat-shaped, apple-crisp persimmons (100-200 chill hours). Self-fruitful 'Chocolate', 'Tamopan' and 'Hachiya' are the acorn-shaped, astringent persimmonsthat need to soften before eating. All are very tasty.

POMEGRANATE
Punica granatum

Hardiness—Zones 9-11

Color—Reddish-orange flowers

Bloom Period/Fruit Period—Spring/Fall

Mature Size (H & W)—10 to 20+ ft. x as wide

Water Needs—Although established Pomegranates are drought-tolerant, they will produce better if watered regularly through the growing season until fall. Decrease water or withhold during winter.

Planting/Care—Grow in a variety of well-drained soil. Plant in winter from bare-root or in spring from containers. Space 4-6 ft. apart for dwarf, 20 ft. apart for standard.

Pests/Diseases—Few disease or insect problems, but remove old fruit during pruning. If leafroller damage is extensive, spray with an organic Spinosad.

Landscaping Tips & Ideas—Beautiful ornamental shrub or tree for backyard gardens. 'Ambrosia' (150 chill hours) bears large, pale pink-skinned, sweet-tasting Pomegranates, 'Desertni' produces large orange rinds with deep red, desert-sweet seeds (100 hours) and 'Eversweet' has clear non-staining juice (150 hours).

RASPBERRY
Rubus idaeus

Hardiness—Zones 5-11

Color—White flowers

Bloom Period/Fruit Period—Spring/ Summer

Mature Size (H & W)—8 to 15 ft. long

Water Needs—Water regularly during growth and fruiting cycles, but keep canes dry to protect against disease.

Planting/Care—Plant bare-root in late winter or from containers in spring and space 4 to 6 ft. apart. In hot climates plant in partial shade and full sun in mild climates. Canes need sturdy supports for training and easy harvest.

Pests/Diseases—If chewing insect damage is a problem, spray with an organic Spinosad. For mildew, spray with a canola-based oil.

Landscaping Tips & Ideas—Remove established second-year canes to the ground in winter and tip the new canes to encourage bud growth. 'Bababerry' and 'Oregon 1030' tolerate the heat of southern and central valleys while 'Chilcotin' and other cultivars do better in cool, coastal areas.

SOUTHERN HIGHBUSH BLUEBERRY

Vaccinium hybrids

Hardiness—Zones 7-11

Color—Pink, white

Bloom Period/Fruit Period—Early spring/ Late spring-summer

Mature Size (H & W)—3 to 6 ft. x 3 ft.

Water Needs—Keep soil moist, not soggy.

Planting/Care—Blueberries do best in full sun, in richly-amended, well-draining and acidic soils. Southern Highbush selections thrive in mild coastal and warm inland regions. To meet their acidic needs, plant in containers, apply a 2-3 in. layer of mulch and fertilize with a cottonseed meal.

Pests/Diseases—Discourage birds and deer by planting in wire cages and covering with bird netting.

Landscaping Tips & Ideas—Although most Southern Highbush are self-fruitful, plant several for an extended harvest season and more bountiful harvest. 'Misty' and 'O'Neal' for early harvest, 'Cape Fear', 'South Moon' and 'Reveille' for mid-to-late harvest. For showy pink blossoms and fruit, select the evergreen 'Sunshine Blue'. Blueberries are beautiful ornamental plants as well as providing delicious fruit.

STRAWBERRY

Fragaria x *ananassa*

Hardiness—Zones 9-11

Color—White

Bloom Period/Fruit Period—Late winter-early spring/Spring-summer

Mature Size (H & W)—4 in. x spreading

Water Needs—Water regularly during growth and fruiting cycles

Planting/Care—Plant from bare-root in winter and from containers in spring and space 8-12 inches apart or in strawberry pots. Soak bare-roots in water for 1-2 hours before planting. Plant the crowns slightly above the soil surface in rows with 4-6 in. irrigation furrows in between.

Pests/Diseases—Rotate plants every 2-3 years to avoid disease and for mold problems, mulch to keep fruit off the ground. Use an organic iron phosphate product to control snails and slugs.

Landscaping Tips & Ideas—Snip off runners with clippers when plants begin to bear fruit for larger berries. Buy new plants every 2-3 years or divide the existing ones. If birds become a problem, plant white cultivars or use plastic netting.

SWEET CHERRY

Prunus avium

Hardiness—Zones 4-9.

Color—White, pink blossoms

Bloom Period/ Fruit Period—Mid-spring/ Late spring-early summer

Mature Size (H & W)—15 to 20 ft. x as wide

Water Needs—Needs regular water during growth and bloom cycles and supplement during fall and winter if rainfall is insufficient.

Planting/Care—Plant from bare-root in winter or from containers in spring and space 25-30 ft. apart. Prefers acid soil so fertilize with cottonseed meal.

Pests/Diseases—Use bird netting and set traps to protect from birds and gophers.

Landscaping Tips & Ideas—Cherry trees are just as ornamental as Flowering Cherries with reddish-brown bark and spectacular flowers. 'Black Tartarian', 'Royal Ann' and 'Bing' need pollinizers and 700 chill hours, but 'Minnie Royal' and 'Royal Lee' produce dark, sweet cherries when planted close to each other or in the same planting pit with 400 or less chill hours.

AVOCADOS

VARIETY	FRUIT TIME	FRUIT TYPE	FRUIT SIZE FRUIT SKIN	FRUIT COLOR TREE SIZE	FRUIT SHAPE COLD HARDY
Bacon	Autumn-Winter	B	8 to 12 oz. Medium thin	Dark green 15 to 20 ft.	Pear form Very
Gillogly (pp)	Summer-Winter	A	8 to 12 oz. Medium	Green 8 to 14 ft.	Obovoid Tender
Gwen (pat. #5298)	Summer-Autumn	A	7 to 12 oz. Medium	Green 6 to 16 ft.	Obovoid Average
Haas	Summer-Autumn	A	5 to 10 oz. Medium	Black 15 to 25 ft.	Obovoid Average
Holiday	Autumn-Winter	A	19 to 24 oz. Medium	Green 10 to 12 ft.	Pear form Tender
Nabal	Summer-Autumn	B	12 to 16 oz. Medium thick	Green 20 ft.	Round Tender
Zutano	Winter	B	8 to 10 oz. Medium thin	Green 20 to 30 ft.	Pear form Very

The term A or B group avocado refers to an avocado's pollinating cycle. Although most avocado varieties are considered self-fruitful, avocado production can be increased 20% by growing an opposite variety amongst the desired crop.

THE PLANTING PIT, BACKFILL AND WATERING BASIN

THE PLANTING PIT

Excavate a rectilinear planting pit 1-to-1½ times the plant's original container depth and 4-6 times the plant's original container width. In a rectilinear pit, the root system grows through the backfill to the corners, encouraging roots to web more quickly into the native soil.

Pile the excavated earth close by so it can be amended for backfill if needed. Roughen the vertical surfaces of the planting pit with a cultivator. The rectilinear form and the roughened surface will encourage the development of lateral roots. Do not place a layer of gravel because it does not solve poor drainage.

THE BACKFILL

The backfill (soil excavated from the planting pit) should be amended to have a texture halfway between that of the native soil and that of the plant's rootball. Backfill is the material that the plant's new roots will first encounter. When the rootball soil, the backfill, and the native soil are similar in texture, it is unnecessary to amend the backfill. If not similar, mix in compost or humus-rich soil amendments and follow package directions to provide a well-draining soil texture. Before planting tamp the soil in the bottom of the planting pit to minimize any settling of the rootball. Plant the rootball 1 inch higher than the surrounding backfill. This 1-in. height accommodates any future settling.

THE WATERING BASIN

Build a berm 4-6 inches high and 4-6 times the plant's original container diameter. Generally 2 inches of surface water gravitates 12 inches in dense, clayey soils, so a watering basin has a 4-in. berm, water will soak down to 2 ft. In porous, sandy soils, it only takes 1 inch of surface water for water to gravitate the same 12 inches. Water a newly transplanted plant thoroughly enough to collapse any air pockets in the backfill.

APPLE

MORE RECOMMENDATIONS

- CARAMBOLA (STAR FRUIT) *Averrhoa carambola*, Zones 10-11 grows up to 20 ft., bears bright yellow, 4-6 in.-long fruit that are star-shaped when sliced in cross-section. Provide full sun with good draining, slightly acid soil. Fruit tastes like a mixture of Pineapple, Kiwi and Apple. Harvests are heaviest in spring, but also summer and winter.

- CHERIMOYA *Annona cherimola*, Zones 9-11, grows 25+ ft., bears pale-green, heart-shaped fruit with sweet, creamy-textured flesh so delicious that it is often called "fruit of the gods." Shelter from winds and protect from cold. Needs full sun with good-draining soil. Harvest in late-fall to winter.

- LOQUAT *Eriobotrya japonica*, Zones 8-11, grows 20 ft., bears tasty orange-yellow fruit in winter or spring. Provide full sun and well-drained soil. Excellent ornamental tree.

- MANGO *Mangifera indica*, Zones 10-11, 10-20-ft. tall, bears long, 9-in., up to 2 lb., yellowish skinned fruits with yellow to orange flesh. Taste is similar to a peach. Needs well-draining soil and full sun.

- PAPAYA *Carica papaya*, Zones 10-11, 10-12 ft. tall, bears bright yellow fruit with sweet orange flesh. 'Red Lady' bears 4-lb. fruits and is a dwarf 6 ft., self-fruitful plant.

- WHITE SAPOTE (SAPODILLA) *Casimiroa edulis*, Zones 9-11, 25-50 ft. tall, bears yellowish fruit with custard-like flesh that tastes like peaches and bananas in mid-fall. Needs well-draining, slightly acid soil in full sun.

STAR FRUIT

JANUARY

- Soak bare-root plants for 2 hours before planting in a prepared hole.

- Cultivate the mulch layer periodically to keep it from crusting over and restricting the exchange of air in and out of the soil.

- Apply a complete organic granular fertilizer 3-4 times a year. First application should be in late winter while the tree is still dormant and just before the flower buds swell and show color.

- Spray Cherimoya, Avocado, Dragon Fruit and other evergreen tropical fruits with an antitranspirant if freezing temperatures are predicted. The film on the leaf surface functions like a layer of insulation. Or cover frost-sensitive plants with a cotton sheet overnight and remove during warmer daytime temperatures. Do not use plastic, clear or black, because plastic is a poor insulator.

- Dormant spray deciduous fruit trees, shrubs and vines with a canola-based or other horticultural oil to smother overwintering insects and lime sulfur spray to control disease (for Apricot use copper sulfate instead of lime sulfur).

- To control bacterial canker on cherry trees, use a copper spray.

FEBRUARY

- Most heavy pruning of mature deciduous fruit trees, shrubs and vines occurs in late winter while they are dormant.

- When planting bare-root fruit trees or vines, trim to about 3 ft. and cut off damaged or broken roots.

- Pruning the first three years of deciduous fruit trees establishes the structure of their canopies. Prune to develop an open-vase form by cutting out interfering branches.

- Berries such as Raspberries need their second-year canes cut to ground level and tops of canes pruned off by 6 inches to force lower buds into growth. Wait on Blueberries until the third year and remove ⅓ of the oldest branches. Avoid cutting back too many shoots and terminals because most of the fruit buds emerge near the ends.

- If space is limited, plant 2-4 semi-dwarf or dwarf fruit trees in the same planting pit. Also salad fruit trees have several different varieties grafted or budded onto a single rootstock.

MARCH

- Early spring is usually the end of the rainy season. Begin supplemental water for young and mature fruiting plants to maintain the flush of spring growth.

- Apply a product containing humic acid to help revitalize the soil and to provide nutrients for beneficial microbes.

- Prevent deer damage by stretching 100-pound test, clear monofilament line, deer-chest high, around plants needing protection. For rabbits and mole use safe, olfactory repellents.

- Plant fruit trees and shrubs from containers after the danger of frost has passed. Plant slightly above the depth of the original container to account for settling of the soil and water 2-3 times the first week.

- Apply a complete, organic granular fertilizer away from the trunks or main stems of all fruit trees, tropical plants, vines and shrubs and spread out to the drip lines and water in thoroughly. For acid-needy fruits such as blueberries fertilize 2-3 times a year with cottonseed meal.

APRIL

- Plant tropical fruit trees and plants now if in hot interior areas, but in cooler climates, wait until May.

- Cull fruit each spring when they reach the size of a nickel. Allow about a hand width between fruits for the largest and plumpest mature fruit.

- Keep diseases and insect infestations at bay for optimum fruit production. Use organic controls such as pheremone traps, Spinosad, canola-based horticultural oils and worm castings whenever possible.

- Systemic products with Imidicloprid (Merit) provides 12-month control for adelgids, aphids, certain borers, Japanese beetles, leafhoppers, leafminers, mealybugs, psyllids, sawfly larvae, scale, thrips and whiteflies on Apple, Crabapple, Loquat, Oriental Pear, Pear, Pecan and Quince. Do not apply on other fruit or nut trees.

- Avocados have shallow root systems and need frequent water. Any level of moisture below field capacity will stress Avocado trees. Supplemental water should be available 2-3 times a week especially during hot, dry weather. for mature trees planted in well-draining, sandy soil, supply 1 inch of water per week every 1-3 weeks depending on soil, growth and climatic conditions.

- Cover the tree canopies where practical with bird netting or try hanging mylar balloons with large eyes painted on them.

MAY

- When fruits develop to about 1-inch in diameter, provide a second application or organic, granular fertilizer. For early fruiting varieties, add an extra feeding of a liquid organic food such as kelp or fish emulsion just after fruits have been harvested.

- Most fruits are ripe when they plop into your hand after a gentle twist, but since Pears ripen from the inside out and Avocados ripen off the tree, it is best to harvest them a week or two before fully ripe.

- Make sure the layer of mulch around the fruiting plants remains at 2-inches, but keep away from the trunks or main stems.

- Espaliered fruit trees require periodic pruning to maintain the flattened growth form.

- Prune back errant growth on mature trees, shrubs and vines during vigorous spring growth.

- Hand-pollinating Cherimoya and Dragon Fruit flowers with a paintbrush increases chances for successful pollination.

JUNE

- Avoid planting during dry, hot weather. If you must plant, wait until late afternoon or early in the morning, spray with an antitranspirant to help retain moisture in the foliage and use a rooting hormone with indolebutyric acid three times, two weeks apart to alleviate transplant shock.

- June drop is when fruits suddenly fall. It occurs when there is a rapid change in moisture or climate or if there is more developing fruit than the plant can accommodate. This is Mother Nature's way of culling to protect the plant. Persimmon, Peach, Nectarine and Apricot are the most susceptible fruits to experience June drop.

- Early- to mid-summer, just after normal fruit drop, thin more by picking off all but one of the developing fruits, spacing the fruits a hand width apart.

- In early summer supplement feed Dragon Fruit, Bananas and other tropical fruits with liquid kelp or fish emulsion as a soil drench around the roots.

JULY

- When temperatures rise, the water needs of fruiting plants can double or triple. Stress from lack of water causes foliage to wilt, fruit to fall and may even be fatal.

- Shortly after fruit has been harvested, summer prune to reduce the volume and height of a plant's canopy. Estimate the perfect height to safely and easily harvest fruit without resorting to ladders by stretching your arm over your head.

- Avocados need an understory of branch support similar to the ribs of an umbrella and should not be pruned unless size reduction is necessary.

- Prune berry vines after harvest removing all wood that produced the current crop and tipping the ends of canes to force out laterals that will bear next season's fruit. To promote larger fruit, around Thanksgiving head back the long laterals at the top of the trellis to 12-15 ft.

- About mid-summer make the third application of organic, granular fertilizer to all fruiting plants.

AUGUST

- Remove fallen fruit and leaves to prevent disease and insect problems.

- Green fig beetles are most active when summer fruits are reaching maturity and swarm around openings of fruit pecked by birds. Control them by netting and disposing of them or use organic Spinosad.

- Wash foliage off with a strong stream of water to rid the foliage of aphids, leaf hoppers and caterpillars and to clean off accumulated dust.

- Avocado leaves begin to show tip-burn during summer. This is a natural occurrence due to salt build-up. Do not exacerbate the problem with chemical fertilizers because this adds to salt build-up. Irrigate to leach out the salts.

- For good quality fruit allow 1-2 Banana stalks per clump to grow and cut off the rest in late summer. After the fruiting stalks have fruited, remove and allow replacement stalks to develop for the following year's fruit. When working on Bananas, wear old clothes because banana sap stains.

SEPTEMBER

- Reset irrigation clocks to adjust for changes in the weather. California's rainy season occurs from late fall to early spring.

- Rebuild and expand the watering basins around plants in anticipation of winter rains. The basin radius should be 10-20% greater than the radius of the drip line of the plant's canopy.

- Maintain a 2-in. layer of compost, humus mulch or other organic material to stabilize soil moisture and temperature.

- An optional additional organic granular or liquid feed in autumn helps winterize your plants. Avoid chemical fertilizers because they encourage frost-tender growth.

- Apply a pre-emergent weed control in fall. Weeds compete with fruiting plants for water and nutrients and are sources of disease and insect infestations.

- Plant Dragon Fruit in 15-gallon containers filled with cactus mix. Set 2 poles 12 inches away and place on opposite sides of the plant. Use a flexible tie in a figure-eight pattern and loosen as the plant's diameter expands.

OCTOBER

- Apply a product containing humic acid because humates revitalize soils and provides nutrients for beneficial microbes.

- Fruiting plants can be planted in early autumn in frost-free zones if they are being transplanted from containers. In areas where early frost is common, delay planting until late winter if the ground is workable or early spring from bare-root stock.

SWEET CHERRY

- Use clippers to avoid tearing fruit and snip off with a small section of their stems. Apples picked with the stem attached to the fruit keep longer.

- Pick Persimmons when they are green to orange but still firm. Ripen indoors by placing them stem side down, leaving them at room temperature away from direct sunlight.

- Avoid staining Pomegranate seeds by cutting off the blossom ends and scoring the rind lengthwise in four to five places. Break apart along the scoring lines underwater, pull back the rind and remove the seeds from the bitter pith.

NOVEMBER

- Drain irrigation lines where grounds freeze.

- Clear accumulated debris around plants, but leave Avocado foliage on the ground. They create a blanket of material over the Avocado's shallow root system.

- Protect deciduous fruit trees – Apple, Pear, Apricot, etc—from overwintering insects and diseases by spraying with a canola-based horticultural or dormant oil three times: in autumn after the leaves have fallen, at the end of December and just before spring buds swell and show color.

- Peach leaf curl blisters and deforms foliage. For Peach and Nectarine trees, spray three times with calcium polysulfide for the same periods as outlined above.

- If planning to plant vigorous berry, Grape or Kiwi vines from winter's bare-root stock, construct structural supports such as posts, trellises or pergolas now. Sturdy supports or wires make training and harvesting easier.

- Bacon, Fuerte and Zutano avocados mature during the cooler seasons. Plant an A and a B variety for increased production.

DECEMBER

- Winter is when bare-root fruit trees and berries are available at nurseries, but plan ahead to insure their success in the garden.

- Determine the percolation rate of the soil by excavating an 18-in.-deep x 18-in.-wide hole. Fill it with water, let it drain and fill again a second time. The second filling should drain at a rate of 1 inch per hour. If water is still standing after 18 hours, plant in a raised bed, on a slope or in containers.

- Select varieties that are suitable for your location noting the chill hours, whether or not it is self-fruitful or if it needs a pollinator.

- To estimate chill hours, use a recording thermometer, total the hours below 45°F during fall, winter and early spring.

- Consider if there is space for a standard, semi-dwarf or dwarf and identify sunny, wind-protected areas.

GROUNDCOVERS
& VINES
for California

GROUNDCOVERS

Groundcover is a carpet for the earth beneath your feet. A less poetic definition of groundcover is this: any dense, low-growing plant that covers an area when planted en masse. To be worthy of the name it must grow quickly, and it is often fiercely aggressive by nature.

A LIVING MULCH

Groundcovers play both practical and aesthetic roles in the garden. Often referred to as "living mulch," once they are established, their dense growth chokes out unwanted weeds, retains moisture, prevents erosion and serves as a fire retardant. They require less maintenance and expense than lawns. They decorate a garden by creating a carpet of foliage and flowers, adding an important landscape dimension by drawing the eye down to themselves and other low-lying neighbors. Without them, landscape grounds can be forlornly barren.

HOW TO GROW

For successful cultivation, prepare the planting area by turning over the soil, raking it free of weeds and adding organic amendments. Whether bare-root, in pint-, quart-, or gallon-size containers, or in flats, the spacing of the plants is determined by variety and mature size. A groundcover normally requires one to two years to cover an area, unless the plants are spaced farther apart than recommended—then an additional 12 to 24 months may be needed. Cuttings are usually spaced eight to ten inches apart on center (measuring from the center of one plant to the center of the next).

After planting, water well, and add two inches of organic mulch. Pull out any weeds or use a pre-emergent product until the groundcover has filled in sufficiently.

MAINTAINING A GROUNDCOVER

Maintenance of an established groundcover is much less demanding than that of a lawn. Some groundcovers—like Vinca Minor and Algerian Ivy—actually tolerate partial shade, and most others consume less water, fertilizer and pesticides than do lawns to keep them looking their best. Fertilize once or twice a year, water during extended periods of drought or high heat, and rake or wash off leaves and debris from the top of a planting.

Woody plants such as Dwarf Coyote Bush, Kinnikinnick, and Shore Junipers need only selective pruning to remove dead wood or to reduce their size if they are beginning to cover a walkway. For vining or trailing groundcovers, carefully use an edger in areas around the base of a tree—the smallest nick can open up a tree to fungal and insect infestations. Set the lawn mower six inches high and mow Dwarf Coyote Bush once a year to improve its appearance and keep it low. Any groundcover that has been scorched brown from a combination of full sun and severely cold winter will also be rejuvenated by a lawn-mower trim, which stimulates fresh growth and removes damaged foliage.

KEEPING A GROUNDCOVER UNDER CONTROL

The yin and the yang of groundcover is that many of them can cover a large area so quickly and thickly that they become pests, invaders of garden areas where they are not welcome. To effectively tame their wild nature, first observe how they grow. Plants like Algerian Ivy that have holdfasts or suckers have a reputation for swallowing anything immobile, including entire buildings, but they can be controlled if their new growth is cut back several times a year. Groundcovers that spread by rhizomes can be stopped with metal or vinyl edging or other physical barriers placed directly in the ground. Others that spread by runners or stolons, like Red Apple, Beach Strawberry, Rosea Iceplant, Trailing African Daisy, and Vinca Minor, can run over edging and settle on the other side—they can be curtailed by trimming their young runners several times a year.

GROUND-LEVEL DIMENSIONS

Whether in a sunny spotlight or shadowy shelter, groundcovers soften a landscape, hide bare soil in all seasons, stabilize soil and provide fire-retardant buffers. Red Apple, Beach Strawberry, Rosea Ice Plant, Trailing African Daisy and Vinca Minor provide a broad expanse of vibrant color. The berries produced by Dwarf Coyote Bush, Kinnikinnick and Shore Juniper are not only attractive but are also food sources for wildlife. Kinnikinnick, Dwarf Coyote Bush, Rosea Ice Plant and Shore Juniper are handsome groundcovers suitable for many different garden designs, including xeriphytic, Mediterranean and woodland. Beach Strawberry and Shore Juniper are excellent choices for seashore plantings or rock gardens. While trees and vines allow us to touch the sky and shrubs capture the "middle" world, floral and foliar carpets encourage us to enjoy the ground-level dimensions of our gardens.

GROUNDCOVER PLANTING SPACE CHART (SQUARE-FOOT COVERAGE PER FLAT)

Spacing Inches On Center	50 Plants Per Flat	64 Plants Per Flat
14 in. oc	5 sq. ft.	7 sq. ft.
18 in. oc	22 sq. ft.	28 sq. ft.
12 in. oc	50 sq. ft.	64 sq. ft.
18 in. oc	112 sq. ft.	144 sq. ft.
24 in. oc	200 sq. ft.	256 sq. ft.
30 in. oc	312 sq. ft.	400 sq. ft.

PLANTING GROUNDCOVER ON BANKS

Prepare the planned site to a depth of 6-12 inches by incorporating an organic soil amendment such as humus, worm castings or compost at a rate of 1 to 2 cubic yards per 1,000 sq. ft. Rake soil surface smooth and water area thoroughly.

Remove any remaining weeds and apply a pre-emergent to keep weed seeds from germinating before putting down a landscape fabric or jute netting to reduce erosion from rainfall or irrigations. Cut out holes in the fabric or netting where plants are to be set.

Spreading groundcovers and vines are available in containers or flats. Flats contain rooted cuttings and are the least expensive. With a clean knife slice them into 2-inch squares before planting at the recommended spacing. Calculate the area's square footage to determine the number of plants necessary for coverage.

Use a 2-inch diameter by 12-to-16-inch auger attached to a portable electric drill for planting from flats.

Transplant all groundcovers at the same depth or slightly above as they were in containers. If planted too deep the plants may rot and if too shallow, the roots may not develop.

Amend the soil to be used to backfill around the rooted cutting with ⅓ sand, ⅓ organic compost or humus mulch and ⅓ native soil.

VINES

Whether they are casting cool shadows, creating privacy, twining up a fence, or arching over a gate, vines can be flamboyant flower factories or sedate evergreen shingles. When space is limited, think about gardening up walls, trellises, arbors, posts or any other structure that begs for highlighting or camouflage. Rambunctious vines can even weave their way through shrubs and trees.

TRAINING YOUR VINES

To keep vines from smothering their supports, other plants, or each other, pinch tender shoots about once a month during their growth cycle, saving the heavy pruning for dormancy. If you prefer a lush, more overgrown look, then relax and subscribe to a laissez-faire style of gardening.

Lavender Trumpet Vines and Clematis are easy to train in small places, but other vines such as Wisteria, Bougainvillea, Scarlet Trumpet Vine, Dutchman's Pipe and Passion Vine, fill larger spaces such as walls and fences. Creeping Fig and Boston

Ivy are self-supporting vines with the help of holdfasts, tendrils with disc-like suction cups or rootlets that enable them to attach to just about anything. Bear in mind that even aggressive vines can be curtailed and confined with annual pruning and frequent pinching back.

Most vines have a natural tendency to grow upward, branch into a tangled mass at the top, and leave their "bottoms" bare. To prevent these growth habits, train and tie their branches horizontally until the desired width is reached. Cover a wall or trellis by laterally spreading and securing the runners, but wrap an arch by training runners upright and spreading them when they reach the top. If multiple branching or denser growth is desired, pinch back regularly, just above the buds— this also promotes more blooms, as the flowers normally emerge at the tips of branches. Once the plant's framework is established, vines can be sheared like a hedge for a dense, compact appearance or clipped to thin out for an open look. To encourage more growth at the base, bend some shoots down and train them to fill in the gaps.

To determine how specific vines perform, check with your nearby nursery or look around your neighborhood—as a rule, the milder your climate, the wider your choices.

CULTIVATION AND CARE

Bougainvillea and Wisteria vines are not self-supporting, grow very large, develop a lot of weight, and must have a sturdy structure on which to grow. Carolina Jessamine, Madagascar Jasmine, Coral and Passion Vines climb by twining or with tendrils, and they grow best up wires or narrow slats. If you use supporting wires, make sure they are insulated; otherwise, they might burn the tender vines in full-sun areas.

For adequate air circulation between a trellis and a wall, allow three to four inches of space, which makes pruning and tying easier and promotes healthier growth. Use insulated wire or rubber tree ties to train and support heavier vines, and stretch plastic or twist-ties for lightweight vines, but check and loosen all ties a couple times a year to prevent any girdling of the stems.

Vines serve as natural sun and windscreens, create inviting entryways, highlight special architectural features, promote privacy and camouflage unsightly walls or fences. Some make appealing combinations, like the brilliant yellow-flowered Guinea Gold Vine and the delicately perfumed white-blossomed Star Jasmine. Once established, they forgive neglect, rebound after overzealous pruning, and often survive short bouts of drought and frost. With proper cultivation and care, they become lush havens that beckon us during glorious springs, sweltering summers, tranquil autumns, or blustery winters. Vines not only weave their way into landscapes, they cling to your heartstrings.

CLEMATIS

ALGERIAN IVY
Hedera canariensis

Hardiness—Zones 7-11

Color(s)—White flowers

Bloom Period—Spring-summer

Mature Size (H & W)—8 to 12 in. (spreading)

Water Needs—Once established, water once or twice a week depending on climate and growth cycles.

Planting/Care—Plant in spring or fall from flats, spacing 10 to 14 in. apart in well-draining soil. Provide semi-shade to shade, but will tolerate full sun in mild climates.

Pests/Diseases—In Southern California control snails with Decollate snails. They prey on brown garden snails and will not harm mature plants. For other regions, control with an iron phosphate molluscicide.

Landscaping Tips & Ideas—When properly tended, Algerian Ivy is a beautiful groundcover for shady slopes, underneath trees and around bushes. Its root system stabilizes steep banks and hides unsightly foundations. Control growth by regularly cutting back and edging borders.

BEACH STRAWBERRY
Fragaria chiloensis

Hardiness—Zones 5-10

Color(s)—White flowers

Bloom Period—Spring

Mature Size (H & W)—4 to 6 in. (spreading)

Water Needs—Needs regular, frequent watering about once a week or more in warm weather.

Planting/Care—Plant in full sun along the coast and partial shade inland in fall or spring from flats, spacing 8-14 in. apart. Provide well-draining, porous soil. Once established, mow in spring to encourage a more compact and dense mat.

Pests/Diseases—Control rust with an organic fungicide or use a canola-based horticultural oil. Bait snails and slugs with an iron phosphate control.

Landscaping Tips & Ideas—Beach Strawberry spreads by offsets making it an excellent choice for rock gardens, as a substitute for lawns, as an attractive groundcover in woodsy or beachfront areas and in front of shrubs and around trees. Thrives in cool, temperate areas and tolerates some foot traffic.

BLUE STAR CREEPER
Isotoma fluviatilis

Hardiness—Zones 5-10

Color(s)—Pastel-blue flowers

Bloom Period—Late spring-early fall

Mature Size (H & W)—3 in. x spreading

Water Needs—Soak thoroughly at planting time and water regularly to establish, but once established decrease watering except during warm, dry conditions.

Planting/Care—Plant in full sun where summers are mild, but set in partial shade where climates are hot. Needs humus or compost-amended, well-draining soil and space 8-12 inches apart.

Pests/Diseases—Few disease or pest problems. Control snails and slugs with an organic molluscicide or hand-pick and squash.

Landscaping Tips & Ideas—Blue Star Creeper's low-growing, mat-forming habit makes it easy to manage. Foliage is similar to Baby's Tears, but is even more attractive because of its pale blue, star-shaped flowers Despite its dainty appearance, it is very cold hardy and spreads easily. It is perfect as fillers between stepping-stones, along pathways or cascading over rocks.

DWARF COYOTE BUSH
Baccharis pilularis

Hardiness—Zones 8-11

Color(s)—Creamy-yellow flowers

Bloom Period—Summer

Mature Size (H & W)—12 to 24 in. x 6 to 10 ft.

Water Needs—Water regularly during the first year of planting, but once established it survives with occasional supplemental watering during summer or Santa Ana conditions.

Planting/Care—Plant in early fall where climates are mild or in spring after the last frost from flats or 1-gallon containers. Space individual plants 3 to 6 ft. apart and closer from flats. Provide full sun and sandy, well-drained soil.

Pests/Diseases—Control aphids by thinning out the plant's woody canopy and spraying with a canola-based horticultural oil.

Landscaping Tips & Ideas—Excellent erosion-control for steep terrains, fire-retardant and water-thrifty landscapes. Don't plant too close together because they grow into each other and thatch. Adapts to a wide range of regions, but does not tolerate foot traffic.

HALL'S HONEYSUCKLE
(JAPANESE HONEYSUCKLE)
Lonicera japonica 'Halliana'

Hardiness—Zones 4-11

Color(s)—Whitish-yellow flowers

Bloom Period—Spring-fall

Mature Size (H & W)—15 to 24 in. spreading

Water Needs—Water regularly once a week or more during hot temperatures.

Planting/Care—Plant from containers in full sun and space 5 ft. apart or closer for faster coverage. Tolerates poor soils, but does best in well-draining, evenly moist soil. Once established, it is somewhat drought resistant. Thin out scraggly, leggy or woody growth by cutting to the ground before spring growth. Semi-evergreen.

Pests/Diseases—Wash aphids off foliage with a strong stream of water or spray with an organic canola-based oil.

Landscaping Tips & Ideas—Shrubby groundcover or vine. Adds delicious fragrance to summer gardens and its sweet nectar attracts hummingbirds and bees. Can be planted to cover fences, walls or slopes and other large areas. For similar positive qualities, but less aggressive behavior, plant *L. periclymenum*.

KINNIKINNICK

Arctostaphylos uva-ursi 'Point Reyes'

Hardiness—Zones 3-9

Color(s)—Small white flowers

Bloom Period—Spring

Mature Size (H & W)—1 ft. x 3 to 6 ft.

Water Needs—Water regularly until established, then water infrequently.

Planting/Care—Plant in fall from containers and space 3-4 ft. apart. Needs full sun and well-drained, sandy loam soil. Withstands some foot traffic, tolerates winds, salt spray and drought.

Pests/Diseases—Low-creeping habit can shelter rats. Set manual or battery-operated traps or even better, find a good hunting cat.

Landscaping Tips & Ideas—A native to California's coastal regions, use this prostrate, low-growing groundcover for drought-tolerant and erosion-resistant landscapes on steep slopes, in rock gardens, along the seashore and in natural and informal landscapes. In the spring it is a lustrous green with white urn-shaped flowers and becomes a reddish color in fall and winter with red berries.

PORK AND BEANS
(STONECROP)

Sedum x rubrotinctum

Hardiness—Zones 9-11

Color(s)—Yellow flowers

Bloom Period—Spring

Mature Size (H & W)—6 to 8 in. x spreading

Water Needs—Very water thrifty once established. Deeply soak after planting, water 2-3 times a week until root system matures.

Planting/Care—Plant in full sun or partial shade from cuttings or from containers, but the soft, succulent leaves will not tolerate foot traffic. Once established, needs little care. Leaves detach and root easily. Plant cuttings in trays with a well-draining medium such as cactus mix and allow to dry slightly between watering.

Pests/Diseases—Few disease or insect problems, but make sure soil is very well-draining to assure longevity.

Landscaping Tips & Ideas—Excellent groundcover for small spaces, rock gardens, in mixed water-thrifty containers and landscapes. Its leaves resemble green jellybeans tipped in a reddish-brown or practically red in full sun.

PROSTRATE ROSEMARY

Rosmarinus officinalis 'Prostratus'

Hardiness—Zones 7-10

Color(s)—Blue

Bloom Period—Spring, fall, winter flowers

Mature Size (H & W)—12 to 24 in. x 4 to 8 ft.

Water Needs—Water regularly to establish about once a week until established and decrease once every 14 days or more depending on climate, soil and growth conditions.

Planting/Care—Plant in spring or fall from containers, spacing 3 ft. apart. Provide full sun with excellent-draining, richly amended soil. Pinch tips regularly during early growth, but once mature, cut selected leafed (not bare wood) branches 50% if becoming too woody to encourage more foliar growth.

Pests/Diseases—Control powdery mildew and aphids with a horticultural or canola-based oil.

Landscaping Tips & Ideas—Rosemary thrives in wind and salt spray, but also does well with inland heat and alkaline conditions. Ideal for seaside landscapes, erosion control, cascading over containers or raised borders and culinary use.

RED APPLE
Aptenia cordifolia

Hardiness—Zone 8-10

Color(s)—Deep-pink flowers

Bloom Period—Spring-fall

Mature Size (H & W)—8 in. x spreading

Water Needs—Soak deeply after planting and water regularly while establishing, but once mature, decrease watering every 10-14 days.

Planting/Care—Plant from cuttings or flats and space them 10-12 in. on center. Requires full or partial sun in well-drained soil.

Pests/Diseases—Control slugs and snails with decollate snails where allowed or an organic iron phosphate bait that is safe to use.

Landscaping Tips & Ideas—An excellent covering for small-large areas, cascading over planters, slopes or nestling in rock gardens. Red Apple is also a bee magnet, so plant with fruiting trees or shrubs like Carambola, Pomegranate, Peach, Avocado and citrus that benefit from pollination. Dry wind and heat is tolerated as long as adequate moisture is available.

ROSEA ICE PLANT
Drosanthemum floribundum

Hardiness—Zones 10-11

Color(s)—Pink

Bloom Period—Summer

Mature Size (H & W)—6 to 10 in. x spreading

Water Needs—Once established, it thrives with a minimum of water. Soak deeply after planting and water regularly until plants become established.

Planting/Care—Plant in full sun in spring or fall from flats, spacing 12-18 in. apart. Grows best in well-drained soil and does not tolerate foot traffic.

Pests/Diseases—Control slugs and snails by applying an organic iron phosphate molluscicide or use decollate snails if in Southern California. (Decollates prey on brown garden snails without harming mature plants.)

Landscaping Tips & Ideas—Because Rosea Ice Plant attracts bees, plant near fruit trees that benefit from pollination such as citrus and Avocado. With intense deep-pink flowers atop fleshy leaves and heat and drought resistance, use to blanket unslightly slopes, as a control for erosion and as fire-retardant landscape.

SHORE JUNIPER
Juniperus conferta

Hardiness—Zones 5-10

Color(s)—None

Bloom Period—None

Mature Size (H & W)—6 to 12 in. x 3 to 6 ft.

Water Needs—Drought resistant once established. Water regularly until plants become established.

Planting/Care—Plant in spring or fall from 1-to 5-gallon containers, spacing 3 to 4 ft. apart. Prefers full sun, but tolerates partial shade. Plant in well-draining soil and fertilize in spring and fall with a complete, granular food.

Pests/Diseases—Subject to occasional attacks from juniper tip moths, but are easily controlled with a systemic insecticide containing Imidacloprid.

Landscaping Tips & Ideas—Its thick, needle-like foliage and architectural form does well in a variety of conditions including seaside bluffs exposed to wind and drought. Use on sunny slopes, for erosion-control and as plantings in front of trees and shrubs and rock gardens. Also when wet, it releases a pleasant, resinous scent.

TRAILING AFRICAN DAISY

Osteospermum fruticosum

Hardiness—Zones 9-10

Color(s)—White, pink, purple, yellow, blue, and bicolor

Bloom Period—Early spring to fall

Mature Size (H & W)—1 ft. x spreading

Water Needs—Soak deeply after planting and water daily the first week. Once established, Trailing African Daisy is drought, wind and heat tolerant, but supplemental watering in summer is best for optimum growth and appearance.

Planting/Care—Plant in spring or fall from flats in full or part sun, spacing 12-20 in. apart. Osteos prefer a moderately rich loam, well-draining soil.

Pests/Diseases—Damping off, a fungal disease, may be a problem if there is poor drainage. Use an organic molluscicide or use decollate snails if in Southern California to control snails and slugs.

Landscaping Tips & Ideas—Often taken for granted as "those freeway daisies," they are excellent soil stabilizers for steep slopes, groundcovers for difficult to reach terraces and salt-tolerant seashore plantings.

TRAILING MYOPORUM (CREEPING BOOBIALLA)

Myoporum parvifolium

Hardiness—Zones 8-10

Color(s)—White flowers

Bloom Period—Summer

Mature Size (H & W)—3 to 6 in. x 9 ft.

Water Needs—Keep soil moist while establishing, but decrease or withhold supplemental water once established depending on growth, fruiting, soil and climatic conditions.

Planting/Care—Plant from flats 6-8 in. apart in well-draining soil. If watered frequently, Myoporum will fill in within 6 months. Do not plant where there is foot traffic, but do provide full sun. Fertilize with an organic, liquid fertilizer 2-3 times per year.

Pests/Diseases—Few pests or diseases, but root rot can occur if established plants are overwatered, especially in clay soils.

Landscaping Tips & Ideas—Its semi-succulent foliage, low-care, drought-tolerance and weed-suppressing qualities make it an excellent groundcover for slopes and banks. Waxy-white, star-shaped flowers smell of honey and in autumn, tiny, purplish berries attract birds.

VINCA MINOR

Vinca minor

Hardiness—Zones 6-11

Color(s)—Lilac, blue or white flowers

Bloom Period—Spring and summer

Mature Size (H & W)—6 in. x spreading

Water Needs—Soak deeply after planting and water regularly until established. Once established they tolerate short periods of drought but produce more flowers and develop more vigorously if adequate moisture is provided.

Planting/Care—Plant in partial sun in rich, well-drained soil. Plant from flats in spring after the last frost, spacing 10-15 in. apart.

Pests/Diseases—Few diseases or insects because of its dense growth habit. Control aphids with a strong stream of water or a canola-based oil and use an organic iron phosphate bait for snails and slugs.

Landscaping Tips & Ideas—Vinca Minor create green carpets sprinkled with splashes of lilac, blue or white flowers along meandering paths, in woodlands, underneath shade trees, cascading over rocks, at the base of hedges or around shrubs.

BOSTON IVY
Parthenocissus tricuspidata

Hardiness—Zones 4-10

Color(s)—Scarlet, purple, yellow, and green foliage

Bloom Period—Colorful foliage in autumn

Mature Size (H & W)—30 to 60 ft.

Water Needs—Water every 7-10 days, but decrease or withhold during dormancy.

Planting/Care—Plant in spring from cuttings, flats or from 1-gallon containers and space 8-10 ft. apart if planting against a structure. For fall color display grow in partial shade or dappled sunlight and plant in well-drained, slightly acidic soil.

Pests/Diseases—Control aphids with a strong stream of water or a horticultural or canola-based oil. For snails and slugs, use decollate snails where allowed or an organic iron phosphate bait.

Landscaping Tips & Ideas—Root system can become invasive so make sure the structures where you plant Boston Ivy are solidly built and avoid exterior wood, stucco or brick walls. Makes a stunning vertical accent especially during fall.

BOUGAINVILLEA
Bougainvillea hybrids

Hardiness—Zones 10-11

Color(s)—Red, pink, white, lilac, or orange bracts

Bloom Period—Spring-fall

Mature Size (H & W)—15 to 30 ft.

Water Needs—Water regularly until established. For optimum bract color, reduce watering established plants in summer, fall and winter.

Planting/Care—Plant in spring from containers in wind- and frost-free areas with full sun and free-draining soil. To keep sensitive roots intact, carefully cut away the container before planting and construct a watering basin. See page 87 for more information. Prune for shape or reduce size after flowering.

Pests/Diseases—Bougainvillea looper feed on foliage and bracts. Spray with an organic Spinosad every 7-10 days until the pest is gone.

Landscaping Tips & Ideas—Show off on trellises, against a wall or fence, on pergolas or arbors and brambling down slopes. Plant Bambino series of Bougainvillea for smaller spaces or containers.

CAROLINA JESSAMINE
Gelsemium sempervirens

Hardiness—Zones 7-11

Color(s)—Yellow trumpet-shaped flowers

Bloom Period—Spring to early autumn

Mature Size (H & W)—20 ft.

Water Needs—Once established, water moderately in spring and summer and sparingly in fall and winter.

Planting/Care—Plant in spring from containers in full sun (tolerates partial shade with less flowering) with well-drained, slightly acidic soil. Space plants 12-30 ft. on center and construct a watering basin. See page 87. After three years, prune hard after blooming to promote future flower development.

Pests/Diseases—To control mealybugs, scale and whitefly during the warmer months, spray with a horticultural or canola-based oil or use a systemic with imidicloprid.

Landscaping Tips & Ideas—Lovely and fragrant vines on trellises, pergolas, fences, walls and as rambling groundcover. Makes a good companion for Crapemyrtle, European Olive and Golden Mirror Plant. All parts of the vine are toxic so keep away from children and pets.

CLEMATIS
Clematis hybrids

Hardiness—Zones 5-11

Color(s)—A rainbow of luscious colors and bicolors

Bloom Period—Late spring

Mature Size (H & W)—3-25 ft., depending on variety

Water Needs—Once a week in spring-summer, less in fall and winter.

Planting/Care—Clematis prefer their roots in shade but their faces in full sun. Plant in spring from containers. Provide well-draining, richly amended normal-slightly alkaline soil and protect with a 3-in. layer of mulch.

Pests/Diseases—Deer-resistant, but if Clematis wilt is a problem, select resistant varieties.

Landscaping Tips & Ideas—Masses of large-flowered (some fragrant) varieties are available in every imaginable color or shape, some like 'Evijohill' look three-dimensional. Their delicate tendrils fasten to fences, pergolas, walls, arbors, trees and in containers. Raymond Evison's Patio Collections are bred to be in containers, while others like 'Avalanche' can weave through trees, roses and tall shrubs.

CREEPING FIG
Ficus pumila

Hardiness—Zones 7-11

Color(s)—Not applicable

Bloom Period—Not applicable

Mature Size (H & W)—20 to 30 ft.

Water Needs—Water regularly about once a week until established. Thereafter water every 14 days depending on climate and growth cycles.

Planting/Care—Plant in spring or fall from 1-gallon containers, spacing 8-10 ft. apart if using as a wall cover, but its invasive roots may damage wood, brick or stucco surfaces. Does well in full sun or shade and needs well-draining, slightly acidic soil.

Pests/Diseases—Few diseases or pests affect Creeping Fig with the exception of snails and slugs. Use an organic iron phosphate molluscicide.

Landscaping Tips & Ideas—Creeping Fig is very hardy and thrives on warm, protected walls, as groundcover over a rock garden, shaped as topiaries or trailing over containers. Softens uninviting structures and deflects heat generated by concrete surfaces.

DUTCHMAN'S PIPE, CALICO FLOWER

Aristolochia spp.

Hardiness—Zones 10-11

Color(s)—Purple, cream, burgundy, and chartreuse combinations depending on species

Bloom Period—Spring, summer

Mature Size (H & W)—8 to 25 ft. long

Water Needs—Supply frequent water during warm months.

Planting/Care—Plant from containers or seed in spring after frost. To control unwanted growth, thin during dormancy. Needs a sturdy structural support like a fence. Grows best in frost-free zones with full sun or partial shade.

Pests/Diseases—If caterpillar damage is extensive, spray with an organic Spinosad. Flies and other insects are attracted to the slight fetid odor of the flowers and serve as pollinators.

Landscaping Tips & Ideas—Giant Dutchman (*A. gigantea*) grows up to 25 ft. with 4-in. diameter heart-shaped leaves and fantastic burgundy 12-in.-long flowers with brilliant yellow throats. Calico Flower (*A. littoralis* or *elegans*) grows almost as long with smaller 3-in. leaves and summer-blooming, creamy-veined purple, flowers.

GUINEA GOLD VINE

Hibbertia scandens

Hardiness—Zones 10-11

Color(s)—Bright-yellow flowers

Bloom Period—Late spring

Mature Size (H & W)—10 to 15 ft.

Water Needs—Water frequently during spring and summer and taper off when temperatures cool.

Planting/Care—Plant in spring or fall from 1-or 5-gallon containers, spacing 4-6 ft. apart. Provide full sun or partial shade and well-draining, slightly acidic, loam soil. Build a watering basin and cover with 2 in. of mulch. See page 87 for more information.

Pests/Diseases—If damage is extensive, control snails with an organic molluscicide and aphids and scale with a horticultural or canola-based oil.

Landscaping Tips & Ideas—Guinea Gold Vine weaves in and out of a wooden or wire trellis, hanging basket or as a groundcover in rock gardens. Since it has a slightly malodorous fragrance, plant the vine downwind. Its value as a sunny ornamental more than compensates for its aromatic nature.

LAVENDER TRUMPET VINE

Clytostoma callistegioides

Hardiness—Zones 8-11

Color(s)—Lavender flowers

Bloom Period—Summer

Mature Size (H & W)—20 to 40 ft.

Water Needs—Water frequently during the first growing season to establish a deep root system. Once established, needs only occasional supplemental water depending on climatic and growth conditions.

Planting/Care—Plant in spring or fall from 1- or 5-gallon containers, spacing 15-20 ft on center. Build a watering basin and apply a 2 in. layer of mulch. Provide full sun for maximum bloom and fragrance, well-draining, loam, slightly-acidic soil.

Pests/Diseases—In spring and summer it is susceptible to aphids, scale and mites. Control with a horticultural or canola-based oil.

Landscaping Tips & Ideas—Effectively covers pergolas, camouflages chain-link fences and other unsightly structures. It is also an excellent groundcover cascading over slopes. Plant with other tropical plants such as Bronze Loquat and Bird of Paradise.

MADAGASCAR JASMINE
Stephanotis floribunda

Hardiness—Zones 10-11

Color(s)—White flowers

Bloom Period—Summer

Mature Size (H & W)—10 to 20 ft.

Water Needs—Water frequently, every 7-10 days when in growth, but reduce watering in the winter months.

Planting/Care—Plant in spring or fall from containers. Because it suffers from transplant shock easily, handle rootball carefully. If growing on a trellis or fence, space the plants 10 ft. apart in part shade. Prune to thin out dense vines in late winter. Tie tendrils for support.

Pests/Diseases—If soft scale or mealybugs cause extensive damage, spray with a canola-based or other horticultural oil or use a systemic containing Imidacloprid.

Landscaping Tips & Ideas—With clusters of fragrant ivory flowers, plant this vine on trellises near a patio or entryway to enjoy their perfume and to snip for cut arrangements. Combine with other tropicals like Hibiscus, Plumeria and Gardenias.

MANDEVILLA
Mandevilla hybrids

Hardiness—Zones 10-11

Color(s)—Pink, red, white and bicolor flowers.

Bloom Period—Late spring-summer.

Mature Size (H & W)—15 to 20 ft.

Water Needs—Water frequently, every 5-7 days while establishing and decrease when mature to 7-10 days during warm weather.

Planting/Care—Plant in spring after frost or in fall in full sun or partial shade. Provide richly amended, slightly acidic soil and apply a 2-in. layer of compost.

Pests/Diseases—Control spider mites with a systemic miticide or spray with a canola-based or other horticultural oil.

Landscaping Tips & Ideas—Showy flowers against deep, glossy-green do best in frost-free climates, but in colder areas plant in containers to move easily for protections. For more compact habit, select one of the Vogue series with saturated red or bright pink and use in containers or trellises. 'Surprise Bouquet' bears white and pink double-flowered beauties to cover an arbor.

PASSION VINE
Passiflora hybrids

Hardiness—Zones 6-11

Color(s)—Pink, lavender, red, orange with contrasting crowns

Bloom Period—Spring-summer

Mature Size (H & W)—6 to 30 ft.

Water Needs—Water once a week during growth and bloom cycles, decrease during cooler seasons.

Planting/Care—Plant in spring from containers spacing 10-15 ft. apart if using on a fence or wall. Provide full sun or partial shade, well-draining and slightly acidic soil. After the second year, prune annually in late winter to lace out.

Pests/Diseases—If caterpillars from the gulf fritillary butterfly become a problem spray with an organic Spinosad.

Landscaping Tips & Ideas—To increase flower production, sever the root system 8-10 in. in the ground and 2-3 ft. from the base and feed with a liquid organic fertilizer. Provides exotic beauty to fences and other sturdy supports. *P. x belotii* is least susceptible to caterpillar damage and *P. edulis* bears edible fruit.

RANGOON CREEPER
Quisqualis indica

Hardiness—Zones 10-12

Color(s)—White, pink, and red flowers

Bloom Period—Summer-autumn

Mature Size (H & W)—20-70 ft.

Water Needs—Water once a week during spring and summer and decrease to every 10-14 days during fall and winter.

Planting/Care—Plant in spring after frost or fall in part sun in well-draining, richly amended slightly acidic soil. Build a watering basin and cover with a 2-in. layer of mulch. See page 87 for more planting information. Provide a sturdy support such as a pergola, arbor or trellis. Does not tolerate frost conditions.

Pests/Diseases—Resistant to deer and rabbits. For spider mite infestations spray with a horticultural oil or a systemic miticide.

Landscaping Tips & Ideas—Fragrant pendant flowers (especially at night) start out white and morph into pink and red over a three-day period. Use near pathways to enjoy its exotic beauty and fragrance on fences, trellises and walls.

SCARLET TRUMPET VINE
Distictis buccinatoria

Hardiness—Zones 9-11

Color(s)—Red, orange-red flowers

Bloom Period—Summer

Mature Size (H & W)—20 to 40 ft.

Water Needs—Water regularly for the first season about twice a week, but once roots are established, decrease to every 10-14 days depending on growth and climate conditions.

Planting/Care—Spring is the best time to plant from containers, spacing 20 ft. apart. Provide full sun in porous, loam slightly acidic soil. Lace out when growth become woody in late winter, prior to flush of new growth.

Pests/Diseases—Chewing insects such as caterpillars can be controlled by spraying with an organic Spinosad.

Landscaping Tips & Ideas—For brilliant summer-long color on gazebos, arbors, walls, fences and in large planters with trellises, Scarlet Trumpet Vines are the essence of warm, tropical landscapes. Avoid planting it on house walls because their clinging tendrils can damage such surfaces.

SNAIL VINE
Vigna caracalla

Hardiness—Zones 9-11

Color(s)—Cream to pale-lavender flowers

Bloom Period—Spring-summer

Mature Size (H & W)—10 to 20 ft.

Water Needs—Water every 5-7 days during growth and warm weather conditions but allow to dry slightly between watering from fall to winter.

Planting/Care—Plant in spring from 1- to 5-gallon containers after frost or in fall. Provide full sun and plant in well-draining, richly amended slightly acid soil. In frost-free areas, it is evergreen, but where winter freeze is common, cut plant to the ground if damaged.

Pests/Diseases—Control spider mites with a systemic miticide or canola-based oil. Root rot may develop if over-watered during winter months.

Landscaping Tips & Ideas—With fragrant, snail-shell-shaped blossoms it makes a lovely summer visual screen, on trellises, arbors or pergolas. Grown by Thomas Jefferson, plant a bit of horticultural history in your warm-weather garden.

STAR JASMINE
Trachelospermum jasminoides

Hardiness—Zones 9-11

Color(s)—White flowers

Bloom Period—Spring-summer

Mature Size (H & W)—10 to 15 ft.

Water Needs—Water once a week during warm weather.

Planting/Care—Plant in spring after the last frost from 1- to 5- gallon containers spacing 4 ft. on center. Does best in full sun, but can tolerate partial shade. Provide well-draining, richly amended, evenly moist soils. It exudes a milky sap that may irritate sensitive skin, so wear a long-sleeved shirt and gloves and wash off pruning shears after clipping this vine.

Pests/Diseases—Control brown soft scale with a horticultural oil. If streams of cotton candy-like strands appear on foliage, apply a systemic specified for giant whitefly.

Landscaping Tips & Ideas—Use as an evergreen groundcover on slopes or train on trellises, gazebos, pergolas, arbors and in hanging baskets or pots. Plant this fragrant vine near pathways and doorways to enjoy its sweet perfume.

WISTERIA
Wisteria sinensis

Hardiness—Zones 5-10

Color(s)—White, blue or lavender flowers

Bloom Period—Spring

Mature Size (H & W)—60 to 100 ft.

Water Needs—Water every 3-4 days during the first season, but once established, allow to dry out slightly before watering again.

Planting/Care—Plant in late winter from bare-root or in early spring from containers, spacing them 15-20 ft. apart. Provide full sun and plant in well-drained, slightly acidic soil. Since seeds and pods are toxic, plant away from pets and small children.

Pests/Diseases—If aphids and brown soft scale appear, control them with horticultural oil.

Landscaping Tips & Ideas—Wisteria's vigorous vines and pendulous, fragrant blossoms need a pergola, archway or gazebo for adequate support. It can also be pruned into an exquisite bonsai. Prune back the new growth in the fall leaving two to four buds for next springs' blooms.

GUIDELINES FOR GROUNDCOVERS AND VINES

- Select only a few varieties to avoid a cluttered or mish-mash appearance, especially groundcovers.

- Consider the area and choose larger specimens for more expansive spaces and smaller varieties for more intimate places. Corsican Mint (*Mentha requienii*) or Blue Star Creeper is ideal between stepping stones or borders, but Myoporum spreads 6-10 ft. and is better suited for wide-open slopes or embankments.

- Two words: *companion planting*. When combining other trees, shrubs, perennials, or bulbs with groundcovers and vines, make sure their growth and maintenance requirements are similar. Combining a vigorous, thirsty spreader such as Boston Ivy with a slower-growing, drought tolerant California Lilac will probably dwarf or kill the latter.

- Assess the condition of the soil: sandy or clayey; free-draining or compacted; alkaline, acidic, or neutral pH. Then determine whether the location is full sun (at least six hours of direct sunshine per day), partial (receives morning or afternoon sun), or heavy shade (little, if any, direct sunlight).

- Find out the hardiness zone of your neighborhood, and make sure it matches the hardiness designation of a particular plant. Also determine the distinctive climatic niches in your garden, either man-made (swimming pools, ponds, sidewalks, roads, foundations) or natural (higher elevations, lower slopes, bare open land).

- Visit other gardens at local arboretums, neighbors or talk to your knowledgeable nursery retailer for appropriate groundcover suggestions.

INSECT AND SPIDER MITE REMEDIES

- EARWIGS, SOWBUGS and SLUGS love warm, dark and moist areas. Roll up a newspaper, moisten it and set it out around vines and groundcover. The next morning throw them away in the trash, paper and all. Grapefruit and orange rinds are another safe way to get rid of these creepy crawlies.

- CATERPILLARS are larvae of moths and butterflies. When found feeding on foliage or stems, pick off or use and organic Spinosad spray or *Bacillus thuringiensis* (Bt).

- APHIDS and MEALYBUGS generally will have ants nearby, since ants harvest their honeydew (excretions). Use an organic insecticide and set out bait stations to get rid of ants. Systemic insecticides are another option as long as there are no plants with edible parts nearby. MITES leave whitish webbings on leaves. Since they are not insects, a chemical insecticide for mite control is best or use a horticultural oil to suffocate them (the oil is also effective against aphids and mealybugs). To prevent leaf burn, spray the oil during cool days or during the late afternoon when the weather is warm and sunny.

- SCALES resemble limpet shells and are difficult to control when they remain under their shell coverings. Systemic insecticide is effective for this stage. When scales are out of their protective shells and crawling around in early spring, use a horticultural or canola-based oil.

- PREDATORY MITES and WASPS, PRAYING MANTIS, LACEWINGS and LADYBUGS are beneficial insects and should be released into the garden as they become available at retail nurseries or mail-order insectaries. Spraying with Spinosad will also control chewing insects, once dry, without harming beneficial ones.

PROSTRATE ROSEMARY

JANUARY

- Discourage browsing deer in smaller areas by setting up a series of posts surrounding prized plants and attaching monofilament line chest-high. When deer brush against the line, it will spook them.

- Dig up existing weeds where you are planning on planting groundcovers and vines and apply a pre-emergent to prevent weed seeds from germinating.

- Spray for overwintering insects with a horticultural or canola-based oil when temperatures are above 45°F. with no rainfall for 72 hours.

- Before planting new groundcovers in spring, make sure they will cover evenly. Stagger plants in parallel rows in a triangular pattern so that they are equidistant from each other or plant in parallel rows in a square pattern so the plants above, below and across are equal from each other.

- If fall-planted groundcovers or vines heave out of the soil due to freezing temperatures, replant right away because cold weather dries and damages tender roots.

FEBRUARY

- Remove dead leaves and debris that have collected on top of established groundcover or around vines. They harbor disease and insects. For established groundcovers, clean off with a strong stream of water.

- Critters become active as soils become workable and temperatures begin to rise. Manual traps are effective against mice, rats, gophers and moles.

- Southern California can use decollate snails to control the brown garden snail, but in Northern California, apply an iron phosphate bait that is safe around children and pets.

- Prune Passion Vine, Clematis and other dormant vines in late winter to lace out and clear away dead, inner, woody vines. This allows sunlight to reach the plant's interior stimulating new growth.

- Protect Bougainvilleas and other frost-sensitive vines overnight when freezing temperatures are predicted with old cotton sheets. If using plastic set up stakes to drape over so the foliage does not touch the plastic and become damaged.

MARCH

- Spring is the ideal season to plant groundcovers and vines once the last day of frost has passed.

- Deeply soak newly planted vines and groundcovers and water frequently to keep roots moist.

- Once roots are established, water only when needed by using the finger test: if the top inch feels dry to the touch, then water again.

- Use a soil conditioner containing humic acid and a root stimulator after planting. Apply the stimulator three times at two-week intervals to encourage root development.

- Fertilize in spring with a complete, liquid organic food every 4-6 weeks to establish new plantings.

- Granular organic or controlled-release fertilizers can be applied to established groundcover or vines once in the spring and another application in the fall. Water in thoroughly.

- Mulch the spaces between new or established plants with a 1- to 2-in. layer of mulch to block out weeds, maintain moisture and protect roots from fluctuating temperatures.

APRIL

- To control Bermudagrass, crabgrass and foxtails in beds of English Ivy, Red Apple, Trailing Gazania or Rosea Ice plant with a post-emergent herbicide with sethoxydim (Grass Getter) as the active ingredient.

- Prune back aggressive groundcovers to keep away from shrubs or trees or spreading in the root systems of existing shrubs and trees.

- Hand-pull weeds as soon as they come up if you forgot to apply a pre-emergent weed control.

- To rejuvenate thick, woody, thatched groundcover, mow with a rotary lawn mower calibrated at its highest setting after their flowering spikes are spent such as Dwarf Coyote Bush, Trailing Gazania and Vinca Minor. For steep slopes, use weed whackers or string trimmers.

- Keep vines and groundcovers vigorous by cutting off spent flowers to divert the energy back to the plants instead of developing seed heads.

- Use plastic or other flexible ties instead of wires to support new vine growth on trellises, pergolas, arbors, etc. Flexible ties will not girdle the canes.

MAY

- Prune off and remove frost-damaged vines and groundcovers once they begin to grow.

- For many spreading and clumping groundcovers and vines, look at the base for small rooted portions that can be detached and re-planted elsewhere.

- Late spring is a good time to root clippings from plants such as Ice Plant and Red Apple. Fill a flat with cactus mix, dip cuttings in rooting hormone, remove foliage below the soil line, water thoroughly, cover with plastic, place under shade and water regularly to make sure cuttings don't dry out. They will root in 10-30 days.

- Blue Star Creeper and English Ivy form plantlets by developing roots along their stems. Simply cut off the ends that have rooted and replant them in the bare spots or wherever they are needed.

- If vigorous groundcovers or vines are beginning to overstep their bounds, prune back and save the cuttings to root more plants.

JUNE

- Grasshoppers are frequent summer visitors and can be caught by hand or spraying with an organic insecticide that has a 7-10 day residual such as Spinosad.

- Watch out for the Bougainvillea looper on its namesake vine. Control with Bt (*Bacillus thuringiensis*) or Spinosad.

- The stream of ants on vines and groundcovers represent just 10% of the entire colony. To be rid of an entire colony, set out baits that worker ants take back to feed the queen and the colony.

- Replenish mulch around newly established plants to 1-2 inches, but keep away from plant stems and crowns to avoid rot problems.

- Crown rot is a fungus that occurs when there is poor drainage. When tugged at, the entire plant falls over or comes out. Remove and dispose of the infected plant. Stop watering the area and solarize. Once the soil is dry, improve drainage by adding more organic material.

JULY

- Shallow-rooted groundcovers and vines may need more frequent supplemental watering. Drought-resistant plants have deeper roots and may not require as much water. Spring-planted plants need water when the soil feels dry to the touch down to one inch.

- Set out shallow tin cans at different locations of the newly planted groundcover or vine to determine the amount of time it takes to deliver ¾ to 1 in. of water. Adjust the automatic sprinkler's timer accordingly.

- Propagate woody-stemmed plants by layering. Bend the stem horizontally to the ground. Cut a shallow ½-inch sliver at the point where the stem is in contact with the soil. Remove all leaves and stems from behind the cut and pin it securely with a u-shaped piece of wire. Cover the nicked stem with backfill soil.

- Layering is complete when roots form at the point of soil contact and new growth emerges, clip off the rooted cutting from the mother plant.

AUGUST

- Rather than planting during the hottest and driest months of the year, spend time properly preparing the soil for planting in autumn.

- Many fragrances infuse the warm summer air such as Rangoon Creeper, Star Jasmine and *Stephanotis*. Incorporate them in your landscape come fall. They will attract bees, butterflies and hummingbirds.

- If Bermudagrass or other stoloniferous grasses are spreading throughout groundcovers or around vines, apply a systemic herbicide and check the label, because most herbicides have temperature guidelines as well as what plants it might harm.

- Protect young groundcovers and tender vines from squirrels or rabbits. Use olfactory repellents, motion-activated sprinklers or lights. For live traps, contact a local animal control center or hire a licensed professional if the problems are causing too much damage.

- Cut back Baby's Tears, Blue Star Creeper, *Coprosma*, Creeping Thyme and other spreaders to encourage new compact growth and prevent them from overstepping their boundaries.

SEPTEMBER

- Re-program irrigation timers to adjust to cooler temperatures.

- Even with cooler temperatures, water established evergreen groundcovers and vines before the rainy season. Decrease watering deciduous selections as they defoliate and enter dormancy.

- Fall is one of the best times to dig and plant groundcovers and vines, especially in frost-free locales while the soil is still warm from summer. Where winters are frigid, hold off until spring.

- Take a walk around the neighborhood and look for groundcovers and vines that turn brilliant colors, such as Boston Ivy and Virginia Creeper to incorporate in your seasonal garden. Bougainvillea and Rangoon Creeper may also be in their flowering glory.

- Fall feeding helps maintain a plant's vigor and prepares them for the colder winter season. Avoid harsh chemical fertilizers that are high in nitrogen, because nitrogen stimulates new and frost-tender growth and harms beneficial microorganisms in the soil. Use an organic granular or liquid fertilizer instead.

OCTOBER

- Continue to water fall-planted groundcovers and vines frequently during the first three months, especially if weather conditions remain hot and dry. If the soil fees dry to the touch down to 1-2 inches, water again.

- Check on spring-planted plants about once a week when there is no fall rainfall and water if necessary.

ALGERIAN IVY

- Mulch over the roots of frost-tender evergreen vines and groundcovers. Replenish mulches so that they remain at 2 inches such as worm castings or soil building compost.

- Move frost-susceptible containerized vines to a more sheltered part of the garden, near walls or trees or wrap with horticultural fleece or cotton sheet.

- Prune back the new, young flexible Wisteria growth in fall after the vines are dormant, but leave 2-4 buds for next spring's blooms. Wisteria flowers more profusely if pruned regularly. The goal is to create stumpy spurs at the base of previous year's growth that will carry flower buds.

NOVEMBER

- If planting toward the end of autumn, make sure to tamp the soil firmly around the roots and water sufficiently to collapse any air holes that might allow cold temperatures to enter and damage the plant's root system.

- Apply a product with humic acid over in-ground plantings and containers twice a year, once in autumn and once in spring. Humic acid revitalizes the soil and helps to proliferate beneficial microbes.

- Aphids, scale and spider mites continue to thrive in fall and their honeydew attracts ants. Treat with an organic canola-based or horticultural oil. Systemic insecticides can also be used if there are no plants with edible parts nearby.

- For acid-needy plants such as *Stephanotis* and Star Jasmine fertilize with cottonseed meal once in autumn and again in spring.

- If humidity and warmth continues, powdery mildew remains a problem. Spray with an organic fungicide or use a horticultural or canola-based oil.

DECEMBER

- Winter is an excellent time to assess the "bare bones" of your yard, when many trees and plants are resting and few flowers are blooming. The right groundcover or vine can soften the stark contrasts between trees, shrubs and hardscape features like fences and sidewalks.

- Peruse plant catalogues and surf the web to garner more ideas for the "highs and lows" of your landscape.

- Apply a pre-emergent weed control on groundcovers and around vines before winter rains arrive if you forgot to apply in fall.

- Protect cold-sensitive groundcovers and evergreen vines from frosts by spraying with an antitranspirant such as Cloud Cover or Wilt-Pruf. The plastic coating will last all winter long.

- During normal winters, supplemental watering is usually not necessary, but when rainfall is below average and the temperature is above freezing, water plants thoroughly except for deciduous or water-thrifty plants. Keep dormant or drought-tolerant plant roots moist, but not soggy.

STONECROP

HERBS,
VEGETABLES &
MELONS
for California

Pundits are proclaiming the current interest in homegrown foods is a sign of economic times, but it is so much more. There is a burgeoning belief that we need to take control of what we are eating—to find out where our foods come from and under what conditions they are grown. In 2007 the New Oxford American Dictionary declared "locavore" as the word of the year. It was coined by Jessica Prentiss from Northern California who sought to promote the idea of eating food harvested within a specified area, about a 100-mile radius.

The locavore movement encourages consumers to either buy from farms close to home or to grow their own food in private or community gardens arguing that such fresh produce is more nutritious and tastes much better. It is also an environmentally responsible way to decrease the use of fossil fuels and non-renewable resources when we no longer purchase and rely on imported food.

SOIL IS ALIVE

Growing edibles organically is vital. Just as the ocean's depth is filled with life that is not visible from its surface, so is the soil. If you are new to the practice of organic vegetable and herb gardening and have traditionally used chemical pesticides and fertilizers as your first line of defense, you need to help build up the population of beneficial bacteria and fungi in the soil. Think of the soil as a living entity, teaming with fungi and bacteria microorganisms working as decomposers, as well as protozoa and beneficial nematodes that are preying on disease-causing bacteria, fungi, root-attacking nematodes, and other bad guys.

By adding organic materials such as humus, worm castings, and compost, we are enhancing the aerobic beneficial microorganisms in soil and returning life and oxygen into it. At the same time, bad anaerobic bacteria and fungi that thrive in oxygen-deprived soils are consumed and crowded out.

Using organic fertilizers and soil builders in liquid or granular form is the other important component to gardening. The main reason is the impact organics have on the soil. Organic fertilizers feed the soil by supplying necessary organic matter and enhancing the soil structure. At the same time, they act as a storehouse for plant nutrients and encourage the proliferation of beneficial soil organisms. Plants take up nutrients as they need them, at their natural rate, building stronger cell walls that results in a higher resistance to attacks by insects and diseases.

Many synthetic or chemical fertilizers are formulated to be fast-acting. Since plants can use only a percentage of the chemical food at once, the rest is wasted and washed away into our waterways and oceans. Besides suppressing beneficial soil organisms, chemical or synthetic plant foods often create harmful side effects by pushing tender, succulent growth that attract chewing and sucking insects. As a result, the plants weaken and become more susceptible to insects and disease.

GARDENING IS FUN

While all of these arguments for creating a vegetable and herb garden are valid, the most important reason is that it is pure, unadulterated fun. Fresh air, sunshine, the relaxing pleasure of enjoying nature's beauty and tasty homegrown harvests—bring joy into our lives, especially when we can share with our family and friends a meal of homegrown Tomatoes, Asparagus, Corn, herbs, and mouth-watering melons.

Surrounded by stressful realities of pollution, economic or personal tribulations, our gardens become a buffering oasis. The beauty of kitchen gardening is you can start small, just dig up a little sunny corner of the yard or pot up a few containers. It is about the joy of puttering in the dirt, the satisfaction of seeing plants flourish and fruit from your own labors and the thrill of harvesting and dining on homegrown delectables.

Herbs can be found in a variety of plant types—trees, vines, shrubs, herbaceous perennials, annuals and biennials. They can also be used for medicinal, culinary or ornamental purposes. Even vegetables have an identity problem. Radishes, Carrots, Celery, and Lettuce are seedless and are—botanically speaking—vegetables. But if they contain seeds such as Cucumbers, Squash, Beans, Peppers, and Tomatoes, are they fruits? Botanists say "yes," but the common perception is that they are all vegetables—seeded or unseeded.

There is no botanical controversy when the topic turns to melons. All belong to the *Curcurbit* family of vines including Cantaloupes (actually muskmelons), Late Melons such as Honeydew, Casaba, 'Crenshaw', Persian and Watermelon and Cucumber, squash and gourds.

Whether fruit, vegetable or herb, medicinal, culinary or ornamental, there are infinite choices of heirloom and hybrid varieties. Tomato plants and seeds alone come from all parts of the world from small cherry-size to meaty behemoth beefsteaks, from striped, streaked or blushed yellows, greens, pinks, oranges, browns, scarlets, blackish maroons and even whites, to round, flat and pear shapes and sweet or acid tastes. Where bell peppers were once the only choice, now there are Habañero, Tabasco, Serrano and Cayenne.

The list is endless and limited only by our imagination. Don't be afraid to experiment, but most of all, have fun. Growing herbs, vegetables and melons is a splendid excuse to get your hands in the dirt. In most areas of California, Mother Nature is particularly kind, allowing us to grow an extensive array of fresh food throughout the year. Let the following chapter heighten all your senses and encourage you to stretch the boundaries of your edible garden.

RECIPE FOR COMPOST TEA

Compost tea increases the population of beneficial microbes, helps suppress foliar diseases and insect infestations on plants and in the soil and increases the amount of nutrients available to your plants. One gallon of compost tea at a dilution ratio of 4:1 should treat 300 square feet with a pressure sprayer. Apply full-strength compost tea every 7-14 days to poor-draining soils. As the soil texture improves, it will become looser. Thereafter, reduce treatments to once a month for 6-12 months, then decrease to about 2-3 times a year.

Many retail nurseries and mail order companies offer compost tea brewers, but you can also make your own.

- Mature compost (turned over several times so that the weed seeds and pathogens have been "cooked") or worm castings
- 2 (5-gallon) buckets
- 1 aquarium pump large enough to run 3 air stones (bubblers)
- Several feet of plastic air tubing
- 1 gang valve to supply air from the pump to the tubes attached to the bubblers
- Unsulfured organic molasses
- Stirring stick or spoon
- Cheese cloth, tea towel or nylon stocking for straining

Brew for 2-3 days and use the tea immediately because the greatest population of beneficial microbes is lost if not used within 24 hours. If the water is chlorinated, allow the bubblers to aerate and evaporate any chlorine before making the tea.

Loosely fill the bucket halfway with compost (do not pack) and attach 1 length of tubing from the pump to the gang valve. Cut 3 more sections of tubing long enough to reach from the rim to the bottom of the bucket. Connect each onto a port of the gang valve and push bubblers into the opposite ends. Hang the gang valve on the bucket lip and bury the bubblers under the compost. Fill the bucket with water 3 inches from the rim and start the pump. Once the mixture is activated, add 1 oz. of molasses and stir it in (molasses is food for the bacteria). Make sure the bubblers are on the bottom and evenly spaced. Stir the tea a couple times a day and after 2-3 days, turn off the equipment and allow the brew to settle for 10-20 minutes. The compost should smell earthy and sweet, never rotten. Strain the mixture with cheese cloth, stocking or tea towel into a bucket and pour the strained mixture into your clean, sterile watering can or sprayer. Makes 2½ gallons of tea. Put the solid residue obtained from straining the tea back on the compost pile or add directly onto the soil.

THE GOOD GUYS

Beneficial insects are effective as the weather warms and daylight hours lengthen. The following chart identifies beneficials and the insects they control.

Beneficial Insect	Controls
lacewings	mites, whiteflies, mealybugs, thrips, aphids, lerp psyllid, scale crawlers
12 spotted lady beetles	aphids, scale crawlers, potato beetles, beetle larvae
looper parasite	cabbage loopers
mealybug destroyer	mealybugs, scale, aphids, thrips, red spider mites
Encarsia formosa	green house whitefly, silver leaf whitefly
big-eyed bug	cabbage loopers, lygus bugs, mites, leafhoppers, boll worms, budworms
ladybird beetle	aphids, soft-bodied insects, scale
spiny soldier bugs	caterpillars, beetle grubs, hornworms, cabbage loopers, webworms
scale destroyer	hard scale, soft scale
western predatory mite	avocado (Persea) mite
beneficial mites	mites, thrips
beneficial nematodes	root-knot nematodes, thrips, fungus gnats, flea beetles

WATERING METHODS

California's average rainfall (10 inches or more) wets the soil by spring to a depth of 6 feet, but if dry weather prevails, supplemental watering becomes a necessity. While the "inch of water per week" is a general guideline for watering herbs and vegetables, adjustments are needed depending on the stage of growth, weather, and cultural conditions of the particular plant. For valuable watering information, visit the Metropolitan Water District's website at www.mwdh2o.com. A tensiometer sold at retail nurseries also helps determine when it is time to water your plants. The following are watering methods to consider.

If you use a sprinkler system, set empty tuna cans under the sprinklers at different locations and record the time the sprinklers are on. When turned off, measure the water depth in the cans and take an average of the various depths to figure the amount of water applied.

For furrow irrigation, create 5- to 6-inch raised beds spaced 32-40 in. apart from center to center. Level the tops of the beds, and spread them to 18-inch widths. Set the seed rows 3 inches from the bedding edges. Raised beds are good during rains because they drain off the excess water. Furrow irrigation avoids wetting the foliage, but more water is needed to moisten the soil to a depth of 2 feet, compared to sprinklers.

Drip irrigation delivers moisture at a slow, water-conserving rate and is applied more accurately in the root zone. These advantages outweigh the initial cost of a drip system and its maintenance.

Soaker hoses are a variation of drip irrigation and are particularly useful for short 20- to 25-foot row plantings where the soil is level, but for longer rows or on sloping soils, use the traditional drip system.

CANTALOUPE

BASIL
Ocimum basilicum

Hardiness—All zones as an annual

Color(s)—Green, purple, variegated foliage

Harvest Period—Spring-autumn

Mature Size (H & W)—24 in. x 12 in.

Water Needs—Water every 5-7 days during growth.

Planting/Care—Where temperatures are 50°+F, sow seeds or plants directly outside and space 10-12 in. apart. Pinch off flowers as they form and young tips to prolong leaf production and encourage a full growth habit. Provide full sun or part shade, well-draining soil and fertilize once with a complete organic food.

Pests/Diseases—Spray with organic Spinosad to control whiteflies and grasshoppers and use canola-based horticultural oil for aphids.

Landscaping Tips & Ideas—Grow in containers or mixed flower or herb gardens. Wonderful in sauces and salads. For a bee magnet, plant 'African Blue', an extremely fragrant basil that flowers without stopping foliar production. Other basils have overtones of lemon, cinnamon or licorice and come in assorted leaf shapes and colors.

CHIVES
Allium schoenoprasum

Hardiness—All zones as an annual

Color(s)—Purplish-rose or white flowers in spring-summer

Harvest Period—Spring-autumn

Mature Size (H & W)—24 to 30 in. x 6 to 12 in.

Water Needs—Water every 5-7 days during growth and bloom cycles.

Planting/Care—Needs well-amended soil with good drainage, spacing 12 in. apart and planted in full sun. Easy to grow from seed in mid-winter or fall or as plants in early spring onward. Divide perennial clumps every 3-4 years to maintain vigor. Let it bloom without sacrificing its mild onion flavor.

Pests/Diseases—Few disease or pest problems. Chives are reputed to resist many insects including aphids.

Landscaping Tips & Ideas—Use as an ornamental edging for borders, containers, cottage or herb gardens. Good companion plant with Tomato, Carrot, Lettuce and ornamentals like Roses. Prized for its mild onion flavor, snip the hollow stems to add in soups, salads, omelets, baked potatoes and sandwiches. Flowers are also edible.

DILL
Anethum graveolens

Hardiness—All zones as an annual

Color(s)—Yellow flowers in summer

Harvest Period—Later spring-autumn

Mature Size (H & W)—2 to 4 ft. x as wide

Water Needs—Water every 7-10 days.

Planting/Care—Sow seeds directly outdoors because it does not like its roots disturbed. For continuous production, sow successively every 4 weeks in spring and summer. For desert or inland areas, sow in late summer or fall. Thin about 8-12 in. apart and plant in well-draining soil in full sun. Apply a 1-2 in. layer of mulch to retain moisture.

Pests/Diseases—Dill is thought to deter cabbage white moth caterpillars, carrot and onion flies and aphids.

Landscaping Tips & Ideas—Aromatic Dill seeds are used for pickling and seasoning vinegars. The leaves are excellent in seafood dishes, salads and sauces. Plant with Carrots, Beets, Lettuce, but avoid planting near Fennel because they tend to cross-pollinate producing "Dennel" seeds.

GOTU KOLA
Centella asiatica

Hardiness—All zones as an annual

Color(s)—Green heart-shaped, serrated leaves

Harvest Period—Year-round

Mature Size (H & W)—6 to 8 in. x spreading

Water Needs—Water every 4-7 days to keep soil moist.

Planting/Care—Grows naturally in the swamps of India and the tropics so provide full sun (partial shade for inland or desert regions), well-drained, humus or compost-amended, loam soil. Provide protection from winter frost or treat as an annual.

Pests/Diseases—As with most herbs, few pests or disease problems, but keep the soil evenly moist.

Landscaping Tips & Ideas—Gotu Kola is an acid-needy plant and does best in containers. Its leaves taste similar to parsley, but tangier and can be served in salads or dried in teas. In India it is a favorite food of elephants and perhaps that is why it is believed to promote longevity, increase intelligence, improve memory and provide energy.

LEMON GRASS
Cymbopogon citratus

Hardiness—All zones as an annual

Color(s)—Not applicable

Harvest Period—Late spring-fall

Mature Size (H & W)—3 to 4 ft. x 3 ft.

Water Needs—Water every 5-7 days during growth and warm weather.

Planting/Care—Needs a humus or compost-amended, well-draining soil planted in full sun. In mild winter regions, this tropical perennial will overwinter, but where winter frosts are common, treat as an annual or bring indoors before the weather gets cold. Start new plants by dividing the clumps.

Pests/Diseases—Control aphids or mealybugs with a strong stream of water or spray with a canola-based horticultural oil.

Landscaping Tips & Ideas—Grass-like leaves are 1-in. wide and stand 3 to 4 ft. tall. Well suited in containers or mixed with heat-loving tropical plants. Every part of this plant has a lemony fragrance and is a must for Thai and Southeast Asian cuisine. Cats also like to chew on the leaves.

MINT
Mentha spp.

Hardiness—All zones as an annual

Color(s)—Grey, yellow, reddish-brown, green, and variegated leaves

Harvest Period—Year-round in mild climates

Mature Size (H & W)—12 to 18 in. x spreading

Water Needs—Water regularly every 5-7 days depending on weather and growth conditions.

Planting/Care—Plant in amended, well-drained soil in full sun or part shade. Divide established plants every 3-4 years in spring. Mulch to retain moisture. Keep contained in pots because of its invasive nature.

Pests/Diseases—For rust, cut the plant back for fresh growth.

Landscaping Tips & Ideas—Harvest throughout the year before flowering for best flavor. Fresh or dried leaves are used in teas, iced beverages and salads. Mints come in a potpourri of flavors and fragrances including Apple, Chocolate, Pineapple, Spearmint and Peppermint. Select several mint species or cultivars for an attractive planting combination as well as for varied flavors and fragrances.

OREGANO
Origanum vulgare

Hardiness—All zones as an annual

Color(s)—Lavender-pink flowers in summer

Harvest Period—During growing seasons

Mature Size (H & W)—18 in. x spreading

Water Needs—Keep moist until established, then allow to dry slightly between watering.

Planting/Care—Where winter frosts are common, plant from seed indoors 6-8 weeks before the soil is workable, but in mild winter regions sow seeds or from plants directly in the garden in spring and fall. Plant in full sun with well-draining, slightly alkaline soil. After blooming, divide this perennial every 3-4 years to encourage full growth.

Pests/Diseases—Control whitefly and thrips with an organic Spinosad and spider mites and aphids with a canola-based horticultural oil.

Landscaping Tips & Ideas—Greek Oregano (*Origanum vulgare hurtis*) is popular in Italian, Greek, Mexican and Spanish dishes. Although it spreads quickly, it is not as invasive as mint and will behave in mixed flower gardens, containers and in front of borders.

PARSLEY
Petroselinum spp.

Hardiness—All zones as an annual

Color(s)—Small, cream flowers in summer

Harvest Period—Year-round in mild temperatures

Mature Size (H & W)—10 to 18 in. x 8 to 10 in.

Water Needs—Regular, even moisture

Planting/Care—This biennial is commonly treated as an annual because it bolts in warm weather. Soak seeds overnight to speed germination before planting in well-amended, good-draining soil in full sun or part shade. Sow in August for the following spring harvest in mild winters, but for frost-prone regions wait until spring. Pinch off flower shoots for a longer harvest.

Pests/Diseases—Control slugs and snails by hand or apply an iron phosphate snail bait. Control aphids with a strong stream of water or spray with Spinosad.

Landscaping Tips & Ideas—Find a different place in the garden every year for optimum vigor or plant in containers. Curled Parsley is pretty, but less aromatic than flat-leafed Parsley.

ROSEMARY
Rosmarinus officinalis

Hardiness—Zones 8-11

Color(s)—Blue, white or pink flowers in winter-spring, fall

Harvest Period—Year-round

Mature Size (H & W)—1 to 5 ft. x as wide

Water Needs—Once established, water sparingly because it is drought tolerant.

Planting/Care—Plant from containers 2 ft. apart and treat root ball gently because roots do not like to be disturbed. Provide full sun in well-drained, amended soil. Tip-prune while plant is young, but for mature plants prune into leafy stems, not bare portions. Adapts to many areas including seaside conditions.

Pests/Diseases—Very few pests due to the resinous leaves, but mildew and root rot are problems if planted in poor-draining soil or poor air circulation.

Landscaping Tips & Ideas—Use this evergreen as an aromatic hedge, topiary, with other water-thrifty perennials or in containers. Flowers and leaves are edible and delicious with lamb, shish-ka-bobs, roasts, barbecues and teas.

SAGE
Salvia officinalis

Hardiness—All zones as an annual

Color(s)—Purple, red, white flowers in late spring-summer

Harvest Period—Spring-early summer

Mature Size (H & W)—1 to 3 ft. x 1 to 2½ ft.

Water Needs—Water regularly until established, them water sparingly.

Planting/Care—Start from seed or cuttings in mid-spring. Needs full sun, well-drained slightly alkaline soil with good air circulation. After flowering, cut back 20% and when new growth begins again, can prune about 50%.

Pests/Diseases—Prone to mildew and root rot if planted in soggy, clay soil and poor air circulation.

Landscaping Tips & Ideas—Clip evergreen foliage for cooking or drying before flowers appear. Use fresh leaves in salads or stuffing. Golden Sage has bright yellow and green variegated leaves and is an ideal companion with cool season annuals. Purple Sage and 'Tricolor' with white, rose and green leaves tolerate hot summers and are pretty additions to butterfly, mixed flower and herb gardens.

SHISO (PERILLA)
Perilla frutescens

Hardiness—All zones as an annual

Color(s)—Purple, white flowers in summer

Harvest Period—Purple or green leaves summer-fall

Mature Size (H & W)—24 to 36 in. x 18 to 35 in.

Water Needs—Water deeply and regularly keeping soil evenly moist.

Planting/Care—Sow seeds in spring-early summer where winters are mild but for desert or inland areas avoid planting until late summer-early fall. Plant directly from seed or pots in full sun and well-draining soil. Encourage more branching structure by periodically pinching off new growth.

Pests/Diseases—Hand-pick off slugs and snails or use an organic iron phosphate bait.

Landscaping Tips & Ideas—Leaves are used in sushi, sashimi, pickling, pink-tinged vinegar (the red leaves bleed with heat) for pickled plums and ginger, as garnish and in salads and tempura. 'Aka Shiso' is purplish-red, 'Ao Shiso' is green and 'Hojiso' is green with a red reverse. Plant in ornamental or herb gardens.

STEVIA
Stevia rebaudiana

Hardiness—Zones 9-10

Color(s)—White flowers

Harvest Period—Summer-autumn

Mature Size (H & W)—30 in. x 18 to 24 in.

Water Needs—Shallow feeder roots need even moisture, but not soggy conditions.

Planting/Care—Plant this frost tender perennial from containers when soil temperatures are above 50°F in full sun spacing 20-24 in. apart. Thrives in full sun in amended, loam soil. Mulch around roots to retain moisture.

Pests/Diseases—Stevia leaves repel most insects.

Landscaping Tips & Ideas—Grow in containers or amidst summer-blooming flowers, cottage or edible gardens. The leaves are 30 times sweeter than sugar and are best harvested in late autumn. Replace after the third year where winters are mild or treat as an annual. Air dry leaves or make a liquid extract by adding 1 cup of hot water to ¼ cup of finely crushed leaves and use within 24 hours.

TARRAGON
Artemisia dracunculus

Hardiness—Zones 6-10

Color(s)—Tiny insignificant flowers

Harvest Period—Early summer-fall

Mature Size (H & W)—2 to 3 ft. x as wide

Water Needs—Once established, allow to dry out slightly between watering about every 7-10 days.

Planting/Care—Perennial herb tolerates poor soil but requires excellent drainage and prefers slightly alkaline soil. Provide full sun and plant in spring after the last day of frost, spacing 2 ft. apart. Top with mulch for cold winters and divide every 3-4 years to maintain vigor.

Pests/Diseases—Few pest problems, but susceptible to powdery or downy mildew and root rot if planted in wet, soggy, heavy soil.

Landscaping Tips & Ideas—Plant in pots, hanging baskets or in mixed beds. Select French Tarragon because Russian Tarragon is flavorless. Flavors mayonnaise, butter, vinegar, oils and mustard and used in salads, poultry, fish and even cheese.

THYME
Thymus spp.

Hardiness—Zones 5-10

Color(s)—White, blue, pink, lilac flowers in spring-summer

Harvest Period—Summer or before flowers bloom

Mature Size (H & W)—12 in. x 24 in.

Water Needs—Once established, allow to dry out before watering.

Planting/Care—Plant from containers or seeds in early spring. Provide full sun (part shade in hot climates) and well-draining soil. Pinch sprigs regularly to promote growth. Cut mature plants as much as 50% in early summer to prevent woody growth.

Pests/Diseases—Few pest problems, but prone to root rot if grown in soggy, heavy soil.

Landscaping Tips & Ideas—Ideal as a small-space ground cover, edging along a border, as fillers between teppingstones, in containers and in herb gardens. Over 350 species to choose including Lemon or Coconut Thyme and for the kitty, Cat Thyme. Use fresh or dried for fish, poultry and stuffing. Add dried thyme with lavender to use as a moth repellent or potpourri.

TOMATO

ARTICHOKE
Cynara scolymus

Hardiness—Zones 7-11

Color(s)—Purple thistle-like flower

Harvest Period—Early fall-late spring

Mature Size (H & W)—4 to 6 ft. x as wide

Water Needs—Water once a week during growth period for a crop, but if grown as an ornamental it is drought tolerant.

Planting/Care—Plant in fall for a spring harvest or plant in spring or winter for a fall crop the following year and space 4-6 ft. apart. Needs full sun in well-draining, richly amended soil. Harvest while buds are tight. After all the buds have been harvested, cut the main stem down to 1 in. above the ground for a second harvest. Apply a 2-in. layer of mulch to protect during cold winters.

Pests/Diseases—Control aphids by spraying with a strong stream of water and snails or slugs by hand-picking or applying an iron phosphate bait. For gophers, use a manual trap.

Landscaping Tips & Ideas—Lovely thistle-like plants with large silvery-sheened foliage is evergreen where winters are mild. Use in back of borders if you have space. Once the artichoke begins to bloom, it is too late to eat, but enjoy the gorgeous purple flower.

ASPARAGUS
Asparagus officinalis

Hardiness—Zones 4-10

Color(s)—Chartreuse flowers

Harvest Period—Spring

Mature Size (H & W)—8 to 12 in. x 18 in.

Water Needs—Keep evenly moist during growth cycle, but decrease during winter dormancy.

Planting/Care—Plant from bare-root crowns labeled "all-male" in late winter-early spring. Dig a 12-ft.-long, 1-ft.-wide, 1-ft.-deep trench and add a 6-in. layer of compost. Place the crowns in the middle of the trench, spread out the roots and space 18 in. apart. Backfill with 2 in. of humus-amended soil. As the plants grow, cover them with more backfill, but do not cover growing tips.

Pests/Diseases—Use a floating row cover in spring to keep insects away.

Landscaping Tips & Ideas—1-year-old crowns take 3 years before harvest. Once mature, harvest for 6-8 weeks from spring-onward. Snap off 6-8 in. spears at soil level. 'UC 157', 'Jersey Knight' and 'Jersey Giant' are "all-male."

BEETS
Beta vulgaris

Hardiness—All zones as an annual

Color(s)—Red, yellow, pink, white and striped

Harvest Period—Fall-winter

Mature Size (H & W)—12 in. x 12 in.

Water Needs—Water every 5-7 days to keep soil evenly moist but not soggy.

Planting/Care—Plant seeds outside when the ground is workable in early spring. Where winters are mild, sow seeds in late summer for fall and winter harvests. Thin seedlings to 6 in. Provide full sun, well-drained and compost-amended soil. Harvest when roots are 1½-3 in. in diameter.

Pests/Diseases—Protect tender seedlings from insects with a row cover in spring.

Landscaping Tips & Ideas—Since all parts are edible, remove beet greens after harvest and prepare similar to Chard. If space is limited, Beets take much less space compared to sprawling vegetables like squash. 'Chioggia' produces concentric circles of red and white, while 'Albino' is pure white and 'Detroit Red' is blood red.

BROCCOLI
Brassica oleracea var. botrytis

Hardiness—Zones 4-10

Color(s)—Green, purple, white flower heads

Harvest Period—Spring and fall

Mature Size (H & W)—2½ ft. x 18 to 24 in.

Water Needs—Water regularly every 5-7 days during growth cycle.

Planting/Care—Prefers full sun but grows best where summers are cool. In hot regions, plant in fall from seed or containers for a spring crop. Provide richly amended, well-draining soil and fertilize with an organic food such as pelletized chicken manure. Space plants 18 in. apart.

Pests/Diseases—Moisten newspaper, roll it up and place by Broccoli plants at night. Earwigs love moist, dark places. In the morning, dispose of them-paper and all-in the trash.

Landscaping Tips & Ideas—After cutting off the main head, continue to fertilize and water to encourage flowering side shoots. Broccoli is an ideal companion with Lettuce and Spinach. 'Arcadia' is slow to bolt and 'Romanesco' bears eye-popping chartreuse spiraling heads.

CABBAGE
Brassica Oleracea Capitata Group

Hardiness—All zones as an annual

Color(s)—Pink, green, red, blue, purple, white heads

Harvest Period—Autumn, winter, spring depending on variety

Mature Size (H & W)—6 to 24 in. x 18 to 24 in.

Water Needs—Water regularly to keep soil moist, but not soggy.

Planting/Care—Plant in amended soil in full sun (part shade for inland areas) from seed (every 3 in.) or from containers (3 ft. apart). Plant early- to late-maturing selections to extend harvest. After heads are cut, leave the stem, continue to water and fertilize for a second crop.

Pests/Diseases—Floating row covers protect tender seedlings against aphids, Cabbage loopers and maggots. Clubroot is a soil-borne fungus that does not thrive in alkaline soils.

Landscaping Tips & Ideas—Colorful Cabbage is ornamental and edible in mixed borders and containers. 'Savoy' is an early variety, but for summer or fall maturity select 'Tundra' or 'Pixie' (great for small gardens).

123

CANTALOUPE
Cucumis melo hybrids

Hardiness—All zones as an annual

Color(s)—Orange flesh

Fruit Period—Summer to early fall

Mature Size (H & W)—6 to 12 in. x 24 to 36 in.

Water Needs—Needs 1-2 in. of water per week.

Planting/Care—Start seeds indoors and transplant in full sun in late spring, but in mild regions, sow seeds directly in the garden. Make a 3-ft. diameter mound from humus-amended, good-draining soil. Water and fertilize regularly around the base of the hill or furrow, but not on the foliage.

Pests/Diseases—Protect seedlings from insect damage with a floating row cover and for mildew, spray with a canola-oil based horticultural oil.

Landscaping Tips & Ideas—Train Cantaloupes on a trellis but support fruits with cloth slings. Select disease-resistant hybrids such as 'Gallery Galia' or 'Solid Gold' or 'Ambrosia' for flavor. It is ripe when it slips off the stem easily.

CARROTS
Daucus carota subspecies *sativus*

Hardiness—All zones as an annual

Color(s)—Red, orange, yellow, purple, white roots

Harvest Period—Spring-fall depending on variety

Mature Size (H & W)—Roots vary from 3 to 8 in.

Water Needs—Deep water 1 in. per week.

Planting/Care—Plant in full sun in well-drained, sandy loam, alkaline soil. Sow seeds in March or June in furrowed rows after frost. Thin seedlings 2 in. apart.

Pests/Diseases—No Carrot fly in California, but control aphids by spraying with a strong stream of water and leafhoppers with organic Spinosad. Plant in another area or a container if root knot nematodes are a problem.

Landscaping Tips & Ideas—Carrots do well in 18-in. container. For a rainbow of colors consider 'Cosmic Purple' (purple skin with yellow and orange flesh), 'Amarillo' (yellow), 'Snow White' (creamy-white) and 'Atomic Red'. Plant an early variety like 'Earlybird Nantes' and a later variety such as 'Rainbow'.

CAULIFLOWER
Brassica oleracea var. *botrytis*

Hardiness—All zones as an annual

Color(s)—Orange, purple, green or white heads

Harvest Period—From seed, matures in 60-100 days

Mature Size (H & W)—6-in.- diameter heads

Water Needs—Water every 5-7 days to keep soil moist.

Planting/Care—Flourishes in long, cool and moist conditions. Plant from containers in rich, amended soil in partial shade to avoid early bolting. Space 2 ft. apart. If summers are hot, grow to harvest before or after the heat of summer.

Pests/Diseases—Same pest problems as Broccoli.

Landscaping Tips & Ideas—Related to Broccoli and Cabbage, it is a bit trickier to grow compared to the other two. For pure white curds (head), pull up outer leaves over the head (blanching) and secure with string. 'Violetta Italia' for purple heads, 'Early White Hybrid' for an early, white head and 'Green Macerata' for bright green heads.

CORN (SWEET CORN)
Zea mays

Hardiness—All zones as an annual

Color(s)—White, yellow, bicolor

Harvest Period—Late summer-fall

Mature Size (H & W)—6 to 8+ft. x 2 ft.

Water Needs—Water regularly especially as tassels emerge from stalks and when silks form.

Planting/Care—Thrives in heat, humus-rich, well-draining soil and full sun. Sow seeds in March and transplant seedlings or plants outside after danger of frost is over. Sow seeds outdoors in May and plant in blocks rather than single rows for better wind pollination. Space 18 in. apart. Fertilize with a complete, granular organic food and supplement with liquid kelp.

Pests/Diseases—If harvested corn is damaged from Corn earworm, cut off the damaged portion.

Landscaping Tips & Ideas—If kernels do not fill out completely, plant more next time in a breezier location for better pollination. Plant one variety because corn cross-pollinates easily. Where summers are cool grow an early hybrid like 'Bonjour' or 'Casino'.

CUCUMBER
Cucumis sativas

Hardiness—All zones as an annual

Color(s)—Green, yellow, white-skinned

Harvest Period—Summer-early fall

Mature Size (H & W)—4 to 6 ft. x as wide

Water Needs—Water every 5-7 days, but not on foliage.

Planting/Care—Plant in full sun, protected from wind in well-draining, rich soil. Soak seeds overnight before sowing outdoors late May-June. Feed with a liquid organic fertilizer when fruits swell every two weeks.

Pests/Diseases—Poor air circulation may cause powdery mildew. Spray with a canola-based horticultural oil. Use a row cover to protect young plants from beetles, slugs and snails, but remove when flowers appear.

Landscaping Tips & Ideas—Train plant on a trellis or make a tepee with 3 poles tied together. Encourage pollinating bees by planting Sage and African Blue Basil nearby. 'Burpless Tasty Green' is disease-resistant, 'Kyoto Three Feet' is aptly named and for containers try 'Bush Champion'.

EGGPLANT
Solanum melongena

Hardiness—All zones as an annual

Color(s)—Purple, green, orange, white, yellow, streaked

Harvest Period—Summer-fall

Mature Size (H & W)—24 to 36 in. x as wide

Water Needs—Water every 5-7 days, especially during growth and fruiting cycles.

Planting/Care—Sow seeds indoors 8-10 weeks prior to the last frost date or plant from containers outdoors in mid-late-spring. Provide full sun, humus-amended and well-draining soil and space 3 ft. apart. Pinch off some blossoms for larger fruits.

Pests/Diseases—Control aphids and whitefly with a canola-based horticultural oil and organic Spinosad.

Landscaping Tips & Ideas—Use in large pots, raised beds or edging a mixed flower border. Besides the popular 'Black Beauty' add other tasty selections like the sweet 'Rosa Bianca' , the white 'Casper', 'Turkish Orange' and for pickling 'Mizuno Takumi'. The strictly ornamental 'Nipple Plant' bears 2-5-ft. spikes of 3-in. yellow-orange fruits resembling a cow's udder and used in dramatic arrangements.

LETTUCE
Lactuca sativa

Hardiness—All zones as an annual

Color(s)—Green, red, yellow, speckled foliage

Harvest Period—Almost year-round

Mature Size (H & W)—Depends on cultivar/variety

Water Needs—Water every 5-7 days at the base of the plant.

Planting/Care—Plant in full sun (in summer provide part shade) in amended, well-draining soil. Sow seeds outdoors from March-July and in late summer-early fall for autumn and winter varieties. Space 12 in. apart.

Pests/Diseases—Mildew may result from poor air circulation or excess humidity. Control slugs and snails with an iron phosphate bait.

Landscaping Tips & Ideas—Lettuce makes a beautiful ornamental in mixed borders and containers and is a lovely filler between other plants. Cut off outer leaves as needed rather than the entire head. 'Dark Lollo Rosso' is red with frilly leaves, 'Forellenschluss' is a romaine with maroon-speckled leaves and 'Val D'Orges' is a light green, French butterhead perfect for overwintering in mild climates.

ONION
Allium cepa

Hardiness—All zones as an annual

Color(s)—White, brown, yellow, red, purple bulbs

Harvest Period—Early summer-fall

Mature Size (H & W)—18 to 24 in. x 12 to 18 in.

Water Needs—Water every 5-7 days, particularly during the bulb growth cycle.

Planting/Care—Plant from onion sets or seeds in mild winter areas in autumn or early spring. Where winters freeze wait until spring. Keep the onion tip slightly above the soil surface. Provide full sun, well-drained soil and a complete organic fertilizer.

Pests/Diseases—Protect from birds by using a net for the first weeks of planting.

Landscaping Tips & Ideas—California cannot produce reliable crops of long-day onions, so plant short-day onions such as 'Grano' and 'Granex'. Medium day-length 'White Sweet Spanish' and 'Italian Red' produce when seeded in early winter in Northern California (wait 4-6 more weeks in Southern California). 'Buffalo' is a day-neutral onion that is not as dependent on daylight length.

PARSNIP
Pastinaca sativa

Hardiness—All zones as an annual

Color(s)—Creamy-white, yellow root

Harvest Period—Late autumn, spring

Mature Size (H & W)—15 to 18 in. long roots

Water Needs—Water during extended periods of drought.

Planting/Care—Plant in full sun or partial shade in sandy, amended, loam soil. Soak seeds for 24 hours before sowing outdoors in May (for fall harvest), but where winters are mild, sow in fall and harvest in spring. Sow a marker row of radishes along the row to mark where parsnip seeds are planted. Thin seedlings to 6 in. apart. Does not like roots disturbed.

Pests/Diseases—If Parsnip canker rots the crown, discard and plant a resistant variety next year such as 'Tender and True'.

Landscaping Tips & Ideas—Related to the Carrot, the parsnip is one of the cold-hardiest vegetables. Interplant with lettuce or spinach. When foliage dies back harvest the roots. Roast, boil or mash cooked Parsnip.

PEAS
Pisum sativum

Hardiness—All zones as an annual

Color(s)—White, pink, purple flowers in spring or winter

Harvest Period—60-70 days from planting

Mature Size (H & W)—3 to 6 ft.

Water Needs—Water in furrows every 5-7 days.

Planting/Care—Some peas are shelled and others have edible pods. Soak seeds overnight before sowing in full sun from February-July in cool climates, but for mild winters plant in October. Provide well-draining, amended soil and space 2 ft. for bush and 5 ft. for vine varieties. Pick pods regularly to keep producing crops.

Pests/Diseases—For powdery or downy mildew spray with a canola-based horticultural oil and control moths with Spinosad.

Landscaping Tips & Ideas—Grow vining peas on supports such as trellises or chicken wire. After harvest, leave the roots because Peas fix nitrogen in the soil. 'Mr. Big' and the petite 'Precovelle' are shelling peas, while 'Mammoth Melting Sugar' and 'Taichung 13' have sweet, edible pods.

PEPPERS
Capsicum spp.

Hardiness—All zones as an annual

Color(s)—Red, orange, yellow, green, purple, and black

Harvest Period—Late summer-fall

Mature Size (H & W)—12 to 36 ft. x 12 to 24 ft.

Water Needs—Water every 5-7 days.

Planting/Care—Plant from containers or seedlings outdoors when evening temperatures are above 55°F and space 18 in. apart. Provide full sun, complete organic fertilizer and well-draining soil. Pinch back young plants for fuller growth and stake for support.

Pests/Diseases—Control whitefly with Spinosad and aphids with a canola-based horticultural oil.

Landscaping Tips & Ideas—Chile Peppers are measured in Scoville heat units from the mild 'Fooled You', slightly hot 'Shishito' to the fiery 'Red Savina' Habañero. Don't drink water to cool the heat of a pepper, instead eat ice cream. 'Big Bertha' is the largest sweet Bell Pepper that begins green and becomes a bright red. Peppers are decorative in mixed flower beds or in containers.

POLE BEANS
(RUNNER BEANS)
Phaseolus coccineus

Hardiness—All zones as an annual

Color(s)—Orange, red, white flowers with purple, green or yellow pods

Harvest Period—Midsummer-fall or winter

Mature Size (H & W)—5 to 8+ft. tall

Water Needs—Water every 5-7 days around the plant's base.

Planting/Care—Prefers cool summers, but where summers are hot, plant in fall. Plant outdoors in full sun in amended, well-draining soil near the end of June and space 12 in. apart. Apply a 1-in. layer of mulch when seedlings are 8 in.

Pests/Diseases—Spray Spinosad on beetle and whitefly infestations and canola-based oil on aphids and spider mites.

Landscaping Tips & Ideas—Sturdy trellises or pole supports bring vertical structure and height to the landscape. Make a foliar bean wigwam out of 3 poles. When beans begin to ripen, pick every 2 days to maintain production. Besides 'Kentucky Blue Wonder', 'White Lady' tolerates warmer temperatures and 'Hestia' is a dwarf good for containers.

POTATOES
Pastinaca sativa

Hardiness—All zones as an annual

Color(s)—Yellow, blue, russet, white, red, purple, multi-colored flesh

Harvest Period—Early summer-fall or spring

Mature Size (H & W)—Depends on variety

Water Needs—Water every 5-7 days.

Planting/Care—Plant in early spring and plant successively for a summer-fall harvest. For mild winters, you can also plant sets in early fall for a winter-spring crop. Provide full sun in fertile, well draining soil, spacing 12 in. apart with the eye pointing up. As the plant grows, add loose soil but keep away from stems and keep tubers covered with soil. Sunlight greens Potatoes and is toxic.

Pests/Diseases—Select blight-resistant varieties to avoid problems.

Landscaping Tips & Ideas—Purchase potato sets (small potatoes to be planted whole) at nurseries, because store-bought potatoes are treated with chemicals to hinder sprouting. Try 'Russet Burbank' for baking, 'Yukon Gold' for an early variety, 'Reddale' for salads and 'All Blue' for colorful fun.

PUMPKIN
Cucurbis spp.

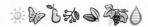

Hardiness—All zones as an annual

Color(s)—Orange, white, red, pink, green, brown, blue

Harvest Period—Late-summer to fall

Mature Size (H & W)—20 to 500 ft. depending on variety

Water Needs—Water every 3-5 days around the plant's base, not on the leaves.

Planting/Care—Sow seeds in mounded, amended, well-draining soil in late May-June and space 3-6 ft. apart. Feed with a liquid kelp every two weeks while growing. Once fruit has formed, slide a block underneath to protect from rot and slugs. When harvesting, leave a 4-in. stem on the fruit.

Pests/Diseases—Control powdery mildew with a canola-based horticultural oil or cut off affected leaves.

Landscaping Tips & Ideas—If size matters and there is plenty of room, plant 'Atlantic Giant' (*C. maxima*) to produce behemoths, 'Musquee de Provence' (*C. moschata*) for 20 lb. pumpkins shaped like a brown-ribbed wheel of cheese and 'Jack Be Little' (*C. pepo*) for 3-in. cuties for baking.

RADISH
Raphanus sativus

Hardiness—All zones as an annual

Color(s)—Red, magenta, pink, yellow, white, green roots

Harvest Period—Spring, fall, winter

Mature Size (H & W)—½ to 4-in.-wide globes and 5 to 24 in. long roots.

Water Needs—Water every 3-7 days depending on growth and weather conditions.

Planting/Care—Sow seeds as soon as ground is workable in early spring, followed with successive plantings until warm weather. Where winters are mild, also sow in fall and winter. Depending on variety, Radish matures in 25-60 days. Plant in full sun in amended, well-draining soil.

Pests/Diseases—Control chewing insects with Spinosad and use an iron phosphate bait for snails and slugs.

Landscaping Tips & Ideas—For spring or summer Radishes plant long, white 'Icicle' or round 'Early Scarlet Globe' Winter varieties include Asian varieties like 'Mantanghong Hybrid' with gorgeous magenta flesh or the world's largest Daikon Radish, 'Sakurajima Mammoth' reaches up to 100 pounds.

SPINACH
Spinacia oleracea

Hardiness—All zones as an annual

Color(s)—Green leaves

Harvest Period—Fall, winter, spring

Mature Size (H & W)—6 to 12 in. x as wide

Water Needs—Water every 5-7 days depending on growth and weather conditions.

Planting/Care—For true Spinach, this cool season annual can be sown from seeds in fall or early spring in rich, well-draining soil. Thin seedlings 3-4 in. apart. Provide full sun but part shade in summer. New Zealand Spinach is more heat tolerant and can be sown in late April-May. Where winters are mild, it is a perennial and grows 18 in. tall and 24 in. wide.

Pests/Diseases—Leaf miner larvae leave tunneling patterns within leaf surfaces. Spray with Spinosad if damage is extensive or cut off affected leaves.

Landscaping Tips & Ideas—Plant between Tomato, Sweet Corn or Beans for summer shade, but keep away from cucumbers because Spinach shares the same diseases.

STRING BEANS
(FRENCH BEANS)
Phaseolus vulgaris

Hardiness—All zones as an annual

Color(s)—Green, red, purple, cream pods

Harvest Period—Late-summer to fall

Mature Size (H & W)—2+ ft. x 1 ft. depending on cultivar

Water Needs—Water every 5-7 days depending on weather and growth condition, especially when flowering.

Planting/Care—Sow from seeds from spring (after frost) to late summer for a continuous crop from late spring to fall. Keep picking as they ripen to continue production. Plant in full sun in humus-amended, well-draining soil. Pick continuously for good production.

Pests/Diseases—Control aphids with a strong stream of water or use a canola-based horticultural oil. Plant non-climbing spring annuals like Nasturtiums to add color between bean plants.

Landscaping Tips & Ideas—Easy to grow and does not need much room. Available in dwarf varieties like 'Purple Tepee' and 'Ferrari' or climbing cultivars such as the red-speckled 'Borlotto di Lingua di Fuoco' or the yellow 'Kingston Gold'.

SUMMER SQUASH
Cucurbis hybrids

Hardiness—All zones as an annual

Color(s)—White, orange yellow, green

Harvest Period—July onward

Mature Size (H & W)—2 to 4+ ft. x as wide

Water Needs—Water regularly every 3-7 days at the base, depending on growth and weather conditions, but keep leaves and stems dry.

Planting/Care—Summer Squash have thinner, edible skins and mature earlier than winter varieties. Includes scallop-edged (Pattypan), crook and straight necks and Zucchini. Sow seeds in full sun, on mounded 4-ft.-diameter hills for trailing and 2 ft. for bush varieties in late spring-early summer. After 1 month, feed with an organic granular or liquid fertilizer every 2-3 weeks.

Pests/Diseases—Control powdery mildew and aphids with a canola-based horticultural oil.

Landscaping Tips & Ideas—'Green Buttons' is a Pattypan , 'Summer Crookneck' and 'Zephyr F1' are neck varieties and 'Genovese' is a trailing Zucchini, while 'Supremo' is a bush selection. For round Zucchini, plant 'Eight Ball'.

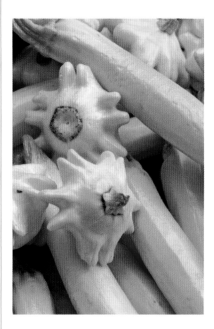

SWISS CHARD

Beta vulgaris subsp. *cicla*

Hardiness—All zones as an annual

Color(s)—Red, green and white, burgundy and green leaves

Harvest Period—Year-round where winters are mild

Mature Size (H & W)—18 to 24 in. x as wide

Water Needs—Water every 5-7 days depending on growth and weather conditions.

Planting/Care—Sow seeds in full sun in amended, well-draining soil from spring-summer. Space thinned-out seedlings 12 in. apart. Cut outer leaves as needed when plants are 12-18 in. In mild winters, sow also for a fall-winter crop.

Pests/Diseases—Control slugs in Southern California with decollate snails, but in Northern California apply an iron phosphate bait.

Landscaping Tips & Ideas—'Swiss Chard' has white stalks, but 'Bright Lights' has green and burgundy leaves with stalks shaded in pink, white, purple, yellow, burgundy, green and orange. Chard is delicious and makes a beautiful ornamental accent in mixed flower beds and containers.

TOMATO

Lycopersicon esculentum

Hardiness—All zones as an annual

Color(s)—A rainbow of colors

Fruit Period—Summer-fall

Mature Size (H & W)—2 to 6+ ft. x as wide

Water Needs—Water every 5-7 days depending on growth and weather conditions.

Planting/Care—Plant in full sun in humus amended, well draining soil. Plant seedlings outdoors after danger of frost has passed. Provide sturdy wire cages or poles. Plant Tomatoes deep (trim off leaves that are below soil surface) for a stronger cane. Fertilize once fruits begin to form.

Pests/Diseases—Hand pick and squash tomato hornworms. There are Tomato varieties that are resistant to Verticillium and Fusarium wilt.

Landscaping Tips & Ideas—'Cherokee Purple', 'Big Zac and 'Sun Sugar' need summer heat. Coastal areas are more successful with 'Murray Smith' and 'Stupice'. 'Heatwave' is for areas where temperatures exceed 85°F. Mild winter regions can also grow 'Taxi', 'Legend' and 'Sasha's Altai' through winter if planted in August.

TURNIP

Brassica rapa

Hardiness—All zones as an annual

Color(s)—White, white and purple, yellow

Harvest Period—Summer, fall or winter

Mature Size (H & W)—3 to 6 ft. x 2 to 3 ft.

Water Needs—Water every 5-7 days depending on growth and weather conditions.

Planting/Care—Plant in full sun or partial shade (inland regions) in humus-amended well-draining, slightly acid soil. Prepare soil to a depth of 12-18 in. Sow seeds in early spring (in cold winter areas) for summer harvest or where winters are mild, plant in fall for a winter crop. Thin seedlings and space 2-6 in. apart. Apply a 2 in. layer of mulch to keep weeds out and to retain moisture.

Pests/Diseases—Control aphids with a canola-based horticultural oil.

Landscaping Tips & Ideas—Turnips are grown for their leaves and roots. 'Shogoin' for delicious white roots and mild greens, 'Petrowski' and 'Ideal Purple Top Milan' for a mild, sweet flavor. Harvest when small for the sweetest flavor.

WATERMELON
Citrullus vulgaris

Hardiness—All zones as an annual

Color(s)—Red, yellow, orange, pink, cream flesh

Harvest Period—Summer-fall

Mature Size (H & W)—5 to 50+ pounds depending on variety

Water Needs—Water every 3-7 days. Do not water the leaves.

Planting/Care—Watermelon needs warm weather and plenty of water. Provide a 6-8 ft. diameter hill with well-draining soil. For cool summers select early varieties. It is ripe when: there is a hollow sound when thumped, the underside patch has turned from white to creamy-yellow and the tendrils around the stem have dried.

Pests/Diseases—Control aphids and mildew with a canola-based horticultural oil and chewing insects with Spinosad.

Landscaping Tips & Ideas—Huge watermelons like 'Carolina Cross' are great if you have the room, but for small areas grow minis such as 'Sugar Baby'. Plant 'Moon and Stars' (red and yellow-fleshed) 'Orangeglo' and 'White Wonder' for more unusual selections. 'Desert King' is drought and sunburn resistant.

WINTER SQUASH
Cucurbita spp.

Hardiness—All zones as an annual

Color(s)—Yellow, orange, green, blue, variegated outer skin

Harvest Period—Late-summer-autumn

Mature Size (H & W)—Varies depending on variety

Water Needs—Water every 5-7 days depending on growth and weather conditions. Do not water foliage or stems.

Planting/Care—Sow seeds outdoors after frost on a 4-6-ft.-diameter mound of well-draining, humus-amended soil in full sun. Fertilize with a complete organic food. Provide sturdy supports for trailing types.

Pests/Diseases—If powdery mildew becomes a problem, cut off affected leaves or spray with a canola-based horticultural oil.

Landscaping Tips & Ideas—Winter Squash include Butternut, Acron, Hubbard, Spaghetti and Pumpkin. Harvest when their skins have hardened and before frost. Leave a 4 in. stem to prevent rotting when cutting Squash. 'Sweet Mama Hyrid' is a Kabocha (Japanese squash) for small spaces and 2½ lb. fruits. 'Marina di Chioggia' and 'Table Gold Acorn' have yummy, yellow flesh.

ORGANIZE AN EDIBLE GARDEN

HOW TO ORGANIZE AN EDIBLE GARDEN

- Record ideas in a journal and include past selections, problems, successes and new ideas.

- Select a location that provides sunshine from sunup to sundown. Most herbs and vegetables produce poorly in the shade, but some cool-season crops such as Lettuce, Spinach and Cabbage tolerate some shade especially inland and desert regions.

- Join a community garden if there is insufficient sunny spaces in your landscape.

- 98% of vegetable and herbs thrive in 6.0-7.0 pH. Acidify alkaline soils by adding humus, compost, worm castings or peat and fertilizing with cottonseed meal.

- Interplant vegetables and herbs among ornamentals, especially when there is not enough space or sunshine for a separate edible garden.

- Visit your public gardens, retail nurseries and neighbors to look for locally adapted favorites and interesting new ones.

- Make sure the tallest growing vegetables and herbs are on the north side of planting beds so they won't shade the smaller plants.

- Never plant members of the Nightshade family (Tomato, Potato, Eggplant) in the same spot year after year. Rotate around in different places in the garden or in containers to avoid the spread of disease.

V,F,N,T WHAT DO THEY MEAN?

- *Verticillium* wilt, fusarium wilt, root knot nematode and tobacco mosaic virus are diseases that affect Tomato, Squash, and Melons and can persist in the soil for years. Vegetables with resistance to these diseases and root knot nematode carry the letter V, F, N or T after the varietal names. FF means it is fusarium 1 and 2 resistant.

HEIRLOOM OR HYBID?

- Heirlooms are open-pollinated varieties meaning when they are grown from seed, they will come back true to type, exactly as the parent plant. Most heirlooms existed before the 1950s.

- Seeds from hybrid varieties will either be sterile or will not exhibit the same characteristics as its parent.

HINTS FOR SAVING SEEDS

- Keep heirloom plants isolated from each other to avoid cross-pollination.

- Wait until seedpods are dry before collecting their seeds.

- Wrap cheesecloth or an old nylon around a ripening pod and securely tie. Collect when the seeds are released.

- Remove pulpy seeds like Tomatoes and Melons and soak in water for 48 hours, stirring occasionally. The pulp will rise to the surface and the seeds will sink. Rinse clean and lay on a paper towel to dry before storing them.

- Store collected seeds in a cool, dry place.

STARTING SEEDS INDOORS

- Plant seeds in peat pots to transplant directly in the soil, container and all.

- Planting trays keeps excess water away from pots.

- Plant several seeds per pot and thin out to the most vigorous seedling.

- When seedlings are 3-4 in. tall, transplant them outdoors, but harden them first by exposing them to outdoor conditions gradually.

- Dig a hole slightly larger than the seedling's peat pot. If in a plastic pot, loosen the soil around the edges with a clean knife, turn upside down while supporting the plant with your fingers and gently set the plant in the hole.

- Tamp the soil around the transplant and water lightly.

- Apply a transplant solution with indolebutryric or alpha-naphthalene acetic acid.

RAISED BED GUIDELINES

- Raised planting beds are space efficient, waterwise and maintenance time savers. Ideal where native soils are poor.

- Rectilinear layouts measuring 8-12 ft. long and 4 ft. wide are generally ideal for care and harvest convenience.

- Orient the long axis east to west to take advantage of the full sweep of the sun and make the short sides narrow enough for your to reach easily into the middle of the bed without walking on it.

- Avoid pressure-treated wood or creosote-soaked railroad ties because of chemical concerns.

- To accommodate a wheelbarrow, design a wide walkway between the raised beds.

- Turn the soil over to the depth of 2-3 ft. and break up any dirt clods.

- Fill with loam soil (40% sand, 40% silt and 20% clay) and blend in 20-30% organic material such as compost, humus mulch and worm castings.

- Apply a humic acid product to activate the beneficial soil microorganisms in the soil.

- Add an organic preplant fertilizer and fertilize thereafter with a complete organic granular or liquid vegetable food following the package directions.

- Rake the surface smooth, create furrows or mounds and water thoroughly.

- Apply a 2-in. layer of mulch after planting to control weeds and retain moisture.

- To protect beds from gophers, line the perimeter with Daffodil bulbs. The high alkaloid content is toxic to gophers.

CONTAINER GARDENING IDEAS

- Combine herbs that have similar moisture, sun and nutrient needs such as French Lavender, Rosemary and Thyme. They are water-thrifty and need full sun.

- Small-leafed herbs, like Thyme and Mint, do well in window boxes or planter bowls, but Tomatoes, Potatoes and Beans need at least 15-gallon containers or half barrels.

- Bush or dwarf Pumpkins, Zucchini and Cucumbers can grow in large containers.

- Bok Choy, Cabbage, Swiss Chard, Lettuce, and Radishes are ornamental and edible and make decorative accents in individual or combination pots.

- For Potatoes, fill a large pot (15-gallon) halfway, plant one seed potato, and when the foliage is 4 in. tall, cover with soil and plant another. Repeat until the container is full.

- Cut out wire mesh to screen the drainage holes at the bottom of containers.

- Fill with a well-draining, organic potting soil.

- Add a humic acid product, pre-plant organic fertilizer and supplement thereafter with a complete organic granular or liquid fertilizer.

- Water and fertilize container plants more frequently than those planted in the ground, because more nutrients and moisture is washed out. During hot, dry weather, it may be necessary to water once a day.

- Apply a 1-to-2-in. layer of mulch to hold in moisture.

TOMATO

JANUARY

- If planning a new vegetable and herb area, prepare the soil first. It takes time to create perfectly textured and nutrient-rich soil.

- Supplemental watering is not as vital in winter because normally there is rainfall. Be careful not to overwater or root rot may result. Once seedlings germinate, water when the soil surface is dry to the touch. Adjust irrigation systems for wet winter.

- After indoor seeds have germinated, give them plenty of bright, indirect light or put them under grow lights for at least fourteen to sixteen hours.

- For indoor seedlings, add a water-soluble organic fertilizer after the first set of true leaves emerge once or twice a week at ¼ the dilution rate.

- Artichokes, Asparagus and Rhubarb are available as bare-root plants at nurseries in late winter. Choose crowns that are solid, rather than soft, and make sure the root systems are intact and evenly distributed. Before purchase, prepare their planting beds.

FEBRUARY

- Continue to plant cool-season vegetables along the coast. For inland or central valleys forego until spring to plant the first summer crops.

- Know your garden enemies. University of California has developed the Integrated Pest Management program to manage pests—insects, diseases, rodents, and weeds. Access their website at www.ipm.ucdavis.edu.

- As soon as Cauliflower heads begin to form, tie their leaves over them to keep them from turning green when exposed to sunlight. Harvest when the white buds are plump and their sections begin to loosen slightly.

- Pick peas for sustained production. The more you pick, the more they will bear.

- When young seedlings collapse suddenly and the soil is moist the problem may be damping off, a fungal disease. Destroy the affected seedlings, increase air circulation, and allow the soil to dry out.

- Provide an extra boost of organic fertilizer if the cool-season herb or vegetable begins to yellow or its growth slows down.

MARCH

- Shore up eroded planting beds and shovel out excess soil in furrows caused by winter rains.

- Clear weeds and debris around herbs and vegetables.

- Sow seeds or set out cool-season Cabbage, Spinach, Broccoli, Peas, etc. for gardens that remain cool during the early summer months.

- After the last day of frost, introduce indoor seedlings to outdoor life. Allow a week in the shade, another week in the sun, but bring them indoors at night. By the third week, leave outdoors through the night before transplanting them.

- To encourage pollinators, offer an herbal bee and butterfly buffet by planting Basil, Borage, Catnip, Hyssop, Lemon Balm, Mint, Summer Savory, and Thyme.

- Dig up and compost any crops that are ready to be replaced from last fall or early winter plantings.

- Thin seedlings to make enough room for the remaining plants. Seed-sown vegetables and herbs need room to properly develop.

APRIL

- Plant warm-season herb and vegetable plants from seed, transplants or indoor-grown seedlings after frost danger is over (Tomatoes, Melons, Corn, Pumpkins, Peppers, Cucumbers, and Eggplant).

- There is still time to plant herbs and vegetables in containers. Add a water-retaining polymer and controlled-release fertilizer with the potting soil for easier maintenance.

- For seedlings hardening outdoors, feed with a water-soluble organic fertilizer once a week at ½ the normal dilution rate.

- For newly planted varieties feed at the normal recommended dilution rate once every four to six weeks or apply a granular organic fertilizer.

- Determinate or indeterminate Tomatoes? Determinates are shorter plants that bear single crops over a period of 4-6 weeks and adapt to small areas. Indeterminate Tomatoes continue to grow, flower, and bear fruit throughout the season and require cages or post supports.

- Spring is a good time to divide and tip-prune herbs such as Chives and Mint to control growth.

MAY

- Before summer, apply a 1-2 in. layer of mulch around vegetables and herbs for moisture retention, weed control and temperature stability.

- Basil, Dill, Oregano, Sage, Thyme, and Sweet Marjoram are herbs that flourish in spring and summer months.

- Towards the end of spring, plant more tropical vegetables such as Squash and Okra.

- Prune back perennial herbs such as Thyme, Rosemary, and Sage that get woody with age. Cut about ⅓ to fresh green wood, just above a leaf node to force new growth.

- Feed potted herbs and vegetables with a liquid organic food once or twice a month depending on the plant's feeding needs.

- Aphids weaken plants and transmit viral disease. Whiteflies hide on the undersides of leaves. When leaves are jiggled, they fly out in a cloud of "plant dandruff." Release ladybugs and lacewings, predators of aphids and whiteflies. Also wipe off or wash off infestations with a strong stream of water.

JUNE

- Cultivate the surface of mulch to prevent crusting and to allow water to percolate.

- As soon as one vegetable or annual herb stops producing, dig it up, amend the soil, and plant warm season varieties, but do not plant the same crop belonging to the same family in the same space. Rotating crops helps slow down or halt the buildup of diseases.

- Where summers remain cool and foggy select warm-season cultivars that are bred to tolerate lower temperatures. 'Murray Smith' and 'Stupice' Tomatoes do very well in cooler weather.

- Plant chile peppers in early summer, and allow about eighty days for them to reach maturity.

- Withhold water on Garlic, bulb Onions and Shallots so that the dry outer layers can form tightly on the bulbs, keeping them fresh for storage.

- Increase the frequency of fertilizer feedings if vegetable or herb foliage pale or if fruit or flower production is low.

JULY

- Once hot summer days arrive, cool-season vegetable plants deteriorate. Remove and place them in a compost pile.

- Cut off spent Pea vines at soil level instead of pulling them out because their roots fix nitrogen in the soil.

- Monitor plants closely during summer heat. If they look perky, hold off watering for a day. A tensiometer is a handy gadget to check soil moisture, but the finger test is also good. Just stick it in the soil about 2 to 4 inches deep and if the soil feels dry, water.

- It is almost impossible to overwater container plants, especially during hot, dry periods. It may be necessary to water once a day and sometimes twice a day.

- Harvest vegetables at their peak flavor. Summer Squash and Zucchini are ripe when their skin is easily nicked with a fingernail. Corn is ripe when you squeeze a couple of kernels and a milky liquid squirts out.

AUGUST

- Share summer's bounty with local food banks, Meals on Wheels and convalescent or retirement homes.

- Sow cool-season crops such as Carrot and Kale seeds and transplant cruciferous vegetables such as Broccoli, Cabbage, and Cauliflower from containers towards the end of summer.

- Plant cool-season Tomatoes now while there is still enough soil warmth to get their roots established. Varieties such as 'Legend', 'Stupice' and 'Galina's Cherry' originate from cold winter regions such as Alaska, Canada, Czechoslovakia, and Russia and bear flowers and fruit as low as 38-45°F.

- Do not dry herbs outdoors in the sun. Wash and set them on a screen indoors where there is good air circulation.

- For large Pumpkins and Melons, leave only one to three fruits per vine.

- Wash foliage off early in the morning with a strong stream of water to blast off aphids, leafhoppers, and caterpillars and apply organic controls such canola-based horticultural oil or Spinosad.

SEPTEMBER

- Time to dig up and compost summer vegetables as their production declines and plant fall-winter crops.

- Along the coast where summer vegetables are still producing, continue harvesting and wait until mid-autumn for cool-season crops.

- Plant only cool-season crops. Do not buy summer vegetable transplants because they cannot tolerate late fall-winter conditions.

- For a continuous supply of winter crops, sow seeds or plants two more times about every two weeks.

- The average first frost date in your area is important for sowing seeds and plants. If you are unsure contact your local University of California Cooperative Extension office to find out.

- Brussels Sprouts, Cauliflower, Cabbage, Celery, Lettuce, and Parsley are available in 4-in. pots or six-pack cells, and Potatoes and Onions are for sale as sets at nurseries.

- Cole crops such as Brussels Sprouts, Cabbage and Cauliflower, as well as Celery and Carrots, dislike their roots disturbed, so think about seeding them instead.

OCTOBER

- Maintain a 1 to 2-in. layer of mulch around herbs and vegetables to prevent weeds and retain moisture. If not sowing seeds, apply a pre-emergent to keep weeds from germinating.

- Dry Santa Ana and Chinook winds are typical this time of year. Water seedlings, established plants and even drought-resistant vegetables and herbs before they wilt.

- Where winters are mild, herbs can be planted year-round, but fall is an excellent time to plant perennial varieties to establish their roots without too much supplemental water.

- Take cuttings and root them indoors like French Tarragon, Stevia, Rosemary and African Blue Basil where winter freezes are common.

POTATO

- Mid-autumn is not too late for vegetable transplants after the hot, dry winds have blown away.

- Allow Pumpkin and Winter Squash to grow to size and harvest when their stems have turned brown because they do not ripen off the vine.

NOVEMBER

- Replenish bedding areas with humus, compost or worm castings at least once a year and add a humic acid product to winterize the plants.

- To promote better drainage loosen compacted soil by lightly tilling without damaging any herb or vegetable root systems.

- Apply a preplant fertilizer (2-4-2), granular organic fertilizer or controlled-release food for newly planted herbs and vegetables. Discontinue additional feedings until early spring.

- Cool-season tomatoes are ready to harvest when they turn color and their skins are slightly soft. If frost is predicted and the tomatoes have turned color, harvest and ripen indoors.

- Extend lettuce and other leafy crops, by clipping the "baby" outer leaves when the plants are about 6 inches. Leave 1 inch at the leaf base and it will re-grow for more cutting opportunities.

- Peas are a "snap" to grow. Supply a trellis and arrange their rows in a north-south direction, 18-24 inches apart. Inoculate Peas and other legumes with rhizobia (powdered bacteria available at nurseries) for better production.

DECEMBER

- If freezes are predicted, cover frost-sensitive herbs and vegetables with cotton sheets or row covers and remove during daytime.

- Dig up, shred and compost any spent plants if they have no disease or insect problems. Otherwise, dispose in the trash.

- Seaside communities are known for their frost-free winters, but the air is laden with salt spray and many plants are salt-sensitive, including Radish and Celery. Beets, Kale, Asparagus, Spinach and Swiss Chard are more tolerant.

- Gather seed-starting supplies including grow lights, peat pots or flats, commercial organic potting soil, perlite, seed-germinating heat pads or cables (never use personal heat pads), spray bottle and water-soluble organic fertilizer.

- Broccoli, Cauliflower, Cabbage, Brussels Sprouts, Basil, Dill, Fennel, Marjoram, Sage, and Thyme grow from seed indoors and take 4-8 weeks before reaching outdoor transplant size. Check seed packets for the best time to sow.

- Check seedlings every day and mist spray to keep evenly moist but not soggy.

SQUASH

LAWNS
for California

Like our freeways, fast-food chains, shopping malls, and multiplex movie theaters, the lawn is an icon of American culture. In spaces as diverse as suburban yards, sport fields, fairways, parks and corporate headquarters, a lawn may be the object of obsessive care and attention. A common image of a perfect landscape is an impeccably manicured velvety lawn, flecked with sunlight amidst the shadows of a couple of trees. Unfortunately, this image of perfection too often comes at the cost of high maintenance: mowing, watering, aerating, fertilizing, weeding, broadcasting and spraying for insects and diseases, which raises some valid economic and environmental concerns.

GO FOR "HEALTHY AND ATTRACTIVE," NOT "PERFECT"

For a lower maintenance and more environmentally friendly lawn, consider reducing its size by incorporating more trees, shrubs, flowers, vines, and ground covers into your landscape. It is helpful to realize that a perfect lawn is an ideal difficult to attain. But even if your lawn has some weeds it can be healthy and attractive. When you mow at the correct height, water properly, fertilize correctly and choose the best-adapted type of grass for your growing conditions, you are providing the optimum components for a healthy lawn that is less susceptible to weeds, pests and diseases.

WHAT KIND OF GRASS SHOULD I PLANT?

To determine the kind of grass you should plant, ask yourself: (1) What is the best match between the grass type and my location? and (2) What do I want from my lawn? Stolons are specialized stems that grow along the ground. At the point where leaf nodes touch the ground, new roots develop creating a dense, thick lawn. If you want rough-and-tumble areas for children, pets, or heavy foot traffic, then a stoloniferous grass is a good choice. Bermuda, Seashore Paspalum, and 'El Toro' Zoysia are stoloniferous warm-season grasses that grow actively during the summer months but go dormant

when temperatures dip below 55 degrees Fahrenheit. Depending on the species and the climate, dormancy will begin in the fall and last until mid-spring.

On the other hand, cool-season clumping grasses like Perennial Rye and Fescue grow most actively during spring and fall, remain green in the winter, and may turn brown during hot, dry summer weather. Unlike warm-weather species, cool-season grasses grow in bunches that tend to clump rather than form a tightly interlaced sod, and they are a much finer-textured turf. Unless they are sown thickly, some bare ground may be exposed. Perennial Rye does well in coastal fog belts and performs adequately elsewhere, but Bermuda and Zoysia grasses do better in the warm regions of California. St. Augustine and Creeping Red Fescue are appropriate for shaded areas, but Bermuda, Seashore Paspalum and Zoysia are better selections for drought tolerance.

When trying to decide, don't forget to talk to neighbors whose lawns you admire and consult your local nursery and University of California Cooperative Extension advisor. Every year there are new and improved grass varieties that better tolerate shade, sun, and drought; slower-growing cultivars that do not require frequent mowing and still others that are more disease or insect resistant.

INSTALLATION AND CARE

Whether planting from seed, stolon, or sod, soil preparation is exactly the same. Once the soil has been raked and cleared of debris and a rough grading has been completed, test the soil's pH. If it is alkaline, apply sulfur. If you have clay soil, improve its texture to allow easy air and moisture movement by blending in gypsum, and mixing about 20 to 30 percent organic material to a depth of eight to twelve inches.

Once planted, firm the soil by pushing a roller over the surface—this enables seeds to germinate or ensures that stolons or sod make close contact with the soil. Before rolling seeds, mulch the surface with one-fourth inch of topdressing such as humus or topsoil; mulch with one-half inch before rolling stolons.

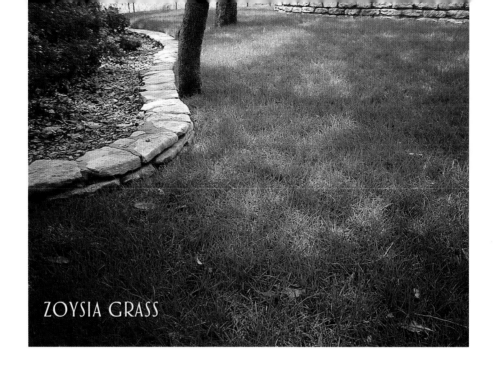

ZOYSIA GRASS

Keep the surface well watered until the seeds, stolons, or sod are established. Do not fertilize until the lawn has been mowed twice. Feed with a granular or liquid lawn fertilizer according to the manufacturer's instructions.

THE REWARDS OF A WELL-KEPT LAWN

Although lawns pose a number of challenges, with proper forethought and care the rewards will be well worth the effort. A well-kept lawn sustains the summer rites of barbecues, water fights, and lawn parties and remains the best possible surface for bare feet, frolicking children, and pets. Grass is the background beat to the grand rhythm of a complete landscape.

THE SOIL REACTION (pH) TEST

Before preparing the soil for planting, check the soil pH, otherwise known as soil reaction. Since California soils tend to become more alkaline over time, it is necessary to monitor the soil reaction twice a year, once in mid-spring and once in early fall. These seasonal readings are an accurate soil pH range for the entire year. Indicate on the site plan of your yard the locations where you obtained these samples, and note the date and readings in your garden journal.

Your garden soil can be acidic, neutral, or alkaline. The pH scale (0 to 14) is actually a measure of the relative concentration of hydrogen ions and hydroxyl ions in soil solution. A reading of 7 is neutral, readings below 7 indicate acid conditions, and readings above 7 indicate alkaline conditions. The scale has another peculiarity: it is logarithmic, which means each increment is ten times greater or lower than the increment before or after it. For example, a pH of 7 is 10 times greater than a pH of 6 and 100 times greater than a pH of 5.

When soils are very acidic, elements such as aluminum and manganese become overly available and may become toxic to plants. Soils that are too alkaline may limit the availability of elements such as iron, zinc, and nitrogen, leading to nutrient deficiencies.

Determining whether your garden soil is acidic, neutral, or alkaline will tell you whether or not nutrients are available to your plants. Take the test samples with a coring tool, at a depth of 10 to 12 inches, from several locations, especially where the topography and growing conditions vary. Use a pH test kit or ask your local garden center if they will test it for you. Analog and digital direct reading pH meters are also available, but they are more expensive. An overwhelming majority of plant species prefer a slightly acidic to neutral (6.5 to 7.0) soil.

BERMUDA GRASS
Cynodon dactylon

Hardiness—Zones 8-11

Season—Warm-season grass

Maintenance Height—¾ to 1½ inches

Water Needs—Water-thrifty, but looks best when watered regularly

Planting/Care—Plant from seed in late spring or summer. Provide a sandy loam soil to a depth of 8-12 in. (pH 7.0), top dress with 1/8 in. of humus and use a water roller to press into the ground. Water immediately and keep moist until the seeds germinate. Plant Hybrid Bermuda from sod or stolons March-November.

Pests/Diseases—Sod webworms are larvae of lawn moths and cause brown or bare patches in lawns. Dethatch the lawn, introduce parasitic nematodes or spray with Spinosad, an organic remedy.

Landscaping Tips & Ideas—Bermuda Grass is a warm-season turf. Grows best in hot summer areas and mild winters. Mow frequently with a rotary lawn mower set ¾-1½ in. high. Fertilize with an organic lawn food once a month while growing, but withhold fall-winter.

FESCUE
Festuca arundinacea x hybrid
(*Festuca elatior*)

Hardiness—Zones 5-10

Season—Cool-season grass

Maintenance Height—1½ to 4 inches

Water Needs—Water 1-2 times weekly

Planting/Care—Provide sandy loam soil down to 8-12 in. (pH 5-7.2). Plant from sod during mild weather or from seed in spring. Sow seeds, top dress with 1/8 in. of humus and press with a water roller. Keep moist until germination. For sod, press with a water roller and water. If seams separate, fill with sand and re-press.

Pests/Diseases—Brown patch or *Rhizoctomia* blight is a fungus that can expand into a large circular or horseshoe shape affecting cool season turfs. Aerate and feed only with an organic fertilizer.

Landscaping Tips & Ideas—Not for low-desert or mountain regions. Excellent for home landscapes and erosion control. Fertilize every 2 months fall-spring. Set rotary mower 2 in. during the cool season and 3-4 in. during warm season.

PERENNIAL RYEGRASS
Lolium perenne

Hardiness—Zones 5-10

Season—Cool-season grass

Maintenance Height—1½ to 4 inches

Water Needs—Water regularly twice weekly.

Planting/Care—Plant from seed any time of the year as long as the weather is mild. Create a sandy loam soil down 8-12 in. (pH 6.5-7.0) for seeding or sodding. Top dress seeds with 1/8 in. of humus and press into the ground with a water roller. For sod, lay the sections on the prepared soil, press with a water roller and water. If seams separate, fill the gaps with sand and re-press with a water roller.

Pests/Diseases—Its quick growth keeps weeds to a minimum, but control rust with a fungicide and sod webworm with Spinosad or parasitic nematodes.

Landscaping Tips & Ideas—Excellent in inexpensive seed mixtures and Bluegrass mixtures. Does best in coastal fog belts, but adapts to other regions except extended hot climates.

SEASHORE PASPALUM
Paspalum vaginatum 'Excalibre' ('Adalayd')

Hardiness—Zones 9-11

Season—Warm-season grass

Maintenance Height—1 to 3 inches

Water Needs—Drought-tolerant, but looks best when watered twice a week during growth cycle.

Planting/Care—Plant from stolons or sod in spring or summer. Create a sandy loam down to 8-12 in. (pH 6.5-7.2). From stolons, distribute evenly across the prepared soil, press with a water roller, top dress with ¼ in. of humus and keep moist until stolons take root. For sod, lay sections down, press with a water roller and water. If the seams separate, fill the gaps with sand and re-press. Fertilize every 2 months from May-October.

Pests/Diseases—For sod webworm, dethatch lawn and spray with Spinosad.

Landscaping Tips & Ideas—Ideal for heavy foot-traffic. Its sea-spray-tolerant grass and deep roots are good for sandy areas along the seashore, rugged coastal sites, dog runs and pockets of light shade.

ST. AUGUSTINE
Stenotaphrum secundatum

Hardiness—Zones 9-11

Season—Warm-season lawn

Maintenance Height—3 inches

Water Needs—Withstands periodic droughts, but looks best when watered every 7-10 days.

Planting/Care—Plant from sod or plugs in spring or summer. Create a sandy loam soil down 8-12 in. (pH 6.5-7.5). For sod, lay the sections over prepped soil, press with a water roller. Plant plugs in holes the same size or in open furrows and tamp down. Water frequently until roots are established. Discontinue mowing during drought.

Pests/Diseases—Since chemical fertilizers cause a surge in tender growth that attracts chinch bugs, feed St. Augustine grass with an organic lawn fertilizer. If infestation persists use an insecticide with cyfluthrin and imidacloprid.

Landscaping Tips & Ideas—Wonderful grass for sandy or alkaline soils in warm climates and withstands partial shade. Since it tolerates salt air and brackish water, it is ideal for beach areas.

ZOYSIA GRASS
Zoysia japonica 'El Toro'

Hardiness—Zones 9-11

Season—Warm-season grass

Maintenance Height—½ to 1 inch

Water Needs—Water once a week.

Planting/Care—Plant from stolon, sod or plugs in spring or summer. Create a sandy loam soil down 8-12 in. (pH 6.5-7.0). From stolons, spread evenly across prepped soil, press with a water roller, top dress with ¼ in. of humus. For sod, lay sections down, press with a water roller. Space plugs 4-6 in. on center, press with a water roller. Water frequently until roots established.

Pests/Diseases—Control billbugs, white grubs, sod webworms and mole cricket infestations with a lawn product containing imidacloprid.

Landscaping Tips & Ideas—Thrives where the days are warm and the nights are mild. It needs less fertilizer, water and mowing than cool-season turf. Withstands heavy foot traffic. Ideal for home landscapes, parks and playgrounds. Mow frequently to maintain a neat appearance.

LAWN PESTS

ANTS

IDENTIFYING CHARACTERISTICS & SYMPTOMS
- Come inside looking for food and moisture, especially in dry weather

SOLUTION
- Home Pest Control Indoor/Outdoor Insect Killer Ready-To-Spray

- PowerForce® Multi-Insect Killer Concentrate or PowerForce® Multi-Insect Killer Ready-To-Spray

- PowerForce® Multi-Insect Killer Granules

** Ants move further into the ground in the summer; mounds should be treated in spring and fall for best results.

BOXELDER BUGS

IDENTIFYING CHARACTERISTICS & SYMPTOMS
- Black, inch long, winged bugs with red stripes

- Feed on flowers, leaves or fruit of boxelder, ash and maple trees

- Congregate in house, on window screens, under porches

SOLUTION
- Home Pest Control Indoor/Outdoor Insect Killer Ready-To-Spray

- PowerForce® Multi-Insect Killer Concentrate or PowerForce® Multi-Insect Killer Ready-To-Spray

CARPENTER ANTS

IDENTIFYING CHARACTERISTICS & SYMPTOMS
- Carpenter Ants are wood-damaging nuisance pests that can destroy wooden structures and ornamental trees. Unlike termites, Carpenter Ants do not digest wood, they carry wood particles away to make their nests. Because colonies require a constant source of moisture, they usually live outside in dead tree limbs, tree holes, stumps, and landscape timbers.

- Symptoms include wood damaging nuisance pests that destroy wooden structures and ornamental trees. Make colonies in dead tree limbs, tree holes, stumps and landscape timbers.

SOLUTION
- PowerForce® Multi-Insect Killer Granules

- Complete Insect Killer For Soil & Turf Ready-To-Spray or Complete Insect Killer For Soil & Turf Granules

- Home Pest Control Indoor/Outdoor Insect Killer Ready-To-Spray

- PowerForce® Carpenter Ant & Termite Killer Plus Concentrate or PowerForce® Carpenter Ant & Termite Killer Plus Ready-To-Use Battery Powered Sprayer

CHINCHBUGS

IDENTIFYING CHARACTERISTICS & SYMPTOMS
- Chinchbugs are surface-feeding lawn pests that damage St. Augustinegrass. You may see them on grasses such as Zoysia, Bermuda, and Centipedegrass, but infestations usually occur where high populations have built up on St. Augustinegrass. Signs of infestation include small, round patches of brownish-yellow grass that first appear in hottest, driest areas of lawn. Left uncontrolled, large areas of lawn may die.

- Symptoms include yellow to brown patches in St. Augustine grass; usually show up in hottest, driest areas of the lawn first.

SOLUTION
- PowerForce® Multi-Insect Killer Concentrate or PowerForce® Multi-Insect Killer Ready-To-Spray

- PowerForce® Multi-Insect Killer Granules

- Complete Insect Killer For Soil & Turf Ready-To-Spray or Complete Insect Killer For Soil & Turf Granules

- PowerForce® Carpenter Ant & Termite Killer Plus Concentrate or PowerForce® Carpenter Ant & Termite Killer Plus Ready-To-Use Battery Powered Sprayer

COCKROACHES

IDENTIFYING CHARACTERISTICS & SYMPTOMS
- Inhabit fields, forests or damp, moist places

- Frequently invade homes looking for food and moisture

- Most active at night; hide in dark, damp places during the day

SOLUTION
- Home Pest Control Indoor/Outdoor Insect Killer Ready-To-Spray

- PowerForce® Multi-Insect Killer Concentrate or PowerForce® Multi-Insect Killer Ready-To-Spray

- PowerForce® Multi-Insect Killer Granules

EARWIGS

IDENTIFYING CHARACTERISTICS & SYMPTOMS
- Small, slender-bodied insects with rear pinchers

- Chew plants and foodstuffs both outdoors and indoors

- Often infest pantries, kitchen cabinets

SOLUTION
- Home Pest Control Indoor/Outdoor Insect Killer Ready-To-Spray

- PowerForce® Multi-Insect Killer Concentrate or PowerForce® Multi-Insect Killer Ready-To-Spray

EUROPEAN CRANE FLY

IDENTIFYING CHARACTERISTICS & SYMPTOMS

- European Crane Fly Larvae are soil insects that feed on the roots of turfgrass from fall to spring. When found in large numbers they can cause extensive damage to turf grass. Signs of infestation are bare spots of yellow patches of grass in the lawn.

- Symptoms include soil insects that feed on the roots of turfgrass from fall to spring and can cause extensive damage.

SOLUTION

- Season-Long Grub Control Granules

- 24-Hour Grub Killer Plus Granules

- Complete Insect Killer For Soil & Turf Ready-To-Spray or Complete Insect Killer For Soil & Turf Granules

FALL ARMYWORMS

IDENTIFYING CHARACTERISTICS & SYMPTOMS

- Fall Armyworms cause damage by consuming foliage. Outbreaks can be sudden and very severe. Damage usually begins to show up as leaves chewed around the edges. Because most feeding is at night, Armyworms can cause significant damage before the problem is ever identified. As the name implies, Fall Armyworms damage is most common from September until hard frost.

- Symptoms include arcs or circles of dead, browned grass.

SOLUTION

- PowerForce® Multi-Insect Killer Concentrate or PowerForce® Multi-Insect Killer Ready-To-Spray

- PowerForce® Multi-Insect Killer Granules

- Complete Insect Killer For Soil & Turf Ready-To-Spray or Complete Insect Killer For Soil & Turf Granules

FIRE ANTS

IDENTIFYING CHARACTERISTICS & SYMPTOMS

- Fire Ants are notorious for the fiery stings they repeatedly inflict on people and small animals who disturb their mound. Many victims require medical attention, but in extreme cases a Fire Ant sting can be fatal. Fire Ants can also cause expensive damage to outdoor electrical equipment (heat pumps, air conditioners, junction boxes, fuses and wiring). The mound is populated by a Queen who can live up to 7 years and can lay up to 1,600 eggs per day. Up to 250,000 ants may inhabit a single mound. Control can only be achieved with an insecticide that kills the Queen.

- Symptoms include fiery stings repeatedly inflected on people and small animals when mound is disturbed.

SOLUTION

- Fire Ant Killer Granules

- Fire Ant Killer Dust

FLEAS

IDENTIFYING CHARACTERISTICS & SYMPTOMS

- Fleas are biting pests that can become a great nuisance to family, pets and home. Skin irritation caused by flea bites can range from minor to severe. Because fleas live and breed both indoors and outdoors, control is best achieved with simultaneous, coordinated effort involving both indoor and outdoor treatments on the same day.

- Symptoms include biting pests that can become great nuisance to family, pets and home. Bites can cause skin irritations.

SOLUTION

- PowerForce® Multi-Insect Killer Granules

- Home Pest Control Indoor/Outdoor Insect Killer Ready-To-Spray

- Complete Insect Killer For Soil & Turf Ready-To-Spray or Complete Insect Killer For Soil & Turf Granules

- PowerForce® Carpenter Ant & Termite Killer Plus Concentrate or PowerForce® Carpenter Ant & Termite Killer Plus Ready-To-Use Battery Powered Sprayer

** It is best to treat pets, house and yard with appropriate products on the same day.

FLIES

IDENTIFYING CHARACTERISTICS & SYMPTOMS

- Life cycles can be as short as eight to 10 days

SOLUTION

- Home Pest Control Indoor/Outdoor Insect Killer Ready-To-Spray

- PowerForce® Multi-Insect Killer Concentrate or PowerForce® Multi-Insect Killer Ready-To-Spray

MOLE CRICKETS

IDENTIFYING CHARACTERISTICS & SYMPTOMS

- Mole Crickets are turf insects that cause severe damage to Bermudagrasses, Bahiagrass, Zoysiagrasses, and Centipedegrass. Some Mole Crickets feed on grass roots, but most feed on a variety of organisms in the soil. As they forage, they tunnel and uproot turf grass which dries out and dies. Infested lawns turn yellow, weedy and eventually die.

- Symptoms include thinning, torn-up looking grass dries out or turns brown in patches where mole crickets form underground tunnels.

SOLUTION

- Complete Insect Killer For Soil & Turf Ready-To-Spray or Complete Insect Killer For Soil & Turf Granules

- Season-Long Grub Control Granules

- PowerForce® Multi-Insect Killer Granules

- PowerForce® Multi-Insect Killer Concentrate or PowerForce® Multi-Insect Killer Ready-To-Spray

- 24-Hour Grub Killer Plus Granules

MOSQUITOES

IDENTIFYING CHARACTERISTICS & SYMPTOMS
- Breed in stagnant water, puddles or ponds

- Eggs can remain dormant and survive out of water for years

- Often hide in shrubs during the day

SOLUTION
- Home Pest Control Indoor/Outdoor Insect Killer Ready-To-Spray

- PowerForce® Multi-Insect Killer Concentrate or PowerForce® Multi-Insect Killer Ready-To-Spray

SOD WEBWORMS

IDENTIFYING CHARACTERISTICS & SYMPTOMS
- Sod Webworms are surface insects that feed on the roots, stems and grass of desirable lawn turf. Signs of infestation include arcs or circles of dead, brown grass. Damage is worse in late summer when grass isn't growing rapidly.

- Symptoms include arcs or circles of dead, browned grass; webbing and threads on grass.

SOLUTION
- PowerForce® Multi-Insect Killer Concentrate or PowerForce® Multi-Insect Killer Ready-To-Spray

- PowerForce® Multi-Insect Killer Granules

- 24-Hour Grub Killer Plus Granules

- Complete Insect Killer For Soil & Turf Ready-To-Spray or Complete Insect Killer For Soil & Turf Granules

SPIDERS

IDENTIFYING CHARACTERISTICS & SYMPTOMS
- Prey on other insects; a few will bite humans

- House spiders hide behind furniture, in corners or around dusty crawl spaces

- Poisonous spiders include black widow and brown recluse

- Black widows nest close to ground

- Brown recluse hides in dark places

SOLUTION
- Home Pest Control Indoor/Outdoor Insect Killer Ready-To-Spray

- PowerForce® Multi-Insect Killer Concentrate or PowerForce® Multi-Insect Killer Ready-To-Spray

- PowerForce® Multi-Insect Killer Granules

TICKS

IDENTIFYING CHARACTERISTICS & SYMPTOMS
- Ticks are frightening and harmful nuisance pests that attach themselves to warm-blooded mammals, humans, and pets to feed on their blood. At minimum, Tick bites cause mild skin irritation. At worst, a Tick bite can transmit Lyme disease. Although ticks live and breed outdoors in lawns, wooded and grassy areas, they can be carried indoors by pets. Effective control requires both indoor and outdoor treatments.

- Symptoms include nuisance pests that attach themselves to warm blooded mammals, humans and pets to feed. Can cause mild skin irritations and possibly transmit Lyme disease.

SOLUTION
- PowerForce® Multi-Insect Killer Granules

- Complete Insect Killer For Soil & Turf Ready-To-Spray or Complete Insect Killer For Soil & Turf Granules

- PowerForce® Carpenter Ant & Termite Killer Plus Concentrate or PowerForce® Carpenter Ant & Termite Killer Plus Ready-To-Use Battery Powered Sprayer

- Home Pest Control Indoor/Outdoor Insect Killer Ready-To-Spray

WASPS

IDENTIFYING CHARACTERISTICS & SYMPTOMS
- Nest outdoors in outbuildings, under leaves, in the ground

- Attracted to food and drink, react when nests are disturbed

SOLUTION
- Home Pest Control Indoor/Outdoor Insect Killer Ready-To-Spray

- PowerForce® Multi-Insect Killer Concentrate or PowerForce® Multi-Insect Killer Ready-To-Spray

- PowerForce® Multi-Insect Killer Granules (Digger wasps)

WHITE GRUBS

IDENTIFYING CHARACTERISTICS & SYMPTOMS
- White Grubs, the larvae of certain Beetles, are the most notorious of all turf-damaging soil insects. In the spring, Grubs live in the top few inches of soil, feeding on the roots of lawn grasses and destroying the turf above. In early summer, Grubs become Beetles that emerge from the larvae to become leaf-feeding adults that dmaage roses, trees and other plants above ground.

- Symptoms include dead or dying grass in brown patches that lifts up easily when pulled; grass wilts even when watered.

SOLUTION
- Season-Long Grub Control Granules

- 24-Hour Grub Killer Plus Granules

- Complete Insect Killer For Soil & Turf Ready-To-Spray or Complete Insect Killer For Soil & Turf Granules

LAWN DISEASES

ANTRACNOSE

TIPS FOR UNDERSTANDING AND CONTROL
- Reddish-brown spots on leaves; Blighted areas of lawn can vary in size from 2 inches to 10 feet

CONDITIONS FOR DISEASE TO APPEAR*
- Warm to hot weather (80 to 90 degrees); Excess rain; Poor drainage; Under-fertilization

SOLUTION
- Fungus Control for Lawns Granules

BROWN PATCH

TIPS FOR UNDERSTANDING AND CONTROL
- Leaves and stems die out in large, circular patches in lawn; One of the most common diseases of fescue lawns

CONDITIONS FOR DISEASE TO APPEAR*
- Warm to hot weather (75 to 95 degrees); High humidity; Excess rain

SOLUTION
- Fungus Control for Lawns Granules

COPPER SPOT**

TIPS FOR UNDERSTANDING AND CONTROL
- Grass blades develop small red spots that enlarge and become darker red; Grass is infested in small, circular patches 1 to 3 inches wide; Grass within the spots dies; Can look like dollar spot

CONDITIONS FOR DISEASE TO APPEAR*
- Mild to warm temperatures (70 to 80 degrees); High humidity

SOLUTION
- Fungus Control for Lawns Granules

DOLLAR SPOT

TIPS FOR UNDERSTANDING AND CONTROL
- Grass dies in small, circular spots 4 to 12 inches wide; Spots may fuse together in big blotches

CONDITIONS FOR DISEASE TO APPEAR*
- Mild to warm weather (60 to 85 degrees); Excess moisture; Under-fertilization

SOLUTION
- Fungus Control for Lawns Granules

POWDERY MILDEW**

TIPS FOR UNDERSTANDING AND CONTROL
- White to light gray moldy-looking growth on grass blades

CONDITIONS FOR DISEASE TO APPEAR*
- Mild temperatures (65 degrees); Damp weather and excess moisture; Shady areas

SOLUTION
- Fungus Control for Lawns Granules

RED THREAD

TIPS FOR UNDERSTANDING AND CONTROL
- Tan to bleached-looking grass blades that shrivel from the tips; Small patches of dead grass; In wet weather you may see small pink thread in the grass

CONDITIONS FOR DISEASE TO APPEAR*
- Mild temperatures (60 to 75 degrees); High humidity; Misty weather; Under-fertilization

SOLUTION
- Fungus Control for Lawns Granules

RUST

TIPS FOR UNDERSTANDING AND CONTROL
- Dust-like orange-colored spores cover grass blades; Affected areas of lawn have a rusty look; Doesn't usually hurt the grass.

CONDITIONS FOR DISEASE TO APPEAR*
- Mild temperatures (60 to 75 degrees); Dry weather or conditions that favor the slow growth of grass

SOLUTION
- Fungus Control for Lawns Granules

STRIPE SMUT**

TIPS FOR UNDERSTANDING AND CONTROL
- Grass blades turn pale green and are stunted; Spores form long black stripes on grass blades; Grass blades curl and die

CONDITIONS FOR DISEASE TO APPEAR*
- Cool temperatures (50 to 60 degrees); Excess moisture

SOLUTION
- Fungus Control for Lawns Granules

SUMMER PATCH OR FROG-EYE DISEASE

TIPS FOR UNDERSTANDING AND CONTROL
- Light green patches form up to 24 inches wide that later turn a reddish brown; Some patches may have green grass in center

CONDITIONS FOR DISEASE TO APPEAR*
- Warm temperatures (80 to 95 degrees); High humidity; Drought-stressed grass

SOLUTION
- Fungus Control for Lawns Granules

WEEDS

BINDWEED

TIPS FOR UNDERSTANDING AND CONTROL
- A vining weed with extensive root system; Very persistent; Shades out lawn; Will climb on nearby flowers and shrubs

SOLUTION
- All-In-One Weed Killer for Lawns Concentrate

- Southern Weed Killer for Lawns Concentrate

RELATED WEEDS
- Hedge, Field or European Bindweed, Creeping Jenny, Creeping Charlie, Wild Morninglory, Woodbine, Greenvine

CHICKWEED

TIPS FOR UNDERSTANDING AND CONTROL
- Very common in new lawns; Sprouts and grows in cool weather

SOLUTION
- All-In-One Weed Killer for Lawns Concentrate

- Southern Weed Killer for Lawns Concentrate

RELATED WEEDS
- Starweed, Satin Flower, Starwort

CLOVER

TIPS FOR UNDERSTANDING AND CONTROL
- Often indicates poor soil, need for fertilizer; Appears in cool weather

SOLUTION
- All-In-One Weed Killer for Lawns Concentrate

- Southern Weed Killer for Lawns Concentrate

RELATED WEEDS
- White Clover, Red Clover, Sweet Clover

CRABGRASS

TIPS FOR UNDERSTANDING AND CONTROL
- Seeds sprout in spring and summer after rain or watering; Very fast growing; Likes bare and weak areas of the lawn

SOLUTION
- All-In-One Weed Killer for Lawns Concentrate

RELATED WEEDS
- Crowfoot Grass, Finger Grass, Pigeon Grass, Polish Millet

CREEPING CHARLIE

TIPS FOR UNDERSTANDING AND CONTROL
- Persistent; Invasive, forms a mat that chokes and shades grass; Worst in moist soil, and partial shade, but also thrives in sun

SOLUTION
- All-In-One Weed Killer for Lawns Concentrate

- Southern Weed Killer for Lawns Concentrate

RELATED WEEDS
- Ground Ivy, Cat's Foot, Gill-over-the-ground, Field Balm

DALLISGRASS

TIPS FOR UNDERSTANDING AND CONTROL
- Appears in summer, but grows year-round in warm climates; Thrives in low, wet areas

SOLUTION
- All-In-One Weed Killer for Lawns Concentrate

RELATED WEEDS
- Paspalumgrass, Watergrass

DANDELION

TIPS FOR UNDERSTANDING AND CONTROL
- Persistent; Appears in early spring and continues through summer, fall, and year-round in warm climates; Will adapt height to escape mowing

SOLUTION
- All-In-One Weed Killer for Lawns Concentrate

- Southern Weed Killer for Lawns Concentrate

RELATED WEEDS
- Blowball, Lionstooth, Cankerwort, Doon-head-clock

DICHONDRA

TIPS FOR UNDERSTANDING AND CONTROL
- Creeps and spreads through lawn to choke it out; One species is used as a substitute for grass in some West coast areas

SOLUTION
- All-In-One Weed Killer for Lawns Concentrate

- Southern Weed Killer for Lawns Concentrate

RELATED WEEDS
- Lawn leaf

GOOSEGRASS

TIPS FOR UNDERSTANDING AND CONTROL
- Loooks like crabgrass except base of stems are lighter green and appears weeks later; Roots are hard to pull; Out-competes lawn in hot, dry conditions

SOLUTION
- All-In-One Weed Killer for Lawns Concentrate

RELATED WEEDS
- Silver Crabgrass, Crowfoot Grass, Yardgrass, Wiregrass, Bullgrass

HENBIT

TIPS FOR UNDERSTANDING AND CONTROL
- Sprouts in fall and grows during cool season; Prefers rich, moist soil and partial shade; Invades bare or weak areas of lawn

SOLUTION
- All-In-One Weed Killer for Lawns Concentrate

- Southern Weed Killer for Lawns Concentrate

RELATED WEEDS
- Dead Nettle, Blind Nettle, Bee Nettle, Giraffe Head

KNOTWEED

TIPS FOR UNDERSTANDING AND CONTROL
- Common in grass where soil is compacted

SOLUTION
- All-In-One Weed Killer for Lawns Concentrate

- Southern Weed Killer for Lawns Concentrate

RELATED WEEDS
- Knotgrass, Doorweed, Matgrass, Yardweed

NUTGRASS

TIPS FOR UNDERSTANDING AND CONTROL
- Most common in damp, compacted soil; Very persistent; Forms colonies by seeds and underground nut-like corns

SOLUTION
- All-In-One Weed Killer for Lawns Concentrate

RELATED WEEDS
- Nutsedge, Cocosedge, Rush Nut, Watergrass

OXALIS

TIPS FOR UNDERSTANDING AND CONTROL
- Persistent; Grows best in cool season

SOLUTION
- All-In-One Weed Killer for Lawns Concentrate

- Southern Weed Killer for Lawns Concentrate

RELATED WEEDS
- Sourgrass, Wood Shamrock

PLANTAIN

TIPS FOR UNDERSTANDING AND CONTROL
- Found in moist soil, shade; Spread by seeding; Appear in spring and continue through summer; Broadleaf plantain common in wet, compacted soil

SOLUTION
- All-In-One Weed Killer for Lawns Concentrate

- Southern Weed Killer for Lawns Concentrate

RELATED WEEDS
- Common Plantain, Rugel's Plantain, Blackseed Plantain, Buckthorn Plantain, Narrowleaved Plantain, Ribgrass

PRICKLY LETTUCE

TIPS FOR UNDERSTANDING AND CONTROL
- Painful if stepped on; often flat and hidden in the grass; Spread by seeding; Appears in spring and continues till fall; Spreads quickly from seed

SOLUTION
- All-In-One Weed Killer for Lawns Concentrate

- Southern Weed Killer for Lawns Concentrate

RELATED WEEDS
- Wild Lettuce, Milk Thistle, English Thistle, Compass Plant, Chinese Lettuce, Wild Opium

PURSLANE

TIPS FOR UNDERSTANDING AND CONTROL
- Makes a mat that chokes lawn; Likes rich soil; Spreads quickly from seed

SOLUTION
- All-In-One Weed Killer for Lawns Concentrate

- Southern Weed Killer for Lawns Concentrate

RELATED WEEDS
- Florida Pusley, Wild Portulaca

SANDBUR

TIPS FOR UNDERSTANDING AND CONTROL
- Appear in spring and remain through fall; Painful to step on the spiny "bur," or seed; Spreads quickly from seed; Worst in sandy soils

SOLUTION
- All-In-One Weed Killer for Lawns Concentrate

RELATED WEEDS
- Sandspur, Burgrass, Field Sandbur

SPEEDWELL

TIPS FOR UNDERSTANDING AND CONTROL
- Dainty runners grow into a solid sheet that chokes grass; Clippings scattered by mower root where they land

SOLUTION
- All-In-One Weed Killer for Lawns Concentrate

- Southern Weed Killer for Lawns Concentrate

RELATED WEEDS
- Veronica, Caucasian Speedwell

SPURGE

TIPS FOR UNDERSTANDING AND CONTROL
- Appear in spring and summer; Prefer sunny areas; Form a stiff mat that chokes and shades grass

SOLUTION
- All-In-One Weed Killer for Lawns Concentrate

- Southern Weed Killer for Lawns Concentrate

RELATED WEEDS
- Prostrate Spurge, Spotted Spurge, Milk Purslane, Milk Spurge

WILD GERANIUM

TIPS FOR UNDERSTANDING AND CONTROL
- Appears in cool weather; Sprouts here-and-there but can spread if uncontrolled; Ruins the look of a uniform winter carpet in warm season lawns

SOLUTION
- All-In-One Weed Killer for Lawns Concentrate

- Southern Weed Killer for Lawns Concentrate

RELATED WEEDS
- Carolina geranium

WILD ONION*

TIPS FOR UNDERSTANDING AND CONTROL
- Appear in late winter; Mar the uniform look of winter lawn; Persistent, smells like onion; Waxy coating protects leaves from spray; Step on leaves to crush lightly before spraying

SOLUTION
- All-In-One Weed Killer for Lawns Concentrate

- Southern Weed Killer for Lawns Concentrate

RELATED WEEDS
- Field Garlic, Wild Garlic, Scallion, Crow Garlic

- * Will probably need repeated treatment for control.

This Information in this section was provided courtesy BayerAdvanced.com.

JANUARY

- Make plans to replace an existing or establish a new lawn.

- If you live at the beach, have alkaline soil, dog or horses, 'Excalbre' ('Adalayd')withstands heavy traffic and is ideal for sandy or coastal areas. St. Augustine is another warm season grass great for sandy or alkaline soils in mild climates.

- For high summer temperatures and mild winters, Bermuda Grass, 'Tifgreen' and 'Santa Ana' hybrids are good drought-tolerant choices. 'El Toro' is a warm-season Zoysia that also does well in much of Southern California and San Joaquin Valley.

- Fescue is a cool season grass with the looks of Kentucky Bluegrass for Southern and Northern California but not low-desert or mountain regions. 'Dwarf Hybrid Tall Fescue' has a more manicured appearance.

- Perennial Ryegrass is another cool-season type that thrives in coastal fog belts and is used to overseed warm-season lawns that turn brown in winter. For mowing ease select hybrids 'Birdie', 'Pennant' or 'Pennfine'.

FEBRUARY

- Set out rain gauges to monitor rainfall and supplement watering lawns if the weather remains dry. Adjust irrigation systems to account for winter rainfall, but during periods of drought maintain the irrigation schedule for warmer, drier weather.

- Rust may appear on blades of cool-season grasses that have not been fertilized. Feed with a complete organic granular lawn food and if rust remains extensive, apply a systemic fungicide with triadimefon.

- Stop lawn weeds now before they start. Apply a pre-emergent for crabgrass, spurge and other broadleaf weeds to stop them before they get established.

- Fertilize cool season grasses such as Fescue, Bluegrass and Rye with a complete, organic granular lawn food.

- During a cold spell, a good indoor activity is to sharpen mower blades.

- Gophers become active in softened soils. Set manual traps and avoid toxic baits.

- Indoor cats appreciate some grass added to their diet. Try kitty grass sold at local pet stores.

MARCH

- Pests that feed on grass blades and roots include chinch bugs, cutworms, leafhoppers, sod webworms and white grubs. Spinosad is an organic control for chewing insects with a residual of 7-10 days. Insecticides containing imidacloprid and cyfluthrin have a 90 day residual.

- For broadleaf (dandelion, clover) and grassy (crabgrass, nutgrass) weeds there are herbicides that kill both, but make sure they are applicable for your lawn type.

- Aerate the lawn to remove small cores of soil to improve water, air and nutrient penetration.

- Remove thatch, a layer of debris and dead stems at the soil surface preventing air, water and nutrients from reaching the roots. Rake clean just as new growth appears or rent a power rake to make the job easier.

- Fix clogged or broken sprinklers and adjust those that are watering sidewalks and other hardscape features. Make sure lawn sprinklers are covering the entire lawn.

APRIL

- Revitalize the soil and provide nutrients for beneficial microorganisms with a humic acid product for lawns, once in spring and once in fall. A healthy soil is more disease and insect resistant.

- Install a warm-season lawn by seed, sod or stolon such as St. Augustine, Bermuda and Zoysia in spring.

- Water only when the lawn needs it (the color will change from bright green to dull gray-green) to encourage deeper roots and better drought-tolerance. Water down to 6-8 inches about once a week (check by probing the soil with a stiff wire; it will move easily through moist soil and stop when it reaches dry), then wait until the soil has dried slightly before watering again.

- Fertilize cool-season lawns in fall and spring with a complete, organic lawn food and feed warm-season lawns like St. Augustine and Zoysia, every other month from late spring into summer.

- Mow at the appropriate height for your lawn type.

MAY

- To conserve water, check irrigation times and set for the early morning.

- White grubs are beetle larva that are white with brown heads and curled into a "C-shape." They live in the top few inches of soil and feed on lawn roots. When present, patches of dead turf can be pulled like a piece of carpet. Apply a grub control with imidacloprid or use beneficial nematodes.

- Warm weather marks the start of ant season and they often thrive in lawns. Set out baits that workers take back to the queen and the rest of the colony. For fire ants use a dust formulated with beta-cyfluthrin.

- Fertilize 'Excalbre' with a complete organic lawn food every other month between May-October.

- Keep rabbits away from lawns with olfactory repellents or live-trap. Relocate them to a more wildlife friendly area. Check with the local wildlife control agency to confirm where they can be moved.

JUNE

- Release beneficial insects such as ladybugs, lacewings, praying mantis, predatory mites and wasps when they become available to control unwanted bugs. They can be mail ordered from insectaries or purchased at nurseries.

- Make sure newly installed lawns are watered frequently to establish root systems. Check with your local cooperative extension or nursery for watering frequency requirements depending on type of lawn, soil condition and temperature.

- If you can't irrigate without having water run into the street, water in intervals, pausing for short periods to let the water soak. Also aerate and dethatch for better absorption.

- If you want to plant warm season grass such as 'Excalbre' (Seashore Paspalum), St. Augustine, Bermuda or Zoysia, there is till time to plant in early summer from stolons or sod.

- Adjust lawn mower blade height for late-spring to summer months depending on the type of lawn. For example Fescue lawns during summer need the blades set at 3-4 inches.

JULY

- Water conservation is vital for California and may mean restrictions affecting lawns, but light sprinkling does little good. To develop deep roots, water to a depth of 6-8 inches.

- Prevent runoff on lawns growing on slopes or heavy clay soils by running sprinklers for 10 minutes turning off for another 10 minutes to allow saturation and repeating the cycle until the soil is moistened to a depth of 6-8-inches.

- 'Turffalo' is a Buffalo Grass hybrid developed for drought and shade tolerance, it grows to 5 inches and can be cut by a rotary or reel mower. Planted by plugs, it will stay green with 2 inches of water per month. Visit www.turffalo.com.

- Identify what kinds of weeds are growing in your lawn and apply a control that is designated for that type.

- Stay away from chemical fertilizers because they can burn lawns especially during summer heat waves. A complete organic lawn food is preferable.

AUGUST

- St. Augustine, 'Excalbre'and Zoysia can establish by winter if seeded, stolonized or sodded in late summer. It is also a good time to fill in the bare spots of these established grasses.

- Feed warm-season lawns like St. Augustine and Zoysia one more time in late summer or early fall with a complete organic fertilizer.

- If skunks, raccoons, possums, moles and other critters are digging up the lawn, they are probably looking for grubs. Apply a grub control with imidacloprid or use beneficial nematodes as an effective biological control.

- Mowing at the upper end of the recommended mowing height for your grass type encourages deeper roots and better heat and drought tolerance since the grass helps shade the soil to reduce evaporation and maximize soil moisture content.

- If you have an automated system occasionally monitor to make sure everything is operating properly and water isn't being wasted through runoff or over-spray.

SEPTEMBER

- Fall is an ideal time to rejuvenate your lawn. Apply a humic acid product over the lawn to help revitalize the soil and provide nutrients for beneficial microorganisms.

- Mow grass only when it's dry because when it's wet the cut is typically very uneven. The wet grass clippings can also clump leaving a soggy mess on the lawn and underneath the mower.

- Early fall is the last chance to plant warm-season grasses such as Bermuda and St. Augustine. Make sure you have prepped the soil properly to create a sandy loam texture and amended with compost or humus.

- Apply a pre-emergent lawn weed control to prevent problems with Annual Bluegrass (Poa annua) or Crabgrass to prevent future problems.

- Dry, hot winds usually occur in the fall in California. Adjust the irrigation timers to accommodate such harsh weather so that there is a sufficient supply of moisture for the lawn.

OCTOBER

- October is a good month to plant a new lawn using cool-season grasses like Perennial Rye or Fescue.

- Begin fertilizing established cool season lawns every other month from fall-spring with a complete organic lawn food.

- Cool fall weather is the prime growing period for cool-season lawns, such as Fescues. Begin fertilizing established cool season lawns every other month from fall-spring with a complete organic lawn food.

- Rake up falling autumn leaves to help the lawn "breathe."

- Watch for fungal lawn diseases such as brown patch. Make sure the brown patch is not the result of poor water drainage leading to root rot, grub damage or poor root development. If it is a fungus, the lawn damage resembles a large donut ring, brown at the edges and green in the center. Brown patch is common during hot, humid weather and can be controlled with a fungicide containing triadimefon.

NOVEMBER

- If lawn damage is extensive from tunneling squirrels, live trap and relocate, but check with the local wildlife control agency to determine where they can be released.

- Re-program irrigation timers and systems to reflect the conditions of shorter days and cooler weather.

- Stop feeding warm season lawns.

- Continue to keep lawnmower blades sharp for a cleaner cut. For rotary mowers, simply replace the blade with a new one. Also lower mower blades for cool-season lawns during autumn and winter.

- As the garden begins to quiet, think about areas in the landscape where a grass might be the perfect accent rather than an expansive lawn. Korean Grass *(Zoysia tenuifolia)* provides a textured appearance that is ideal in rock gardens where mowing is unnecessary. Dichondra is a cool season evergreen turf with distinctive round leaves. Although it is not for high foot traffic and requires well-drained acidic soils, it is lovely in small rock or oriental landscapes.

DECEMBER

- Bermudagrass, St. Augustine and Zoysia look beautiful during summer months, but they brown in winter. The solution is to overseed the warm season grass with annual or perennial Ryegrass to keep the lawn looking green. Once spring arrives, the Ryegrass will die back and the warm season grass will take over.

- The exact timing for overseeding varies depending on your location, so contact the local university cooperative extension or nursery for the best time frame.

- If your lawn is very dense or has a thick thatch layer, aerate or dethatch prior to overseeding.

- If your lawn has weeds, apply a weed killer appropriate for warm-season lawns about 3-4 weeks before overseeding.

- Mow the lawn as low as possible and overseed at rates recommended on the grass seed package. Lightly topdress with humus or other organic matter and water about once a day until the seeds germinate.

Many gardeners love the look of an attractive manicured lawn.

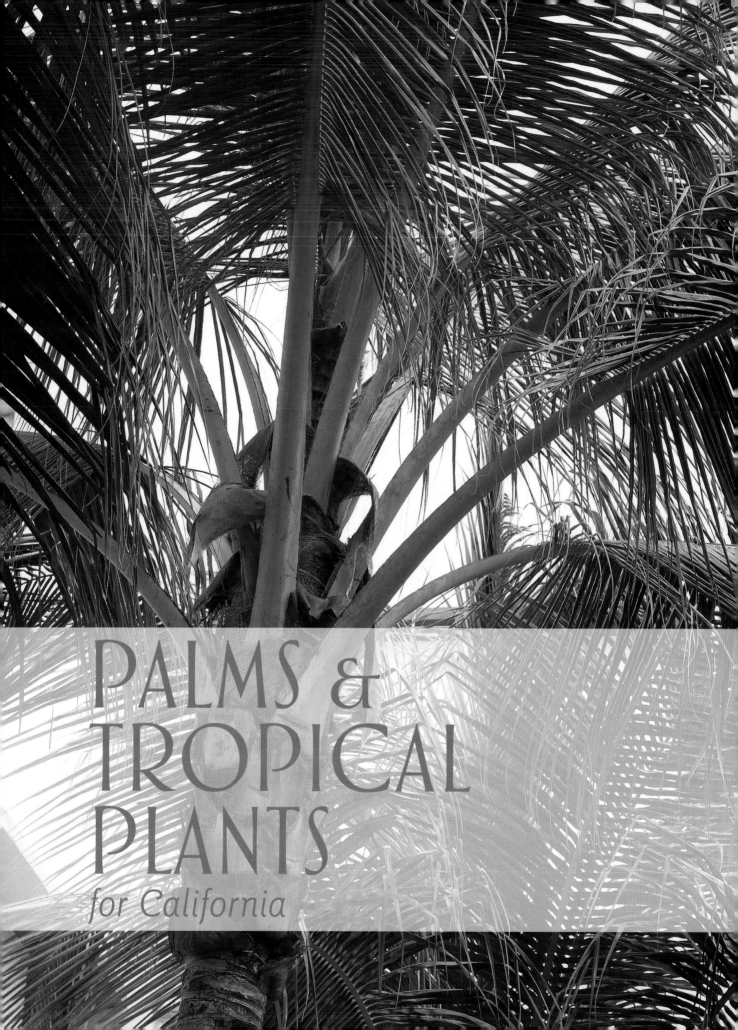

PALMS &
TROPICAL
PLANTS
for California

The lure of lush tropical landscapes in Hawaii, Bali, and other exotic locales is the stuff dreams are made of, and universally appealing for those of us who do not live in such places. Most people associate the flamboyant and contrasting silhouettes of Palms with the tropics. Languorous landscapes of swaying Palms are synonymous with that South Seas island atmosphere. This is because the majority of the world's 2,800 Palm species are found in tropical and subtropical regions, although their natural range is from as far north as Southern Europe to as far south as the North Island of New Zealand.

PRINCES IN THE LANDSCAPE

Palms are regarded as the "princes" of plants. In fact, the noted Swedish botanist and founder of the modern binominal system of nomenclature, Carl Linnaeus, labeled them "Principes." Following his lead, the members of the Palm Society had named their quarterly journal *Principes*, until it was recently changed to *Palms.*

California has many areas that are ideal for the culture of Palms. Rather than describe all Palm species, we have chosen those that behave themselves in average home landscapes with temperate climates—not the 150-foot "Paul Bunyan" varieties or the vining or twelve-inch miniature types.

DISTINCTIVE FEATURES OF PALMS

Palms are fibrous monocotyledons, members of the *Arecaceae* family of plants, which makes their appearance easily recognizable. We have also included the unrelated Sago Palm, a Cycad, because of its similar appearance.

Superficially these plants may all seem to look alike because many have clustering or clumping trunks with stalks of long evergreen fronds. On closer inspection you can see there are differences. Palms can be categorized according to frond shape: the fan-frond, also called palmate, like the Lady Palm, and the feather-frond or pinnate, like the Pygmy Date. Palmate fronds are round or semicircular in outline, while pinnate fronds are linear or oblong with segments arranged like the pattern of a feather. Although Sagos are a unique group of plants that form seed-bearing cones rather than flowers, they have evergreen pinnate fronds.

Despite the fact that Palms are usually used in garden designs for their form rather than color, there are many Palms with bright fruits such as the stranded clusters of ruby-red jewels on the Fishtail Palm, the brownish-orange fruits of the Mediterranean Fan Palm, and the bright-red, egg-shaped seeds of the Sago Palm.

Palms are monocots, which means they lack a main taproot. Instead, Palms grow fibrous, adventitious roots from the trunk bases. They do not produce successive layers of growth in their trunks or stem; their trunks enlarge over time because their tissues expand, not because of the new wood development. This is why injuries to the trunk should be avoided—such damage is permanent and cannot be repaired.

CARE FOR YOUR PALMS

Since Palms are primarily surface feeders, they need regular supplies of moisture and soil nutrients, although some, like the Mediterranean Fan Palm, are drought resistant. All palms do well on organic palm food.

Palms lack a deep root system allowing them to be moved relatively easily and transplanted successfully as long as a planting hole has been prepared in advance and the trunks are buried a little deeper than before. They may be transplanted any time of the year, but the warm spring or summer months are best since root growth is highest during those months.

Once a Palm is established, use a pruning saw to cut off dead or damaged leaf stalks and make sure the cuts are flush with the trunk. Mulching is beneficial since it conserves water, stabilizes root zone temperatures, adds nutrients, and improves the soil's porosity and water infiltration. Lawns, ground covers, and weeds should be kept away from Palm trunks because they compete for water and nutrients and increase the danger of damage from mowers and weed-whackers.

TROPICAL MAGIC FOR THE LANDSCAPE

Smaller Palms such as the Fishtail, the Mediterranean Fan, and Pygmy Date Palms normally grow only ten to twenty-five feet tall and are ideally suited for average-size yards. Others, like the Lady Palm and Sago Palm, are also excellent on the patio in containers or near the house. Palms have great value for use near swimming pools or other bodies of water because they rarely drop fronds or other litter. Their graceful foliage is beautiful when silhouetted by back lighting. Palms play a variety of roles in the landscape that few other plants can duplicate. Whether indoors or out, sun or shade, coastal to interior areas, there are species to fill many landscape situations. All Palms cast a spell of tropical magic.

ORCHIDS ARE OLD FRIENDS

Orchids leave us speechless and awestruck. Perhaps because they express themselves in such different forms and structures, but these differences—however dramatic—are merely different looks for old familiar friends.

BLOOM CATEGORIES

Orchids can generally be categorized into three groups according to bloom period: cool-season flowering Orchids, warm-season flowering Orchids and continuously flowering Orchids. After blooming, Orchids generally enter a resting state for one to two months followed by several months of a vegetative growth period. Depending on environmental factors and the Orchid variety, this entire process will take from eleven to fourteen months.

GROWTH CONDITIONS

Orchids can also be categorized into four groups according to their growing conditions—epiphytic (which thrive in rainforest canopies), terrestrial (which grow in soil), geophytic (which grow on rocks) and saprophytic (which grow on decaying organic material). Epiphytic and terrestrial Orchids are the varieties most commonly available to California gardeners.

THE MYSTERIOUS ALLURE

Their alluring, yet strange, gnarled roots, variety of leaf shapes, and, of course, their elegant and extraterrestrial flower forms and limitless colors inspire plant hunters to risk their lives in search of these exquisite beauties. Once we understand the nature and specific needs of Orchids, gardeners do not have to be obsessed plant hunters to unravel the "orchid mystery" and successfully grow these beauties.

MORE TROPICAL PLANTS

Besides swaying Palm trees and other-worldly Orchids, lush jungle-scapes are also teeming with giant Banana leaves, Frangipani flowers, and neon-colored Hibiscus. They provide a panorama of brilliant foliage and spectacular flowers. Nor can one ignore the tropical fragrances of Angel's Trumpet or Plumeria or forget the exotic beauty of pricklier tropicals such as Bromeliads as well as the "prickle-free" Orchid Cactus.

TROPICAL OASIS IN COOLER ZONES

For Californians in Zone 9 or higher, there are dozens of tropical plants from which to choose, but even those living in cooler zones can create a tropical oasis by planting cold-tolerant varieties or by utilizing containers to move sensitive tropicals into temporary winter quarters. A greenhouse, conservatory, enclosed courtyard, atrium, or entryway offers yet another solution.

The exotic Canna Lily looks at home under a Hawaiian sunset but can survive freezing weather by dying back to the ground and resprouting from its roots. Bromeliads and Epiphyllums are epiphytic rainforest plants, but they also adapt to the shaded canopies of trees in southern California. The unusual Crown of Thorns was hybridized in Thailand, but—with a little care—it will bloom on a California patio.

So dare to dabble in Palms, Orchids and other tropicals—you will be in for an exciting journey that will captivate all your senses.

PLUMERIA

HUMIDITY TRAY FOR INDOOR PLANTS

Most tropicals come from rainforests as understory plants making them adaptable to the low light conditions of homes. However, they require 50 to 60 percent humidity, a condition that is not available indoors, particularly with air conditioning and forced air heating. Humidity trays are a simple way to increase moisture around indoor plants. Available from retailers or make your own.

Supplies:
- Low-profile water-proof container such as a saucer or tray
- Coarse gravel, decorative pebbles or marbles
- Rack, brick or block of wood

Fill the saucer with gravel, pebbles or marbles and add water up to the gravel surface. Place brick, rack or wood block on the gravel and set the potted plant on top to prevent water from wicking up into the potting medium and the roots from sitting in water. Humidity trays help to create a continuous column of humidity surrounding the plants. Misting plants around the soil and under the leaves with a spray bottle adds needed humidity for indoor plants.

HOW TO RE-POT WINTER-BLOOMING ORCHIDS

Re-pot winter-blooming orchids such as Cymbidium and Miltoniopsis after their bloom cycles are completed and when the pots are completely filled with pseudobulbs or it has been longer than two years since the growing medium was changed.
- Gently remove the plant and swirl the root mass in a bucket of water to clean off the old potting mix or bark
- Cut off any brown or shrivelled pseudobulbs
- Divide with a clean knife or shovel into clusters of 3-4 pseudobulbs and pull apart gently to untangle the roots
- Sterilize knife or shovel between cuts to prevent the spread of disease (Physan sterilizes without rusting tools)
- Fill the bottom of the pot with orchid mix or orchid bark
- Fan out the roots and spread them over the mix
- Center the plant and fill around the edges of the pot with more mix or bark
- Soak deeply and allow to dry slightly before watering again

*New planting mixes are constantly being introduced. There are some ready-to-use orchid, tropical or houseplant mixes that are 100% organic and highly absorbent. Some of these mixes are combined with diatomite, a sedimentary rock composed of the fossilized remains of microscopic algae impregnated with silica. Diatomite-based orchid mixes do not deteriorate or break down over time, are pH neutral, non-toxic, high in silica matter and provide excellent air penetration. Unlike orchid bark, diatomite-based mediums do not need to be replaced when repotting plants. Available from retailers or make your own.

FISHTAIL PALM

Caryota mitis

Hardiness—Zone 10-11

Color(s)—Dark green fronds.

Fruit Period—Ruby-red fruits

Mature Size (H & W)—10 to 20+ ft. tall (clumping)

Water Needs—Water every 7-10 days depending on growth and weather conditions.

Planting/Care—Plant in spring from containers. Construct a watering basin (page 87) and apply a 2-in. layer of mulch. Needs partial shade or full sun outdoors and bright, indirect light indoors. Thin fronds to control extra dense, clump growth.

Pests/Diseases—Control spider mite and scale with a Neem or canola-based horticultural oil or a systemic insecticide.

Landscaping Tips & Ideas—Each stem is monocarpic (it dies after fruiting) and takes about 30 years before the entire palm dies, but not before it is replaced by basal suckers. Distinctive, uneven leaves is true to its namesake and makes a graceful focal plant outdoors or as a dramatic container for tall, indoor spaces.

FOXTAIL PALM

Wodyetia bifurcata

Hardiness—Zones 9-11

Color(s)—Shiny green fronds

Fruit Period—Orange-red fruits in summer

Mature Size (H & W)—15 to 30 ft. x 15 ft.

Water Needs—Wait until soil dries slightly before watering.

Planting/Care—Although drought tolerant, looks best when watered and fed regularly and grown in full sun. Needs well-draining, sandy loam, slightly acidic soil. Not cold-hardy, but will survive short period of 28°F.

Pests/Diseases—Wash off mealybugs, aphids and scale with a strong stream of water or spray with a canola-based horticultural oil.

Landscaping Tips & Ideas—8-10 ft. plume-like fronds resemble its namesake's tail. Combined with its columnar trunk it is a handsome specimen outdoors in containers or planted in the ground as a focal point by swimming pools, planted amidst other evergreen plants or planted along a driveway or road. If there is bright, indirect light, the Foxtail can also be grown indoors.

LADY PALM

Rhapis excelsa

Hardiness—Zones 9-11

Color(s)—Glossy light-green fronds

Fruit Period—Reddish berries in summer

Mature Size (H & W)—5 to 8 ft x clumping

Water Needs—Water regularly every 7-10 days depending on growth and weather conditions.

Planting/Care—Plant in spring or summer from containers. Construct a watering basin (page 87) and apply a 2-in. layer of mulch. Needs well-drained, slightly acidic soil. Does best in partial shade and mild temperatures, but withstands short bouts of freezing weather.

Pests/Diseases—Few pests or diseases outdoors, but indoors watch for mealybugs or spider mites. Control with Neem or canola-based horticultural oil or a systemic insecticide.

Landscaping Tips & Ideas—Small stature and graceful appearance makes Lady Palms a popular dwarf palm for foundation planting, as focal points for small gardens and container plants for indoors or patios. Also use palmate fronds in exotic or formal cut-flower arrangements.

MEDITERRANEAN FAN PALM

Chamaerops humilis

Hardiness—Zones 8-11

Color(s)—Blue-green fronds

Fruit Period—Brownish-orange fruits from green and yellow flowers summer-fall

Mature Size (H & W)—8 to 15 ft. x clumping

Water Needs—Water regularly, but after 1-2 years, wait until slightly dried before watering.

Planting/Care—One of the hardiest of all palms, they can withstand temperatures down to 15°F, short periods of drought, hot sun, wind and salt spray. Needs full sun or partial shade in well-draining, amended, slightly acidic soil.

Pests/Diseases—If leaf spots caused by fungus seriously affect the palm, consult the local university cooperative extension for recommendations. For mites or scale use a Neem or canola-based horticultural oil.

Landscaping Tips & Ideas—Low-growing clustering palms that need male and female plants to pollinate. Lightly fragrant male flowers are an added bonus. Plant near pools, by seashore or in containers.

PYGMY DATE PALM

Phoenix roebelenii

Hardiness—Zones 9-11

Color(s)—Light-dark-green fronds

Fruit Period—Black fruits from small, yellow flowers in fall

Mature Size (H & W)—4 to 10 ft. (single trunk)

Water Needs—Water 2-3 times per week depending on climate and growth cycles.

Planting/Care—Plant anytime where winters are mild or in spring after the last frost from containers. Construct a basin (page 87) and apply 2 in. of mulch. Thrives best in full sun or partial shade along the coast or complete shade for inland areas. Provide well-draining slightly acidic soil. Feed with a complete, organic palm food every other month from March-October. Needs both male and female plants for pollination.

Pests/Diseases—Control spider mites and mealybugs with a Neem or canola-based horticultural oil.

Landscaping Tips & Ideas—Beautiful as night-lit silhouettes in smaller gardens, as foundation plantings, beside a swimming pool and as container plants indoors or outside.

SAGO PALM

Cycas revoluta

Hardiness—Zones 9-11

Color(s)—Olive-green fronds

Fruit Period—Red fruit from female

Mature Size (H & W)—4 to 6 ft. tall (clumping)

Water Needs—Allow soil to dry out slightly before watering.

Planting/Care—Plant anytime where winters are mild or in spring after the last frost. Requires deep, sandy, well-draining slightly acidic soil from 1-5-or-15-gallon containers. Provide a watering basin (page 87) and apply a 2-in. layer of mulch. Needs full sun or partial shade and organic palm food every other month during growth cycle.

Pests/Diseases—Avoid overhead watering to prevent rot problems and apply chelated iron to correct chlorosis.

Landscaping Tips & Ideas—Sago tolerates high temperatures, drought, and cold weather down to freezing. Ideal for oriental-style landscapes, tropical gardens and containers for patio or as bonsai specimen. All parts are toxic, so keep away from small children or pets.

ANTHURIUM
Anthurium x hybrida

Hardiness—Zone 11 or indoors

Color(s)—Red, pink, yellow, green, orange, brown, white, and bicolors

Bloom Period—On and off year-round

Mature Size (H & W)—1 to 4 ft. x as wide.

Water Needs—Water regularly every 5-7 days depending on growth and weather.

Planting/Care—Provide an organic, well-draining medium such as equal parts peat moss, perlite and coir. Needs partial shade outdoors and bright indirect light indoors.

Pests/Diseases—For aphid, scale or mealybug infestations, spray with a Neem or canola-based horticultural oil. Control thrips with Spinosad.

Landscaping Tips & Ideas—Where cold weather is common, plant in containers, bring indoors during winter and place on humidity trays. Fill plastic saucers with gravel, add water and set Anthuriums on blocks to prevent roots from sitting in water. For large, multi-hued Anthuriums, consider 'Obake' and for dainty flowers and compact growth, select 'Krypton'.

BANANA SHRUB
Michelia figo

Hardiness—Zones 8-10

Color(s)—Creamy-yellow blossoms

Bloom Period—Spring-early summer

Mature Size (H & W)—6 to 12 ft. x 4 to 12 ft.

Water Needs—Water regularly every 5-7 days from spring-summer, but decrease frequency during fall-winter.

Planting/Care—Plant in humus-rich, well-draining soil in full sun along coastal regions and part shade inland. Needs slightly acid soil and a feeding of cottonseed meal before and after the bloom cycle.

Pests/Diseases—Few pests or diseases except mealybug or aphid infestations. Spray with a strong stream of water or Neem or canola-based horticultural oil. Root rot may be a problem if there is poor-draining soil.

Landscaping Tips & Ideas—Plant this shrub protected from the wind and place it close to walkways or entries where its intense banana perfume can be appreciated during spring. Or plant it in a pot and place on the patio.

CAST IRON PLANT
Aspidistra spp.

Hardiness—Zones 7-11 or indoors

Color(s)—Gray-violet flowers

Bloom Period—Not applicable

Mature Size (H & W)—2 to 3 ft. (clumping)

Water Needs—Water every 10-14 days depending on growth and weather conditions.

Planting/Care—Plant from containers spring-fall. Provide well-draining, humus-rich, slightly acidic soil and shade. Indoors, it tolerates low light levels, but grows best in bright, indirect light. Fertilize every other month from spring-fall with a complete, organic liquid food.

Pests/Diseases—Control spider mites, scale, mealybugs or aphids with a canola-based horticultural oil or a systemic insecticide.

Landscaping Tips & Ideas—Use in a shaded garden or in containers for the home. 'Akebono' has large green leaves with yellow stripes running down the center and 'Asahi' is a favorite among flower arrangers for its long, deep green leaves tipped in white. Cast-Iron plants thrive on neglect but still provide tropical-looking beauty in shaded nooks and crannies.

CHINESE GROUND ORCHID
Bletilla striata

Hardiness—Zones 6-11

Color(s)—Magenta, yellow, pink, white

Bloom Period—Spring

Mature Size (H & W)—12 to 20 in. x as wide

Water Needs—Keep moist spring-summer, but decrease water in the fall and withhold during winter dormancy.

Planting/Care—Very hardy orchid to grow in containers or in the ground. Provide part shade and plant the pseudobulbs with tips up about 1 in. below the soil surface. Where winter freezes are common plant 2 in. below. Needs humus-amended, well-draining, slightly acidic soil. Feed monthly with an organic, liquid fertilizer spring-summer.

Pests/Diseases—Protect from snails and slugs with an iron phosphate bait or hand-pick. If in Southern California, decollate snails are an effective control.

Landscaping Tips & Ideas—Perfect choice for a low-maintenance orchid in a shade garden or in a pot in dappled light. The flowers resemble mini Cattleyas atop wiry stalks rising from pleated, strap-like foliage.

CHINESE YELLOW BANANA
Musa lasiocarpa

Hardiness—Zones 7-11

Color(s)—Golden-yellow flower

Bloom Period—Summer

Mature Size (H & W)—3-4 ft. x as wide

Water Needs—Water regularly during spring-summer, allow to dry out slightly before watering in fall and withhold in winter.

Planting/Care—Prefers cool, mild regions but adapts to many different zones if maintained properly. Needs full sun (along the coast) or part shade (inland) and excellent-draining soil. Apply a 2-in. layer of mulch and feed from spring-summer with a complete, organic granular fertilizer.

Pests/Diseases—Root rot problems occur when soil drainage is poor.

Landscaping Tips & Ideas—This ornamental banana adds tropical flair even for those areas where true tropical plants are difficult to grow. Its yellow blossoms resemble giant artichokes that remain in flower all summer long. Once the flowers are spent, the stem dies, but not before new growth occurs at the base.

CYMBIDIUM ORCHID
Cymbidium x hybrida

Hardiness—Zones 9-10

Color(s)—Almost all colors of the rainbow and combinations

Bloom Period—Winter-spring

Mature Size (H & W)—12 to 48 in. x 8 to 36 in.

Water Needs—From spring-summer, keep moist and decrease during winter.

Planting/Care—Needs partial shade and a well-draining orchid mix. Flowering spikes develop when night temperatures dip in the 50s outdoors. Bring indoors during extended winter frost or to enjoy the blossoms. Feed a complete, organic liquid fertilizer every 2-3 weeks or granular fertilizer once a month.

Pests/Diseases—Control slugs and snails by handpicking or using iron phosphate bait.

Landscaping Tips & Ideas—Upright Cymbidiums add winter-early spring beauty under the shaded canopy of a tree and can be brought indoors to enjoy their clusters of blossoms. Miniature Cymbidiums are ideal for small spaces and cascading varieties are lovely in hanging baskets.

161

EPIDENDRUM
Epidendrum x hybrida

Hardiness—Zones 9-11 or indoors

Color(s)—Orange, yellow, pink, red, lavender, white

Bloom Period—Year-round in temperate climates

Mature Size (H & W)—8 to 36 in. x as wide

Water Needs—Water every 5-7 days depending on growth and weather conditions.

Planting/Care—Plant in an orchid potting mix and provide some shade in the afternoon, particularly inland regions to avoid burning the foliage. Along the coast plant with their roots in the shade and faces in the sun. Use a complete, liquid organic fertilizer (½ the recommended rate) when watering about every other time.

Pests/Diseases—Control aphids, mealybugs and scale with Neem or a canola-based horticultural oil.

Landscaping Tips & Ideas—Epidendrums can grow directly in planting beds, but light, soil and climate needs are better met if grown in containers. Cut back spent flowers down to one or two leaf joints above the soil.

HELICONIA
Heliconia spp.

Hardiness—Zones 10-11

Color(s)—Orange, yellow, red bracts

Bloom Period—Spring-summer

Mature Size (H & W)—3-6 ft. x as wide

Water Needs—Water regularly every 5-7 days depending on growth and weather conditions.

Planting/Care—Plant in full or part sun in amended, well-draining, slightly acidic soil. Where frosts are common, plant in containers so they can be moved to protected areas.

Pests/Diseases—For ants use baits and spray aphids with a Neem or canola-based horticultural oil.

Landscaping Tips & Ideas—Grown for their large, colorful, upright or drooping, bracts like 'Lobster Claw' or 'Parrot's Beak' or exotic banana-like foliage and used in gorgeous flower arrangements. Most require warm, humid days and evenings, but one of the cold hardiest is the smaller, but striking *H. scheideana* 'Fire and Ice' It bears bright red bracts with yellow sepals and grows to 4 ft. 'Christmas Holiday' has red and white bracts and blooms during winter.

HIBISCUS
Hibiscus rosa-sinensis

Hardiness—Zones 10-11

Color(s)—Red, yellow, orange, purple, pink, blue and bicolors

Bloom Period—Summer-autumn

Mature Size (H & W)—3 to 10 ft. x 3 to 6 ft.

Water Needs—Water every 5-7 days during warm months and decrease watering during the cool seasons.

Planting/Care—Plant in well-draining, humus-amended soil in full or part sun. Bloom and growth cycles stop when temperatures fall below 50°F. Use a complete, organic Hibiscus fertilizer during growth and bloom periods.

Pests/Diseases—Giant whitefly produces cotton candy-like strands underneath leaves. Control with Spinosad or a systemic insecticide.

Landscaping Tips & Ideas—Grafted selections like 'Rainbow Christie' (pink with red eye edged in white or yellow) and 'Dragon's Heart' (deep burgundy) are available with 8-12 in, single or double flowers in a rainbow of color combinations and grow 4-8 ft. tall in the ground and 3-4 ft. in containers.

LADY'S SLIPPER ORCHID
Paphiopedilum insigne

Hardiness—Zones 10-11 or indoors

Color(s)—Wide array of colors, shapes, patterns and textures

Bloom Period—Autumn or spring depending on variety

Mature Size (H & W)—4 to 16 in. x 8 to 12 in.

Water Needs—Water every 5-7 days.

Planting/Care—Plant from containers and provide a well-draining orchid medium. During warm spring and summer months, grow outdoors in shady spots, but bring indoors during winter. Find a place indoors with bright, indirect light. Fertilize during growth with an organic or slow-release food.

Pests/Diseases—Control mealybugs or scale with a canola-based horticultural oil or use a systemic insecticide for indoor use.

Landscaping Tips & Ideas—Group with other orchids outdoors in shady nooks and indoors for exotic colors in white, yellow, green or combinations. *P. insigne* is among the cold-hardiest and least fussy of Lady's Slipper Orchids.

MOTH OR BUTTERFLY ORCHID
Phalaenopsis amabilis

Hardiness—Zone 11 or all zones indoors

Color(s)—Magenta, lavender, pink, white, green, yellow, brown, red

Bloom Period—On and off year-round

Mature Size (H & W)—8 to 12 in. x 12 to 18 in.

Water Needs—Water every 7-10 days allowing soil to dry slightly.

Planting/Care—Repot every 2 years when the plants are growing, remove dead or decayed roots and plant in a well-draining orchid mix. Fertilize with an organic orchid or slow-release food from fall-winter.

Pests/Diseases—Problems may occur if the air is too dry. Set on trays filled with gravel and water and use a block to keep the plants from sitting in water.

Landscaping Tips & Ideas—Grow Moth Orchids indoors during cooler months in bright, indirect light and take outdoors to a shady area during summer. When flowers are spent, leave spikes so additional buds will form.

ORCHID CACTUS
Epiphyllum hybrids

Hardiness—Zones 10-11

Color(s)—White, yellow, pink, red, orange, lavender, magenta, bicolors

Bloom Period—Spring, summer or fall

Mature Size (H & W)—2 to 6 ft. x as wide

Water Needs—Water every 5-7 days, keeping roots moist but not soggy.

Planting/Care—Plant from cuttings or containers in spring or summer. Provide a rich, free-draining, slightly acidic soil. Remember they are tropical plants, not drought tolerant Cacti and thrive best when watered and fertilized regularly (organic Cactus food before and after bloom cycles).

Pests/Diseases—Control scale with a canola-based horticultural oil and keep slugs away from foliage.

Landscaping Tips & Ideas—The long, arching stems with spectacular blossoms show off well in hanging baskets, large tubs or pots. Flowers range in size from small to dinner-plate 10 in. or more. Some are quite fragrant such as 'Gold Chain' and most hybrids bloom during the day.

PEACE LILY

Spathiphyllum floribundum hybrids

Hardiness—Zone 11 or indoors

Color(s)—White spathes

Bloom Period—Spring-fall

Mature Size (H & W)—2 to 3 ft. x clumping

Water Needs—Water every 5-7 days to keep moist, decrease during winter.

Planting/Care—Plant outdoors from containers in late spring in shade or indoors anytime. Provide a well draining, slightly acidic, organic soil. Indoors, find a spot with filtered light.

Pests/Diseases—Tip burn is caused by salt accumulation in the soil. Drench the soil to leech out and if indoors, change from tap water to de-ionized water (steam iron water sold at grocery stores).

Landscaping Tips & Ideas—The giant 'Mauna Loa' stands 3 ft. tall, with huge leaves and 4 ft. stems with pale green-white spathes. 'Petite' is a smaller, more compact variety. Native to tropical rainforests, plant in containers for shaded spots outdoors and move indoors during the cooler months.

PLUMERIA (FRANGIPANI)

Plumeria rubra

Hardiness—Zones 10-11

Color(s)—White, yellow, red, pink, orange and multi-colored

Bloom Period—Spring-autumn

Mature Size (H & W)—6-40 ft. x 10 to 15 ft.

Water Needs—Water every 5-7 days during growth and bloom periods. Withhold water when dormant, but keep roots moist if there is an extended drought.

Planting/Care—Plant from cuttings or containers in late spring or summer in full sun. Provide well-draining, slightly acidic soil and a frost-free location. Prune in late spring or summer for shape or to remove damaged branches.

Pests/Diseases—Control whiteflies with a strong stream of water or use an organic insecticide such as Spinosad.

Landscaping Tips & Ideas—Since Plumeria bear generous clusters of fragrant flowers, set near entryways or walkways to enjoy their perfume. 'Daisy Wilcox' produces huge 4½-in. flowers in pastel pink blending to white with yellow and 'Candystripe' bears deep pink, yellow and white blossoms.

PRINCESS FLOWER

Tibouchina urvilleana

Hardiness—Zones 9-11

Color(s)—Bright-purple

Bloom Period—Spring-summer

Mature Size (H & W)—12 to 15 ft. x 5 to 6 ft.

Water Needs—Water once a week depending on growth and weather conditions.

Planting/Care—Plant from containers in spring or fall and provide rich, well-draining, slightly acidic soil. Needs full sun and protections from wind or frost. Prune for shape or to control size and feed with a complete organic fertilizer after bloom period. Pinch back new growth for bushier appearance.

Pests/Diseases—Geranium budworm prevents flower buds from opening. Control with Spinosad if damage is extensive.

Landscaping Tips & Ideas—Can be grown as a specimen tree or shrub. Use as a hedge, screen or focal point, especially near a pool for tropical beauty. Combine with Hibiscus and Plumeria. Its large 3-in. purple flowers and soft, ciliated leaves are also ideal for a sensory garden.

SILVER VASE
Aechmea fasciata

Hardiness—Zones 10-11 or indoors

Color(s)—Pink or purple bracts.

Bloom Period—Summer-fall or fall-winter

Mature Size (H & W)—12 to 24 in. x as wide

Water Needs—Keep center foliar cup filled with water and surrounding soil evenly moist.

Planting/Care—Provide partial shade with an excellent-draining, planting medium such as cactus mix. Where frost is common, keep in a container and move indoors during winter months.

Pests/Diseases—Protect from snail or slug damage with an iron phosphate bait or hand-pick. Use decollate snails in Southern California.

Landscaping Tips & Ideas—There are numerous bromeliads, including *Aechmea* and *Tillandsia* in a rainbow of colorful bracts and shapes. Most are epiphytes that grow in rainforests. For frost-free regions, place them in hanging baskets or in tree elbows with bits of moss attached to their roots. 'Silver King' has unique silvery foliage and 'Marginata' have leaves edged in cream.

TASMANIAN TREE FERN
Dicksonia antarctica

Hardiness—Zones 9-11

Color(s)—Not applicable

Bloom Period—Not applicable

Mature Size (H & W)—8-15 ft.

Water Needs—Water 2 in. per week or more when becoming established. Prefers soil evenly moist.

Planting/Care—Most cold-hardy of all the tree ferns and withstands temperatures down to 20°F. Dig a hole twice as large as the rootball, fill with humus-rich, well draining, slightly acidic soil and plant in late spring at the same level as the original container. Keep the shaggy trunk moist until established and during hot, dry weather. Find a partial-full shady spot.

Pests/Diseases—Generally free from pests and diseases, but susceptible to root rot in poor draining soil.

Landscaping Tips & Ideas—Lacey-textured, arching fronds lend beauty to the tropical landscape in atriums and enclosed courtyards. Plant in a grouping with other ferns or as a companion to Gardenias, cold-hardy Heliconia and Vireya.

VIREYA
Rhododendron hybrid

Hardiness—Zones 10-11

Color(s)—Yellow, orange, pink, red, white, bicolors

Bloom Period—On and off year round

Mature Size (H & W)—2 to 5 ft. x as wide

Water Needs—Water every 5-7 days to keep soil moist but not soggy.

Planting/Care—Requires excellent draining, acidic potting mix and prefers morning sun and afternoon shade. Apply 2-3 in. of mulch to protect roots from temperature fluctuations. Prefers morning sun and afternoon dappled shade.

Pests/Diseases—Control mildew, rust, aphids, scale and mealy bugs with Neem or canola-based horticultural oil and spray thrips with Spinosad.

Landscaping Tips & Ideas—Vireyas are tropical Rhododendrons that bear brilliant-colored clusters of trumpet-shaped flowers and thrive in frost-free climates. Use as tropical accents in partially sunny gardens or in containers. For prolonged winter freezes, bring indoors to protect. 'George Budgen' (bright orange-yellow), 'Ne Plus Ultra' (deep red) and 'Purple Splendor' are among the many hybrids available.

MORE ORCHID RECOMMENDATIONS

- BEALLARA ORCHID (x *Beallara* 'Howard's Dream) Zones 10-11 or indoors, bright dappled light, 18 inches x 18 inches, flowers late spring or summer, plant in fine orchid bark.

- CATTLEYA (*Laeliocattleya*) Zones 10-11 or indoors, bright dappled light, 4 to 12 inches x 4 to 24 inches, flowers spring and summer, some hybrids are fragrant, plant in medium grade orchid bark.

- CHOCOLATE ORCHID (x *Oncidium* 'Sharry Baby') Zones 10-11 or indoors, bright dappled light, 10 to 30 inches x 10 to 24 inches, flowers late spring to summer, flowers smell like chocolate, plant in medium grade orchid bark.

- COCONUT ORCHID (*Maxillaria tenufolia*) Zones 10-11 or indoors, bright dappled light, 6 to 10 inches x 6 to 10 inches, flowers late spring or early summer, flowers smell like coconut, plant in medium grade orchid bark.

- NUN'S ORCHID (*Phaius tankervilleae*) Zones 10-11 or indoors, full shade outdoors, bright indirect light indoors, 12 to 40 inches x 8 to 32 inches, flowers late winter to early spring, plant in equal parts bark and potting soil.

- PANSY ORCHID (*Miltoniopsis* x *hybrida*) Zone 11 or indoors, full shade outdoors or bright indirect light indoors, 8 to 16 inches x 8 to 16 inches, flowers in winter, plant in medium grade orchid bark.

- SPIDER ORCHID (*Brassia* x *hybrida*) Zones 10-11 or indoors, bright dappled light, 8 to 12 inches x 8 to 16 inches, flowers spring to summer, plant in medium-grade orchid bark.

CATTLEYA

JANUARY

- When there is little rain, provide supplemental water to tropical plants. They are susceptible to frost damage, insect and disease problems if allowed to dry out completely.

- Install outdoor lights to highlight Palm trees' structural beauty at night.

- Catalogues and websites specializing in tropical plants are a nice escape from dreary winter days. There are more than 200,000 species to make your tropical dreams a reality.

- Cattleya, Paphiopedilum and Phalaenopsis orchids prefer evening temperatures 15°F to 20°F cooler than daytime. If possible, move them at night to a cooler area to encourage flowering spikes.

- Fungus gnats lay their eggs in houseplant soil. Spread a layer of horticultural sand (not beach sand) over the soil and use yellow sticky traps to capture the adults.

- Control slugs and snails by placing mesh screens in the bottom of pots, wrapping copper tape around the pots (copper's electrical charge keeps snails from crossing) and spreading poison-free baits containing iron phosphate.

FEBRUARY

- Collect rainwater and use to water tropical plants that have moved indoors as well as outdoor container Palms and Orchids.

- Blooming Cymbidiums are available at nurseries. Make your choices now for the best selections and feed with an organic orchid fertilizer every 2-3 weeks, January-June.

- Pull or hoe existing weeds before using a pre-emergent to prevent future weeds from germination.

- Mark the spots where dormant tropicals are "resting" because you don't want to accidentally dig around or step on those areas.

- If frost has damaged tropicals, do not trim back until new foliage emerges in spring to determine how far back to prune.

- Discourage nibbling deer and rabbits with motion-activated sprinklers or lights, olfactory repellents or surrounding tropical plants with mesh fencing (Angel's Trumpet, Bougainvillea, Euphorbia and Hibiscus are deer resistant). Set out manual traps rather than toxic baits when burrowing gophers and moles become active.

MARCH

- Adjust irrigation clocks to accommodate spring's change in weather and plant growth conditions. Apply a product with humic acid twice a year, once in spring and once in fall. For clay soils also add organic amendments such as humus, compost, peat moss or worm castings.

- Fertilize tropical plants with an organic liquid every 30-45 days or a granular organic food every 45 days from early spring. In containers, apply every other week if liquid and once a month if granular.

- When evening temperatures are 50°F move indoor orchids outside. *Cattleya*, *Oncidium* and *Maxillaria* prefer dappled sunlight, but *Beallara*, *Phalaenopsis*, *Miltoniopsis*, Phaius and *Paphiopedilum* like cooler, shaded spots.

- Plant Chinese Ground Orchid (*Bletilla*) from corms in bright, dappled light or morning sun.

- Every 7-10 days, soak potted orchids in a tub or sink of water and let sit for 30 minutes before draining.

APRIL

- For interior regions, plant tropicals such as Palms, Hibiscus and Bougainvillea, but for cooler areas wait another month. Pygmy Date or Sago Palms are ideal for smaller spaces.

- Build watering basins for newly planted tropical plants and water every 2-4 days until roots are established (for free-draining, loam soil). In clay soils, water less to keep the root ball moist but not soggy.

- Re-pot an established tropical in a container one size up or the same container after root pruning. Cut the lower ⅓ of the root ball, loosen the outer roots and plant in an organic potting soil or Cactus mix.

- Replant winter-stored Cannas and Plumeria after the last frost date in full sun.

- Established, drought-tolerant tropical Crown of Thorns, Bougainvillea and Bird of Paradise need water twice a month during spring (if no rains).

- Wait to water and fertilize Plumeria until new leaves emerge.

MAY

- Maintain a 1-2 in. layer of mulch around tropical plants, but keep away from the trunk or main stems.

- Remove sucker growth that appears below grafts of tropical. Wait until new growth appears before pruning frost damaged branches.

- Fertilize Palms with an organic food every other month during the growth cycle, spring-summer.

- After 2-3 years, divide Cymbidiums and re-plant just after blooming. Prune off dead roots, cut out shriveled, brown pseudobulbs and divide into 3-4 clusters with a clean, sterilized knife or shovel.

- Remove old fronds on Palms to expose the trunks' structure. Wear protective gloves and arm shields because of sharp, spines or the presence of calcium oxalate, a skin irritant.

- If winds or salt spray are pitting or tearing large-leafed plants like Banana and Canna Lilies, set up wind baffles and wash the foliage frequently. If damage is persistent, move to the leeward side of the house or other structures.

JUNE

- Re-program irrigation timers for summer.

- Select tropical plants at nurseries or plant sales at local Orchid, Plumeria, Bromeliad, Epiphyllum and Palm clubs.

- Transplant in late afternoon or early evening and spray with an anti-transpirant to help avoid transplant shock.

- Divide Chinese Yellow Banana, Ginger, Canna Lily and other clumping tropical plants in early summer.

- Phalaenopsis often rebloom off an old floral stalk, if it remains green. Sometimes a keiki emerges from one of the nodes. Cut just below the node where the keiki formed and bend the stalk so that the keiki can be planted in a separate pot (use an orchid mix) while still attached to the stalk. Once the keiki's root system is established, cut the floral stalk to release the new plant from its parent (*Epidendrum* also bears keikis).

- Control aphids, scale and mealybugs and should be washed off or sprayed with a canola-based horticultural oil or Neem oil.

JULY

- Visit arboretums and other public gardens with tropical collections for more landscaping ideas.

- Make sure automatic irrigation systems are functioning properly to avoid stressing tropical plants.

- Take cuttings from Plumeria, tropical Crown of Thorns and Angel's Trumpet and allow to callus over for 24-48 hours before planting in moistened perlite or Cactus mix.

- Continue fertilizing with a complete, organic granular food every 45 days or with a liquid fertilizer, once a month during growth and bloom cycles. Feed container-grown tropicals every 2 weeks with a liquid or every 4 weeks with a granular food.

- Many tropical flowers are most fragrant and beautiful during summer. Harvest in early morning when their stems have peak moisture content. Do not use toxic Angel Trumpet's flowers.

- Remove errant or damaged branches and pinch back new growth to encourage fuller growth. If cutting off foliage infected with rust or mildew is ineffective, spray with a canola-based horticultural oil.

AUGUST

- Clean up fallen flower and clippings regularly because they harbor pests and diseases.

- Yellowing foliage may indicate chlorosis. Apply a chelated iron product.

- Monitor soil moisture by using a soil probe or shovel to determine if the soil is drying (roots of Ginger and Cannas are just below the surface, but the roots of Angel's Trumpet may be 6-12 in.).

- Keep all newly planted tropicals well-watered to avoid plant stress during hot weather. Canna Lilies demand so much water during summer that they are often grown along the edges of shallow ponds or in water gardens with water barely covering their soil.

- Keep Bromeliad cup reservoirs filled with water and mist during periods of low humidity.

- Grow epiphytic *Tillandsia* and *Bromeliad* under the shaded canopy of a tree or set them in the nooks and crannies of tree branches. Others such as Silver Vase do best in containers.

SEPTEMBER

- Water tropical plants thoroughly and apply an anti-transpirant when Santa Ana or Diablo winds are predicted. Also apply an anti-transpirant where practical.

- Withhold fertilizer for tropical plants in autumn to slow their growth in preparation for cooler weather.

- Along the coast where mild weather prevails in autumn and winter, it is possible to plant tropicals in containers or in the ground such as Palms, Bougainvillea, Hibiscus and Plumeria by early fall. For inland or central regions, wait until spring.

- Time to bring frost-sensitive orchids and container tropical plants indoors where there is bright indirect light. Cattleya, Oncidium, Beallara and Maxillaria prefer the sunnier east and west windows, while Miltonia, Phalaenopsis and Paphiopedilum prefer cooler north and east facing windows.

- Before bringing outdoor plants indoors, check for insects on foliage, stems and soil. Spray with Spinosad or use a systemic plant stake formulated for houseplants.

- Keep *Epidendrum*, *Cymbidium* and *Bletilla* outdoors throughout the year.

OCTOBER

- Dropping temperatures and shorter days signal spring and summer blooming orchids to slow their metabolism. Many become dormant and even drop a few leaves.

- For winter-blooming orchids like Cymbidium and Miltoniopsis, feed with an organic liquid or granular fertilizer once a month in autumn.

- Give indoor orchids and tropicals a quarter turn each time they are watered for even growth and light exposure.

ANTHURIUM

- Periodically wash indoor orchids and other tropicals and dry off with a soft cloth foliage.

- Crown rot occurs when too much water has been left to stagnate in the crown of a plant, especially orchids. Soak them in a water-filled tub or sink rather than watering overhead.

- Allow Bromeliad pups to remain attached to the parent or carefully remove them when they are ⅓ as large as the parent and plant them upright in cactus mix. Move pups to a more protected area when temperatures dip below 55°F or above 90°F.

NOVEMBER

- Rebuild watering basins and replenish mulch 1-2 inches before winter rains. For freezing winters, increase mulch to 4 inches out to the drip lines, but leave a 4-in. space around the trunks.

- Clean up plant debris, pull out weeds and apply a pre-emergent.

- Mark the plants that are struggling to move them in late spring.

- Dig up Canna Lilies and other rhizomatous plants in autumn and store indoors where temperatures dip below freezing during winter and early spring. Cover rhizomes with loose burlap or compost.

- Don't be afraid of incorporating tropical plants. There are many to select for coastal regions, but there are also cold-tolerant specimens such as Canna Lily and Chinese Yellow Banana and others that can be dug up or moved until warm weather returns.

- Soil pH (most prefer 6.0-6.8 range) and percolation rates are additional considerations.

DECEMBER

- Tropical plants available this time of year are usually greenhouse-grown. Keep indoors through winter in bright indirect light and wait until spring to take outdoors.

- When frost is predicted, cover smaller Palms, Cymbidiums and other frost-sensitive tropical outdoor plants with cotton sheets or frost cloths to prevent damage. Spraying with an anti-transpirant such as Wilt-Pruf or Cloud Cover will offer extra protection as well.

- Purchase stakes to support winter-blooming Cymbidiums (mature Cymbidiums can produce 10-15 floral spikes, each laden with 5-12 blossoms).

- When needed re-pot spring and summer blooming orchids (*Dendrobrium*, *Epidendrum*, *Beallara*, etc.) during winter dormancy and water just enough to keep the roots moist.

- Fertilize winter and early spring-blooming orchids with a half-strength dilution of an organic liquid fertilizer or foliar feed with a seaweed extract about once a month.

- Remember to water all the frost-tender plants you have stored under the eaves and patio covers.

PERENNIALS
for California

Perennials are flowering or foliage plants with life spans of more than two years; they are technically herbaceous, since they lack the woody stems and branches characteristic of shrubs and trees. Although some perennials will last only a few years, others survive for decades. Some have top growth that dies back every winter, but their roots live from year to year and send up new shoots each spring. Perennials give color and texture to gardens in shady spots, slopes, and meadows, and take center stage in casual cottage landscapes. Their abundant foliage and flowers bursting forth from intimate or expansive spaces produce a glorious potpourri of scents, textures, and colors.

GOOD MARRIAGES BETWEEN PLANTS

Before planting, determine if your perennial selections are compatible with each other and with the site, considering light, soil, and water needs. Study the bloom times of perennials in your neighborhood and select plants that flower together, as well as those that flower when nothing else is in bloom. Shasta Daisies, Coreopsis, Delphiniums, and Yarrow bloom from late spring through the end of summer, while Daylilies blossom early, midseason, or late depending on the variety, and Candytuft blooms throughout the year in warm-winter regions.

While some, like Coreopsis, bloom for up to twelve weeks, others, like Delphiniums, rebloom after their first flush of flowers are cut back and before they set seed. Clivia, Lilies and Impatiens are perfect for shaded nooks and crannies under trees or shrubs, but if you need heat lovers and drought-tolerant types, Gerbera Daisies and Wallflowers are better choices.

Perennials ease the transition from one space to another. Because of their more limited longevity, nestle perennial plantings as color, texture, and size accents in front of more permanent shrubs and trees.

Think about foliage as well as flowers, and mix bold-leafed Ivy Geraniums with fine-textured Marguerite Daisies. When designing a perennial border, start with tall, long-lived specimens such as Delphinium, Foxglove, and Daylilies, and stand them in the back. To support their taller neighbors

and peek over their tinier friends, Lily of the Nile, Coreopsis, and Shasta Daisies are great fillers for the middle. Toward the front, plant ground huggers like Candytuft, Ivy Geraniums, or Impatiens. Near ponds, a tropical stand of thirsty Canna Lilies can effectively show off their lush, bold foliage and burgeoning flowers of eye-popping reds, oranges, yellows, and pinks.

In most mild-winter western regions, October is the best time to plant perennials or to divide or take cuttings from established ones. Planting or propagating in autumn gives perennials a head start over those that are planted in the spring.

HEIRLOOMS AND CUT FLOWERS

Part of the joy of gardening is being able to share your plants with others and, in turn, to receive plants from family and friends. Our parents grow an Ivy Geranium variety called 'Rouletta' with magnificent semi-double white-and-magenta-striped clusters of blooms. They gave us some cuttings, and we think of them every time we pass the hanging basket brimming with its trailing foliage and blossoms. Gifts of plants from people who mean so much give a whole new meaning to the word "heirloom."

A drift of Daisies, Lilies or Woolly Yarrow is not only a feast for our eyes, but the petals are perfect cushions for fluttering butterflies, whirring hummingbirds and buzzing bees. Nectar- and berry-rich perennials are important food sources for your garden wildlife. Whether they are flowering or fruiting, we enjoy cutting them to use in colorful mixed bunches of flowers arranged loosely in a favorite vase or in formal, more elegant designs. From the ornate to the minimal, from hot, intense splashes of yellows, reds, oranges, magentas and rusts to cool whites, delicate lavenders, pinks, salmons and creams, perennials make excellent cut-flower arrangements suitable for any decor.

THE SPICE OF LIFE

Perennials prove that "variety is the spice of life." They add color and texture for mass planting

COREOPSIS

displays in meadow and woodland gardens, provide punctuation points for beds and borders, brighten pond and rock landscapes, nourish neighborhood wildlife and beckon the outdoors in with fresh-flower arrangements. Whether you find them while treasure hunting at local nurseries or propagating them from seed, division, or cuttings, perennials serve as precious threads in your garden tapestry.

Nor should we forget how perennials provide the "sigh-factor" in casual cottage landscapes. Without Canterbury Bells, Delphiniums, Foxgloves, Coneflowers, Daisies, Heliotrope, and wandering

Geraniums, there would be no need for white picket fences.

Perennials give color and texture to gardens in shady nooks, sunny slopes, and meadows and brighten pond and rock landscapes. Choosing perennials is limited only by one's imagination. Weave in an abundance of perennials as the more permanent threads in your garden tapestry. From the ornate to the starkly minimal, from the floriferous to the evergreen, perennials provide the "spice" and threaded continuity in a garden.

BLUE MARGUERITE DAISY
Felicia amelloides

Hardiness—Zones 9-11

Color(s)—Blue

Bloom Period—Spring, summer, fall

Mature Size (H & W)—3 ft. x 4 ft.

Water Needs—Initially water Marguerite Daisies frequently, but once established provide deep, infrequent watering rather than shallow, frequent irrigation.

Planting/Care—Plant in spring after danger of frost is over from containers and space 3 ft. apart. Provide full sun, well-draining, slightly acidic soil. Deadhead spent flowers to prolong blooms. Following the bloom cycle, prune to shape and lace out dense growth.

Pests/Diseases—Control snails and slugs with the "pick and squish" method, organic iron phosphate bait or in Southern California use decollate snails.

Landscaping Tips & Ideas—Once established, *Felicia* tolerates drought, seaside and windy conditions and are spectacular in mass plantings as well as lovely companions in mixed flowerbeds a nd containers. Cut them just before their petals unfurl for loose bouquets.

BUTCHER'S BROOM
Ruscus spp.

Hardiness—Zones 7-11

Color(s)—Light- to dark-green foliage

Bloom Period—Insignificant greenish-white flowers off and on during the year

Mature Size (H & W)—1 to 4 ft. x as wide

Water Needs—Water regularly every 7-10 days, and decrease every 10-14 days once established.

Planting/Care—Plant in spring-summer from containers in part to complete shade. Provide well-draining, slightly alkaline soil. Drought tolerant once established.

Pests/Diseases—Few disease or insect problems

Landscaping Tips & Ideas—Adapts and grows underneath established tree roots. *R. hypoglossum* has flattened, leaflike branches (cladodes) and bears tiny flowers in centers of cladodes. It makes an attractive ground cover (18 inches tall) and also used by florists for long-lived greenery (1 month or more). *R. aculeatus* has spine-tipped cladodes and is much slower growing, but will eventually reach 4 feet. It will also bear bright red, marble-like fruits if male and female plants cross-pollinate.

173

CANDYTUFT

Iberis sempervirens

Hardiness—Zones 3-10

Color(s)—White

Bloom Period—Spring-Summer

Mature Size (H & W)—6 to 10 in. x 10 in.

Water Needs—Water frequently until established, then water every 7-10 days depending on growth, bloom and weather conditions.

Planting/Care—Growth is slow, so it is best to plant in the spring or summer from color packs or larger containers and space 8-12 inches apart. Candytuft thrives in hot, sunny, southerly locations in well-draining, slightly acidic soil.

Pests/Diseases—There are no serious pest or disease problems, provided the soil drains well and there is good air circulation.

Landscaping Tips & Ideas—Perennial Candytuft are perfect as accents for rock gardens, en masse as foreground plants or in mixed containers. Their pure white flowers contrast beautifully with the dark-green foliage and mixed colors of other plants. Their candy-scented blossoms last for 5-6 days as cut flowers.

CANNA LILY

Canna x generalis

Hardiness—Zones 9-11

Color(s)—Red, white, pink, yellow, orange, bicolors

Bloom Period—Spring and summer

Mature Size (H & W)—3 to 6 ft. (rhizostomatous, clumping)

Water Needs—With good drainage, it is practically impossible to overwater.

Planting/Care—Plant rhizomes in spring after the last frost from containers, spacing 2 ft. apart. Provide full sun in rich, moisture-retaining, slightly acidic soil. Fertilize in early spring after frost with a complete, organic granular food.

Pests/Diseases—Control giant whitefly with an organic insecticide such as Spinosad or a systemic product containing imidacloprid. For slug and snails use iron phosphate bait, hand-pick or in Southern California use decollate snails.

Landscaping Tips & Ideas—Canna Lily's statuesque banana-like leaves and fiery-hued spikes of flowers add exotic looks to the tropical garden, foliage border and because they are thirsty plants, thrive along ponds and streams.

CHRYSANTHEMUM

Dendranthema x grandiflorum

Hardiness—Zones 5-10

Color(s)—Yellow, orange, white, bronze, green, purple, pink, and red

Bloom Period—Late summer-fall

Mature Size (H & W)—2 to 8 ft. x as wide

Water Needs—Water every 7-10 days.

Planting/Care—Plant from containers in spring, provide full sun and well-draining, humus-amended soil. On large-flowered types, disbud by removing all lateral buds from each stem, leaving only the center bud for the largest bloom and stake stems to support.

Pests/Diseases—Control aphids with a neem or canola-based horticultural oil and use baits to get rid of ants.

Landscaping Tips & Ideas—The true "Queen of Fall Flowers" such as football mums, exotic spiders, Fujis are spectacular in flower beds or containers or flowing cascades in hanging baskets or tumbling over walls. The giant-flowered 'Kokka Bunmi' with light lavender petals and purple reverse, the white spider 'Icicles' and cascading orange-red 'Firefall' are just a few selections.

CLIVIA LILY
Clivia miniata

Hardiness—Zones 9-11

Color(s)—Red, orange, yellow

Bloom Period—Spring

Mature Size (H & W)—2 ft. (clumping)

Water Needs—Water every seven days during spring and summer, but decrease frequency during winter.

Planting/Care—Plant spring-fall from containers in shaded or dappled-light locations and space 2-3 ft. apart. From seed, it needs 3-5 years before flowering. Make sure the soil is well draining and slightly acidic. Fertilize from late winter-early spring with a complete organic granular food.

Pests/Diseases—Control mealybugs with a Neem or canola-based horticultural oil or a systemic insecticide. Get rid of snails and slugs with an iron phosphate molluscicide.

Landscaping Tips & Ideas—Plant these shade lovers under trees or along dappled light borders. When few flowers are in bloom, their trumpet-shaped clusters of red, orange or yellow blossoms provide a floriferous display.

COREOPSIS
Coreopsis grandiflora

Hardiness—Zones 4-10

Color(s)—Orange, yellow

Bloom Period—Spring-fall

Mature Size (H & W)—1 to 2 ft. x 1 ft.

Water Needs—Once established, water deeply once a week at the base of the plant.

Planting/Care—Plant in the spring from seed, color packs or larger containers, spacing 15-18 inches apart and provide full sun in sandy loam, well draining, slightly acidic soil. Fertilize from spring-fall with a complete organic granular food about every other month. Deadhead blooms regularly.

Pests/Diseases—Powdery mildew, aphids and mealybugs can be controlled with neem or canola-based horticultural oil.

Landscaping Tips & Ideas—Coreopsis is one of the easiest perennials to grow. Plant en masse at the edges of lawns, country meadow gardens, background for borders and in mixed containers. Their bright, yellow or orange flowers contrast nicely with Shasta Daisies, Daylilies and Delphiniums.

DAYLILY
Hemerocallis hybrids

Hardiness—Zones 5-10

Color(s)—Yellow, red, orange, pink, white, purple, brown, bicolors

Bloom Period—Spring-Summer

Mature Size (H & W)—2 to 3 ft. (clumping)

Water Needs—Water regularly every 7-10 days, depending on growth and weather conditions.

Planting/Care—Plant in late winter or early spring as soon as soil is workable from containers, spacing 2-3 ft. apart. Daylilies will tolerate partial sun, but thrive best in full sun in well-amended, well draining, slightly acidic soil. Fertilize in early summer with a complete, organic granular food.

Pests/Diseases—Control snails and slugs with an iron phosphate bait or in Southern California use decollate snails.

Landscaping Tips & Ideas—Include Daylilies in planting beds, borders, along meandering paths, at the edges of lawns or woodland, next to shrubs, mass plantings on slopes or near water gardens. Cut flowers when buds are beginning to show color (they bloom for a day).

DELPHINIUM
Delphinium elatum

Hardiness—Zones 3-10

Color(s)—Blue, purple, pink, lavender, magenta, red, white

Bloom Period—Summer, fall

Mature Size (H & W)—2 to 8 ft. x 2 to 4 ft.

Water Needs—Water every 5-7 days at the base of plants.

Planting/Care—Plant in spring from seed, color packs or larger containers and space 2-3 ft. apart. Provide full sun and well-drained, humus amended, slightly acidic soil. Thin out all but 3-4 stalks for air circulation and deadhead spent flowers. Keep away from young children and pets because all parts are toxic.

Pests/Diseases—Control leaf miners and caterpillars with Spinosad and powdery mildew and scale with a canola-based oil.

Landscaping Tips & Ideas—Delphiniums are must-haves for cottage gardens, particularly for cool, moist climates such as the coastal areas of northwest California. Also use for tall background plants in flowerbeds and combine with Foxglove.

FOXGLOVE
Digitalis purpurea

Hardiness—Zones 4-10

Color(s)—Purple, pink, white, rose, yellow

Bloom Period—Spring-midsummer

Mature Size (H & W)—2 to 4 ft. x 2 ft.

Water Needs—Water every 5-7 days depending on growth and weather conditions.

Planting/Care—Plant in early spring from seed or containers spacing 18 inches apart. Provide in full sun or dappled shade in humus amended, well draining, slightly acidic soil. After initial bloom, cut off spike and side shoots will develop and bloom Fertilize in early spring with a complete, organic granular food. Self-seeds freely. Keep away from small children and pets because of toxicity.

Pests/Diseases—Control slugs and snails with an iron phosphate molluscicide.

Landscaping Tips & Ideas—Foxglove is another iconic cottage garden plant, in mass plantings in meadows and woodlands and colorful punctuation accents as medium-height perennials in beds, borders and containers. Mix with Phlox, Roses and Delphiniums.

GERBERA DAISY
(TRANSVAAL DAISY)
Gerbera hybrids

Hardiness—Zones 9-11

Color(s)—Yellow, pink, red, white, orange

Bloom Period—Spring-fall

Mature Size (H & W)—8 to 12 in. x 12 to 16 in.

Water Needs—Once established, water every 5-7 days, depending on growth and weather conditions.

Planting/Care—Plant in spring form containers, spacing 12 inches apart. Plant the crown slightly higher than the surrounding soil level to help prevent root rot.

Pests/Diseases—Control earwigs by rolling up a moistened newspaper and setting it out in the evening. Earwigs are attracted to dark moist spaces. In the morning, throw the paper away in the trash.

Landscaping Tips & Ideas—The large, florist type flowers are excellent in container, but to plant in gardens select the *Gerbera* Everlast series, bred to thrive year after year in borders, planting beds and rock gardens. Their red, orange, pink or white flowers are smaller, but lovely in arrangements.

HELIOTROPE
Heliotrope arborescens

Hardiness—Zones 10-11

Color(s)—Purple, blue, white

Bloom Period—Summer-fall

Mature Size (H & W)—1 to 4 ft. x 1 to 2 ft.

Water Needs—Water regularly every 5-7 days, particularly while plant is immature and from summer-fall.

Planting/Care—For inland regions, plant in part shade and along the coast, full sun. Needs well-draining, humus-amended soil. Fertilize with a complete organic granular food from spring-summer. Trim at the end of bloom cycle for a more compact growth habit. All parts are toxic so keep away from small children and pets.

Pests/Diseases—Control whiteflies by washing off with a strong stream of water or spray with Spinosad. If rust occurs, spray with a canola-based horticultural oil.

Landscaping Tips & Ideas—Heliotrope is a shrubby perennial that lends its purple-flowered cherry or vanilla-like fragrance to flower beds, window boxes, as an edging plant or camouflaging leggier shrubs and vines.

IMPATIENS
Impatiens walleriana

Hardiness—Zones 10-11

Color(s)—Crimson, violet, pink, white

Bloom Period—Spring-fall

Mature Size (H & W)—2 ft. x 3 ft.

Water Needs—Provide frequent water while establishing and water every 5-7 days once established.

Planting/Care—Plant in spring from color packs and space 18 inches on center. Along the coast, plant in full sun, but partial shade inland. Provide amended, well draining and slightly acidic soil. Fertilize once a month spring-summer with an organic liquid food. Pinch back tip growth for a more compact habit.

Pests/Diseases—Spray with a canola-based horticultural oil to control spider mites and use an iron phosphate molluscicide to get rid of snails and slugs.

Landscaping Tips & Ideas—Their bright colored flowers add to sunny or shaded color beds, borders, windowboxes or containers on patios. Combine with English Ivy and Geranium. Known to re-seed readily and also grows easily from cuttings.

IVY GERANIUM
Pelargonium pelatum

Hardiness—Zones 10-11

Color(s)—Red, pink, lavender, white

Bloom Period—Summer

Mature Size (H & W)—8 to 12 in. (spreading)

Water Needs—Water every 7-10 days, depending on growth and weather conditions once established.

Planting/Care—Plant in spring after last frost from color packs or larger containers, spacing 18 inches on center. Provide full or partial shade in well-draining, slightly acidic soil. Feed with a complete liquid fertilizer once a month from spring-fall. Deadhead spent blooms including stalks.

Pests/Diseases—Control snails and slugs with an iron phosphate bait or in Southern California, use decollate snails.

Landscaping Tips & Ideas—Pelargonium flowers have two irregular-shaped upper petals that are different in size and shape from the three lower ones (Geranium flowers have symmetrical petals). Use Ivy Geranium cascading in color baskets, trellises or window boxes. Shasta Daisies, Lilies of the Nile and Pink Indian Hawthorn are ideal companions.

LEOPARD PLANT

Farfugium japonicum
(Ligularia tussilaginea)

Hardiness—Zones 7-10

Color(s)—Green foliage with yellow or cream markings

Bloom Period—Yellow daisy-like flowers fall-winter

Mature Size (H & W)—2 ft. x 2 ft. (spreading rhizomes)

Water Needs—Water regularly every 5-10 days, depending on growth and weather conditions.

Planting/Care—Plant in spring from containers in partial shade. Does best in moist, well-drained, humus-amended slightly acidic soil. Provide a 1-2-in. layer of mulch in hot, dry regions or where prolonged freezes are common.

Pests/Diseases—Keep snails and slugs away with an iron phosphate bait or in Southern California use decollate snails.

Landscaping Tips & Ideas—Prized for their bold and attractive foliage, grow Leopard Plants in borders, containers, along edges of ponds or streams or under the shaded canopies of trees. 'Argenteum' has white markings, 'Aureomaculatum' has yellow speckles and 'Crispatum' has ruffled foliage. Also, use in stylized flower arrangements.

LENTEN ROSE

Helleborus hybrids

Hardiness—Zones 4-10

Color(s)—Lavender, pink, white, purple, black, green

Bloom Period—Winter, spring

Mature Size (H & W)—12 in. x 12 to 18 in.

Water Needs—Water regularly every 5-7 days until established, then decrease to every 7-10 days.

Planting/Care—Plant in late winter-spring from containers. Provide humus-amended, excellent draining, slightly alkaline soil and partial shade. Unlike its Christmas Rose cousin (*H. niger*), it tolerates warm-winter climates and is easier to transplant.

Pests/Diseases—To avoid root rot by provide excellent drainage. For powdery mildew, spray with a canola-based horticultural oil.

Landscaping Tips & Ideas—Lenten Rose adds color to the winter-early spring garden, when few other plants are blooming with their nodding or upright cup or bell-shaped flowers. Deer and rabbit resistant, Plant under trees, in shaded flowerbeds or in containers. Also lovely in cut flower arrangements.

LILY OF THE NILE

Agapanthus africanus

Hardiness—Zones 9-11

Color(s)—Blue, violet-blue, white

Bloom Period—Summer

Mature Size (H & W)—18 in. x (clumping)

Water Needs—Water once a week from spring-summer and during winter every 10 days.

Planting/Care—Plant is spring from containers, spacing 18 inches apart. Provide full sun in well-drained, slightly acidic soil. Feed spring-summer every 45 days with a complete organic granular fertilizer.

Pests/Diseases—Control snails and slugs with an iron phosphate molluscicide.

Landscaping Tips & Ideas—Ideal to use as a foreground plant in front of larger shrubs or in mass plantings near water features, along a wall, fence or driveway. They also combine beautifully in cut-flower gardens or in containers. 'Peter Pan' is a mini grower 8-12 inches tall with 18-in. lavender-blue flowering stems, 'White' and 'Queen Anne' (blue flowers) are moderate growers and 'Streamline' is a rapid grower with grayish-blue flowers.

MADEIRA GERANIUM

Geranium maderense

Hardiness—Zones 9-11

Color(s)—Lavender

Bloom Period—Summer

Mature Size (H & W)—24 to 48 in. x 24 to 48 in.

Water Needs—Water once a week, but once established it is drought tolerant.

Planting/Care—Provide well-draining, slightly acidic soil. It is an understory plant in its native habitat, so plant where there is morning sun and part shade in the afternoon. Do not clip off the lower, brown leaf stalks because they serve as a support for its top-heavy canopy of leaves.

Pests/Diseases—Spray with a canola-based horticultural oil for sawfly and powdery mildew.

Landscaping Tips & Ideas—One of the true Geraniums, this biennial or short-lived perennial gives lots of pizzazz as a stand alone specimen in a large container or as a focal plant in mixed flower beds. It bears hundreds of pink blossoms rising from large leaves so give it plenty of room.

SHASTA DAISY

Chrysanthemum maximum
(Chrysanthemum x superbum)

Hardiness—Zones 4-10

Color(s)—White

Bloom Period—Summer-fall

Mature Size (H & W)—2 ft. (clumping)

Water Needs—Once established, water every 7-10 days. Keep evenly moist but not soggy.

Planting/Care—Plant in spring from seed or containers spacing 12 inches apart. Provide full sun in humus-amended, well draining and slightly acidic soil. Deadhead regularly to encourage a longer flowering cycle and feed once a month with a complete, organic fertilizer spring-fall.

Pests/Diseases—If leaf miner damage is extensive, spray with Spinosad, an organic remedy that will not harm most beneficials (do not spray when bees are present).

Landscaping Tips & Ideas—Developed by Luther Burbank, these large 3-4-in. daisies on 16-in. stems are used by florists for cut flower arrangements and for edging a walkway, in front of hedges or shrubs or grouped in cottage-style perennial borders. Ideal companions are Wallflower and Wooly Yarrow.

WALLFLOWER

Erysimum linifolium

Hardiness—Zones 3-10

Color(s)—Orange, purple, violet, white

Bloom Period—Spring-fall

Mature Size (H & W)—1 to 2 ft. x 2 to 3 ft.

Water Needs—Once established, water every 7-10 days and allow to dry out slightly between watering.

Planting/Care—Plant in spring or fall from seed or containers spacing 2 feet apart. Provide full sun along the coast, part shade inland in well-draining, slightly acidic soil. Fertilize every month with a complete, organic food spring-summer. After blooming, prune back about 20% to prevent woody thatch and to encourage new growth.

Pests/Diseases—Control aphids, spider mites and mealybugs with a Neem or canola-based horticultural oil.

Landscaping Tips & Ideas—Wallflowers are effective in drier areas such as rock gardens, planted in walls, on slopes or combined with other drought tolerant plants such as Shasta Daisies and Lavender. They also make lovely, easy maintenance container plants.

WOOD VIOLET
Viola odorata

Hardiness—Zones 4-10

Color(s)—Violet

Bloom Period—Spring

Mature Size (H & W)—4 to 6 in. x 8 to 24 in.

Water Needs—Water every 5-7 days depending on growth and weather conditions and decrease frequency in winter.

Planting/Care—Plant in spring or fall from containers spacing 6-10 inches apart. Provide humus amended, slightly acidic, well draining loam soil in partial shade. To lengthen bloom season, remove spent flowers and feed monthly with a complete organic liquid fertilizer from spring-summer.

Pests/Diseases—Protect from snails and slugs with an iron phosphate bait or hand-pick. In Southern California use decollate snails or bait but not both.

Landscaping Tips & Ideas—Nestle Wood Violets under the canopy of trees or peeking out of shaded rock gardens, border edges or containers. Cut their purple, aromatic flowers just as they are beginning to open and enjoy indoors.

WOOLY YARROW
Achillea tomentosa

Hardiness—Zones 3-10

Color(s)—Yellow

Bloom Period—Summer

Mature Size (H & W)—4 to 12 in. (spreading)

Water Needs—Once established, allow to dry slightly before watering, about every 10 days, depending on growth and weather conditions.

Planting/Care—Plant in spring from seed or containers spacing 10 to 12 inches apart. Provide full sun is well draining, sandy loam, neutral soil. Feed once in spring with a complete organic fertilizer and deadhead unless you want seeds to spread. Divide overgrown clumps every 3-4 years in early spring or fall.

Pests/Diseases—Control powdery mildew or rust with a canola-based horticultural oil or use an organic fungicide.

Landscaping Tips & Ideas—Plant along pathways so that you can brush up against Wooly Yarrow to release their spicy fragrance. They also look wonderful in cut flower, herb or meadow gardens, as well as ground cover or in containers.

MORE RECOMMENDATIONS

- BERGENIA (*Bergenia cordifolia*) Zones 4-10. 6 to 12 in. x as wide. Bold cabbage-like leaves are perfect in partial shady areas. 'Evening Glow' bears bell-shaped red flowers in spring and 'Tubby Andrews' has golden variegation or entirely pale gold foliage with pale-pink flowers in spring and fall.

- HOSTA (*Hosta* hybrids) Zones 4-9. 1 to 2 ft. x 1 to 5 ft. Hostas are made for the shade, easy to grow and require little care in rock gardens and massed plantings. 'Guacamole' is one of the most fragrant with large, white and lavender flowers. 'Sieboldiana Elegans' has large, corrugated blue-green leaves that are slug-resistant once established.

- LAVENDER (*Lavandula* spp.) Zones 5-9. 2 to 3 ft. x as wide. Fragrant lavender blue spikes from late spring to summer. 'Hidcote Superior' is very floriferous and compact, 'Provence' is used for sachets or in herb gardens, 'Winter Bee' bears dark purple flowers and tolerates heat, humidity and cold wet weather and 'Hazel' is ideal for water-thrifty gardens.

- PEONY (*Paeonia* spp.) Zones 3-8. 1 to 3 ft. x 2 to 3 ft. Large, double or single-petaled gorgeous and fragrant blossoms. The Chinese or French Peonies (*P. lactiflora* hybrids) die back in the fall. 'Avalanche' is one of the most fragrant white peonies, 'Victor de la Marne' is dark pink and 'Pillow Talk' is pale pink. For Southern California gardeners, some grafted tree peonies can grow successfully as long as winter temperatures are in the 30-40°F range.

- PURPLE CONEFLOWER (*Echinacea purpurea*) Zones 3-9. 2 to 4 ft. x 1 to 2 ft. This sun-loving, deer-resistant perennial bears long-lasting blooms with vigorous stems that do not need staking and perfect for butterfly and water-thrifty gardens. 'Magnus' bears 4-in. magenta flowers, 'Ruby Star' has carmine red blossoms and 'Fragrant' offers white, perfumed flowers.

DELPHINIUM

JANUARY

- Catch up on plant catalogues, scan websites and your garden journal to make decisions about next year's perennial garden.

- Grow perennials in areas that can be renovated periodically because at some point, they must be replaced.

- Intersperse with more permanent shrubs like Pink Indian Hawthorn or Wheeler's Dwarf Pittosporum to make renovation periods less obvious.

- For a perennial border design, start with tall specimen such as Delphinium in the back, mid-high Shasta Daisies to support the taller neighbors and compact or ground-hugging Candytuft toward the front or as fillers for blank spaces.

- Winter is a good time to test the condition of the irrigation system. Remove, clear, reinstall and adjust all clogged irrigation or drip system heads.

- Keep out deer by erecting stakes 10 ft. apart and attaching monofilament line 3 ft. off the ground around perennial beds. When deer approach, they feel it but cannot see, frightening them away.

FEBRUARY

- Start Coneflower, Coreopsis and other perennials from seed indoors and follow the package directions.

- No fertilizing of perennials is necessary except for seedlings. Use a water-soluble organic fertilizer diluted to ¼ the normal rate and begin feeding once every 2 weeks after two sets of true leaves have emerged.

- If deer and rabbits are a problem, add perennials such as Candytuft, Foxglove, Lenten Rose, Lavender, Purple Coneflower and Yarrow that are resistant, particularly if physical barriers are impractical.

- Prepare the soil in perennial beds when the ground is workable by turning it over to a depth of 1 ft., blending in 2 cubic ft. bags of organic amendment per 100 square ft.

- Continue to water container plants and keep seedlings, divisions and newly rooted cuttings evenly moist.

- Cut off old perennial flower spikes and divide overgrown clumping perennials.

MARCH

- Spring is when many perennials are in their full glory. Visit local public gardens and walk around the neighborhood for fresh ideas.

- Plant summer and fall flowering and foliar perennials after the danger of frost has passed, which can be as early as St. Patrick's Day or as late as Mother's Day, depending on the region.

- Select and plant perennials such as Geraniums and Shasta Daisies that have long bloom periods. Also look for Garden Gerberas because they are bred to flourish in the ground, unlike pot-cultured florist-type varieties.

- Newly planted or transplanted perennials should be thoroughly watered. Apply enough water to wet the soil to a depth of 8-10 inches to settle the soil and collapse any air pockets around the roots.

- Follow planting with an application of a root stimulator containing indolebutyric or naphthalene acetic acid, three times two weeks apart to develop new roots and protect the existing ones.

APRIL

- Remove weeds and grasses that have survived the winter by hand pulling or carefully hoeing them out of your perennial bed. Use a pre-emergent if you are not starting perennials from seed to prevent future weed seeds from germinating.

- Make sure there is a 2-in. layer of mulch around perennials from the root flare to the drip line (leave a 2-3-in. space at the trunk or main stem) to stabilize soil temperature, retain moisture and prevent weeds.

- Fertilize perennials with a complete organic granular or liquid food about once a month to keep the soil and plants healthy.

- Divide and transplant summer and fall blooming perennials such as Hostas and Shasta Daisies, but leave spring bloomers alone until fall. Keep evenly moist but not waterlogged.

- Pinch back new growth when it reaches 4-6 inches for more branch development and compact growth. As frost-damaged perennials begin to grow, prune and remove the damaged parts.

MAY

- Protect perennials from rabbits, deer and squirrels with physical barriers, olfactory repellents, traps or motion-activated lights or sprinklers. If using live traps, contact the California Department of Fish and Game to find out if live-trapping and releasing is allowed in your area.

- Control insect pests by releasing beneficial insects like lady beetles and lacewings available at nurseries and insectories.

- The stream of ants that you see represents just ten percent of the entire colony. Follow the ant stream to the back of the line and place ant baits near the nest. The workers will carry the bait to the nest killing the queen and the entire colony in a few days.

- Some tall or sprawling perennials need extra help against wind. Stake Delphinium and other stately growers to help them stand tall.

- Deadhead perennial flowers as they fade to prolong their bloom production and to divert energy back into the plants rather than into seed production.

JUNE

- Ask a friend or neighbor to water your garden perennials while away on vacation, especially those in containers.

- Soak perennials every 7-10 days, depending on weather, humidity and soil conditions, but be aware that established plants such as Yarrow and Wallflower are drought tolerant and prefer to dry out slightly before watering.

- Water container plants whenever soil has dried 1 inch below the surface, but during prolonged, hot dry spells, water as often as once a day.

- Studies indicate that the optimum time to water containers during summer is between noon and 6 PM increasing growth and photosynthesis production by as much as seventy percent compared to morning watering. Also it was found that the beads of water are not magnified by sunshine, nor do they cause sunburn.

- Remove spent flowers once a week to encourage more blooms.

- Control weeds by mulching and removing by hand if there was no application of a pre-emergent.

JULY

- Prune back spring-blooming perennials to encourage re-blooming such as Geraniums.

- Broadcast a complete organic granular fertilizer around perennials planted in the soil or containers. Water in immediately after application and rinse off foliage.

- Control powdery mildew by spraying with an anti-transpirant in the morning or with a canola-based horticultural oil.

- Local nurseries and garden club plant sales are great places to look for colorful perennials that are "in the zone," but plant them late in the afternoon or early evening to avoid rapid moisture loss during summer. Apply a root stimulator and spray with an anti-transpirant to keep the foliage moist and supple.

- Release beneficial predators such as lady beetles to control aphids or wash off with a stream of water or spray with a canola-based horticultural oil.

- For exhibition-sized Chrysanthemum flowers, select 1-3 stems and remove any side branches. Take off all flower buds except the terminal flowering bud.

AUGUST

- Trim overgrown plants now allowing time to put out new growth before winter. Lace-out woody growth to increase air circulation and allow sunlight to enter the interior of plants.

- Consider replacing perennials in late summer or early fall when they become less vigorous, woody or when they don't respond with new growth after being fertilized and pruned.

- Trap earwigs by setting a wet, rolled up newspaper under perennials—they love cool, humid environments. Then pick up the roll and discard it.

- Whether using an automatic drip irrigation system or hand watering, make sure there is enough water percolating to a depth of about 8 inches. Determine this by shoveling down or using a tensiometer or soil probe.

- Avoid watering perennials from overhead to help prevent black spot, mildew and rust.

- For established perennials that have completed their grow and bloom cycles, fertilize one last time at summer's end with a complete, organic granular food.

SEPTEMBER

- Next to spring, fall is the best time to plant perennials in the garden. In regions where winter freezes are common, delay until spring.

- If perennials with different growing needs are planted in the same area, regroup them so that they are more compatible. Cluster the thirstier perennials and separate them from the more drought-tolerant ones.

- Consider replacing annuals with perennials to fill in the spaces among shrubs and under trees. Butcher's Broom grows under established trees where nothing else will grow. Growth is slow, but worth the wait.

- Apply a humic acid product twice a year around perennials to provide nutrients to beneficial soil microbes, once in fall and once in spring. Humic acids also help protect tender plants from freezing.

- Divide and transplant spring-blooming perennials and plant them at the same level as their original location.

- Water perennials thoroughly the afternoon or evening before predicted hot, dry winds or low humidity.

OCTOBER

- Spread or rebuild a 2-in. fresh layer of organic mulch around perennials to insulate roots from cold weather.

- Apply a pre-emergent weed control to save backbreaking work in spring. Do not apply if starting perennials from seeds.

IVY GERANIUM

- There is a wide selection of blooming Chrysanthemums available in autumn. Select the color, shape and sizes of your choice and plant at the same level as their original containers.

- Once cool weather settles in and the danger of Santa Ana or Diablo winds have passed, adjust the irrigation clocks to accommodate the change in weather, daylight hours and the slowdown in plant growth.

- Decrease the amount and frequency of watering but maintain enough to keep roots moist. Withhold water from perennials that go dormant.

- Continue to stake perennials that are still growing and blooming such as Chrysanthemums. Pull up stakes and supports that are no longer being used, rinse off and store.

NOVEMBER

- Prepare perennials for the upcoming winter by clearing and disposing of dead or diseased branches, foliage, stems and spent flowers. Add them to compost piles if there are no signs of disease or insects.

- Withhold fertilizer until early spring for perennials.

- Protect plants that are still blooming from frost by covering them overnight with a cotton sheet, horticultural blanket or spray with an anti-transpirant.

- Move containers of frost tender perennials to more protected areas under eaves or if practical, indoors.

- Cut Chrysanthemums back to just a few inches above the soil after their bloom cycle is over and they will rebound in spring. Prune back any other perennials that bloomed in the fall after their flowers are spent.

- If plants suddenly collapse, root rot or water molds may be the cause. Remove the plants, dry the soil and treat with compost tea, humic acid and worm castings to increase the population of beneficial microorganisms.

DECEMBER

- Record overnight temperatures and rainfall with a high-low thermometer and a rain gauge to chart the results in a garden journal for future reference.

- Adjust watering pattern for winter conditions, decreasing water and frequency to plants no longer growing.

- Make sure containers moved under eaves and patios receive sufficient moisture.

- Test the pH of the soil with a test kit, because many California soils are alkaline. The optimum pH range for most perennials is 6.5-7.0.

- Spray with a canola-based horticultural oil if insects and diseases were prevalent during the growing season such as soft brown scale, aphids and thrips. Spray when there is no rain predicted for 72 hours.

- Look for pockets in the garden that have poor drainage. Mark the areas with stakes and take steps to improve drainage now or in spring by amending the soil with more organic material, cutting drainage trenches or re-grading if necessary.

CHRYSANTHEMUM

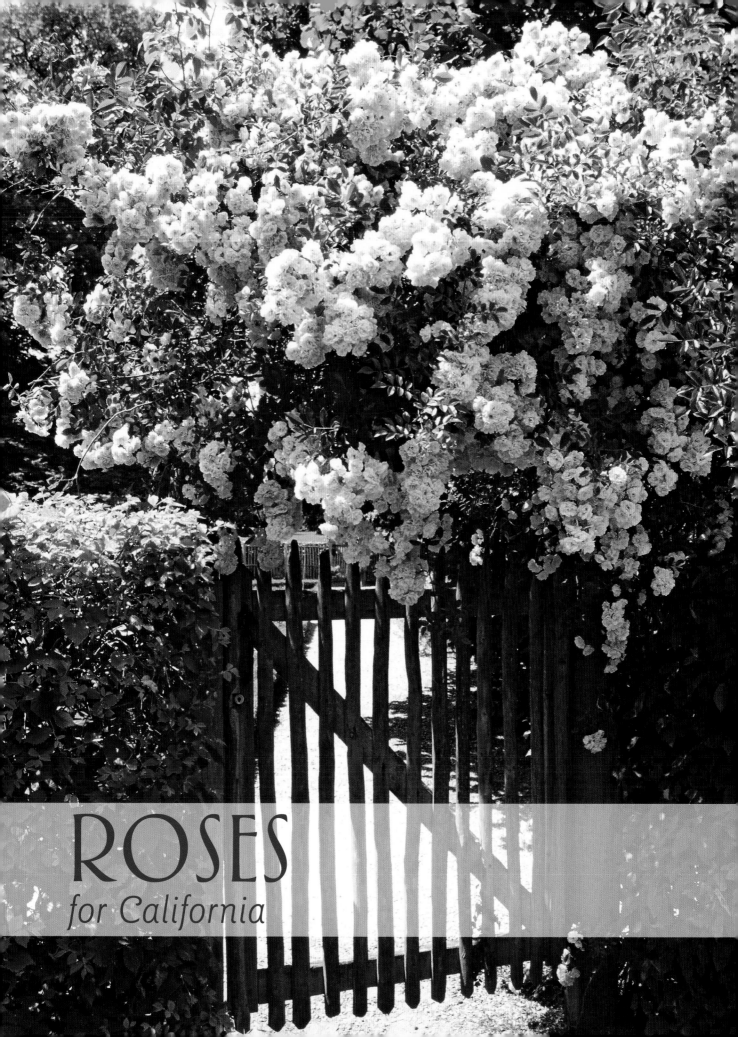

ROSES
for California

There is never a time when the sun isn't shining on roses somewhere in the world. As the sun glides from east to west, its rays continually bathe buds of the world's most popular flower. Roses can be found on just about every continent, but there is one location that can be called the "Rose Growing Capital of the World"—towns with names like Visalia, Wasco, Reedley, Del Rey, and Shafter.

During winter the magnificent snow-capped Sierra Nevadas lie to the east of Visalia. The ancient Kern River once flowed from these mountains into the San Joaquin Valley between Bakersfield and Oildale. Its flow transported rich soil down to the valley floor, creating an immense alluvial fan. Southward is the rain-shadow side of Southern California's Transverse mountain ranges and westward is the eastern side of California's Coastal range. These mountains block the ocean breezes originating along California's central coast. All of these factors have created the perfect area to grow roses and this region is home to millions of roses that eventually find their way into rose gardens around the world.

CALIFORNIA WEATHER

Most years the seasons are as they should be, crisp and clear in the spring and fall, warm in the summer and cold and rainy in the winter. When normalcy prevails, spring and summer are the seasons in which roses need the most water.

Two events create obstacles to producing perfect roses. The first event occurs when Central and Southern California experience an El Niño phenomenon that produces exceptionally wet weather or dry weather and warmer than average winters. When the effect is very wet and temperatures are mild, roses tend not to go dormant or roses begin an early growth and bloom season. So in late December or early January, force dormancy by pruning and stripping off the foliage. La Niña causes above-average rainfall in Northern California and below-average precipitation in Southern California.

The second event occurs in the late summer or early fall, when high-pressure cells build up over the Nevada Mountains. The pressure differential with the air mass over California generates the "foehn phenomenon," otherwise known as the Santa Ana winds in southern California, the Diablo wind in the East Bay hills and the Chinooks from the Pacific Northwest. These are fast moving winds that desiccate everything in their paths. Fortunately the winds can be predicted, so roses can be irrigated and protected prior to the event.

Along the Pacific Coast, Saint Patrick's Day is usually a marker for the last frost day. The further inland your garden is, the further into the year the last frost date moves. If an El Niño or La Niña event leads to increased rainfall, it may over saturate the soil, particularly if drainage is poor, increasing harmful pathogens and destroying root systems. By adding organic amendments such as humus and compost as well as applying mycorrhizal fungi, saponin and humic acid products, the soil will be well-draining, healthy and better able to withstand above average rainfall or drought.

HOW TO CHOOSE

It is easy to become overwhelmed by the thousands of roses available for the garden and the best advice is to first do some homework. Visit several public and private rose gardens in your area and contact the local Rose Society chapter, the University Cooperative Extension and your nearby nursery. From Rose Hills in Whittier, Huntington Gardens in San Marino to the Golden Gate Park Rose Garden in San Francisco and Filoli Center in Woodside are just a few of many gardens to visit for ideas.

Fragrance might be another consideration since the first thing one does when passing a rose is to tenderly cup its beckoning blossom in hand and inhale its fragrance. To encourage the hybridization of more fragrant roses, Dr. James Gamble established the James Alexander Gamble Fragrance Medal under the auspices of the American Rose Society with the stipulation that the winning selection must also have an ARS rating of at least 7.5 on a 1 to 10 scale.

When a rose has won your heart and nose, purchase only Grade #1 plants from a source, which guarantees the success of the plant. #1 canes are husky and vigorous, #1½ are thinner and less vigorous, and #2 are very small. With roses, you get what you pay for, and buying cheap is usually not economical in the long run.

BRINGING OUTDOOR BEAUTY INDOORS

To insure the maximum longevity of cut roses, pick them in the early morning or late afternoon. Use sharp, sterilized shears to snip the stems just above a leaf that has five or more leaflets, because a new branch will not form if you cut above a three-leaflet leaf. Also cut above a leaflet that is facing outward from the center of the bush, the direction where replacement roses are to grow. Once indoors, immerse in tepid water mixed with a powdered floral preservative. Give the stems a fresh cut under water at an angle before arranging them to prevent air bubbles from forming and to allow them to uptake water.

CLASSES OF ROSES

Although roses can be classified into numerous categories, it is impossible to cover everything. This chapter includes several climbing roses, floribundas, grandifloras, groundcovers, hybrid teas, miniatures and shrubs with additional recommendations for English, minifloras, old garden roses and polyanthas.

Climbers have large arching stems that frame windows, outline arches, poles, fences, pergolas, walls and old trees. They also serve as background for border plants, including bush roses and add spectacular vertical color.

Floribundas bloom abundantly and, in most cases, in clusters. If you remove the center bud, the surrounding buds will open simultaneously, creating an instant bouquet.

Grandifloras are taller than hybrid teas or floribundas and bear blossoms that resemble hybrid tea flowers on long stems, but they are borne in clusters.

Although certain climbers have been anchored and trained to cover expansive areas, recent groundcover roses have been developed to grow horizontally in low, dense habits without any training fuss and carpeting bare ground easily.

Hybrid teas are erect growers with single, often large-headed flowers typically used in florist arrangements. With their long stems and elegant blooms, they make classic cut flowers, and can be combined with other perennials in border plantings.

The word "miniature" refers to the bloom size, not the bush size. Ranging in height from six inches to four feet, miniatures allow a gardener to have an extensive rose display in a tiny space in low borders, window boxes and hanging baskets, climbing on small trellises or nestling in rock gardens.

Shrub roses, often known as landscape roses have been bred to be easy growing, disease resistant, summer and winter-hardy. They are perfect for areas where disease and weather conditions make other types of roses more of a growing challenge.

The allure of roses is irresistible and when its perfume matches its beauty, then the blending of these two traits creates an alchemy that transports us to a world of magical wonder. With recent developments among rose hybridizers and effective organic methods of gardening, successful rose culture is relatively simple. Hopefully this chapter will transform "rosy" dreams into landscape reality.

ALTISSIMO (CLIMBER)
Rosa hybrid

Hardiness—Zones 5 and higher

Color(s)—Crimson

Bloom Period—Spring-fall

Mature Size (H & W)—8 to 15 ft. x 6 to 8 ft.

Water Needs—Water 3 times weekly during the first few weeks, once established water every 5-7 days, depending on growth and weather conditions.

Planting/Care—Plant in late winter-early spring from bareroot stock or just about any time from containers. Provide full sun, sandy loam soil and ties to train on supports. Fertilize with a complete, organic granular rose food from spring-summer. Climbers usually bloom on second-year or older growth. Leave 4-8 structural canes, including some of last year's laterals.

Pests/Diseases—Disease resistant, but for chewing insects spray with Spinosad.

Landscaping Tips & Ideas—With large, abundant flowers and repeat blooming habit, 'Altissimo' is stunning as an espalier, trellis or pillar plant, as well as tumbling over a fence or wall.

FOURTH OF JULY (CLIMBER)
Rosa hybrid

Hardiness—Zones 5 and higher

Color(s)—4 inch red and white striped flowers

Bloom Period—Spring-fall

Mature Size (H & W)—10 to 15 ft. x 6 ft.

Water Needs—Water regularly during spring-summer, but decrease during fall and withhold during winter.

Planting/Care—Follow planting instruction for 'Altissimo' and plant with the bud union slightly above the surrounding soil.

Pests/Diseases—Disease and pest resistant, but if aphids become a problem, wash off with a stream of water or spray with a canola-based horticultural oil. Stop ants from "farming" the aphids by setting out baits for the workers to take back to the queen and the rest of the colony.

Landscaping Tips & Ideas—One of the best striped climbers with semi-double, apple-scented, repeat-blooming flowers. It was the first climber to win an AARS award in 23 years. Provide a pergola, arch or trellis for years of beauty.

SALLY HOLMES
(CLIMBER)
Rosa hybrid

Hardiness—Zones 5 and higher

Color(s)—Opens pale apricot and ages into white.

Bloom Period—Spring-fall

Mature Size (H & W)—10 to 15 ft. x 6 ft.

Water Needs—Soak deeply after planting. Water 3 times the first week and adjust thereafter according to climatic and growth conditions. Keep evenly moist spring-summer, decrease in fall and withhold during winter dormancy.

Planting/Care—Same planting instructions as 'Altissimo'.

Pests/Diseases—Few disease problems, but if thrips and sawfly larva are damaging the flowers, spray with Spinosad.

Landscaping Tips & Ideas—Huge 40-50 clusters of sweetly fragrant white blossoms tinted with a hint of apricot. Can grow as a shrub, but this repeat bloomer shows off best as a climber along a fence, arbor or pillar. Use a darker façade or support as a contrast to these bright, creamy-white flowers.

JOSEPH'S COAT
(CLIMBER)
Rosa hybrid

Hardiness—Zones 5 and higher

Color(s)—Multi-colored orange, pink, yellow, red and white flowers

Bloom Period—Spring-fall

Mature Size (H & W)—4 to 10 ft. x 3 to 10 ft.

Water Needs—Soak deeply after planting. Water 3 times the first week and adjust thereafter according to climatic and growth conditions. Keep evenly moist spring-summer, decrease in fall and withhold during winter dormancy.

Planting/Care—Follow planting instructions for 'Altissimo'. Wear rugged thorn-proof gloves when handling and training this tough climber.

Pests/Diseases—Deer resistant, but susceptible to mildew and blackspot. Spray with a canola-based horticultural oil.

Landscaping Tips & Ideas—Joseph's Coat is a repeat bloomer that brightens an arbor or pergola with its rainbow of colors and light fruity fragrance. Because of its thorny habit, it is also ideal for establishing boundaries and property lines.

ENCHANTED EVENING
(FLORIBUNDA)
Rosa hybrid

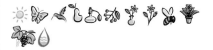

Hardiness—Zones 5 and higher

Color(s)—3½-in. lavender flowers

Bloom Period—Spring-fall

Mature Size (H & W)—3 to 4 ft. x as wide

Water Needs—Soak deeply 3 times weekly the first few weeks, once established adjust frequency and amount according to climatic and growth conditions.

Planting/Care—Plant from bareroot stock in late winter or early spring or almost any time of the year from containers. Provide full sun, sandy loam and slightly acidic soil. Fertilize with a complete organic granular rose food spring-summer. After 12 months, prune lightly for shape and remove ⅓ of its height if necessary.

Pests/Diseases—Resistant to black spot, mildew and rust.

Landscaping Tips & Ideas—One of the best mauve-lavender floribundas with large clusters of lavender, citrus-scented, ruffled blossoms. Plant toward the front of mixed perennials, beds, borders or in containers to enjoy its heavenly perfume.

HOT COCOA
(FLORIBUNDA)
Rosa hybrid

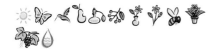

Hardiness—Zones 5 and higher

Color(s)—Chocolate with tints of purple and cinnamon-orange

Bloom Period—Spring-fall

Mature Size (H & W)—3 to 4 ft. x as wide

Water Needs—Same as Enchanted Evening

Planting/Care—Same as Enchanted Evening. 2003 AARS winner. Continues to bloom even in warmer weather.

Pests/Diseases—As a recent AARS winner, it has been tested throughout the United States and has been found to be disease and insect resistant.

Landscaping Tips & Ideas—Hot Cocoa's unique color, strong growth, lovely thick, velvety petals and moderate old-rose fragrance makes it a must for a focal spot in the garden. Mix this bold-colored rose with bright orange or lavender roses or other hot-colored perennials and shrubs or against a white fence or wall as a contrast to Hot Cocoa's blossoms.

JULIA CHILD
(FLORIBUNDA)
Rosa hybrid

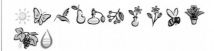

Hardiness—Zones 5 and higher

Color(s)—Butter-gold

Bloom Period—Spring-fall

Mature Size (H & W)—3 to 4 ft. x as wide

Water Needs—Same as Enchanted Evening

Planting/Care—Same as Enchanted Evening. A consistent, floriferous and hardy rose in all climates.

Pests/Diseases—Very disease resistant, but if thrips or sawfly larva damage the blossoms, spray with Spinosad, an organic remedy that will not harm most beneficial insects. For bees, spray in the late afternoon or early evening when they have returned to their hive.

Landscaping Tips & Ideas—Julia Child personally selected this butter gold floribunda with a strong licorice candy and spicy perfume. It has an old-fashioned rose form with an over 35 petal count. Think outside the box and plant this beautiful yellow rose amidst a vegetable and herb garden or combine with other fragrant orange, peach or yellow roses or perennials.

TRUMPETER
(FLORIBUNDA)
Rosa hybrid

Hardiness—Zones 5 and higher

Color(s)—Scarlet orange

Bloom Period—Spring-fall

Mature Size (H & W)—3 ft. x 2 to 3 ft.

Water Needs—Same as Enchanted Evening

Planting/Care—Same as Enchanted Evening

Pests/Diseases—Very disease resistant, but if aphids or scale become problems, spray with a canola-based horticultural oil. If temperatures exceed 85°F, wait until late afternoon or early evening to prevent burning the foliage.

Landscaping Tips & Ideas—One of Trumpeter's parents is 'Satchmo' and it is known to blow its own horn by blooming from early spring to winter as long as the weather is mild. It is a low maintenance plant that blends in well with other companions or as the centerpiece in containers. For eye-popping color, mass them along walkway, entrances, as low hedges or border plants. Although Trumpeter has a light fragrance, its main appeal is brilliant color and easy care.

191

CRIMSON BOUQUET
(GRANDIFLORA)
Rosa hybrid

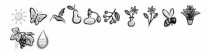

Hardiness—Zones 4 to 10

Color(s)—Red

Bloom Period—Spring-fall

Mature Size (H & W)—4½ ft. x as wide

Water Needs—Same as 'Cherry Parfait'

Planting/Care—Same as 'Cherry Parfait'. As with other grandifloras, do not prune when newly planted, but once established, prune to cut out old, dead or interfering branches. In mild winter areas, prune the remaining canes by ⅓ in late winter, but where winter freezes are common, prune back 40-50% in early spring.

Pests/Diseases—Very disease resistant in a wide range of climates, but if chewing insects become a problem, spray with Spinosad. Once dry, Spinosad is not harmful to bees.

Landscaping Tips & Ideas—A 2000 AARS award winner, 'Crimson Bouquet' flowers in large masses of fabulous double clear red blooms. Since it is not as tall as other grandifloras, it is ideal for hedges or combined with other perennials, shrubs or roses in the landscape.

CHERRY PARFAIT
(GRANDIFLORA)
Rosa hybrid

Hardiness—Zones 5 and higher

Color(s)—White edged in red

Bloom Period—Spring-fall

Mature Size (H & W)—5 ft. x 4 to 5 ft.

Water Needs—Soak 3 times weekly the first few weeks after planting and once established, water every 5-7 days, depending on growth and weather conditions.

Planting/Care—Plant from bareroot stock in late winter or early spring or almost any time of the year from containers. Provide full sun, sandy loam and slightly acidic soil. Fertilize with a complete organic granular rose food late winter-summer. Once established, prune before new growth and cut to an outward-facing bud, about ⅓ of its original height.

Pests/Diseases—Excellent disease resistance. Use a miticide or horticultural oil for spider mites.

Landscaping Tips & Ideas—'Cherry Parfait' bears bouquets of lightly fragrant, 4-in. flowers spring-fall. They blend well with other perennials, shrubs, as well as other roses.

FAME!
(GRANDIFLORA)
Rosa hybrid

Hardiness—Zones 5 or higher

Color(s)—Deep-pink

Bloom Period—Spring-fall

Mature Size (H & W)—4 ft. x as wide

Water Needs—Same as 'Cherry Parfait'

Planting/Care—Same as 'Cherry Parfait' and 'Crimson Bouquet'

Pests/Diseases—Disease resistant, but if rust or mildew begins to spread, spray with a canola-based horticultural oil underneath and on the surface of foliage. During temperatures above 85°F, spray in the late afternoon or early evening. Also pick up and dispose of leaves around the plant.

Landscaping Tips & Ideas—When 'Fame' unfurls its 4½-in. blossoms, it has lovely ruffled edges. It is also one of the longest-lived cut roses and holds up very well in the landscape. Its beauty and continuous flowering more than compensate for a mild, slight fragrance. A 1998 AARS award winner, use as a focal point in an entryway or as a foundation plant in a mixed landscape.

QUEEN ELIZABETH
(GRANDIFLORA)
Rosa hybrid

Hardiness—Zones 5 and higher

Color(s)—Pink

Bloom Period—Spring-fall

Mature Size (H & W)—5 to 8 ft. x 4 to 6 ft.

Water Needs—Same as 'Cherry Parfait'

Planting/Care—Same as 'Cherry Parfait' and 'Crimson Bouquet'

Pests/Diseases—Despite its robust growth, it can be susceptible to powdery mildew, rust or aphid infestations. Spray with a canola-based horticultural oil or a systemic fungicide and insecticide.

Landscaping Tips & Ideas—'Queen Elizabeth' was the first designated grandiflora in 1955 in honor of the real Princess's accession to the throne and deserves to be the reigning monarch with 4-in., clear pink blossoms and a gentle tea-rose perfume. On long, almost thornless stems, 'Queen Elizabeth' flowers are marvelous in bouquets. Because of her statuesque height, use as a stand-alone specimen near a doorway or garden entrance or as a background plant behind lower-growing plants.

BABY BLANKET
(GROUNDCOVER)
Rosa hybrid

Hardiness—Zones 5 and higher

Color(s)—Pink

Bloom Period—Spring-fall

Mature Size (H & W)—3 ft. x 6 ft.

Water Needs—Thoroughly soak after planting, water 3 times weekly the first few weeks and once established every 5-7 days, depending on growth and climate conditions.

Planting/Care—Plant from bareroot stock in late winter or early spring or almost any time of the year from containers. Provide full sun, sandy loam and slightly acidic soil. Fertilize with a complete organic granular rose food spring-summer. For groundcovers, prune only dead wood and any vertical-growing stems.

Pests/Diseases—Excellent disease resistance, but protect from snail and slug damage with an iron phosphate bait.

Landscaping Tips & Ideas—One of the first groundcover roses, 'Baby Blanket' is ideal for difficult slopes, rocky areas and steep banks as well as cascading over hanging baskets or mixed containers. Also, perfect bordering along driveways.

HAPPY CHAPPY
(GROUNDCOVER)
Rosa hybrid

Hardiness—Zones 5 and higher

Color(s)—Bright-orange, pink and yellow flowers

Bloom Period—Spring-first frost

Mature Size (H & W)—2 ft. x 3 ft.

Water Needs—Same as 'Baby Blanket'

Planting/Care—Same as 'Baby Blanket'. Holds up to summer heat and keeps on blooming. Gives quick, wide-spreading coverage.

Pests/Diseases—Same as 'Baby Blanket'. Tough disease resistance, but watch out for browsing deer, rabbits, moles and gophers. Discourage deer and rabbits with olfactory repellents or motion-activated lights or sprinklers. For gophers and moles use manual traps.

Landscaping Tips & Ideas—Same as 'Baby Blanket'. A unique multicolored groundcover rose that remains covered in flowers from spring through first frost. Not only is 'Happy Chappy' a bright, colorful groundcover in orange, pink and yellow flowers, it is a quick-growing solution for any problem area. Use to cover bare spaces in between perennials and shrubs or in between taller roses.

PEACH DRIFT
(GROUNDCOVER)
Rosa hybrid

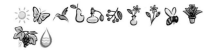

Hardiness—Zones 5 and higher

Color(s)—Peachy-pink

Bloom Period—Spring-first frost

Mature Size (H & W)—18 in. x 24 in.

Water Needs—See 'Baby Blanket'

Planting/Care—See 'Baby Blanket'. As with all groundcovers, plant at the same level as its original container and make sure the soil drains very well.

Pests/Diseases—Relatively disease resistant, but rose midges (larvae of tiny flies) and thrips (yellow or brown insects) cause deformed leaves and buds, often falling off before opening. Most common during summer, spray with Spinosad every 7-10 days until the problem has been remedied.

Landscaping Tips & Ideas—Drift roses have been crossed with normal-sized groundcover roses, miniatures and polyanthas for use in small garden spaces such as a sunny atrium and mixed containers on patio decks. The Drift series ('Ivory', 'Pink', 'Red' and 'Peach') are petite-growers and among them, 'Peach' is the most floriferous of the series.

SNOW CONE
(GROUNDCOVER)
Rosa hybrid

Hardiness—Zones 5 and higher

Color(s)—Pure-white

Bloom Period—Spring-fall

Mature Size (H & W)—2 ft. x as wide

Water Needs—Same as 'Baby Blanket'

Planting/Care—Same as 'Baby Blanket'

Pests/Diseases—Excellent disease resistance, but spider mites may cause problems particularly during dry weather. They leave a silvery sheen on leaves and fine, white webbing on the undersides. Since spider mites are spiders, not insects, insecticides are ineffective. Spray with a canola-based horticultural oil or a miticide.

Landscaping Tips & Ideas—Cream-colored buds unfurl into petite white, dogwood-like flowers that bloom prolifically in uniquely cone-shaped, clusters resembling hydrangea flower heads. Its vigor and re-blooming characteristics are perfect in combination planters or as groundcovers, but it can also be used as a low-growing, mounding shrub in mixed borders or in front of leggier perennials or as space fillers.

DOUBLE DELIGHT
(HYBRID TEA)
Rosa hybrid

Hardiness—Zones 5 and higher

Color(s)—White with creamy-yellow edged in strawberry-red.

Bloom Period—Spring-fall

Mature Size (H & W)—3 to 4 ft. x as wide

Water Needs—Soak after planting, water three times the first few weeks and once established water every 5-7 days, depending on growth and weather conditions.

Planting/Care—Plant in later winter or spring from bare-root stock or almost any time of the year from containers where weather is mild. Provide full sun, well draining and slightly acidic soil. Fertilize with a complete organic rose food winter-summer. After a year, prune canes in late winter into a vase shape.

Pests/Diseases—Susceptible to mildew. Spray with a canola-based horticultural oil to keep it under control.

Landscaping Tips & Ideas—An AARS winner in 1977, it also became the Gamble Fragrance Award recipient in 1986. Plant close to pathways or entryways to enjoy its spicy fragrance.

MISTER LINCOLN
(HYBRID TEA)
Rosa hybrid

Hardiness—Zones 5 and higher

Color(s)—Deep-red

Bloom Period—Spring-fall

Mature Size (H & W)—5 ft. x 4 to 5 ft.

Water Needs—See Double Delight

Planting/Care—See Double Delight. Prune back to three or four feet. To shape and for growing long blooming stems, make cuts ¼ inch above a growth bud that is pointed away from the center axis of the plant so that its growth is encouraged outward.

Pests/Diseases—Prone to mildew and rust, but both can be controlled with a canola-based horticultural oil or systemic fungicide.

Landscaping Tips & Ideas—It has been many years since 'Mister Lincoln' was named the 1965 AARS award winner, but it continues to be one of the most popular hybrid red teas of all time and its strong melon perfume won a recent Gamble Fragrance Award. Plant where one can inhale its fragrance and appreciate its statuesque beauty.

POPE JOHN PAUL II
(HYBRID TEA)
Rosa hybrid

Hardiness—Zones 4 and higher

Color(s)—White

Bloom Period—Spring-fall

Mature Size (H & W)—4½ to 5 ft. x as wide.

Water Needs—Same as 'Double Delight'

Planting/Care—Same as 'Double Delight'

Pests/Diseases—Good disease resistance. Control aphids by washing off with a strong stream of water or spraying with a canola-based horticultural oil. Prevent ants from farming aphid "honeydew" (aphid excretions) by placing ant baits close to their nests.

Landscaping Tips & Ideas—'Pope John Paul II' is one of the best white hybrid teas. Each high-centered, exhibition-quality flower bears up to 50 petals that unfurl into a 5-in. bloom. Adding to its physical beauty is a heavenly, fresh citrus perfume that fills the garden air. Plant close to a walkway, entryway or under a window, so that its fragrance can be fully appreciated. Its white flowers and dark-green foliage also contrasts beautifully among brightly colored perennials and annuals.

YVES PIAGET
(HYBRID TEA)
Rosa hybrid

Hardiness—Zones 5 and higher

Color(s)—Deep-pink

Bloom Period—Spring-fall

Mature Size (H & W)—3 ft. x as wide

Water Needs—See 'Double Delight'

Planting/Care—See 'Double Delight'. Wait until your hybrid teas are older than one year before cutting for flower arrangements.

Pests/Diseases—Good disease resistance. If larvae of the sawfly, known as the rose slug, skeletonizes the leaves, spray with Spinosad.

Landscaping Tips & Ideas—'Yves Piaget' is in honor of the Swiss watch and clockmaker that makes the trophy for the best rose in the Geneva rose competition and fittingly won the year it was entered. It has the look of an old-fashioned rose with improved disease resistance and hardiness. The large double, ruffled flower has a petal count of 80 with a wonderful old rose perfume. Plant near the front of borders, pathways or in containers where its intoxicating fragrance and incomparable beauty can be appreciated.

COFFEE BEAN
(MINIATURE)
Rosa hybrid

Hardiness—Zones 5 and higher

Color(s)—Smoky red-orange and glistening rust-orange reverse

Bloom Period—Spring-fall

Mature Size (H & W)—12 to 16 in. x as wide

Water Needs—Soak thoroughly after planting, then every other day during the first few weeks. Once established, water every 3-5 days, depending on growth and weather conditions.

Planting/Care—Plant in winter or spring from bare roots or in spring-summer from containers. Provide full sun and sandy loam, slightly acidic soil. Fertilize weekly from spring-summer with a complete organic liquid food at half-strength. Do not prune until after 12 months.

Pests/Diseases—For disease problems such as rust and mildew, spray with a canola-based horticultural oil.

Landscaping Tips & Ideas—The colors and flowers of 'Coffee Bean' are genetically linked to 'Hot Cocoa' in miniature form. It brightens any container or mixed border and "percolates" a light tea fragrance.

GIZMO
(MINIATURE)
Rosa hybrid

Hardiness—Zones 5 and higher

Color(s)—Scarlet-orange with a white eye

Bloom Period—Spring-fall

Mature Size (H & W)—20 in. x as wide

Water Needs—Same as 'Coffee Bean'

Planting/Care—Same as 'Coffee Bean'. If a mature miniature plant grows taller than what the space or container needs, cut its length similar to a hybrid tea to a height of 10-16 inches. Otherwise prune off old or damaged stems and for shape.

Pests/Diseases—Same as 'Coffee Bean'. If gophers and moles become active around roses, set manual traps rather than toxic baits.

Landscaping Tips & Ideas—Winner of the Rose Hills Memorial Park's Golden Rose Award, 'Gizmo' bears 5-petaled single lowers covering a round mounded plant with glossy green leaves. The brilliant scarlet-orange, white-eyed blossoms also offer a light, apple perfume. Use to brighten mixed borders or containers.

SUN SPRINKLES
(MINIATURE)
Rosa hybrid

Hardiness—Zones 5 and higher

Color(s)—Bright, deep-yellow

Bloom Period—Spring-fall

Mature Size (H & W)—24 in. x as wide

Water Needs—See 'Coffee Bean'. Water container plants as often as once a day during hot, dry weather. In the landscape, water more frequently than other roses because of shallower roots.

Planting/Care—See 'Coffee Bean'

Pests/Diseases—Good disease resistance, but to control chewing insects such as rose slugs and thrips, spray with Spinosad.

Landscaping Tips & Ideas—In 2001, 'Sun Sprinkles' became one of the few miniature roses to win AARS honors. Although the blossoms are small in size, the orange-red centers with a deep-yellow reverse are packed with 30-35 petals and perfume the air with a light, spicy scent. It has a rounded, tidy growth habit with lush flowers. Plant this ray of sunshine in the front of borders, rock garden accent or in mixed containers or planter boxes.

TROPICAL TWIST
(MINIATURE)
Rosa hybrid

Hardiness—Zones 5 and higher.

Color(s)—Apricot pink-coral orange

Bloom Period—Spring-fall

Mature Size (H & W)—20 to 24 in. x as wide

Water Needs—Same as 'Coffee Bean'

Planting/Care—Same as 'Coffee Bean'. Lightly shear established miniature roses for shape, but to keep their diminutive plant size, it may be necessary to cut back by 20-40% in late winter (for mild winter areas) or early spring (where winter freezes are common).

Pests/Diseases—There are many beneficial insect controls available at nurseries or insectories for rose protection: predator lacewings and lady beetles prey on aphids; green lacewings and predatory mites control thrips.

Landscaping Tips & Ideas—'Tropical Twist' was the 1998 ARS Award of Excellence winner. Its bright shades of apricot-pink and coral-orange more than compensate for its light fragrance. Plant this sparkler in a rock garden, planter or container to make a big statement.

BONICA
(SHRUB)
Rosa hybrid

Hardiness—Zones 4 and higher

Color(s)—Peachy-pink

Bloom Period—Spring-fall

Mature Size (H & W)—4 ft. x 5 ft.

Water Needs—Soak thoroughly after planting, water 3 times the first few weeks and once established, water every 5-7 days, depending on weather and growth conditions.

Planting/Care—Plant in winter or spring from bareroot stock or spring-summer from containers. Provide full sun and sandy loam, slightly acidic soil. Fertilize spring-summer with a complete organic food.

Pests/Diseases—Excellent disease resistance, but if ants are a problem, place baits near the ant nest.

Landscaping Tips & Ideas—The first shrub rose to win the AARS award in 1987, 'Bonica' bears clusters of semi-double blossoms on arching canes with a fresh apple fragrance. It is a heavy bloomer and hardy even in harsh climates. Planted in an informal style garden or mix with other perennials and shrubs.

CAREFREE SPIRIT
(SHRUB)
Rosa hybrid

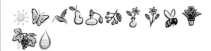

Hardiness—Zones 4 and higher

Color(s)—Cherry-red

Bloom Period—Spring-fall

Mature Size (H & W)—Up to 5 ft. x as wide

Water Needs—See 'Bonica'

Planting/Care—See 'Bonica'. Wait for 12 months before pruning shrub roses. Trim off dead, interfering or damaged stems and branches.

Pests/Diseases—Even better disease resistance than its cousins 'Carefree Delight' and 'Carefree Wonder'. For aphid infestations, wash off with a strong stream of water or spray with a canola based horticultural oil or organic insecticide.

Landscaping Tips & Ideas—'Carefree Spirit' is a mounding shrub that blooms prolifically with huge clusters of cherry-red single, five-petaled flowers and contrasting golden stamens. An AARS award winner for 2009, include 'Carefree Spirit' in containers or edging lawns, ponds, patios, pathways and embankments. Group in threes or fives along fences or mixed in with perennial beds.

KNOCK OUT
(SHRUB)
Rosa hybrid

Hardiness—Zones 4 and higher

Color(s)—Cherry-red

Bloom Period—Spring-fall

Mature Size (H & W)—3 to 4 ft. x as wide

Water Needs—See 'Bonica'. 'Knock Out' is drought tolerant once established.

Planting/Care—See 'Bonica'. No need to deadhead because it is self-cleaning.

Pests/Diseases—Excellent resistance to black spot. For mildew and rust, spray with a canola-based horticultural oil or organic fungicide.

Landscaping Tips & Ideas—'Knock Out' is known for its extreme hardiness and easy care as well as disease resistance. A 2000 AARS award winner, it bears beautiful red blossoms from early spring until first frost and sets beautiful hips in autumn ('Rainbow Knockout' was the 2007 AARS award winner with coral pink petals and yellow eyes). Sets beautiful hips in autumn for fall and winter color. Although there is no fragrance, its bright good-looks fit perfectly in an informal garden setting, along fences, in mixed perennial beds and in containers.

THE IMPOSTER
(SHRUB)
Rosa hybrid

Hardiness—Zones 4 and higher

Color(s)—Medium-pink or salmon with deep-rose splatters

Bloom Period—Spring-fall

Mature Size (H & W)—18 to 24 in. x as wide

Water Needs—Same as 'Bonica'

Planting/Care—Same as 'Bonica'. The Imposter' will stop bloom production if deadheaded.

Pests/Diseases—Good disease resistance, but control thrips and rose slugs with Spinosad. Although organic, protect bees while Spinosad is wet by spraying in the early evening after the bees have returned to their hive.

Landscaping Tips & Ideas—This single-flowered shrub rose is named 'The Imposter' because the blossoms resemble a clematis or is it a clematis pretending to be a rose? It also adapts to a variety of climates including triple-digit temperatures. While other roses wilt in the heat, 'The Imposter' keeps on blooming as if it was the first day of spring. Plant habit remains compact and uniform, so little pruning is needed.

MORE RECOMMENDATIONS

ENGLISH ROSES

English roses have been developed by hybridizers such as David Austin to have the appearance and fragrance of Old Garden Roses such as Gallicas, Albas and Damasks, but the repeat-blooming and extensive color palates of hybrid teas and floribundas. Generally, they grow much wider than hybrid teas or floribundas, so allow plenty of room. 'William Shakespeare 2000' is a gorgeous deep, crimson-purple selection with Old Garden Rose perfume.

MINI-FLORA

A new classification established by the American Rose Society in 1999 to recognize roses that have intermediate bloom size and foliage between miniatures and floribundas and usually about 3 to 5 ft. tall. Great garden roses such as the 'Sunblaze' and 'Memphis' series are perfect for pots or in the landscape as edgings, low borders or mixed in perennial borders.

OLD GARDEN ROSE

An Old Garden Rose is any variety or cultivar that existed prior to 1867, the year that 'La France' was recognized as the first hybrid tea. 'Aimee Vibert' is a Noisette that climbs, rambles or can be pruned into a large shrub and bears pure-white, very fragrant repeat-blooming flowers. 'Mutabilis' is a China Rose with single flowers resembling butterflies that "morph" into a rainbow of colors from orange, red, yellow and copper with all the colors on the bush at the same time. Blooms early and continuously from spring-fall.

POLYANTHA

Polyanthas are the parents of floribundas and are generally small in size, but their trusses of tiny blossoms are perfect for low borders, cascading over retaining walls, in hanging baskets or other containers. 'Crystal Fairy' with pure white trusses and 'Mlle. Cécile Brünner with pink sprays add delicate beauty to the landscape.

CLIMBING ROSE

HOW TO PLANT YOUR ROSES

Once you've selected a location based on sunlight, soil drainage and spacing, follow the simple steps below and you'll have beautiful healthy, blooming roses in no time!

Step 1
After bringing your bareroot roses home, immediately soak roots in lukewarm water for 12 to 24 hours! Some gardeners add soil polymer powder, mud, or a little fertilizer.

Step 2
Dig a hole about 12 inches deep and 24 inches wide. Make sure it's large enough to give the plant's root system plenty of room to develop after planting. Loosen the soil at the bottom and sides with your shovel.

Step 3
Fill the hole with water. It should drain in one hour. If the water remains longer, dig deeper to improve the drainage—or add some amendments, such as compost or peat moss.

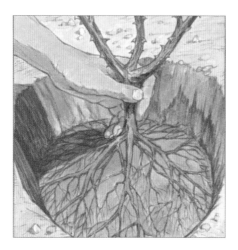

Step 4
Build a mound in the center of the hole to support roots. Set rose on top, making sure the crown (the point where canes join together at the shank) is at ground level, or a little lower in cold climates.

Step 5
Fill the hole with two-thirds of the remaining soil mixed with peat moss or compost. Tamp down gently with hands. Add water, let it soak in, then finish filling the hole with soil. Tamp down lightly and water well.

HOW TO SPACE YOUR ROSES

Step 6
Spread mulch, compost or bark chips around to suppress weed growth and help retain moisture. Water three to four times a week until leaves begin to grow.

Step 7
Your plants will leaf out faster if you mist the canes as often as possible while they're getting started. Roses need plenty of moisture both above and below the soil to develop fully.

SUGGESTED ROSE SPACING

Hybrid Teas & Grandifloras
Space: 3 feet apart
Coverage: 6-10 square feet

Floribundas
Space: 2-2 ½ feet apart
Coverage: 4-6 square feet

English Roses
Space: 3½ feet apart
Coverage: 10 square feet

Climbers
Space: 4-5 feet apart
Coverage: 12-15 square feet

Hedges
Space: 2-3 feet apart
Coverage: 4 square feet

Large Shrubs
Space: 3-3 ½ feet apart
Coverage: 6-10 square feet

Small Shrubs
Space: 2-2 ½ feet apart
Coverage: 4-6 square feet

Miniatures
Space: 12-18 inches apart
Coverage: 1-2 square feet

Standard Tree Roses
Space: 3-5 feet apart
Coverage: 10-15 square feet

Patio Tree Roses
Space: 3-4 feet apart
Coverage: 10-12 square feet

Miniature Tree Roses
Space: 2½-3 ½ feet apart
Coverage" 6-10 square feet

This information was provided courtesy of Jackson & Perkins,
www.jacksonandperkins.com.

ROSE PRUNING GUIDELINES

- Where winter and spring freezes are typical, prune roses after the last day of frost, but for mild winter and spring locales, prune soon after the New Year or early spring.

- Use sharp, sterile cutting tools: hand prunes for ¾ in. canes, loppers for up to 1¾-in. canes and for larger canes, use a saw.

- Cut out any damaged, diseased, dead, spindly, inward or interfering wood.

- Hybrid teas, floribundas, grandifloras and many other varieties have been grafted onto hardy rootstock that generate suckers. Remove all sucker growth above or below the bud union. Own-root and most shrub roses do not have problems with sucker growth.

- Cut at a 45-degree angle whenever possible to avoid the accumulation of water and possible decay around the cut.

- Bud eyes are where new growth emerges and are small, brown or red. Prune ¼ in. above an outward-facing bud to encourage fresh growth away from the center of bush.

- Shorten lanky or disproportionate stems to keep the plant looking neater, more compact and to encourage new growth.

- For most roses (climbers and ramblers are exceptions), prune to create a vase shape, spacing the flowering canes evenly on all sides of the bush and keeping the center of the plant open for good air circulation.

- In most cases, prune back flowering branches of climbers or ramblers that are growing from the main canes after the bloom cycle is complete (usually in summer). Wait until they are 4 years old before pruning heavily.

- After floribundas bloom, remove the oldest canes, leaving 6-8 of the younger, more vigorous ones and keep them about 20-30 inches tall with a rounded shape to encourage floral coverage over the entire plant.

- Grandifloras are generally larger and taller than hybrid teas or floribundas, so allow 4-5 canes to remain after pruning and keep them 36 inches tall.

- Ground cover roses are meant to spread, so prune just the dead wood and any vertical growing stems.

- Once a year cut back hybrid teas to 3-5 of the healthiest canes that are 12-18 inches tall.

- Miniature roses can be cut similar to hybrid teas and if desired kept to a height of 10-16 inches.

- Old Garden Roses should be pruned after their bloom cycle.

- Reduce polyanthas to 6-8 healthy 20-28-in.-long canes.

- Shrub roses appreciate a yearly trim and thinned to prevent thick, inner growth. If used as a hedge, trim ⅓ to ½ their growth with hedge clippers.

PRUNING FOR ROSE EXHIBITIONS

- Timing and technique is important when it comes to showing off roses at a rose show. Also contact the garden group that is hosting the show for additional helpful hints.

- Prune the roses 4-6 weeks before the date of the show.

- Encourage exhibition-sized hybrid tea and grandiflora flowers by disbudding. Select a stem with a large flower bud and cut off any buds that are forming along its side stems.

- Do not disbud roses that grow in clusters such as floribundas or polyanthas (except remove the center bud of a floribunda if you want the surrounding flowers to open at the same time).

PROPAGATING ROSES FROM CUTTINGS

- Early autumn is an excellent time to harvest rose cuttings, but hybrid teas and floribundas are more challenging and may need more time to root from cuttings. It is illegal to propagate patented roses until the patent expires (twenty years from the introduction date) without paying a royalty to the patent holder.

- Select healthy stems about the diameter of a pencil that have recently flowered or have hips (seed pods) beginning to form.

- Remove the flower heads or hips down to the first set of 5-or 7-leaflet leaves and make the first cut.

- Make the second cut at a 45-degree angle 4-5 leaf sets down from the first cut (6-9 inches).

- Miniature rose cuttings need 2-4 in. lengths and planted 1-2 inches deep.

- Take six cuttings to increase the chances for one or more successful rootings.

- Snip, do not yank off, the leaves from the stem to avoid tearing the protective outside layer of the cutting.

- Dip cuttings into a rooting hormone.

- Fill a 2-gallon black plastic nursery pot or something similar with an organic, well-draining and sterile potting mix. Water to moisten mix thoroughly but not soggy.

- Make six 1-in. diameter holes, 3-4 inches deep.

- Place the lower half of the cutting into the hole. Tamp down the surrounding planting mix. Remove the cap and cut the bottom off a plastic 2-liter soda bottle. Place over the cutting.

- Set the potted cuttings in a filtered, lightly shaded area and keep moist. Do not allow the cuttings to dry.

- Once the roots are established, remove soda bottle to harden the cuttings. Transplant each plant into individual containers.

PROPAGATING SEEDS FROM ROSE HIPS

- Seeds extracted from rose hips is another propagation method recommended especially for species roses. When the flower petals fall off, reddish-orange or yellow hips develop, typically during fall-winter.

- Harvest after the hips have changed color from green to red, orange or yellow.

- Open the hips with a sterile knife or your fingers and take out the seeds.

- Drop the seeds in a cup of water (can add 1 tsp. of bleach) and keep only the seeds that sink (the floaters are sterile).

- Wrap the seeds in a moistened coffee filter or paper towel and store in a sealable baggie.

- Label each baggie with the rose species or variety and store in a refrigerator's crisper at 40°F for 45-60 days.

- Remove the seeds and sow them in sealable, large-sized baggies filled ⅓ with moistened (not soggy) perlite, spacing 1-inch apart and cover with ½-in. moistened perlite and seal the bag (can also sow in seed trays or peat pots).

- Set outdoors in filtered light or keep indoors where there is bright, indirect light or under grow lights.

- Continue to spray with a mister to keep the medium moist and open periodically if excess moisture accumulates on the surface of the baggie. Germination occurs in 2-4 weeks.

- After 2 or more sets of leaves emerge, transplant them into plastic pots, keep seedlings moist and fertilize with an organic, liquid food at 25% the normal dilution rate once a week.

- Seedlings will bloom in 3-4 months. Keep them in larger containers or transplant into the ground after 1-2 years.

PEGGING OR LAYERING*

- Select a long, pencil-thin rose cane. Bend without snapping it.

- Clip off the foliage from the part that will be buried in the ground.

- Slice a small knick at the elbow of the bent cane and insert a toothpick or stick to keep the wound open.

- Dip the elbow in a rooting hormone then bury 8-12 inches under the ground.

- Cover and brace it with a wire hoop or fashion a wire coat hanger into a bobby pin to secure the plant in place underground.

- Tamp the soil around it making sure there is enough leafy portion of the plant stem sticking out of the ground.

- Water regularly until new roots form, in 4-6 weeks.

- The portion of the plant that is sticking out of the ground will continue to grow as its roots form.

- Once rooted, it can be cut off from the mother plant, but wait a few days to make sure the plant is doing well before transplanting to another location or into a container.

* (used for climbing or rambling roses)

HOW TO MIX ROSES WITH OTHER PLANTS

- Choose roses that have similar growing conditions with prospective annual, perennial and shrub companions.

- Pastel-colored roses recede and give the illusion of depth when planted toward the front of beds.

- Bright-colored roses advance and give the illusion of proximity when planted at a distance.

- Design the garden with the taller roses on the north side and the lowest growing roses on the south side to provide the most sun exposure as the sun moves from east to west.

JANUARY

- Bareroot roses are available at local nurseries and mail order companies. Shop early for the best selection.

- Roses need 6 hours of full sun each day. To make sure they have enough sunshine, plant roses on the south side of a wall or building and set taller roses toward the back of planting beds and use the miniature, groundcover or polyantha roses toward the front.

- Plant in late winter-early spring where weather is mild, but wait until spring where winter freezes are common.

- In mild winter regions, remove old foliage and prune back roses now if the weather hasn't triggered dormancy, but wait until early spring where freezes are common.

- Once planted, apply 2 inches of mulch from the root flare to the drip line. This organic blanket stabilizes soil temperature and soil moisture.

- Spray rose bushes with a canola-based horticultural oil to smother insects and diseases that may overwinter.

FEBRUARY

- When established rose plants become woody and less productive with increased age, rub bud unions with coarse steel wool to encourage more basal break development. Don't rub too hard, apply just enough pressure to loosen the flaking protective covering.

- Snails and slugs become active during rainy months. Control with a non-toxic iron phosphate bait or use decollate snails in Southern California.

- Apply a granular pre-emergent to keep spring weeds from germinating. Use every 3-4 months to make weeding chores easier.

- Fertilize established roses with an organic granular rose and flower food in late winter or early spring just before buds break. For containers, use a liquid organic rose fertilizer every 2 weeks or a granular food once a month.

- For newly planted roses or miniature roses, cut the recommended fertilizer amounts to half.

- A slow-release synthetic rose fertilizer is another option because the nutrients become available slowly and re-application rate is between 3-6 months.

MARCH

- Rebuild watering basins keeping berms at 4-6 inches and diameter equal to the rose's drip line. Pitch basins away from root flares.

- Replenish mulch to 2 inches around roses and apply mulch to newly planted roses.

- Apply a complete organic rose and flower fertilizer three times from late winter or early spring-summer around the inside perimeter of watering basins. Supplement with a liquid organic foliar fertilizer during growth and bloom cycles.

- Encourage beneficial microbes in the soil with a humic acid product and if soil is clayey, loosen the texture by digging in organic amendments and adding a product with saponin (yucca extract).

- Once roses are fully leafed out, supply moisture down to 15 inches. Determine how long it takes for water to penetrate down to that level with a tensiometer or shovel.

- Check climbers and ramblers regularly because they sprawl quickly and need to be tied to supports and trained.

APRIL

- Release beneficial insects like big-eyed bugs, lady beetles and lacewings that prey on harmful insects.

- Get rid of ants that are feeding on honeydew-secreting insects such as aphids. Ants harvest honeydew and will attack beneficial insects to protect the food source. Use a bait that will be taken back to the nest to kill the queen and the entire colony.

- Another effective control for aphids is a disc impregnated with a pheromone that causes aphids to stop feeding. Effective for 3-4 weeks.

- Pull out weeds while they are still young. For Bermudagrass and other stoloniferous weeds, use a systemic weed control, but apply carefully to avoid plant damage. Set a piece of cardboard around the weed before spraying with a systemic.

- Set manual traps for gophers and moles to avoid secondary kill.

- For rabbits use olfactory repellents or live trap. Check with the California Department of Fish and Game for local regulations.

MAY

- Control powdery mildew by washing off foliage, early in the morning with a stream of water. Anti-transpirants and canola-based horticultural oils are also effective for powdery and downy mildew and rust.

- Rose slugs chew holes and skeletonize rose leaves and resemble small black or green caterpillars, but are the larvae of sawflies. Spray with Spinosad or a systemic with imidacloprid. Do not apply imidacloprid if harvesting flowers or rose hips for cooking.

- Keep deer away with olfactory repellents or motion activated light or water sprinklers.

- After feeding roses and clearing weeds, apply a pre-emergent to prevent summer weed seeds from germinating.

- Southern California can use decollate snails to prevent snail infestations. In Northern California, use an organic iron phosphate bait, safe around pets and wildlife.

- Harpin is an organic protein that boosts a plant's immune system against pests and diseases and stimulates growth. Use for roses prone to various fungal or insect infestations.

JUNE

- Remove spent flowers and hips unless collecting the seeds.

- Select roses resistant to diseases that are common in your area. For example, if you live where summers are dry or overcast, choose selections that resist rust and mildew.

- When planning vacations include public rose gardens and arboretums to see which roses are looking their best in summer's heat and which are not. Visit www.rose.org for a list of accredited public rose gardens around the United States.

- Ask someone to watch over your roses and other plants while you are away.

- Early summer is the second time to apply a complete, organic granular rose and flower fertilizer and continue with a supplemental feeding every 2-4 weeks with a liquid, organic foliar feed such as kelp. For roses that bloom just once a year, do not supplement with a foliar feed.

- Deep water roses and all other plants in the garden especially during warm summer months.

JULY

- During summer plant roses on a cool overcast day and use an anti-transpirant to help prevent transplant shock.

- When transplanting roses into containers, provide pots with drainage holes, well-draining organic potting soil and set at the same level or slightly above as they were in their original containers.

- Water container roses as often as daily because they dry out so rapidly when compared to in-ground plants. Adding coir (coconut husk) to the planting mix, may cut watering by 50%.

- Roses planted in sandy loam soil need an inch or more of water to percolate down 12-15 inches.

- Make sure the irrigation or drip system is functioning properly, especially before going on vacation. Determine beforehand how long the timers need to be on in order for the water to reach 12-15 inches in depth.

- If a slow release fertilizer was applied in early spring, apply again between early summer-fall depending on the formulator's recommendations.

AUGUST

- Roses often take a short nap during the heat waves of late summer or early fall. Exceptions would be heat tolerant roses such as The Imposter.

- Help resting repeat-blooming roses by giving them a light trim to stimulate autumn blossoms. Prune off spindly or lanky growth back to a plump outside leafbud or eye.

- Cut back blossoming stems that have ceased flowering by ⅓ unless from an older, large bush, then prune as much as 50%.

- Rebuild watering basins before winter keeping berms at 4-6 inches and diameter equal to the rose's drip line. Pitch basins away from root flares.

- Continue attaching climbers and ramblers to their supports. Tie securely, but loose enough to avoid damaging the stems and train the growth horizontally or in a fan shape to increase bloom production.

- Remove and dispose of any foliage that is yellowed or diseased on the rosebush and any that have fallen to the ground.

SEPTEMBER

- Remove spent flowers and hips unless collecting seeds or using the hips as seasonal color for fall and winter. Many roses such as Rugosas have beautiful hips.

- Decrease the amount and frequency of watering to accommodate shorter days and cooler temperatures.

- In cold winter regions, withhold fertilizing until early spring except provide a supplemental feeding of kelp meal to increase the plant's sugar content, which in turn increases its tolerance to cold.

- For mild winters, withhold fertilizing and decrease watering roses during autumn to encourage dormancy by mid-winter, but feed one more time to extend the bloom season through the winter holidays.

- Harvest rose stems for cuttings and collect and prepare rose hips and seeds for germination.

- Spider mites proliferate in dry weather conditions, leaving a silvery sheen or stippling on the leaves. They have fine, white webbing on the undersides of leaves. Control with a canola-based horticultural oil or a miticide.

OCTOBER

- Time to select and preorder new roses from local garden centers or online mail orders. Look over the landscape to decide if there are sites to plant climbers, groundcovers, floribundas, hybrid teas, Old Garden Roses, shrubs and miniatures. Think about combining them with existing perennials and structures.

- AARS winners are great selections because they have been tested in a variety of gardens throughout the United States and Canada for at least two years for disease, insect resistance and soil and climatic variables.

- If fragrance is important to you, choose James Alexander Gamble Fragrance Award winners including 'Crimson Glory', Chrysler Imperial', Sutter's Gold', 'Fragrant Cloud', 'Papa Meilland', 'Sunsprite', Double Delight', 'Angel Face' and 'Mister Lincoln'.

- Stop deadheading by mid-autumn if you live where winter freezes are common because it encourages roses to continue their growth rather than going dormant

- Rake, pick up and dispose of fallen foliage to curtail overwintering insects and disease.

NOVEMBER

- Replenish mulch to 2 inches around roses in the landscape and in containers to prevent weeds, protect against temperature fluctuations and prevent moisture loss.

- Apply a humic acid product to encourage the proliferation of beneficial microbes in the soil, revitalize the soil and to prepare plants for the upcoming winter months.

- If soil is clayey, improve the texture by digging in plenty of organic humus or compost amendments and adding a product with saponin (yucca extract). Saponin helps loosen the soil, permits better percolation and leaches salts from the soil.

- Apply a pre-emergent weed control every 3-4 months to keep weed seeds from germinating. It will save work later.

- Where winter freezes are common, do not plant roses again until spring. Instead prepare your soil for future rose plantings and excavate the planting holes.

- Continue to water container roses as long as they are blooming.

DECEMBER

- Keep a garden journal because seasonal events in the rose garden over several years will provide important information about successfully growing roses.

- Join a local rose society. Members are generous with their knowledge and expertise. Also, websites such as www.ars.org are great resources and www.rose.org lists all the AARS award winners as well as the best roses for specific regions.

- Organize the tools necessary to prune roses and keep them sharp and clean. Physan sterilizes tools without rusting them (sold at nurseries).

- If rainfall is insufficient, supplement 1-1½ inches of water per week for roses in good-draining soil in cool weather, but increase up to 3 inches when the weather warms up. In containers, water every 2-3 days during the growing season.

- Use a tensiometer or shovel just outside the root zone down to a depth of 12 inches. If the soil is beginning to dry at that level, water again.

CLIMBING ROSE

TREE ROSE

SHRUBS
for California

While at New Zealand's Taranaki Rhododendron Festival, my husband and I visited several private gardens, including one owned by a sprightly eighty-five-year-old. Originally her land was a pastureland, but now it was like entering a painting, filled with a variety of textures and a rainbow of colors, all accomplished by massive plantings of Azaleas and Rhododendrons interspersed with areas of lush lawns, brilliant pink and red Camellias and lemon-scented Mock Oranges as well as alabaster-white Gardenias and canary-yellow Hibiscus.

With forethought, dedication, and a gifted painter's eye, she used her shrubs as more than mere multi-trunked woody plants plopped in a landscape between trees, flowers, and lawns. Instead they were grouped in borders and hedges, interplanted in flower beds, highlighted as specimen and clustered in foundation plantings—proving that shrubs can be the base coat, top coat or colorful trim for any garden.

FIRST DO YOUR HOMEWORK

Most of us don't have acres of pastureland from which to create an expansive estate-sized landscape, but it is possible to incorporate shrubs that meld beautifully with other plants rather than treating them as separate entities.

Before purchasing and planting a shrub, carefully consider local climatic conditions, site locations, and the shrub's particular needs and habits. A little homework beforehand will save time, money and effort afterward as you try to maintain the plant's health or prune it to keep it within bounds.

A cute little Yew Pine or Hollywood Twisted Juniper from a one-gallon-sized container can grow much taller, just as a young child grows until reaching full adulthood. If such a shrub is planted as a foundation shrub in front of an average-sized home, in a few years it might be much too tall, obscuring the house or blocking window views. For foundation plantings and borders, it is wiser to plant low to medium-height evergreen or deciduous shrubs.

A MULTITUDE OF CHOICES

Whether the landscape calls for evergreen or deciduous, berry or flower-bearing, screening or showcasing, there are shrubs for every purpose. For showy spring flowers and deep-green foliage in shaded areas, few plants can compete with Azaleas, Camellias, and Hydrangeas.

Others are known less for their flowers but have variegated foliage, including Gold Dust and Golden Mirror Plants that look as if a painter took a paintbrush and stippled the leaves with gold dust. Some, like Heavenly Bamboo, Laurustinus, and Cotoneaster, provide blazing autumn color and bright berries.

If fluttery visitations from ruby-tinged hummingbirds, plump bees, and boldly patterned monarch and swallowtail butterflies are important to you, find sunny areas for the Butterfly Bush, Pride of Madeira, and California Lilac—their delicate fragrant, spiked flowers and sweet nectar are perfect metaphors for the sweetness of life.

For those who think good hedges make good neighbors, Hibiscus, Rose of Sharon, Yew Pines, and Laurustinus are ideal choices. Dwarf Jade Plants, Silverberry, Rock Rose, California Lilac and Pride of Madeira make good companions for other drought-tolerant trees, shrubs and ground covers. Hollywood Twisted Junipers are excellent accent plants in areas that allow for their mature dimensions, often grouped or planted in pairs on opposite sides of driveways and walkways in formal landscapes. On warm California spring and summer days, the blossoms of Saucer Magnolias, Mystery Gardenias and Japanese Mock Orange scent gentle breezes with their perfumes.

A MULTITUDE OF USES

By definition a shrub is a woody plant smaller than a tree; yet, a shrub is so much more. Shrubs manufacture life-sustaining oxygen, mitigate nuisance noise, define spaces and boundaries and surprise us with their individuality.

Instead of planting in linear, single-file formations, draw eyes skyward by intermixing taller, bolder shrubs toward the back of groupings.

To spotlight more earthbound visions, cluster identical varieties for focal points or group smaller, subtler plants toward the front or along walkways or combine with trees to create a shade garden or wooded landscape.

Evergreen shrubs that prefer pruning are great when planted for formal hedges or verdant walls. And taller evergreen shrubs make perfect backdrops for the seasonal changes of shorter, deciduous shrubs, annuals and bulbs. Use shrubs as a gifted conductor would use his orchestra —to create a composition of undulating rhythms, modulating diminuendo tones, and accentuating fortissimo notes—a symphony for your garden.

Avoid combining drought-tolerant shrubs with thirsty ones, or shade-lovers with sun-seekers. While upright and pyramidal shapes draw the eyes skyward and lend themselves to the more formal landscape, the weeping, mounding or spreading shapes anchor our vision to ground level and reflect a more relaxed plan.

Leaf shapes, textures, sizes, and colors bring contrasts to gardens. Shrubs offer colors that cover the spectrum from gold to blue-gray to all shades of green as well as red, burgundy, purplish-bronze and variegated splashes, stipples or stripes. In winter, many deciduous plants have colorful bark patterns or interesting branch structures that more than compensate for their leafless state.

To soften or camouflage, to brighten or shade, to flower or evergreen, whatever the purpose, there are shrubs for every need. More importantly, they serve as artful bridges between sentinel trees, smaller perennials and annuals and ground-hugging lawns and also shine as gregarious floral showpieces or hide in the muted shade of more forceful plants. Use them as a gifted artist would use a rainbow palette of texture and color.

AZALEA

ANGEL'S TRUMPET
Brugmansia suaveolens

Hardiness—Zones 9-11

Color(s)—Pink, white, yellow, peach

Bloom Period—Spring-fall

Mature Size (H & W)—8 to 12 ft. x 8 ft.

Water Needs—Deep water 1-2 times a week, depending on weather and growth conditions.

Planting/Care—Plant in spring from containers in a frost-free, wind-protected site. Provide full sun in loam, slightly acidic soil and space 6-10 ft. apart if planting more than one. Fertilize 3 times with a complete, organic granular food early spring-fall.

Pests/Diseases—Control spider mites with a canola-based horticultural oil or a systemic miticide.

Landscaping Tips & Ideas—Angel's Trumpet is a large bush with single or double (hose in hose) pendulous, funnel-shaped blossoms and a musk-like fragrance. For a small tree form remove the lateral branches up to 4 ft. with pruning shears. Since all parts are toxic, wear gloves when handling and plant away from children and pets.

AZALEA
Rhododendron indica

Hardiness—Zones 8-11

Color(s)—Red, white, pink, orange, variegated

Bloom Period—Spring

Mature Size (H & W)—4 to 6 ft. x as wide

Water Needs—Once established, keep evenly moist but not soggy.

Planting/Care—Azaleas require well-drained, humus-amended, slightly acidic soil. Mix equal parts peat and sandy loam soil. Plant rootball 2-inches above the soil surface to account for settling. Begin feeding every 6-8 weeks from April-September with an organic, acid fertilizer or cottonseed meal. For chlorotic foliage, supplement with a chelated iron.

Pests/Diseases—Control spider mites with an organic horticultural oil or systemic miticide and use Spinosad for thrips.

Landscaping Tips & Ideas—One of the most popular shade plants used in formal and informal landscapes as shrubs or topiaries and in containers. 'Rosea' have rose-red semi-double flowers and 'California Snow' is a midseason bloomer with large, double, pure-white blossoms.

BURFORD HOLLY
Ilex cornuta 'Burfordii'

Hardiness—Zones 7-10

Color(s)—White flowers in spring, red berries

Bloom Period—Autumn-winter berries

Mature Size (H & W)—15 to 20 ft. x 6 to 10 ft.

Water Needs—Needs regular water, about once a week or more during warm weather until established.

Planting/Care—Plant from containers in spring or in fall where winters are mild. Provide full or part sun and amended, well-draining, slightly acidic soil. Prune for shape and fertilize just before growth in spring.

Pests/Diseases—Few pests or diseases, but wash off periodically to clean.

Landscaping Tips & Ideas—'Burford Holly' is perfect for winter floral designs with shiny , dark green, almost spineless leaves and Christmas-red berries. It also provides fruit and nectar for birds and bees and is a wonderful landscape accent or evergreen hedge. For a smaller version, select the 4-6 ft. 'Dwarf Burford Holly'.

CAMELLIA
Camellia spp.

Hardiness—Zones 8-11

Color(s)—Red, white, pink, salmon, yellow, variegated

Bloom Period—Late winter-early spring, depending on species

Mature Size (H & W)—3 ft. to 15 ft. x 4 ft. to 8 ft, depending on species

Water Needs—Water regularly, especially during the summer growth cycle. Keep moist but not soggy.

Planting/Care—Same as for Azalea planting care

Pests/Diseases—Camellia blight prevents buds from opening, turning them brown or mushy. Pick off infected buds and pick up fallen buds and foliage. Use a fungicide and apply a 2-in. layer of mulch, but allow a 2-4 in. space around the base.

Landscaping Tips & Ideas—*C. japonica* 'Kramer's Supreme' has large, deep red, mildly fragrant flowers. Hybrids like 'High Fragrance' bear very fragrant, small, pink Peony-form flowers on a 3-4 ft. tall bush. *C. sasanqua* is more sun-tolerant like 'Shishi Gashira', a low-growing shrub with semi-double red flowers.

CRIMSON BOTTLEBRUSH
Callistemon citrinus

Hardiness—Zones 8-11

Color(s)—Red

Bloom Period—Spring-summer

Mature Size (H & W)—6 to 10 ft. x 8 ft.

Water Needs—Water frequently when newly planted, but once established, water every 7-14 days, depending on growth and weather conditions.

Planting/Care—Plant in fall (in mild winter regions) or spring from containers and space 10-12 ft. apart in well-draining, slightly acidic soil. Provide full sun and fertilize in early spring and early summer with a complete, organic granular food.

Pests/Diseases—Deer resistant. Few pests and diseases, but wash off periodically to clean out accumulated debris.

Landscaping Tips & Ideas—Crimson Bottlebrush is a large shrub or can be pruned into a small tree. Useful as a visual screen. Their citrus-scented leaves can be mixed with dried citrus for potpourri. Plant with other water-thrifty shrubs such as Cotoneasters, Rock Rose and Silverberry. 'Little John' is a dwarf 3-ft. cultivar.

FIRETHORN (PYRACANTHA)
Pyracantha coccinea

Hardiness—Zones 5-10, depending on cultivar

Color(s)—Cream flowers, red, orange berries

Bloom Period—Flowers in spring, berries late summer-winter

Mature Size (H & W)—2 to 12 ft. x as wide depending on cultivar

Water Needs—Water deeply and regularly when newly planted, but once established, water every 7-10 days, depending on growth and weather conditions.

Planting/Care—Plant from containers in spring or in fall where winters are mild. Provide full sun, well-drained, slightly acidic soil. Feed with a complete, organic granular fertilizer before new growth in spring.

Pests/Diseases—Control aphids and scale with a canola-based horticultural oil.

Landscaping Tips & Ideas—Dense, thorny growth is perfect for barriers, hedges and visual screens and can be trained as an espalier. Birds and flower arrangers love the colorful clusters of berries. "Rutgers' and 'Red Elf' are 2-3 ft. tall, but 'Mojave' and 'Kasan' grow 8-12 ft. tall.

FRAGRANT OLIVE
Osmanthus fragrans

Hardiness—Zones 8-10

Color(s)—White, yellow

Bloom Period—Spring-summer

Mature Size (H & W)—10 to 15 ft. x 6 to 10 ft.

Water Needs—Water when top 3 inches of soil is dry.

Planting/Care—Plant in spring from containers in slightly acidic soil. Can tolerate different soil types, including heavy clay. Provide full sun along coastal regions, but for hot, dry inland areas, afternoon shade is best.

Pests/Diseases—Few disease or pest problems, but wash off periodically to get rid of accumulated debris and spray with Spinosad for chewing insects.

Landscaping Tips & Ideas—Broad upright form is densely branched and covered with dark, green finely toothed foliage. Tiny white flower clusters have a heady apricot-like fragrance. Use for background screening, hedges and adding perfume to the garden. 'Conger Yellow' has the same characteristics, but bears tiny, buttery yellow clusters of flowers.

GLOSSY ABELIA
Abelia x grandiflora

Hardiness—Zones 7-10

Color(s)—White

Bloom Period—Summer-fall

Mature Size (H & W)—4 to 10 ft. x 5 to 8 ft.

Water Needs—Water 1-2 times a week when newly planted, but once established Abelias are drought tolerant needing water every 10-14 days depending on weather and growth conditions.

Planting/Care—Plant from containers in spring in full sun and provide well-draining, slightly acidic soil. Lace plants out after flowers are spent to allow more light to reach into the center of the plants.

Pests/Diseases—Wash off aphids with a strong stream of water or use a canola-based horticultural oil.

Landscaping Tips & Ideas—Good for just about any California region, even when temperatures dip below freezing. Sweet-scented white flowers on arching branches, bloom from June through first frost. Structurally they make ideal low-maintenance hedges or combine with Japanese Mock Orange and Rock Rose.

GOLD DUST PLANT
Aucuba japonica 'Variegata'

Hardiness—Zones 6-10

Color(s)—Green with yellow splattered foliage.

Bloom Period—Not applicable

Mature Size (H & W)—3 to 4 ft. x as wide

Water Needs—Deep soak to leach out salts from the root zone and avoiding salt burn on the foliage.

Planting/Care—Plant in spring from containers spacing 4 ft. on center. Provide sandy loam, well-draining, slightly acidic soil in a shaded location. Feed with an organic, acid fertilizer or cottonseed meal in spring and in fall.

Pests/Diseases—Control mealybugs by washing off with a strong stream of water or spray with a canola-based horticultural oil. An iron phosphate bait is effective against snails and safe to use.

Landscaping Tips & Ideas—Particularly effective in Asian-style landscapes when combined with several species of bamboo in dappled shade areas. Gold Dust's yellow-splattered foliage is an excellent companion for Azaleas, Camellias and Clivia Lilies.

HEAVENLY BAMBOO
Nandina domestica

Hardiness—Zones 7-11

Color(s)—White flowers, red berries

Bloom Period—Flowers in spring, berries in fall

Mature Size (H & W)—4 to 6 ft. (clumping)

Water Needs—Water 2 times a week when newly planted, but thereafter, water every 7-10 days, depending on weather and growth conditions.

Planting/Care—Plant from containers spring-summer and also in fall where winters are mild. Prefers partial shade and loam soil, but it grows in full sun and adapt to denser soil. In groupings, space them 4 ft. on center.

Pests/Diseases—Deer resistant and few disease or insect problems. Wash periodically to clean out debris.

Landscaping Tips & Ideas—Heavenly Bamboo resembles bamboo, but is hardier with colorful foliage and bright red berries. Plant *en masse* as foundation plantings or combine with Prostrate Natal Plum, Shore Juniper and Pink Indian Hawthorn. 'Sienna Sunrise' ('Monfar') bears fiery red new foliage and grows to 3 ft.

HOLLYWOOD TWISTED JUNIPER
Juniperus chinensis 'Torulosa'

Hardiness—Zones 6-10

Color(s)—Fleshy, bluish berry-like cones

Bloom Period—Summer

Mature Size (H & W)—8 to 15 ft. x 6 to 10 ft.

Water Needs—Water regularly once or twice a week until established, then deep water every 7-14 days, depending on growth and weather conditions.

Planting/Care—Plant from containers spring-summer or where winters are mild, in fall. Provide full sun, well draining, loam and slightly acidic soil. Feed in spring, just before growth.

Pests/Diseases—Few pest or disease problems, but spray with water periodically to clean out accumulated debris.

Landscaping Tips & Ideas—Hollywood Juniper adapts to Mediterranean and seaside climates. Use as an accent plant in large spaces, as a topiary or plant in pairs on opposite sides of driveways, windows and walkways. 'Torulosa Variegata' has similar characteristics with splashes of yellow variegations in the foliage.

HYDRANGEA
Hydrangea macrophylla hybrids

Hardiness—Zones 5-10

Color(s)—Pink, blue, red, lavender, greenish-white, white

Bloom Period—Spring

Mature Size (H & W)—4 to 6 ft. x 6 to 8 ft.

Water Needs—Water deeply and regularly about 1-2 times per week, depending on growth and weather conditions.

Planting/Care—Plant in spring after the last frost from containers and plant 6 ft. on center. Provide partially shaded sites in well-draining, humus-amended and acidic soil. Fertilize with an organic acid food in spring and in summer. Prune after blooms are spent.

Pests/Diseases—Control aphids with a canola-based horticultural oil.

Landscaping Tips & Ideas—To change the floral color from pink to blue, apply aluminum sulfate, but blue turns pink in alkaline soils. 'Endless Summer' (blue mophead flowers), 'Blushing Bride' (white mophead) and 'Twist-n-Shout' (pink or blue lacecap) bloom on old and new wood. Combine with Gardenias, Camellias and Saucer Magnolias.

JAPANESE BOXWOOD
Buxus microphylla japonica

Hardiness—Zones 5-10

Color(s)—Dark green foliage, yellow inconspicuous flowers

Bloom Period—Not applicable

Mature Size (H & W)—4 to 6 ft. x as wide when unpruned

Water Needs—Once established water every 7-10 days, depending on weather and growth conditions.

Planting/Care—Plant from containers in spring-fall. Provide full or part sun in well-draining, amended, slightly acidic soil. Fertilize with an organic, granular food in spring just before new growth.

Pests/Diseases—More disease resistant than English Boxwood, provide well-draining soil to prevent root rot and spray with Spinosad to protect against leafminer damage.

Landscaping Tips & Ideas—If kept natural in shape, use as a backdrop in planting beds with Rosemary and other herbs, Lilacs or perennials. As a formal hedge, it defines spaces in knot gardens, parterres or defines boundary. Also makes a lovely topiary. 'Green Beauty' is an excellent Japanese Boxwood.

JAPANESE MOCK ORANGE
Pittosporum tobira

Hardiness—Zones 8-10

Color(s)—White

Bloom Period—Spring

Mature Size (H & W)—6 to 8 ft. x 6 ft.

Water Needs—Water deeply every 7-10 days.

Planting/Care—Plant from containers from spring-fall and space 6 ft. apart on center if used as a hedge, 10 ft. if used as a single focal plant. Provide full sun or partial shade in well-draining, amended, slightly acidic soil. Fertilize with a complete, organic granular food in spring.

Pests/Diseases—Avoid planting in areas where water accumulates to prevent root rot. Control aphids by washing off with water or spraying with a canola-based horticultural oil.

Landscaping Tips & Ideas—'Wheelerii' is a dwarf, dense plant with a mounded form available as solid green or variegated. Japanese Mock Orange has the intense fragrance of citrus and makes an excellent hedge or as a focal plant in a fragrance garden.

LILAC
Syringa vulgaris hybrids

Hardiness—Zones 3-10

Color(s)—Lavender, blue, pink, white, purple

Bloom Period—Spring

Mature Size (H & W)—10 to 20 ft. x 6 ft. to 15 ft.

Water Needs—Once established water every 7-10 days and decrease or withhold near the end of summer to encourage dormancy.

Planting/Care—Plant in winter-early spring from bareroot stock or spring-fall from containers. Provide well-draining, alkaline soil and plant in full sun. Prune after flowers are spent. Feed with an organic fertilizer just before buds form.

Pests/Diseases—Spray with Spinosad to control downy mildew, scale and aphids.

Landscaping Tips & Ideas—French hybrids like the purplish-red and white-edged 'Sensation' or the lilac-colored 'President Lincoln' need winter chill. Descanso hybrids are developed for mild winter regions such as 'Lavender Lady', 'White Angel' 'Blue Skies' and 'Blue Boy'. Use fragrant lilacs as hedges or specimen plants.

MYSTERY GARDENIA

Gardenia jasminoides 'Mystery'

Hardiness—Zones 9-11

Color(s)—White

Bloom Period—Summer

Mature Size (H & W)—4 ft. x as wide

Water Needs—Water deeply every 5-7 days, depending on weather and growth conditions.

Planting/Care—Plant in spring or early summer from containers, spacing 4 ft. on center in full or part sun. Provide an acidic, well-draining, humus-amended soil. Feed with an organic, acid fertilizer mid-spring.

Pests/Diseases—Control leafminers with Spinosad and aphids with a canola-based horticultural oil. For chlorotic leaves, spray with a chelated iron.

Landscaping Tips & Ideas—Mystery Gardenias are the favorite of florists and gardeners for their elegant beauty and unforgettable perfume. Combine with other sun-loving perennials and shrubs like Hibiscus, Japanese Mock Orange and Viburnum or use as a focal plant near entryways, along pathways and under windows to better enjoy its heady fragrance.

PINK INDIAN HAWTHORNE

Rhapiolepsis indica 'Enchantress'

Hardiness—Zones 7-11

Color(s)—Rose-pink

Bloom Period—Spring-summer

Mature Size (H & W)—2 to 4 ft. x 3 ft.

Water Needs—Once established, water down to a depth of 6 inches.

Planting/Care—Plant in spring or fall from containers and space 3-4 ft. on center for mass planting. Provide full sun or part sun in loam, humus-amended, slightly acidic soil. Feed with a complete organic fertilizer.

Pests/Diseases—Control snails and slugs with an iron phosphate molluscicide and spray aphids and scale with a canola-based horticultural oil.

Landscaping Tips & Ideas—Pink Indian Hawthorn makes ideal border plants or large groupings on banks and also popular with bonsai enthusiasts. Deadhead only if you do not want the blue-black berries that develop after the spring-summer flowers. *R. umbellata* (*R. ovata*) is known as Yeddo Hawthorn with fragrant white flowers and bright pink-red stamens.

PINK POWDER PUFF

Calliandra haematocephala

Hardiness—Zones 9-11

Color(s)—Pink

Bloom Period—Summer-fall

Mature Size (H & W)—6 to 10 ft. x 8 ft.

Water Needs—Deep, thorough soaking about once a week, depending on growth and weather conditions.

Planting/Care—Plant form containers in spring. Provide full sun and well-draining, slightly acidic soil. Feed twice a year in spring and summer with a complete organic granular fertilizer. Prune while young if growing as shrubs and pinch back tips when new growth reaches 12 inches. Deadhead to extend bloom cycle.

Pests/Diseases—Control aphids and scale with a horticultural oil.

Landscaping Tips & Ideas—With its clusters of reddish-pink stamens, Pink Powder Puff is most effective as an espalier on south-facing walls or fences. Although self-supporting, prune regularly to keep within bounds or to maintain the espalier form. Combine with tropical plants like Hibiscus and Bird of Paradise.

PROSTRATE NATAL PLUM

Carissa macrocarpa 'Prostrata'

Hardiness—Zones 10-11

Color(s)—White flowers, red fruit

Bloom Period—Summer

Mature Size (H & W)—2 to 3 ft. x 4 to 6 ft.

Water Needs—Water once a week , but once extend watering to every 10-14 days.

Planting/Care—Plant after the last frost from containers spacing 6 ft. on center. Provide full sun in well-drained, slightly acidic soils. Feed twice a year, in spring and summer, with a complete, granular organic fertilizer. Prune errant, vertical shoots at the base.

Pests/Diseases—Deer resistant. Few disease or pest problems.

Landscaping Tips & Ideas—Prostrate Natal Plum is a dense, low-growing plant with sharp thorns and is an excellent evergreen border or barrier plant. The delicately scented white flowers give way to red fruits and can be made into jelly if grown organically. Ideal for seaside and other frost-free regions.

ROSE OF SHARON

Hibiscus syriacus

Hardiness—Zones 5-9

Color(s)—White, mauve, violet, pink

Bloom Period—Summer

Mature Size (H & W)—6 to 10 ft. x 8 ft.

Water Needs—Water regularly once a week or more to establish and thereafter water according to growth and weather conditions.

Planting/Care—Plant in fall or spring from containers spacing 8-10 ft. on center or if growing as a hedge, 6-8 ft. on center. Provide full or part sun in well-draining, slightly acidic soil. While 2-3 years old, prune in late winter-early spring to increase branching and bloom production.

Pests/Diseases—Control giant whitefly with Spinosad and spray with a canola-based oil for mealybugs, aphids and scale.

Landscaping Tips & Ideas—Combine with other sun-loving plants such as Canna Lilies, Hibiscus and Birds of Paradise for a tropical-looking landscape. To restore its vigor, prune canopies back 40-60% while dormant.

ROUNDLEAF LAURUSTINUS

Viburnum tinus 'Robustum'

Hardiness—Zones 7-11

Color(s)—White flowers, blue fruits in summer

Bloom Period—Fall-spring

Mature Size (H & W)—6 to 12 ft. x 3 to 6 ft.

Water Needs—Once established, water deeply every 7-10 days.

Planting/Care—Tolerant of various soils, but needs well-draining soil. Plant in early spring or fall from containers and space 6-8 ft. on center for a hedge or 4-6 ft. if using as a single specimen. Provide shade inland, but along the coast, full sun.

Pests/Diseases—Control mildew and spider mites with a canola-based horticultural oil.

Landscaping Tips & Ideas—Can train into a small patio or garden tree. Fragrant clusters of pink-blushed white flowers in spring and bright red fruit in summer-fall. Use dense foliage for screens, hedges or topiaries. Lace the plant in fall to open the canopy and provide good air circulation. 'Robustum' is less prone to mildew.

SAUCER MAGNOLIA
Magnolia x soulangiana

Hardiness—Zones 5-11

Color(s)—Lavender, white

Bloom Period—Spring

Mature Size (H & W)—15 to 20 ft. x 12 to 15 ft.

Water Needs—Water established plants every 7-10 days, depending on weather or growth conditions, but reduce frequency when dormant fall-winter.

Planting/Care—Plant in spring or fall from containers spacing 6-8 ft. on center. Provide full sun or partial shade in amended, well-draining, slightly acidic soil. Prune after the flowers are spent.

Pests/Diseases—Few pest and disease problems, but sensitive to salt build-up. Leach salts out with deep, thorough soakings and apply products containing humic acid and saponin.

Landscaping Tips & Ideas—Grow as large shrubs or small trees with multiple trunks resembling graceful, spreading candelabras. Saucer Magnolia's delicate, raspberry-pineapple-like fragrance and fresh green foliage is spectacular as a focal point or planted near an entryway.

TINY TOWER ITALIAN CYPRESS
Cupressus sempervirens 'Tiny Tower'

Hardiness—Zones 7-10

Color(s)—Blue-green foliage

Bloom Period—Not applicable

Mature Size (H & W)—8 ft. x 2 ft.

Water Needs—Water newly planted Cypress every 5-7 days, then every 10-14 days, depending on growth and weather conditions.

Planting/Care—Plant from containers in spring or fall spacing 3 ft. apart. Provide full sun in well-draining, amended, slightly acidic soil.

Pests/Diseases—Deer resistant and few disease or insect problems. Wash off accumulated debris in the interior.

Landscaping Tips & Ideas—Compact Italian Cypress is slow growing reaching 8 ft. in 10 years. Its stiff, columnar form is ideal for architectural accents along driveways or grouped together as focal points in formal gardens. Pairs of 'Tiny Tower' are also used as welcoming topiaries by front doors, backdrops in small spaces or as a centerpiece in specialty gardens such as kitchen gardens.

YESTERDAY-TODAY-AND-TOMORROW
Brunfelsia australis

Hardiness—Zones 9-11

Color(s)—Deep purple, pale lavender, white

Bloom Period—Spring-summer

Mature Size (H & W)—4 to 6 ft. x 4 ft.

Water Needs—Water every twice a week until established, decrease to 7-10 days, depending on weather and climate conditions.

Planting/Care—Plant in spring from containers spacing 4-5 ft. on center if using multiple specimen. Provide partial or full shade in amended, well-draining, acidic soil. Feed every 4-6 weeks spring-fall with a complete organic granular fertilizer. Pinch off branch stems for more prolific blooms.

Pests/Diseases—Control snails and slugs with an iron phosphate molluscicide, hand-pick or in Southern California, use decollate snails.

Landscaping Tips & Ideas—Displays purple, lavender and white blossoms at the same time. It combines well with Hydrangeas, Azaleas and Camellias. *B. pauciflora* 'Macrantha' bears flowers 2-3 times larger than *B. australis*.

MORE RECOMMENDATIONS

- AUSTRALIAN FUCHSIA *Correa pulchella* Zones 9-10. Hardy down to 20°F and drought tolerant once established. Grows 2-3 ft. tall and as wide, its pendant, bell-shaped salmon-pink flowers bloom from winter through spring. 'Pink Flamingo' is also deer resistant. Provide full sun and well-draining soil.

- CALIFORNIA DREAMERS FUCHSIAS *Fuchsia hybrida* Zones 9-11. Fist-sized-flowered Fuchsias on 6-12-in. tall plants are ideal for coastal areas and have no equal when it comes to size. Provide part shade to full shade and well-draining, acidic soil. 'Bella Rosella' bears pale pink petals with lavender centers, 'Deep Purple' is has white sepals, 'Rocket Fire' has red blooms and 'Flamenco Dancer' bears white sepal and red-marbled centered flowers. 'Snowburner' is more heat tolerant with pale inner pinkish petals and bold red outer petals.

- SHARK BAY BORONIA *Boronia crenulata* 'Shark Bay'. Zones 9-10. A dense, compact shrub 2-4 ft. tall and as wide with aromatic foliage and pale-pink flowers. Blooms year-round, but especially prolific from winter-spring. Hardy to 20°F, Shark Bay Boronia thrives in evenly moist soil, even clayey soil in full or part sun and performs beautifully in hanging baskets or in the landscape.

- SHRIMP PLANT *Justicia brandegeana* Zones 10-11. Shrub grows 3 ft. x 2 ft. and bears drooping red, rust, pink, salmon or yellow bracts with white inner flowers resembling colorful shrimps. Provide full or part sun in well-draining, humus-amended soil. Blooms year-round in mild climates.

WATERING GUIDELINE FOR BASINS

The following gives an idea about how much water it takes to fill basins depending on their diameters and berm heights. The volume of water a plant requires is the volume of water that transpires off its canopy and evaporates from the ground.
- 3 ft. diameter, 4 in. berm watering basin takes 20 gallons to fill.
- 3 ft. diameter, 6 in. berm watering basin takes 30 gallons to fill..

- 4 ft. diameter, 4 in. berm watering basin takes 30 gallons to fill.
- 4 ft. diameter, 6 in berm watering basin takes 50 gallons to fill.
- 6 ft. diameter, 4 in. berm watering basin takes 70 gallons to fill.
- 6 ft. diameter, 6 in. berm watering basin takes 150 gallons to fill.

SOIL MOISTURE TEST

The following helps to determine the wetness or dryness of the soil or use a tensiometer or dig down with a shovel.
- Take a handful of soil and try to form a ball with it. If soil does not form a ball, less than 50% of water is available to the soil and it is time to water (or if soil is gritty and drops through the fingers, it is dry and needs water).

- If the soil forms a ball but does not hold together it indicates 50-70% of water is available to the soil. Wait to water for another day or two.
- If the soil forms a ball without a shiny surface and crumbles apart, 75% water is available. Wait to water for a few days.

JANUARY

- Survey and repair irrigation systems to make sure they are in working order for spring.

- Where winters are mild, move or plant coniferous shrubs. Make sure they are planted at the same level as their original location.

- When transplanting an established shrub, tie a ribbon to the north side of the plant to maintain the same north orientation when positioning it in its new planting pit.

- Protect tender shrubs from damaging frosts with a cotton sheet or floating horticultural blanket just before the predicted freeze, but remove the covering during the day.

- Also spray cold-sensitive foliage with an anti-transpirant and where practical, string Christmas tree lights for a couple of extra degrees protection.

- Pick up and dispose of Camellia flowers and buds that are infected with Camellia petal blight. Break the soil-borne fungal cycle by applying a 2-in. layer of mulch and spray with compost tea.

FEBRUARY

- Rebuild watering basins and maintain 2-4 inches of organic mulch, but keep mulch 4-6 inches away from the base of a shrub's trunk or stem.

- Prune shrubs that bloom on current-season wood in late winter or early spring (40-60%) before the new flush of growth appears.

- Withhold fertilizing shrubs during winter, especially Camellias because they will drop their buds and flowers and begin to grow.

- Select Camellias and Azaleas while in bloom for color and form. When their blooms are spent, they start growing. Consider Satsuki Azaleas to extend the Azalea floral display as late as May.

- Water molds like *phytophthora* are fungi that destroy a plant's root system in dense, clay and continually wet soil. Apply compost tea, worm castings, humic acid and saponin to the soil.

- Populations of aphids and scale may overwinter and explode in spring. Get ahead of them by spraying shrubs with a canola-based horticultural oil.

MARCH

- Spring is the best time to plant (after the last frost) because the soils are warming and pliable.

- Test the pH of soil with a test kit available at nurseries. If the pH falls between 6.5-6.8, nutrients in the soil will be available for 95% of all shrubs.

- Cultivate the soil to suppress weeds and use a pre-emergent to eliminate the next generation of weeds, but do not apply if planting seeds in that area.

- If autumn and winter rainfall was below normal, supplemental watering is necessary, particularly when new growth emerges.

- Do not wait until a shrub's foliage wilts. Use a tensiometer or a shovel and dig down away from the shrub, to a depth of 12-18 inches. If dry at that level water again.

- Water shrubs in containers 2-3 times a week if the planting medium is well-draining and porous.

APRIL

- To improve soil texture, amend the soil with humus or mulch, add products with humic acid and saponin and apply compost tea.

- Determine the percolation rate by digging an 18-in.-deep hole and fill with water. After it drains, fill again. The second filling should drain at 1 inch per hour. If the pit drains at a slow rate, expand the planting pit deeper and wider.

- Excavate planting pits for new shrubs when the soil has warmed to 55°F and is workable.

- Increase the width of the planting pit to 3-4 times the breadth of the rootball to encourage rapid lateral growth, but the depth need not be any deeper than the height of the rootball.

- Scratch the inside surface of the hole with a cultivator so new roots will grow into the native soil.

- For mass plantings, excavate a trench 2-3 times the width of the rootballs.

MAY

- Other than California natives and plants that evolved from arid regions such as South Africa, Australia, southern Europe, fertilize with a complete, organic granular food three times, spring-summer. If a liquid organic fertilizer is used, increase to about 4-5 times, spring-early fall.

- For acid-loving shrubs such as Hydrangea, Azalea and Camellias, use an organic acid fertilizer or cottonseed meal after the flowers are spent.

- If not collecting seeds, clip off the faded flowers to direct the shrub's energy back into bud and growth development rather than seed production.

- To reduce moisture stress, maintain a 2-in. layer of mulch on the ground and below the canopy of all shrubs where practical, but keep the mulch away from their trunks or stems.

- Prune plants that bloom on second-year wood like Lilacs after their flowers are spent, but some Descanso hybrids may repeat bloom in the fall. If it is a repeat-bloomer, prune after autumn.

ROSE OF SHARON

JUNE

- Since most shrubs bloom during spring and summer, visit public gardens, local nurseries and walk the neighborhood for ideas that might work in your landscape.

- Photograph pleasing combinations of plants that have a useful scale for residential landscapes as well as similar maintenance and growth requirements.

- Plant shrubs during summer's heat in the morning or late afternoon, spray with an anti-transpirant and remove ⅓ of the foliage to reduce water loss through transpiration.

- When transplanting, apply a root stimulator containing indolebutyric acid or naphthalene-acetic acid three times, two weeks apart.

- The most efficient time to water shrubs in the summer is in late afternoon or early morning when there is time for absorbing roots to move moisture into their canopy.

- For containers, water between noon and 6 PM. Research indicates that morning watering stresses plants retarding their growth, whereas afternoon watering increases growth by as much as 70%. Afternoon showers are refreshing!

JULY

- Drip irrigation system is an effective method of conserving water during high-demand months. Use emitters that release 2 gallons per hour for shrubs.

- A programmable irrigation clock is an easy way to make seasonal and climatic adjustments.

- When weather is hot and dry, adjust irrigation clocks to water more frequently, except do not overwater established drought-tolerant shrubs such as Italian Cypress and Australian Fuchsia.

- High salt readings causes leaf burn or stunted growth. Irrigating deeply and infrequently benefits most shrubs because it dissolves and leaches soluble salts.

- Continue to apply organic liquid fertilizer once a month or a dry organic fertilizer every 6-8 weeks. Controlled-release fertilizers can be applied every 4-6 months, depending on the formulation.

- Treat weeds with a contact or systemic herbicide if there is sufficient space between the landscape shrubs. If not, physically remove the weeds and apply a pre-emergent weed control to eliminate the next generation of weeds.

AUGUST

- Prune in summer to control a shrub's size or shape after they have bloomed.

- Prune out dead, diseased branches and errant growth and open up the dense interior to allow sunlight to reach latent interior branch buds.

- Continue deadheading spent flowers, unless berries form to feed birds and other wildlife.

- Give shrubs a shower with an adjustable nozzle or hand-held fan sprinkler to wash off dust and debris.

- For gifts to yourself, family and friends, take semi-hardwood cuttings. Cut 4-6-in. sections (taken about 6 inches down or wherever the woody sections are less flexible). Clip off the bottom leaves and callus ends 12-24 hours.

- Dip ends in rooting hormone and cluster three cuttings in the middle of a 1-gallon black plastic nursery container. Fill with moistened perlite (50%) and organic potting soil (50%) and place a 2-liter soda pop bottle over pot for an instant greenhouse. Cuttings will root in 3-4 weeks.

SEPTEMBER

- Autumn is California's second best season to plant shrubs. The soils are still warm from summer's sun and root growth accelerates. Plant native and other water-thrifty shrubs now.

- Test soil pH levels in fall because salts accumulate during summer as watering frequencies increase and should be at their highest levels. High pH levels are indicators of problems with nutrient absorption.

- If pH levels are higher than 7.2-7.5, add soil sulfur 1 to 2 pounds per 100 square feet or calcium chloride 1 quart per 2½ gallons of water per 1000 sq. ft. Add 2-3 cubic yards of mulch, compost or worm castings.

- Add a humic acid product to all shrubs and the entire garden once in spring and once in fall.

- When the weather cools and rainfall is average, turn off the automatic irrigation and water manually if there is a dry spell.

OCTOBER

- After the Santa Ana, Diablo or Chinook winds but before winter's cold snap, shape espaliered shrubs like Pink Powder Puff.

- Control spider mites on Azaleas, Italian Cypress, Brugmansia, Rose of Sharon and Australia Fuchsias with a canola-based or other horticultural oil or systemic miticide. When using oil, wait until there are 3 days of clear weather before spraying.

- Discontinue fertilizing Camellias, Azaleas and other plants that are beginning to develop flower buds and beginning to go dormant.

- To increase the size of your Camellia blossoms, thin the developing buds where there are clusters of 5-7 buds. Cull 2-3 of them, making space for the remaining buds to fully open. Disbudding also directs the plant's energy toward producing large, perfect flowers.

- Plant fall-colorful shrubs like Cotoneaster, Nandina, Pyracantha, and Viburnum.

- Fall is the second or third time to apply a pre-emergent, but withhold if planting seeds in that area.

NOVEMBER

- Transplant germinated seedlings in peat pots and grow indoors in bright, indirect light or plant outdoors in mild winter regions.

- Keep Italian Cypress and other dense-leafed shrubs free of debris by washing with a strong stream of water into the dense foliage and branching structure.

- Move frost-tender shrubs in containers such as Shark Bay Boronia, Shrimp Plants and Fuchsias to more protected areas.

- Set up a 3 ft. x 3 ft. x 3 ft. composting bin to put in brown matter such as dried leaves and chipped branches, green matter like grass clippings and vegetative kitchen refuse (never meat) and livestock manure. The ratio of green to brown matter is 50-50 and layered like a lasagna. Turn the material over once a week. After 2-4 months (depending on the weather), it is ready to add to your garden as a soil amendment or as mulch.

DECEMBER

- Review your gardening journal for rainfall patterns and amounts, pest and disease problems and assess how new and established shrubs are faring as well as decide what new shrubs to plant.

- California's rainy season is November to mid-March. Unless there is a prolonged dry spell, supplemental watering is usually unnecessary.

- If rainfall is light it is more efficient to water deeply and infrequently rather than to water frequently and shallow amounts.

- During extended periods of drought, native and other established shrubs will have roots that extend well beyond their driplines and much deeper than the initial planting depths, so a deep soaking once a month should be sufficient.

- Cool, damp weather is the perfect environment for snails and slugs. Use an iron phosphate molluscicide because it is safe around pets and children and degrades into fertilizer. Available in Southern California, decollate snails prey on young brown garden snails, but don't use snail baits.

FIRETHORN

TREES
for California

Surrounding us in perfect botanical harmony are splendid trees that are either native to California or more often than not, transplanted from all over the world. In early spring, country roads and city streets light up when the golden flowers of Bailey's Acacias from Australia burst forth and smother their branches, followed by the hazy violet glow in late spring when the Jacarandas, our welcome travelers from Brazil, are in bloom. Summer's heat opens up the pink pompons of the Persian Silk Trees and the citrus-scented alabaster flowers of the Southern Magnolia.

By fall, the Sweet Gums and Japanese Maples are ablaze with shades of reds, oranges, and yellows, a final energetic burst before slumbering through the winter months. As if to celebrate the winter holidays, the Incense Cedars, nature's living garlands, are particularly aromatic after the rains. And Hong Kong Orchid Trees bear their spectacular lavender and pink flowers in defiance of cool winter and early spring months.

LOVELY PLANTS OF INESTIMABLE VALUE

No matter which season, trees are among the loveliest of living things—but they are not here as mere cosmetics, just to make our parks, streets and gardens look nice. They help produce the air we breathe, trap and hold pollutants, offset the buildup of carbon dioxide, control and stabilize the world's climate and feed and shelter much of the world's wildlife. An acre of trees supplies enough oxygen each day for eighteen people.

Trees reduce water loss caused by surface runoff, soil erosion by wind and water and the amount of harmful substances that wash into waterways. In addition to their economic value as lumber and sources of fuel, they screen unsightly views, soften harsh outlines of buildings, absorb and block noise and define space. Where would humankind be without trees?

As gardeners and tree lovers, our own gardens should contain at least one tree, and preferably more. Trees add beauty to homes and shelter us from the harsh sun and cold winds. If planted along the eastern and western walls of a house, they provide shade from the morning and afternoon sun. In winter, tall thick trees can deflect blustery winds over and around your home.

LEAVE A BOTANICAL FOOTPRINT

Planting trees is a way of leaving a botanical footprint long after we are gone. They link us to past events and eras. An old, gnarled, vase-shaped Common Olive Tree with multiple trunks stood in our Grandmother Asakawa's backyard. Every fall she and her friends would patiently gather its purplish-black bounty and cure them in an alkaline solution. Throughout the year, she would proudly share her jars of delicious home-preserved olives with her family. Even though it has been almost forty years since her passing, whenever we see an Olive Tree, it conjures up fond recollections of her.

In the spirit of our grandmother's tree as a connecting legacy from her to us, we recently planted a Crapemyrtle and a 'Pink Cloud' Flowering Cherry Tree—since they live for several hundred years, ours will probably remain to serve the next generation long after we are gone. There is comfort in knowing we have planted something with such beauty and longevity, connecting us to both the near and distant future.

PLANNING AHEAD

To ensure that your trees will live long and well, give them a helping hand by planning ahead. Since trees come in a variety of shapes and sizes from a few feet tall to towering giants, choose carefully so as not to underwhelm or overwhelm the location you have in mind. Whatever function you want the tree to fulfill—shade, privacy, shelter from wind—select the one most suitable and take into careful consideration the ultimate size, both height and width. That dainty Chinese Weeping Banyan Tree, otherwise known as a *Ficus benjamina*, is often sold in a six-inch pot, but it will eventually reach forty feet in height. Madrone and Camphor Trees have been known to touch the skies at sixty feet. If trees are planted too close to each other, they will compete for space, light, food, and water and may become deformed or stunted.

Avoid planting trees directly in front of windows and doors or close to paths, driveways, electrical wires, drainage pipes and gas lines. Careful placement is important because once trees are established they are difficult and often expensive to move.

Consider what the effect on both sides of the fence will be when your tree is mature. Be a considerate neighbor and think about whether or not your tree will cast unwelcome shade on the property of others, will block their view or if there will be bothersome flowers or fruits that may drop messily in their yard. Stepping in their shoes beforehand prevents feuds later.

TREES OF LIFE

Trees have tenaciously survived and adapted to many modern-day environmental stresses. They continue to inspire us, touch our spirits and connect us to our past, present, and future. The phrase "tree of life" is no exaggeration, for without them, there would be no miracle of life. Although this chapter includes only a minuscule sampling of the thousands of trees available, hopefully these few will inspire you to expand your repertoire of landscape sentinels.

OLIVE

Trees are astonishingly diverse and adaptable. One grove of Bristlecone Pines—the oldest living of trees—has survived an estimated 4,000 to 5,000 years in the gale force winds of California's White Mountain Range. The world's tallest trees, California's Coastal Redwoods, flourish under incessant rainfall. And the California Fan Palm endures searing desert heat.

Sacramento—known as the "City of Trees"—has a unique organization called "The Right Tree in the Right Place Committee." Charged with maintaining the city's urban forest, it works to maintain a diversity of tree species. Some municipalities have allowed one species of tree to cover an entire city—with often tragic results. If insects or pathogens invade one tree, the malady can quickly decimate an entire urban forest. Just like Sacramento's Tree Committee, we believe there is the right tree for the right place somewhere in your garden.

Of all the plants we cultivate, trees are the most dominant embellishment and the most permanent. They are the scene-setters and the mood-makers. Trees are also our spiritual sanctuaries, teaching us to reach for the skies. In one of our favorite stories, Jean Giono's *The Man Who Planted Trees*, Elzeard Bouffier spends his entire life transforming a desolate region of barren land and raging winds. By planting a forest of trees, life around him is reborn, filled with gentle breezes rustling though the leaves like the sound of water from the mountains. And in the process, he too is reborn.

As gardeners and lovers of trees, our family has planted many trees. They are the source of gardening inspiration and the connection to our past, present, and future—because without trees, there would be no miracle of life.

BAILEY'S ACACIA
Acacia baileyana

Hardiness—Zones 9-11

Color(s)—Canary-yellow flowers

Bloom Period—Early spring

Mature Size (H & W)—20 to 30 ft. x 25 to 40 ft.

Water Needs—Water about once a week until roots are established, then water once every two weeks or longer, depending on weather and growth conditions.

Planting/Care—Plant in fall or early spring from containers and space 15-20 ft. on center if planting in multiples. Provide well-draining, loam soil and protect from blustery winds. Fertilize in early spring with a complete, organic granular food.

Pests/Diseases—Few pests, but root rot may result from poor-draining soil.

Landscaping Tips & Ideas—Bailey's Acacia is a medium-sized, drought-tolerant ornamental that adapts to many California communities, including seaside. It is not a long-lived tree and should be replaced in 15-20 years. Use as a single specimen or combine with Bottlebrush, Silverberry and Japanese Mock Orange.

BRONZE LOQUAT
Eriobotrya deflexa

Hardiness—Zones 9-11

Color(s)—Creamy-white flowers, gold fruits

Bloom Period—Summer-early fall flowers, fall-winter fruits

Mature Size (H & W)—15 to 30 ft. x 20 ft.

Water Needs—Drought tolerant once established, but water every 7-10 days when newly planted.

Planting/Care—Plant in spring from containers, spacing multiple trees 20 ft. on center and single plants 15 ft. from structures or paved areas. Feed in late winter or early spring with a complete, organic granular fertilizer.

Pests/Diseases—Dieback among the branches may be due to fireblight. Cut off infected branches, disinfecting pruner after each cut with Physan and spray tree with compost tea.

Landscaping Tips & Ideas—Upright, vase-shaped form with bronze-tinted foliage and non-aggressive root system makes it an ideal medium-sized shade tree. For a smaller Loquat tree, select 'Coppertone' an evergreen that grows up to 15 ft.

CALIFORNIA SYCAMORE
Platanus racemosa

Hardiness—Zones 7-10

Color(s)—Greenish-yellow

Bloom Period—Spring

Mature Size (H & W)—60 ft. to 80 ft. x 60 ft.

Water Needs—Water every 5-7 days until established, thereafter water every 7-14 days, depending on weather and growth conditions. Withhold water during winter dormancy.

Planting/Care—Plant in fall or spring from containers and space 30-40 ft. on center and 30 ft. from any structure or paved area. Never plant over leach lines or under power lines. Provide full sun and well-draining soil.

Pests/Diseases—Sycamore blight attacks the ends of new growth annually, especially along the coast, but should not cause permanent harm. The wood growth becomes gnarled and irregular, creating an interesting silhouette.

Landscaping Tips & Ideas—One of the best shade trees for drier soils and climates and can be planted in lawns if there is excellent soil drainage.

CANARY ISLAND PINE
Pinus canariensis

Hardiness—Zones 9-11

Color(s)—Brown cones

Bloom Period—Late fall-early winter

Mature Size (H & W)—50 to 70 ft. x 20 ft.

Water Needs—Water once a week until established, thereafter water every 10-14 days, depending on weather and growth conditions.

Planting/Care—Plant in fall or spring from containers and space 15 ft. on center if planting in groups or 20 ft. from structures if planting a single tree. Provide full sun and well-draining soil.

Pests/Diseases—Clean out accumulated debris with a strong stream of water to get rid of havens for insect and disease.

Landscaping Tips & Ideas—Canary Island Pine comes from an area where rainfall is unpredictable and soil is thin, porous and volcanic. Use to give proportion to the house in relationship to the yard and to give depth by planting them in groups in the back.

CAMPHOR TREE
Cinnamomum camphora

Hardiness—Zones 9-11

Color(s)—Chartreuse

Bloom Period—Spring

Mature Size (H & W)—40 to 60 ft. x 50 to 80 ft.

Water Needs—Once established, water deeply and infrequently to encourage deep root development,

Planting/Care—Plant in fall or early spring from containers and keep it 30 ft. from structural or paved areas. Never plant over leach lines or under power lines. Provide full sun in well-draining, neutral soil and fertilize in late winter or early spring with a complete organic food.

Pests/Diseases—Generally insect free, but if mites become a problem in spring use a systemic miticide for mature trees.

Landscaping Tips & Ideas—Camphor Tree is a slow-growing evergreen that is a stunning ornamental if there is room. The essence of camphor oil is released when the leaves are rubbed. For a more uniform-growing tree, plant 'Majestic Beauty'.

CRAPEMYRTLE
Lagerstroemia indica

Hardiness—Zones 6-10

Color(s)—Magenta, pink, white, lavender, red

Bloom Period—Summer

Mature Size (H & W)—15 to 20 ft. x 20 ft.

Water Needs—Water deeply every 5-7 days until established, thereafter water every 7-10 days, depending on weather and growth conditions. Withhold water during winter dormancy.

Planting/Care—Plant in spring from containers and space multiple trees 15-20 ft. on center and keep 15 ft. away from a structure. Plant in full sun for optimum bloom, although it will survive in partial shade. Provide 6.7-7.2 pH, well-draining and porous soil.

Pests/Diseases—Susceptible to mildew and aphids, but can be controlled with a canola-based horticultural oil.

Landscaping Tips & Ideas—Deciduous, long-living, medium-sized tree that is beautiful any season of the year, even when barren in winter. Many hybrids such as 'Zuni' (dark lavender floral trusses) and 'Glendora White' (snow-white flowers) are more resistant to mildew.

DEODAR CEDAR
Cedrus deodara

Hardiness—Zones 8-10

Color(s)—Purplish-brown cones

Bloom Period—Fall-winter

Mature Size (H & W)—60 to 80 ft. x 25 to 40 ft.

Water Needs—When newly planted, soak deeply once a week until established, thereafter water every 10-14 days.

Planting/Care—Plant in spring from containers spacing 20-30 ft. on center and 20 ft. from structures. Provide full sun in well-drained, neutral soils.

Pests/Diseases—Few pest or disease problems, except if mites cause needle dieback, spray with a canola-based horticultural oil or use a systemic miticide.

Landscaping Tips & Ideas—Deodar Cedar grows rapidly and its pyramidal shape and outstretched branches is an ideal specimen for a large space and makes a good companion with Cotoneasters or in hybrid Tall Fescue lawns. 'Glauca' is the Blue Atlas Cedar and 'Aurea' is slower-growing with golden needles and 25 ft. tall.

EUROPEAN BIRCH
Betula alba

Hardiness—Zones 2-10

Color(s)—Insignificant

Bloom Period—Not applicable

Mature Size (H & W)—20 to 30 ft. x 15 to 20 ft.

Water Needs—Birches are riparian trees and need deep watering every 7-10 days once established. Withhold water during winter dormancy.

Planting/Care—Plant from bare-root or balled-and-burlapped stock in winter or from containers in spring. Space 10-20 ft. apart on center and 15-20 ft. away from structures. Provide full sun in well-draining, slightly acidic soil.

Pests/Diseases—Birch borers may attack when the tree is stressed from lack of moisture. Use a systemic with imidacloprid.

Landscaping Tips & Ideas—Deciduous Birches are graceful and pyramidal in shape and their winter-bare branches create an elegant silhouette against a dormant landscape. Select a Birch with multiple trunks for a visually interesting focal point. Plant with Saucer Magnolia, Silverberry and Cotoneaster.

FIREWHEEL TREE
Stenocarpus sinuatus

Hardiness—Zones 10-11

Color(s)—Reddish-orange

Bloom Period—Summer-fall

Mature Size (H & W)—20 to 30 ft. x 15 ft.

Water Needs—Water once a week until roots are established, thereafter water every 10-14 days, depending on weather and growth conditions.

Planting/Care—Plant from containers in spring or fall and space 15 ft. apart and 15 ft. away from structures. Provide full sun, humus-amended, well-drained and slightly acidic soil. While immature, prune for shape and be patient because it needs several years before bloom, but the wait is worth it.

Pests/Diseases—Few pests or disease problems but wash off accumulated debris periodically.

Landscaping Tips & Ideas—Native to Australia, the evergreen Firewheel Tree is slow-growing and bears tubular-shaped, red and yellow floral clusters resembling spokes on a wheel. Because of its flashy blossoms and little leaf drop, plant near patio, deck or pool.

FLOWERING CHERRY TREE

Prunus spp. x *hybrida*

Hardiness—Zones 4-10 depending on variety

Color(s)—Pink, white flowers.

Bloom Period—Spring

Mature Size (H & W)—12 to 25 ft. x as wide

Water Needs—To establish, water every 5-7 days, thereafter water every 7-14 days, depending on weather and growth conditions. Do not water during winter.

Planting/Care—Plant from bare rootstock in late winter or from containers in spring-fall. Provide full sun along coastal regions and partial shade for hot inland areas. Make sure the soil is rich, well-draining and slightly acidic.

Pests/Diseases—Root rot may occur with poor-draining soil.

Landscaping Tips & Ideas—Flowering Cherry Trees are must-haves for Japanese gardens or as shade trees. 'Kwanzan' bears double rose-pink flowers, while 'Snow Fountains' bears double-white blossoms. For mild winter regions, select the 20 ft. tall 'Pink Cloud' with deep-pink flowers.

FOREST PANSY REDBUD

Cercis canadensis 'Forest Pansy'

Hardiness—Zones 5-10

Color(s)—Deep-pink, white, lavender

Bloom Period—Spring

Mature Size (H & W)—12 to 20 ft. x 15 ft.

Water Needs—Water once a week until established, thereafter water every 10 days, depending on weather and growth conditions. Withhold water during winter dormancy.

Planting/Care—Plant from containers in spring or fall spacing 12-15 ft. apart and 10 ft. from structures. Provide full sun for maximum blooms and porous, neutral pH, well-draining soil.

Pests/Diseases—If leaf hoppers and grasshoppers destroy foliage, spray with Spinosad.

Landscaping Tips & Ideas—Western Redbuds (*C. occidentalis*) need winter chill for prolific blooms in early spring, but *C. canadensis* 'Forest Pansy' adapts to mild winter areas. Spring blossoms are replaced with scarlet-purple, heart-shaped leaves and morph in a blaze of autumnal hues. 'Forest Pansy' is perfect as an ornamental specimen for small gardens.

GINKGO (MAIDENHAIR TREE)

Ginkgo biloba

Hardiness—Zones 3-10

Color(s)—Gold leaves

Bloom Period—Fall

Mature Size (H & W)—35 to 50 ft. x 17 to 40 ft.

Water Needs—Water deeply every 7-10 days until 20 ft. tall, thereafter water once a month depending on growth and weather conditions. Withhold during winter dormancy.

Planting/Care—Plant from containers in spring spacing 20-30 ft. apart and 30 ft. away from structures. Provide full sun and porous, loam soil with a neutral pH. Prune for shape in late winter.

Pests/Diseases—Pest, disease, salt and smog resistant.

Landscaping Tips & Ideas—Female trees bear messy, odiferous fruit, so plant male trees. Known for its graceful, fan-shaped leaves, they are lovely in cut-flower arrangements and beautiful in the summer and fall garden. Use as a focal garden tree, street tree or bonsai. 'Jade Butterfly' grows to half the length of a standard Ginkgo.

GOLDEN RAIN TREE
Koelreuteria paniculata

Hardiness—Zones 5-10

Color(s)—Yellow

Bloom Period—Summer

Mature Size (H & W)—20 to 40 ft. x 30 ft.

Water Needs—Water every 5-7 days until established, thereafter every 7-10 days.

Planting/Care—Plant in spring or fall from containers spacing 30-40 ft. on center and 20-30 ft. away from structures. Provide full sun in well-draining acid or slightly alkaline soils (6.5-7.2 pH).

Pests/Diseases—Red-shouldered bugs suck on the leaves, stems and developing seeds. Rake up the fallen pods and spray with a canola-based horticultural oil or use a systemic insecticide with imidacloprid.

Landscaping Tips & Ideas—Deciduous Golden Rain Tree bears large clusters of fragrant, small, clear-yellow flowers with lush green compound leaves that turn a burnished gold in autumn. Use in a tropical landscape or as a patio or lawn tree. 'Rose Lantern' bears pinkish pods and 'Beachmaster' is a dwarf variety.

GRECIAN LAUREL
(SWEET BAY OR BAY LAUREL)
Laurus nobilis

Hardiness—Zones 8-11

Color(s)—Lemon-yellow, black fruit

Bloom Period—Spring flowers, fall fruit

Mature Size (H & W)—20 to 30 ft. x 25 ft.

Water Needs—Water 1-2 times a week until established, thereafter water every 10-14 days.

Planting/Care—Plant in spring or fall from containers, spacing 10-15 ft. apart and 15 ft. from structures. Provide full sun or part shade in loam, well-draining, neutral soil.

Pests/Diseases—Control brown soft scale with a canola-based horticultural oil. It is safe to use with plants with edible parts.

Landscaping Tips & Ideas—Use the foliage for seasoning sauces or marinades. Its handsome form and adaptability to a variety of soil types makes it a perfect companion to Prostrate Natal Plum, Glossy Abelia and English Ivy. 'Saratoga' is a smaller variety and makes an excellent patio tree and 'Aurea' bears yellow-tinged foliage.

HONG KONG ORCHID TREE
Bauhinia x blakeana

Hardiness—Zones 9-11

Color(s)—Wine-red, purple, pink

Bloom Period—Late winter-spring

Mature Size (H & W)—20 to 30 ft. x 25 ft.

Water Needs—Water established tree once a week or more during hot weather.

Planting/Care—Plant in spring or fall from containers spacing 15 ft. on center and 20 ft. away from structures and paved areas. Provide full sun with a well-draining, slightly acidic to neutral soil. In December, remove branches below 4-5 ft. to expose the trunk.

Pests/Diseases—Borers may attack when the tree is stressed from drought. Water regularly and use a systemic with imidacloprid.

Landscaping Tips & Ideas—One of the most beautiful trees, with large, fragrant, orchid-like flowers. Use *en masse* as a visual screen or plant a single tree as a focal point amidst other tropical plants like Angel's Trumpet, Plumeria and Hibiscus. and Banana Shrub.

INCENSE CEDAR
Calocedrus decurrens
(Libocedrus decurrens)

Hardiness—Zones 5-9

Color(s)—Brown cones

Bloom Period—Fall-winter

Mature Size (H & W)—60 to 70 ft. x 20 to 30 ft.

Water Needs—Water deeply every 7-10 days for the first two years, thereafter water every 10-14 days depending on weather and growth conditions.

Planting/Care—Plant in spring or fall from containers spacing 30-50 ft. on center and 35 ft. from structures or paved areas. Provide full sun in well-draining, porous and slightly acidic soil.

Pests/Diseases—Bark beetle attack trees under stress from drought or poor-draining soil. Add more organic amendments to the soil, water regularly and use a systemic insecticide with imidacloprid.

Landscaping Tips & Ideas—Incense Cedar has dense coniferous, cone-bearing branches with a shapely, pyramidal form. Found on 4,000-8,000-foot elevations, its aromatic fragrant branches are used in holiday décor. Makes a tall screen and windbreak.

JACARANDA
Jacaranda mimosifolia

Hardiness—Zones 9-11

Color(s)—Mauve-purple

Bloom Period—Spring

Mature Size (H & W)—25 to 40 ft. x 30 to 40 ft.

Water Needs—Water once a week until established, thereafter water every 10-20 days, depending on weather and growth conditions. Withhold water during winter dormancy.

Planting/Care—Plant in spring from containers spacing 20-30 ft. on center. Provide full sun in well-draining, sandy loam, neutral pH soil. Keep away from paved areas or structures.

Pests/Diseases—Control aphids by spraying with a canola-based horticultural oil or a systemic with imidacloprid.

Landscaping Tips & Ideas—Its gorgeous haze of trumpet flowers and fern-like green leaves provides spring and summer beauty to a water-thrifty garden. Combine with other waterwise plants such as Butterfly Bush, Echium and Cotoneaster. Do not plant in lawns, because it prefers to remain on the dry side. 'Alba' bears white, trumpet-shaped flowers.

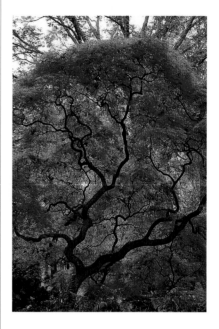

JAPANESE MAPLE
Acer palmatum

Hardiness—Zones 5-10

Color(s)—Purple, bronze, yellow, red leaves

Bloom Period—Fall

Mature Size (H & W)—15 to 30 ft. x 15 to 20 ft.

Water Needs—Once established, water every 5-7 days, depending on weather and growth conditions. Withhold during winter dormancy.

Planting/Care—Plant in spring or fall from containers. Space 10-12 ft. apart and provide part shade in humus amended, well-draining, slightly acidic soil.

Pests/Diseases—Control chewing insects with Spinosad.

Landscaping Tips & Ideas—Japanese Maples with their delicate canopies and autumnal blaze of brilliant-colored foliage thrive in raised beds or containers and shine in Asian-style landscapes, bonsai or rock gardens. Combine with Camellia, Azalea and Rhododendrons. 'Emperor I' adapts well to Southern California climates with dark red foliage that turns bright scarlet in fall. In cooler regions 'Sangokaku' has a stunning red trunk.

MADRONE
Arbutus menziesii

Hardiness—Zones 8-11

Color(s)—Cream flowers, orange-red fruits

Bloom Period—Spring flowers, summer fruits

Mature Size (H & W)—60 to 80 ft. x 60 ft.

Water Needs—Water deeply once a week until established, thereafter water every 14-30 days, depending on weather and growth conditions.

Planting/Care—Plant in fall from containers spacing 30-40 ft. from any structure and never over leach lines. Provide full sun in porous, loam-textured and acidic soil. Prune for shape.

Pests/Diseases—Few pest and disease problems, especially resistant to oak root fungus.

Landscaping Tips & Ideas—A California native, Madrone has an open canopy and airy branching structure. Its bark sheds revealing a smooth, rust-brown trunk. Fragrant blossoms bloom in spring followed by orange-red fruit. A beautiful specimen for large, open spaces along coastal areas. Combine with other natives like California Lilac, Silverberry and Prostrate Manzanita.

NEW ZEALAND CHRISTMAS TREE
Metrosideros tomentosa

Hardiness—Zones 10-11

Color(s)—Bright-red stamens

Bloom Period—Winter

Mature Size (H & W)—20 to 30 ft. x 25 ft.

Water Needs—Water once a week until established; thereafter water every 14 days or longer, depending on weather and growth conditions.

Planting/Care—Plant in spring from containers spacing 15-20 ft. on center and keep 20 ft. from a structure or paved area. Provide full sun in well-draining, acidic soil. Prune for shape and lace out to open up the dense canopy.

Pests/Diseases—If Eugenia Psyllid or Longhorned Borer attack, use a systemic with imidacloprid.

Landscaping Tips & Ideas—Medium-sized tree with multiple trunks that prefers coastal regions and adaptability to sandy soil, salt spray and prevailing ocean winds. It can also be trained into a hedge or visual screen. Ideal companion plants include Rock Cotoneaster and Gold mirror Plant. 'Variegata' has variegated-edged leaves.

OLIVE TREE
Olea europaea

Hardiness—Zones 9-11

Color(s)—Off-white flowers, blackish olives

Bloom Period—Spring flowers, summer olives

Mature Size (H & W)—15 to 25 ft. x 20 ft.

Water Needs—Water deeply once a week until established, thereafter water every 2 weeks or longer depending on growth and weather conditions.

Planting/Care—Plant from containers in spring or fall 15-20 ft. apart and 20-30 ft. from structures and paved areas. Provide full sun in well-draining, loam, slightly acidic soil.

Pests/Diseases—Control aphids and scale with a canola-based horticultural oil. Do not use a chemical systemic if harvesting olives.

Landscaping Tips & Ideas—A Mediterranean native, Olive trees take 10 years before producing fruits. Cure and process olives before eating. Spray with a plant growth regulator like Florel or Olive Stop if you do not want to harvest. Perfect for Mediterranean and water wise landscapes.

PEPPERMINT TREE
Agonis flexuosa

Hardiness—Zones 10-11

Color(s)—Small white flowers

Bloom Period—Summer-winter

Mature Size (H & W)—15 to 25 ft. x 15 ft.

Water Needs—Water once a week until established; thereafter water every 10-14 days or longer, depending on weather and growth conditions.

Planting/Care—Plant in spring or fall from containers and keep 15-20 ft. away from structures or paved areas. Provide full sun and well-draining humus-amended soil.

Pests/Diseases—For extensive spider mite damage, use a canola-based horticultural oil or a systemic miticide.

Landscaping Tips & Ideas—Native to Australia, the Peppermint Tree is an evergeen ideal for California gardens. Drought and heat resistant once established, use this spreading, medium-sized tree with weeping, willow-like foliage in a lawn, container for the patio or as an espalier. Leaves smell like peppermint when crushed. 'After Dark' has dramatic deep burgundy leaves.

PERSIAN SILK TREE
Albizia julibrissin

Hardiness—Zones 7-11

Color(s)—Pale-pink

Bloom Period—Summer

Mature Size (H & W)—30 ft. x 30 ft.

Water Needs—Water every 5-7 days until established, then water every 7-10 days. Withhold water during winter dormancy.

Planting/Care—Plant from containers in spring, spacing 20 ft. apart and 15-20 ft. away from structures, paved areas and leach lines. Provide full sun in loam-textured, well-draining and slightly acidic soil.

Pests/Diseases—Few pest or disease problems except for aphids in the spring. Spray with a canola-based horticultural oil or systemic insecticide with imidacloprid.

Landscaping Tips & Ideas—Persian Silk Tree is a beautiful addition to a tropical landscape with its pom-poms of white and deep pink, silky stamens, pea-like seedpods and feathery green foliage. Its spreading canopy provides shade and in the winter its deciduous, bare branches create an architectural silhouette. 'Rosea' bears deep-pink puffball flowers and 'Alba' floral clusters are white.

SOUTHERN MAGNOLIA
Magnolia grandiflora

Hardiness—Zones 7-11

Color(s)—Creamy-white

Bloom Period—Summer

Mature Size (H & W)—40 to 60 ft. x 50 ft.

Water Needs—Water every 5-7 days until established thereafter water every 7-10 days, depending on weather and growth conditions.

Planting/Care—Plant from containers in early spring or fall spacing 40 ft. apart and 30 ft. away from structures. Provide full sun in good-draining, humus-amended soil with a pH of 6.5-7.2.

Pests/Diseases—For scale spray with a canola-based horticultural oil if practical or use a systemic insecticide with imidacloprid.

Landscaping Tips & Ideas—Southern Magnolia is an evergreen tree with green lacquered foliage and plate-sized, citrus-scented blossoms. Flowers, seedpods and leaves are used in fresh arrangements. Makes a stately focal point in lawns or an attractive shade tree. 'St. Mary' and 'Little Gem' are good choices for smaller trees, but 'Majestic Beauty' lives up to its name at 35-40 ft.

SWEET GUM
Liquidambar styraciflua

Hardiness—Zones 6-10

Color(s)—Greenish flowers, brown spiky seed capsules

Bloom Period—Spring flowers, fall-winter seed capsules

Mature Size (H & W)—40 to 60 ft. x 50 ft.

Water Needs—Water once a week until established, thereafter water every 10-14 days, depending on weather and growth conditions. Withhold water during winter dormancy.

Planting/Care—Plant in spring or fall from containers spacing 20-30 ft. on center and 30-40 ft. from structures or paved areas. Provide full sun in rich loam, slightly acidic soil.

Pests/Diseases—Control the larvae of leaf rollers with a canola-based horticultural oil or use a systemic insecticide with imidacloprid.

Landscaping Tips & Ideas—The deciduous Liquidambars are used in expansive areas. For reliable fall color plant grafted varieties: 'Burgundy' bears purple-red foliage and 'Palo Alto' has extra large leaves that turn a bright orange-red in fall.

TABEBUIA (TRUMPET TREE)
Tabebuia spp.

Hardiness—Zones 9-11

Color(s)—Pink, yellow

Bloom Period—Late winter-spring

Mature Size (H & W)—25 to 50 ft. x 20 to 50 ft.

Water Needs—Water once a week until established; thereafter water every 10-14 days or longer, depending on weather and growth conditions.

Planting/Care—Plant in spring or fall from containers and keep 30 ft. away from structures or paved areas. Provide full sun in well-draining, loam-textured, slightly acidic soil. Feed with a complete organic fertilizer before buds swell.

Pests/Diseases—Few pests or diseases.

Landscaping Tips & Ideas—Tabebuia's bright clusters of large, trumpet-shaped flowers in pink with yellow throats and spreading canopy makes it a showy color-accented, semi-evergreen specimen tree, along driveways, in expansive lawns or in containers on patios. Flowers even more profusely as it matures. Other species bear yellow or purple blossoms. Drought tolerant once established.

TIPU TREE
Tipuana tipu

Hardiness—Zones 9-11

Color(s)—Yellow

Bloom Period—Late spring-early summer

Mature Size (H & W)—25 to 40 ft. x 30 to 60 ft.

Water Needs—Water once a week until established, thereafter water every 7-14 days, depending on weather and growth conditions.

Planting/Care—Plant in spring or fall from containers, spacing 30 ft. apart and 30 ft. away from structures or paved areas. Provide full sun in rich, well-draining, slightly acidic soils.

Pests/Diseases—Alkaline soils may cause yellowing of interveinal leaves. Feed with an organic acid or cottonseed meal fertilizer rather than chemical fertilizers.

Landscaping Tips & Ideas—Beautiful spring-to summer-blooming, semi-evergreen tree with lush panicles of sweet pea-like blossoms in apricot to yellow hues. Tipuana Tipu is a perfect lawn tree or shade tree for the deck or patio. Also use as a tropical accent.

TULIP TREE
Liriodendron tulipifera

Hardiness—Zones 5-10

Color(s)—Lime-green with orange centers

Bloom Period—Late spring

Mature Size (H & W)—60 to 80 ft. x 60 ft.

Water Needs—Water deeply once a week until established, thereafter water every 10-14 days, depending on weather and growth conditions. Withhold water during dormancy.

Planting/Care—Plant in spring or fall from containers spacing 40-60 ft. apart and 50 ft. from structures, paved areas and leach lines. Provide full sun and well-drained, loam, slightly acidic soil.

Pests/Diseases—Control aphid and leaf hopper damage with a canola-based horticultural oil and Spinosad or a systemic insecticide with imidacloprid.

Landscaping Tips & Ideas—Tulip Tree's flowers resemble Magnolia cup-shaped blossoms and cone-like seeds appear after flowers are spent. It is a stunning shade tree in a large landscaped area. 'Arnold' has a more compact appearance and 'Aureomarginatum' bears green leaves edged in bright yellow.

VICTORIAN BOX

Pittosporum undulatum

Hardiness—Zones 9-11

Color(s)—Cream

Bloom Period—Spring-early summer

Mature Size (H & W)—20 to 30 ft. x 30 ft.

Water Needs—Water deeply once a week until established, thereafter water 10-14 days, depending on growth and weather conditions.

Planting/Care—Plant in spring or fall from containers spacing 20 ft. from structures or in groups 12-15 ft. on center. Provide full sun (coastal regions) or part shade (inland areas) in loam, well-draining, slightly acidic soil.

Pests/Diseases—Black sooty mold results from aphid or scale excretion. Wash off the foliage with water and spray with a canola-based horticultural oil.

Landscaping Tips & Ideas—Victorian Box is a dense, bushy-crowned, evergreen tree with very fragrant, citrus-like blossoms. Use as a landscape tree or as a large shrub. Ideal companions include Japanese Mock Orange and Pink Indian Hawthorn. 'Variegatum' bears leaves with undulating white margins.

WHITE ALDER
Alnus rhombifolia

Hardiness—Zones 6-10

Color(s)—Deep-green foliage

Bloom Period—Not applicable

Mature Size (H & W)—25 to 40 ft. x 40 ft.

Water Needs—Water 1-2 times a week until established, thereafter water every 7-10 days, depending on growth and weather conditions. Withhold or decrease water during winter dormancy, but do not allow to dry out completely.

Planting/Care—Plant in spring or fall from containers spacing 20-30 ft. on center and 30 ft. away from structures and leach lines. Provide full sun in well-draining, loam, slightly acidic soil.

Pests/Diseases—Control chewing insect damage with Spinosad if practical or use a systemic insecticide with imidacloprid.

Landscaping Tips & Ideas—White Alders are fast-growing trees. Use as shade trees, as windbreaks, along waterways for erosion control and as background trees. These deciduous trees are riparian and do not tolerate drought conditions.

QUESTIONS TO ASK BEFORE SELECTING A TREE

1. Is the tree evergreen (E) or deciduous (D)?
2. Does the tree have a vertical (excurrent (X)), umbrella (decurrent (D)), or (O) form?
3. Does the tree tolerate drought? (Yes (Y) or No (N))
4. What is the average mature height and width of the tree?
5. Is the tree readily available? (Y) (N)
6. Are the branches brittle? (Y) (N)
7. Does the tree have brilliant flowers (Y) (N)? or foliage? (Y) (N)
8. Does the tree require yearly pruning? (Y) (N)
9. Will the tree survive freezing weather? (Y) (N)
10. Does the tree require a host-specific mycorrhizal fungus? (Y) (N)

	1	2	3	4	5	6	7	8	9	10
African Tulip Tree	D	X	Y	50'h–20'w	Y	Y	YN	N	N	N
Firewheel Tree	E	X	Y	30'h–20'w	N	N	YN	N	N	N
Forest Pansy Redbud	D	D	Y	15'h–10'w	Y	N	YY	N	Y	N
Japanese Black Pine	E	O	Y	30'h–20'w	Y	N	NN	N	Y	Y
Japanese Maple	D	D	N	20'h–20'w	Y	N	NY	N	Y	N
Karo Tree	E	O	Y	15'h–15'w	N	N	NN	N	N	N
Peppermint Tree	E	O	Y	20'h–20'w	Y	N	NN	N	Y	N
Pink Trumpet Tree	D	D	Y	30'h–40'w	Y	N	YN	N	Y	N
Tipu Tree	D	D	Y	40'h–60'w	Y	N	YN	N	Y	N
Toon Tree	D	D	Y	30'h–20'w	N	N	YY	N	Y	N

TREE SIZES

SMALL TREES (10 TO 12 FEET)
- Crapemyrtle (*Lagerstroemia indica*)
- Flowering Crabapple (*Malus floribunda*)
- Hawthorn (*Crataegus* spp.)
- Saucer Magnolia (*Magnolia* x *soulangiana*)

MID-SIZED TREES (20 TO 40 FEET)
- Bailey's Acacia (*Acacia baileyana*)
- Bronze Loquat (*Eriobotrya deflexa*)
- Chinese Weeping Banyan (*Ficus benjamina*)
- European Birch (*Betula alba*)
- Firewheel Tree (*Stenocarpus sinuatus*)
- Flowering Cherry Tree (*Prunus* spp. x *hybrida*)
- Forest Pansy Redbud (*Cercis canadensis* 'Forest Pansy')
- Golden Rain Tree (*Koelreuteria paniculata*)
- Grecian Laurel (*Laurus nobilis*)
- Hong Kong Orchid Tree (*Bauhinia* x *blakeana*)
- Jacaranda (*Jacaranda mimosifolia*)
- Japanese Maple (*Acer palmatum*)
- New Zealand Christmas Tree (*Metrosideros tomentosa*)
- Olive Tree (*Oleo europaea*)
- Peppermint Tree (*Agonis flexuosa*)
- Persian silk tree (*Albizia julibrissin*)
- Scarlet Flowering Eucalyptus (*Eucalyptus ficifolia*)
- Tabebuia (*Tabebuia* spp.)
- Tipu Tree (*Tipuana tipu*)
- Sweet Gum (*Liquidambar styraciflua*)
- Victorian Box (*Pittosporum undulatum*)
- White Alder (*Alnus rhombifolia*)

TALL TREES (OVER 40 FEET)
- California Sycamore (*Platanus racemosa*)
- Camphor Tree (*Cinnamomum camphora*)
- Canary Island Pine (*Pinus canariensis*)
- Deodor Cedar (*Cedrus deodora*)
- Ginkgo (*Ginkgo biloba*)
- Incense Cedar (*Calocedrus decurrens*)
- Italian Cypress (*Cupressus sempervirens*)
- Madrone (*Arbutus menziesii*)
- Southern Magnolia (*Magnolia grandiflora*)
- Tulip Tree (*Liriodendron tulipifera*)

PRUNING TIPS

PRUNING TOOLS

Pruning Tool	Branch Diameter	Blade Type	Use
Hand pruner	¾ in.	bypass	for general pruning
Hand pruner	½ in.	bypass	for thinning
Hand pruner	½ in.	bypass	for cut and hold (flowers & fruit)
Loppers	1½ in.	bypass	for heading back leaders
Hedge clippers	½ in.	bypass	for shearing hedges & ground covers
Knob cutter	1 in.	pinch	for close cutting bonsai pruning
Telescoping Pole pruner	1½ in.	bypass	for pruning branches from the ground
Telescoping Pole pruner	½ in.	bypass	cut and hold / fruit harvesting
Pruning saw	2 in.	pull	for removing branches
Chain saw	4 in.	gas/electric	for removing scaffolds

GENERAL PRUNING FOR ALL PLANTS

- Remove diseased, dead or interfering wood.

- Prune by thinning or heading.

- Thinning cuts open a plant's canopy to lower a plant's height, reduce the weight on branches, stimulate new growth and increase flowering and fruiting.

- Heading back (also known as shearing) increases the density of a plant's perimeter improving its ability to provide shade or screening. It removes current or one-year-old shoots down to a bud or stub and helps train young trees and shapes flowering trees and hedges.

- Cuts made flush with the surface of the supporting branch (flush cuts) are not recommended.

- Expose the least amount of surface to insect or disease by cutting just outside the branch bark ridge (the wrinkle of bark extending from the "V" at its point of attachment) and the collar (the raised bark below the V"). Cut up from the lower side of the branch 10-20% of the diameter and finish by cutting down from the upper side to meet the first cut.

PRUNING TIPS FOR TREES

- Do not apply a sealing compound over pruning cuts because it slows down natural compartmentalization (a tree or shrub's method of sealing of injured areas) unless there is insect or disease activity.

- If flowering trees bloom in clusters at the ends of branches, do not head back in fall or winter because you lose the next spring's blooms. Instead, prune shortly after blooms are spent.

- Lacing allows light to penetrate the tree's canopy stimulating new growth, improving air circulation and controlling pests.

- Prune off suckers that are growing from the lateral surface roots or from the area between a root flare and a bud or graft union.

- After pruning off the sucker, apply a sucker suppressant containing naphthalene acetic acid.

- If possible, wait until nesting birds have finished raising their young.

- To control the height and shape of pine trees, remove their candles (upright new growth).

- Trees growing in your garden that have branches or roots extending beyond your property line are normally your responsibility.

- Do not prune back a tree's branches when transplanting because this removes auxins (plant growth hormones concentrated in branch and twig tips that stimulate new root development) and hinders cytokinins (plant growth regulators in the root system that stimulates new canopy growth if it is damaged) from re-establishing the root system.

- When transplanting a tree, reduce moisture loss by pruning off 60-90% of its foliage.

THE PLANTING PIT

- Dig a rectilinear-shaped planting pit, not circular, to avoid roots from growing round and round and binding.

- In a rectilinear pit, the root system grows through the backfill to the corners enabling the roots to web into the native soil.

- Excavate a planting pit 1-1½ times the plant's original container depth and 4-6 times the plant's original container width to encourage important lateral roots.

- Roughen the pit's surfaces with a cultivator to further help the roots web into the native soil.

- Do not use rocks or gravel at the bottom of the planting pit because they do not improve drainage.

THE BACKFILL

- Amend backfill with organic material like humus or compost to create a texture halfway between that of the native soil and the plant's root ball.

- Tamp down the soil at the bottom of the pit to minimize settling of the root ball.

- Set the tree so its root ball is 1-2-inches higher than the finished elevation of the surrounding backfill to accommodate any future settling.

- Add humic acid and a product with saponin to encourage the proliferation of beneficial microbes and to increase the soil's porosity.

- Spread a complete organic, granular fertilizer along the inner perimeter of the watering basin.

- Water thoroughly to collapse any air pockets and apply a root stimulator containing indolebutyric or naphthalene acetic acid three times, two weeks apart.

TREE HAZARD CHECKLIST

- If a tree is leaning and its root system is lifting the surface soil, consult a certified arborist to determine if the situation is repairable or whether or not the tree and roots should be removed.

- A tree's branching structure over the roof of the house not only sheds debris on the roof, it may be a fire hazard.

- If a tree develops a coppice (an expanding group of trees)— a common trait of Aspen, Chinese Tree of Heaven, Toon Tree and Birch Trees—they can cover a large area very quickly.

MIMOSA

- When a tree has two leaders of equal importance, they can be bolted together with extra-long threaded ⅝-in.-diameter bolts or the branching structure can be guyed with steel cables and turnbuckles.

- When a tree has been topped and hat racked (pruned leaving a stubby portions of the tree's scaffold), the new growth is weak and breaks off easily during windy conditions.

- Even if a tree weathers the stress of wind, rain or drought, it is wise to survey for damage before planning any activity below or near the tree.

- If a tree has suffered mechanical damage from construction activity, hit by a vehicle or weed-whacked near its base, check for injury or insect infestation.

JANUARY

- Watering established trees during winter is usually not necessary, particularly dormant trees.

- If there is little or no rain, a thorough supplemental soaking of a tree's root zone once every 45-60 days should sustain most trees during winter.

- Do not fertilize trees during winter, especially deciduous trees because fertilizing them stimulates new tender growth that is vulnerable to freezing weather.

- Evergreen trees are in a state of suspended growth except for their root systems, which keeps growing while the trees take advantage of the rainy season.

- Do not stake and tie young trees tightly because it weakens them and may cause the trunks to snap as soon as the supports are removed. If it requires support, refer to the month of March for proper support techniques.

- Do not prune trees in winter unless there is a predicted hazardous situation such as torrential rains or ferocious winds. In those cases, reduce the trees' canopies.

FEBRUARY

- Wait until spring when new growth occurs before pruning off frost-damaged limbs. New growth indicates how far into the branches to prune.

- Also delay pruning until fledgling birds have left their nests. Contact your local Audubon Society for more information.

- When a tree is cut for firewood, stack in full sun away from structures, cover with plastic and secure to prevent critter and insect problems. Do not use for firewood if treated with chemicals.

- Discourage deer with olfactory repellents or motion-activated sprinklers or lights. Also, physically exclude them by surrounding trees with wire mesh baskets or by stretching clear, 100-pound-test monofilament line, deer-chest high around stakes surrounding the trees.

- Control boring insects like bark beetles with an insecticide containing imidacloprid. Pour mixture directly around the base of an ornamental tree. It translocates over 100 ft. and lasts for a year.

- Keep sucking insects and diseases from overwintering by applying a canola-based horticultural oil.

MARCH

- Planting trees in spring is ideal because it gives them until fall to re-establish.

- Drive around the neighborhood and list the mature trees that exhibit the form, color, proportion and size you believe will work well in your landscape.

- Also look for established tree roots that are breaking apart concrete, retaining walls or asphalt areas.

- Be aware of the positives and negatives of specific trees before purchasing. For example, Ginkgo Trees tolerate many climate and soil conditions, but female Ginkgos bear malodorous nuts, so plant only male Ginkgos.

- After the last freeze date, prune out frost-damaged branches just above the point where the new growth is emerging.

- In late winter or early spring, feed most trees with a complete, organic and granular fertilizer. Distribute the fertilizer in a band just inside the berm that surrounds the watering basins. A controlled-release fertilizer in another option and is applied every 4-6 months depending on the formulator.

APRIL

- Deep soak trees every 7-10 days during the growing season as long as the soil drains well.

- Apply a humic acid product to revitalize the soil twice a year, once in spring and again in autumn.

- Keep weed seeds from germinating by using a pre-emergent or hoe the weeds out, but avoid injuring the tree's root system.

- If a young sapling is tied to a single stake, remove to avoid girdling, instead install (2) 6-ft. stakes on opposite sides of the tree and 1 ft. away from its trunk. Using flexible garden ties, create a figure-eight pattern around the trunk and the two stakes to loosely support the tree.

- Before planting a container tree, thoroughly water, make three evenly spaced vertical cuts down its side and slip the plant out.

- If the root layer is matted loosen with a knife or a cultivator before setting the tree in the planting pit.

MAY

- 2-4 hours after watering established trees use a tensiometer near the tree's drip line to determine if the water has percolated down 18-24 inches. If the soil is dry at that depth, then extend the watering time the next time you irrigate.

- Do not overwater established drought-tolerant trees such as Olive and Jacaranda trees, especially in dense, clay soil. Allow them to dry out slightly between waterings.

- Contact your local utility company if a tree is growing too closely to power lines and do not plant a new tree under power lines unless approved by the utility company.

- No cause for alarm when mature Acacia and Magnolias drop their leaves each time a new flush of growth occurs.

- Do not plant deciduous trees like Silk Oak, Sycamore, Ash, Willow and Alder upwind from a swimming pool.

- If planting a California native or water-thrifty tree in free-draining soil, there is no need to amend the backfill.

JUNE

- When planting trees in summer thoroughly water them the day before, remove 40-60% of their foliage and spray the remaining foliage with an anti-transpirant to reduce moisture loss.

- Plant in the late afternoon rather than summer's midday heat or when it is dry and windy.

- Specimen trees may be costly, but they become the garden focal points and supporting plants can be incorporated later if budgets are limited.

- Repeat fertilizing established trees with a complete, organic granular fertilizer, but wait until summer-flowering trees like Pink Trumpet Tree and Tipuana Tipu have completed their bloom cycle.

- Solarize firewood logs in summer by covering with 4- to 6-millimeter clear plastic sheeting. Never apply pesticides to firewood because of potential toxic fumes when burning.

- For salt-sensitive trees such as Japanese Maples and Forest Pansy Redbud, add a surfactant with saponin when watering to help dissolve and leach out the salts every other month, from summer to fall.

JULY

- Summer is usually hot and dry. Irrigate under the tree's canopy and beyond the dripline where many of its absorbing roots are located.

- If unsure how much to water, monitor weekly for three months using a tensiometer to probe down 12-14 inches. If the soil is dry at that depth, give the entire root zone a thorough soaking.

- Be careful when using a weed-whacker around trees because it can damage the trunk and possibly destroy it.

- Sudden Summer Limb Drop is caused by increased pressure inside heavy horizontal limbs when there is hot, still air and minimal moisture loss through the tree's canopy. Weakened limbs may crash to the ground.

- Minimize Sudden Summer Limb Drop by not overwatering and increase transpiration by reducing insect and disease damage to the tree.

- Prune off suckers flush at the point of origin and spray with a plant growth regulator (alpha-naphthalene acetic acid) to suppress re-growth.

AUGUST

- Prune out vertical shoots that grow up through a tree's canopy or head back to fill a void in its canopy.

- Chimeras are peculiar mutant growths that have no common characteristics with the parent tree. Remove to maintain a uniform character.

- Prune back spring-and-summer-blooming trees after their flowers are spent. Also prune for shape and remove any dead, diseased or interfering branches.

- Some trees like California Sycamore and Crapemyrtles are prone to powdery mildew, especially when hot and humid. Wash with a strong stream of water or spray with a canola-based horticultural oil.

- Protect newly planted trees from sun scorch by spreading breathable horticultural cloths over their canopies and covering their trunks with a white water-based paint or wrapping them with a protective gauze.

- Roosting crows scare off other birds and prey on fledglings. Set up hawk or owl decoys or play a tape such as Johnny Stewart's "Death Cry of a Crow."

SEPTEMBER

- Autumn is an excellent time to plant California native and water-thrifty trees while the soil is still warm and just before the rainy season.

- When selecting a container tree, do not purchase if its roots are protruding out of the drainage holes, a sign of being root-bound.

- Where winters are mild, transplant sapling and dwarf (2- to 4-ft.) trees from one location to another (ground to ground). Orient at the new location in the same direction as it was before.

- Early fall is the third time to apply a complete, organic granular fertilizer for trees, except do not fertilize tropical trees because new growth is susceptible to cold damage.

- The Santa Ana, Cascade and Diablo winds common during fall dries and stresses trees. Thoroughly water the day before the wind's arrival.

- Apply a product with humic acid to help revitalize the soil and to help prepare trees for the winter months.

OCTOBER

- Mid-autumn to early spring is the rainy season in California. Native trees such as Coast Live Oaks and Black Walnuts have evolved to survive in this annual wet-then-dry weather cycles.

- Australian Firewheel, Peppermint and Pink Trumpet Trees come from similar wet-dry conditions and have little problem adapting to California regions where winters are mild.

- During a drought, provide supplemental irrigation for established water-thrifty and native trees.

- For trees that begin their dormancy in autumn, over-saturated soils may lead to anaerobic fungi, known as water molds. Open the berms surrounding the watering basins, allowing water to drain away from the soil around their trunks.

- Adjust irrigation clocks to accommodate changing weather conditions and growth patterns of the trees.

- Study the structural integrity of your trees, especially if you live in California's snow country. Contact a certified arborist at www.isa-arbor.com to properly assess suspected weak trees like hazardous cantilevers, uneven weight distribution and errant directional growth.

NOVEMBER

- Suppress annual and perennial weeds before the seasonal rains with a pre-emergent.

- Time to rake up the blanket of leaves and debris that have accumulated around your trees and chip or shred and then compost for future sources of mulch or soil amendment.

- Autumn is a good time to prune, but do not head back flowering trees that bloom in clusters at the ends of their branches such as Crapemyrtle, Saucer Magnolia, Jacaranda and Hong Kong Orchid trees. You will lose next spring or summer's flowers.

- Pollarding controls fast-growing trees such as Elm or Fruitless Mulberry trees. It heads back all the tree's growth to the same point on the primary scaffolds or trunk, but it will need to be done annually.

- Wrap a 3- to 4-in.-wide copper band around the base of tree trunks to keep snails out of trees. Copper generates a mild electrical current when a snail's slimy foot tries to cross.

DECEMBER

- At year's end, think about creating more pockets of shade and replacing or moving trees that are too close to structures, paved areas and leach lines.

- Many deciduous trees and conifers are available at nurseries as bareroot, balled-and-burlapped (B & B) or container stock.

- Most B & B trees are conifers grown in Oregon and shipped to communities with similar growing and soil conditions.

- Before selecting a new tree, consider the following: is it susceptible to insects or diseases; does it shed seeds (like Sweet Gum); does it spread pollen (such as Acacias); are the roots aggressive (like California and Brazilian Pepper trees); and does it produce allelopathic substances (certain trees deter other plants from growing around it such as California Black Walnut).

- Add water to make a slurry as the backfill is shoveled into the planting pit to collapse air pockets around and between the roots.

DEODAR CEDAR

JAPANESE MAPLE

WATERWISE
PLANTS
for California

Limited water supply, recurring drought, dry summers and firestorms are some of the challenges of living in our Golden State. Fortunately, there are many native and non-native plants that are not only waterwise and fire resistant but also add unique beauty and provide welcoming bird, bee and butterfly habitats to our gardens.

Average annual rainfalls in California vary greatly from region to region: Redding traditionally receives 33 inches; San Francisco normally has 20 inches; San Diego receives a mere 10.77 inches; Los Angeles County is anywhere from 13 to 20 inches.

Periodic droughts are a way of life for California. Since the 1920s, droughts spanning several years have occurred in the Sacramento and San Joaquin valleys from 1929 to 1934, 1976 to 1977, and 1987 to1992. Another drought lasted from late 1999 through 2004, south of Sacramento. During that period, the average for San Diego was below its average rainfall by as much as 5 to 7 inches. Now California is facing another drought and many experts are predicting it will be worse than those in 1987 and 1999.

Additionally, much of the state relies on the Sierra Nevada snowpack, particularly during summer. If Northern California's mountains experience light snowfall and a warm, dry, early spring, water supplies are compromised even more by a lack of snow, early thaw and runoff. Water agencies throughout the state are beginning to adopt conservation mandates.

Unlike other natural disasters such as floods, earthquakes, and fires—which require an immediate response with little time to prepare—the good news/bad news is that droughts occur slowly over a number of years. Rather than forget about the bad times during the years of plentiful rainfall, plan to incorporate plants that adapt to arid environments into your landscape design as a first line of defense against extended dry weather and firestorms.

XERISCAPE IS NOT "ZERO-SCAPE"

Xeriscape is a word that has become part of the popular vernacular for water-conscious gardeners.

It was coined and trademarked by the Denver Water Department in 1983 so that their carefully developed "Seven Principles of Xeriscape Landscaping" would remind everyone that the principles and the term, Xeriscape, would be forever linked together.

In 1986, the trademark was transferred to the National Xeriscape Council, Inc., a nonprofit entity that serves as a source of information about Xeriscape landscaping and as a support for the development of Xeriscape demonstration gardens across the United States.

The seven Xeriscape landscaping principles are:

- Start with a good design
- Improve the soil
- Limit lawn use
- Choose low-water need plants
- Water efficiently
- Mulch
- Practice good maintenance

These guidelines promote the idea that water conservation in the landscape is not "zero-scape" gardening. Instead they provide alternatives that are just as exciting as water-thirsty plants with an endless variety of flower and foliar color and texture.

BEAUTIFUL AND COLORFUL WATERWISE PLANTS

Despite the efforts of water departments and other water conservationists, myths abound when it comes to waterwise plants. They are not just prickly cacti sticking out of concrete or gravel beds, nor are they limited to the blah color spectrum from lackluster brown to gloomy grey. Instead of barren landscapes and wind-swept sand dunes, water-thrifty plants create colorful and beautiful gardens with lower water demands.

Besides stunningly colorful or fragrant California natives, many exotic species with similar low water and fertilizer needs endemic to Australia, New Zealand, South Africa, and the Mediterranean are adaptable to our soil and climate.

When you combine natives with these compatible out-of-towners, you lengthen the flowering season and brighten up the landscape.

DIAMOND FROST

There are additional reasons to consider water-thrifty plants. Many such as Sage and Lavender have resins that saturate the surrounding air with their fragrance on sultry afternoons, encouraging you to inhale nature's aromatherapy and exhale all of life's tensions. Others are nectar and seed factories that advertise their bounty to birds and butterflies. Butterfly Bush and Tower of Jewels will lure so many winged flutterers your garden may look like a wildlife refuge. Water-efficient shrubs, perennials, and trees will quiver with the activity of finches, hummingbirds, sparrows, butterflies, hover flies, honeybees, and other beneficial birds and insects.

PROBLEMS SOLVED

Drought-tolerant species are also problem solvers. Mahonia, Coyote Bush, New Zealand flax, Manzanita or Sumac stabilize slopes. If there are swaths of dry, light shade, Bush Anemone or Pacific Coast Iris will happily bloom for you in hot inland areas. Near wind-swept coastal areas and salt spray, Butterfly Bush and Lemonade Berry are ideal choices. For high elevations at 6,000 to 7,000 feet, Flannel Bush has survived for 60 million years while meeting additional challenges such as dry, granitic slopes and rocky ridges. If your garden is filled

with rocks and serpentine soils, Siskiyou Lewisia provides petite, daisy-like flowers growing from rosettes of greenery. Rock Purslane and Elephant Bush are attractive water-efficient succulents that thrive in the desert and other areas that average fewer than 10 inches of annual rainfall.

One of the most critical issues confronting California is making homes fire safe by creating a 100 feet of defensible space. Local fire departments suggest:

- Clear an area of 30 ft. immediately surrounding your home and incorporate low-growing plants with high moisture content.
- For the remaining 70 ft. or to the property line, create horizontal and vertical spacing between plants depending on slope grades and plant size to prevent fire from spreading.
- It is not necessary to cut down large trees as long as all of the plants beneath them are removed eliminating vertical "fire ladders."
- Remove all accumulated debris from the roof and gutters.
- Keep tree limbs trimmed 10 ft. from chimneys and remove dead limbs hanging over the home, garage or other structures.

BE WATERWISE

Indigenous plants offer a striking range of color for the drought-tolerant landscape and diverse plant groups have adapted well to California's seasonal rhythms of wet winters and dry summers. They all can be very useful in designing an easily maintained drought-tolerant, fire-resistant landscape.

When planning a new landscape or renovating part of an existing one, consider plants that do not require much water or maintenance, and yet are just as colorful and interesting as more water-thirsty plants. Hopefully, this chapter will inspire you to incorporate more waterwise plants that are also known for their "oohs-and-aahs" beauty.

AEONIUM
Aeonium hybrids

Hardiness—Zones 9-11

Color(s)—Depends on hybrid

Bloom Period—Spring-fall

Mature Size (H & W)—6 to 12 in. x as wide

Water Needs—Allow soil to dry slightly before watering. During winter dormancy, decrease to once a month.

Planting/Care—Plant from containers anytime from spring-summer or in fall where winters are mild. Provide full sun along the coast, but morning sun inland and plant in well-draining, cactus mix. Keep compact by pruning back leggy branches.

Pests/Diseases—Wash off aphids and mealybugs with a stream of water or spray with a canola-based horticultural oil.

Landscaping Tips & Ideas—Low-growing, mounded Aeoniums are decorative in rock gardens, combined with other waterwise plants in containers or in the front of borders. 'Kiwi' has rosettes of fleshy leaves with yellow centers that progressively transitions from lime-green to pink and edged in red. 'Zwartkop' bears dark maroon rosettes with chartreuse centers.

AFRICAN AZALEA
Ruttya fruticosa

Hardiness—Zones 8-11

Color(s)—Yellow, orange

Bloom Period—Spring-fall

Mature Size (H & W)—4 to 8 ft. x as wide

Water Needs—Water every 3-5 days until established, thereafter water every 7-10 days, depending on weather and growth conditions.

Planting/Care—Plant from containers in spring or fall. Provide full sun or part shade in well-draining, slightly acidic soil.

Pests/Diseases—Spider mites leave a silvery sheen on the foliage and webbing underneath. Spray with a canola-based horticultural oil or use a systemic miticide.

Landscaping Tips & Ideas—Endemic to Eastern Africa, *Ruttya* is drought tolerant once established. Where winters are mild, *Ruttya* bears clusters of brilliant-orange or yellow tubular flowers almost year-round. Nicknamed "Jammy Mouths" because of the dark, purplish black centers resembling mouths smeared with jam. Use in mixed containers or stand-alone pots or plant among other water-thrifty perennials and shrubs.

AFRICAN DAISY
Arctotis hybrids

Hardiness—Zones 8-11

Color(s)—Yellow, red, orange, hot pink, gold, peach

Bloom Period—Fall-spring

Mature Size (H & W)—12 to 14 in. x 12-16 in.

Water Needs—Water every 5-7 days until established, thereafter water every 7-10 days, depending on growth and weather conditions.

Planting/Care—Plant from containers in spring or fall. Provide full sun and well-draining, sandy loam, slightly acidic soil.

Pests/Diseases—Few insect or disease problems except poor-draining soil may lead to root rot.

Landscaping Tips & Ideas—Native to South Africa, it is an ideal plant choice for areas with mild winters. During the cooler months of the year, its colorful flowers heat up the landscape when other perennials have faded or are just beginning to bud. Use this colorful, compact plant with silver-green leaves to liven up mixed plantings in containers or in bedding plant areas.

AGAVE
Agave hybrids

Hardiness—Zones 7-11

Color(s)—Blue-green foliage

Bloom Period—Not applicable

Mature Size (H & W)—2 to 3 ft. x as wide

Water Needs—Once established wait until soil dries out slightly before watering again. During winter dormancy, water as little as once a month.

Planting/Care—Plant from containers anytime from spring-summer or in fall where winters are mild. Provide full sun along the coast, but morning sun inland and plant in well-draining, cactus mix.

Pests/Diseases—Agave snout weevil lays eggs at the base of the plant. Use a grub control with imidacloprid.

Landscaping Tips & Ideas—Agave hybrids add structure to containers, as single specimen focal points or in rock gardens with other water-thrifty plants. 'Blue Glow' is 2 ft. tall with blue-tinted spines and leaves edged in red. 'Shark Skin' bears smooth, bluish-grey, shark-like skin and 3 ft. upright leaves tipped in black.

ALOE
Aloe hybrids

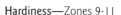

Hardiness—Zones 9-11

Color(s)—Foliage varies depending on hybrid.

Bloom Period—Winter-spring, but some species bloom summer or fall.

Mature Size (H & W)—2 to 8 in. x as wide depending on hybrid

Water Needs—Allow soil to dry out slightly before watering. During winter dormancy, water as little as once a month.

Planting/Care—Plant from containers anytime from spring-summer or in fall where winters are mild. Provide full sun along the coast, but morning sun inland and plant in well-draining, cactus mix.

Pests/Diseases—Control mites with a canola-based horticultural oil or a miticide.

Landscaping Tips & Ideas—Aloe hybrids are available with beautiful variegations on green to reddish foliage and add rich, colorful texture to containers or rock gardens. Sizes range from the petite 2-3-in. 'Diego' with white ridges on dark-green leaves and 4-6-in. 'Red' bearing bronze-orange ridges on light green foliage to the 6-8-in. 'Carmine' with silvery-green leaves edged in reddish-orange.

AUSTRALIAN FAN FLOWER
Scaevola hybrids

Hardiness—Zones 9-11

Color(s)—Lavender, periwinkle

Bloom Period—Spring-summer

Mature Size (H & W)—8 to 14 in. x as wide

Water Needs—Water about twice a week until established, thereafter water every 7-10 days, depending on weather and growth conditions.

Planting/Care—Plant from containers in spring-fall. Provide full sun in well-draining, loam, slightly acidic soil.

Pests/Diseases—Avoid root rot by planting in well-draining soil and do not overwater. Control caterpillars and thrips with Spinosad. Spray Spinosad in late afternoon after the bees have returned to their hives.

Landscaping Tips & Ideas—Australian Fan Flowers make a floriferous groundcover and an outstanding hanging basket specimen with branches smothered in fan-shaped flowers. Also use in combination planters with other heat-and-drought-tolerant plants. 'New Wonder' bears pastel flowers and the more diminutive 'Spring Secret' has deep periwinkle blossoms.

BACOPA (SUTERA)
Sutera hybrids

Hardiness—Zones 9-11 or treat as an annual

Color(s)—White, blue, pink, lavender

Bloom Period—Late spring to frost

Mature Size (H & W)—1 to 2 ft. x as wide

Water Needs—Water every 5-7 days until established, thereafter every 7-10 days, depending on weather and growth conditions.

Planting/Care—Plant from containers in spring-summer and fall where winters are mild. Provide full or part sun in well-draining, humus-amended, slightly acidic soil. Keep compact by pinching back branches regularly.

Pests/Diseases—Few insect or disease problems. Wash aphids off with a strong stream of water or spray with a canola-based horticultural oil.

Landscaping Tips & Ideas—Some Suteras are water thrifty once established like the Mighty Mights series bearing blue, lavender and mauve flowers and 'Gold 'n Pearls' with variegated yellow and green foliage and yellow-eyed white blossoms. Lovely as groundcover in small areas, mixed containers and hanging baskets.

BIRD OF PARADISE
Strelitzia reginae

Hardiness—Zones 10-11

Color(s)—Orange

Bloom Period—Spring, fall

Mature Size (H & W)—3 to 5 ft. (clumping)

Water Needs—Water deeply every 7-10 days once established during spring-summer, less frequently in winter.

Planting/Care—Plant from containers in spring and fall spacing 6 ft. on center. Provide full sun in porous, well-draining slightly acidic soil. Remove spent flowers and stems all the way down to the base. After about 3-5 years, divide in summer.

Pests/Diseases—In southern California control snails with decollate snails and in northern California use an iron phosphate bait.

Landscaping Tips & Ideas—A native of South Africa, there are few flowers more dramatic in form with their pointed beak-like flowers crowned with orange petals and blue-spiked corolla. It is a long-lived cut flower, a stunning accent in a tropical garden or in large terracotta pots on patios or decks.

BUTTERFLY BUSH
Buddleia davidii

Hardiness—Zones 5-10

Color(s)—Pink, blue, purple, red, white

Bloom Period—Summer

Mature Size (H & W)—4 to 8 ft. x 3 to 6 ft.

Water Needs—Water once a week until established, thereafter allow to dry slightly before watering, every 10-14 days.

Planting/Care—Plant from containers in spring or fall. Provide full sun and well-draining, loam, slightly acidic soil. Prune back in late fall-early winter to control size.

Pests/Diseases—Do not overwater because saturated soils can lead to root or crown rot. If encouraging butterflies, do not spray with any insecticides.

Landscaping Tips & Ideas—Butterfly Bush bears showy panicles of fragrant flowers and are good background, screening or accent plants. They are ideal in cottage gardens as well as a butterfly gardens. 'Black Knight' with violet-purple blossoms, 'Petite Snow' bears showy white flowers and 'Petite Plum' grows to 5 ft. with reddish-purple floral spikes.

CALIFORNIA LILAC
(WOOLLYLEAF CEANOTHUS)
Ceanothus tomentosus

Hardiness—Zones 8-10

Color(s)—Lilac-blue

Bloom Period—Spring

Mature Size (H & W)—6 to 12 ft. x 10 ft.

Water Needs—Water every 7-10 days until established, thereafter water once every 2-3 weeks, depending on weather and growth conditions. During normal rainy seasons, withhold water.

Planting/Care—Plant from containers in fall or spring spacing 10 ft. on center in a triangular or rectangular pattern if planting several. Provide full sun or part shade and well-draining, sandy loam soil. Fertilize in winter with a complete, organic granular food. Prune only to shape.

Pests/Diseases—In hot inland regions, do not water foliage because it may lead to fungal dieback. Root rot may also result from poor-draining soil.

Landscaping Tips & Ideas—Plant California Lilac in a waterwise landscape behind groundcovers and medium-sized shrubs. Combine with other drought-tolerant plants like Red Clusterberry Cotoneaster, Silverberry and Rock Rose.

CALANDRINIA
(ROCK PURSLANE)
Calandrinia grandiflora

Hardiness—Zones 8-10

Color(s)—Magenta

Bloom Period—Spring-fall

Mature Size (H & W)—1 to 3 ft. x 2 to 3 ft.

Water Needs—Water every 5-7 days until established, thereafter allow to dry slightly before watering (about 10-14 days). Withhold water during winter dormancy.

Planting/Care—Plant from containers in fall or spring spacing groups 2-3 ft. apart. Provide full sun in humus-amended, excellent-draining soil. Propagate by cuttings in spring.

Pests/Diseases—Few pests, but root or crown rot may develop as the result of overwatering or poorly draining soil.

Landscaping Tips & Ideas—Calandrinia bear gorgeous magenta flowers on tall, wiry stems that wave in gentle breezes. Even though the flowers are short-lived (24 hours), there are several buds on 18-36 in. stems that open up one at a time, for a long bloom period. Plant *en masse* in front of borders, as focal point in rock gardens or in containers.

CAPE MALLOW
Anisodontea hybrids

Hardiness—Zones 9-11 or treat as an annual.

Color(s)—Rose, light pink, cranberry

Bloom Period—Spring-fall

Mature Size (H & W)—2 to 3 ft. x 2 ft.

Water Needs—Water every 5-7 days until established, thereafter water every 7-10 days, depending on weather and growth conditions.

Planting/Care—Plant from containers spring-summer as well as fall where winters are mild. Provide full sun and well-draining, humus-rich, slightly acidic soil. Self-cleaning, no deadheading.

Pests/Diseases—Control spider mites and aphids with a canola-based horticultural oil.

Landscaping Tips & Ideas—Unlike many other *Anisodontea*, 'Barely Boysenberry', 'Slightly Strawberry' and 'Very Cranberry' are heat and drought tolerant. They all are upright, fast-growers and bear striking clusters of miniature hollyhock-like blossoms. Perfect for the back or mid-areas of mixed perennial beds or in large containers.

CARMEL CEANOTHUS
Ceanothus griseus

Hardiness—Zones 8-11

Color(s)—Blue

Bloom Period—Spring

Mature Size (H & W)—4 to 6 ft. x 6 to 10 ft.

Water Needs—Water every 7-10 days until established, thereafter water once every 2-3 weeks, depending on weather and growth conditions. During normal rainy seasons, withhold water.

Planting/Care—Plant from containers in fall or spring spacing 10 ft. apart. Provide full sun in humus-amended, well-draining soil. No need to deadhead or prune, except for shape.

Pests/Diseases—Wash off aphids with a strong stream of water or use a canola-based horticultural oil. Read about disease prevention under California Lilac.

Landscaping Tips & Ideas—Carmel Ceanothus is drought and seaside tolerant. Combine with other water-thrifty plants such as Rock Cotoneaster, Rock Rose and Dwarf Coyote Bush. 'Horizontalis' makes an excellent ground cover (2-3 ft.) with blue flowers and 'Frosty Blue' bears large blue flowers on 2-3-ft.-long spikes.

DIAMOND FROST
Euphorbia hypericifolia hybrid

Hardiness—Zones 9-11 or treat as an annual

Color(s)—White

Bloom Period—Year-round in mild climates

Mature Size (H & W)—10 to 14 in. x as wide

Water Needs—Water 1-2 times a week until established, thereafter water every 7-10 days, depending on weather and growth conditions.

Planting/Care—Plant in spring, summer or fall from containers. Provide full sun or part shade in well-draining loam and slightly acidic soil.

Pests/Diseases—Deer resistant with few disease or insect problems.

Landscaping Tips & Ideas—Diamond Frost is a *Euphorbia* with exceptional heat and drought tolerance and beautiful too! Its delicate, airy-white flowers cover lime-green foliage almost year-round in mild climates. During winter, combine Diamond Frost for a flurry of snowflake-like flowers with Poinsettias in mixed borders or containers. Combines well with other waterwise plants no matter what the season.

DWARF JADE PLANT

Crassula argentea 'Nana'

Hardiness—Zones 10-11

Color(s)—Pink

Bloom Period—Fall

Mature Size (H & W)—1 to 2 ft. x 2 to 3 ft.

Water Needs—Keep moist but not soggy until established, thereafter allow to dry out slightly before watering again (about once every 2-3 weeks).

Planting/Care—Plant from containers in fall or spring spacing 18 in. on center. Provide full sun, part shade or shade and do best in good-draining, loam, slightly acidic soils. Propagate from cuttings.

Pests/Diseases—Keep snails away with an iron phosphate bait or use decollate snails in southern California.

Landscaping Tips & Ideas—Dwarf Jade Plants are compact and have a natural rounded shape. Use as border plants as well as in rock gardens and containers. Because the fleshy leaves are high in moisture, they are perfect to plant within 30 ft. of a home or other structure as a fire-resistant barrier.

FLANNEL BUSH

Fremontodendron

Hardiness—Zones 8-11

Color(s)—Bright-yellow

Bloom Period—Spring

Mature Size (H & W)—Up to 20 ft. x 12 ft.

Water Needs—Water only during periods of extended drought.

Planting/Care—Plant from containers in fall or spring. Provide full sun and excellent-draining, sandy loam, slightly alkaline soil. If possible plant on a slope. While young, stake plant for extra support and protection during windy periods. To control size and encourage more branching, pinch back new growth regularly.

Pests/Diseases—Root rot is a common problem when soils are poor-draining and wet.

Landscaping Tips & Ideas—Flannel Bush bears brilliant yellow, 5-petaled flowers in spring that gives way to ciliated brown seedpods with dark green, fuzzy foliage. Plant where it has plenty of room to stretch. In chilly climates, place against a sunny wall for extra warmth. For people with sensitive skin, it is best to wear gloves when handling Flannel Bush.

GOLDEN MIRROR PLANT

Coprosma repens 'Aurea'

Hardiness—Zones 9-11

Color(s)—Green, gold foliage

Bloom Period—Not applicable

Mature Size (H & W)—3 to 4 ft. x 4 to 6 ft.

Water Needs—Water every 7 days until established, thereafter water when soil dries slightly (every 10-14 days). Withhold water during rainy season.

Planting/Care—Plant in fall or spring from containers spacing them 6 ft. on center. Provide full sun or part shade in well-draining, slightly alkaline soils.

Pests/Diseases—Control snails and slugs with an iron phosphate molluscicide.

Landscaping Tips & Ideas—The Golden Mirror Plant is a low-growing, spreading shrub with shiny, green-and-gold foliage. Found naturally along the seacoast, it tolerates strong winds, but not freezing temperatures. Use *en masse* as hedges and windbreaks and with other waterwise plants. 'Marble Queen' bears variegated green and white leaves and 'Pink Splendor' has deep-green leaves with yellow margins that turn pink.

GUMI (GOUMI)
Elaegnus multiflora

Hardiness—Zones 4-9

Color(s)—Cream flowers, red berries

Bloom Period—Spring flowers, fall berries

Mature Size (H & W)—6-8 ft. x as wide

Water Needs—Water every 7-10 days until established, thereafter water when soil dries out slightly. Withhold water during rainy season.

Planting/Care—Plant from containers in spring or fall spacing them 6 ft. apart or 4 ft. for hedges. Provide full sun and well-draining, slightly acidic to alkaline soil.

Pests/Diseases—Rarely has insect or disease problems

Landscaping Tips & Ideas—From China and Japan, Gumi is a deciduous shrub with silvery-green foliage on top and brownish-silver underneath. The tiny, fragrant spring flowers give way to reddish-orange berries summer-fall. A very ornamental plant that also functions beautifully in an edible, wildlife-friendly or drought-tolerant landscape and bonsai. 'Sweet Scarlet' berries are slightly tart and used in sauces, juices, pies and jelly. Birds love them too.

LAVENDER STARFLOWER
Grewia caffra

Hardiness—Zones 10-11

Color(s)—Lavender-blue

Bloom Period—Spring-fall

Mature Size (H & W)—6 to 10 ft. x as wide

Water Needs—Water every 5-7 days until established, thereafter water every 10-14 days, depending on weather and growth conditions.

Planting/Care—Plant in spring or fall from containers spacing them 6-8 ft. on center. Provide full sun in well-draining, humus-amended, slightly acidic soil. Flowers are self-cleaning.

Pests/Diseases—Susceptible to root rot in poor-draining soils, but otherwise few pest or disease problems.

Landscaping Tips & Ideas—Native to South Africa, the Lavender Starflower is a fast-growing shrub with tiered branches. It is a wonderful espalier plant or trained against a wall, fence or trellis. Perfect for a small space area and in large containers. Combine with other low water usage plants like Gumi, Rock Rose and Silverberry.

LEWISIA
Lewisia cotyledon hybrids

Hardiness—Zones 3-10

Color(s)—White, pink, red, peach, yellow with contrasting stripes

Bloom Period—Spring-fall

Mature Size (H & W)—12 in. x 10 in.

Water Needs—Water every 7-10 days until established, thereafter wait until soil dries out slightly before watering.

Planting/Care—Plant in spring or fall from containers spacing them 10-12 inches apart. Must be grown in fast-draining, slightly acidic soil mixed with gravel. Provide full sun along the coast and partial shade inland.

Pests/Diseases—Prevent root or crown rot by providing excellent drainage and planting them at the same level or slightly higher than its original container.

Landscaping Tips & Ideas—Lewisia comes in a rainbow of colorful flowers rising from green rosettes and are perfect in rock gardens, as drought-tolerant container plants and planted in the cracks of walls. 'Sunset Strain' bears apricot, rose and yellow blossoms and 'Little Plum' boasts purple-pink flowers.

MATILIJA POPPY
Romneya coulteri

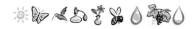

Hardiness—Zones 7-10

Color(s)—White

Bloom Period—Spring-summer

Mature Size (H & W)—8 to 10 ft. x 3 ft.

Water Needs—Once established, no supplemental water is necessary.

Planting/Care—Plant from containers in spring or fall. Provide full sun and well-draining soil. Cut down to the plant's base in late fall. New growth emerges during winter rains.

Pests/Diseases—Deer resistant. Wash off mealybugs and aphids with a strong stream of water or use a canola-based horticultural oil.

Landscaping Tips & Ideas—Matilija Poppy is known as the "fried egg plant" because of its spectacular 4-9-in. diameter, chalk-white flowers with golden eyes. Its blooms are the largest of any California native. The caveat is that it can be invasive and is not recommended for small gardens. Excellent as erosion control on slopes and in expansive water-thrifty gardens. Also lovely in cut flower arrangements.

PRIDE OF MADEIRA
Echium candicans

Hardiness—Zones 9-10

Color(s)—Blue

Bloom Period—Spring-summer

Mature Size (H & W)—6 to 8 ft. x 12 ft.

Water Needs—Water about once a week until established, thereafter water when soil dries slightly once every 2-3 weeks. Withhold water during seasonal rains.

Planting/Care—Plant in fall or spring from containers spacing them 8-10 ft, on center. Provide full sun and porous, slightly acidic soil. Prune to control size and shape in fall and deadhead.

Pests/Diseases—Few pests and diseases. The pubescent foliar texture discourages chewing insects.

Landscaping Tips & Ideas—Pride of Madeira's stature and spectacular spikes of clustered lavender-blue flowers are excellent for steep slopes, in hummingbird-butterfly gardens, seaside areas and as background plants with Butterfly Bush and Glossy Abelia. It can also be used in cut flower arrangements. Tower of Jewels is another *Echium* species that bear salmon-colored flower heads.

PTILOTUS (MULLA MULLA)
Ptilotus 'Platinum Wallaby'

Hardiness—Zones 9-11 or treat as an annual

Color(s)—Purple

Bloom Period—Spring-summer

Mature Size (H & W)—12 to 18 in. x 12 in.

Water Needs—Water every 5-7 days until established, thereafter every 10-14 days, depending on weather and growth conditions.

Planting/Care—Plant in spring or fall from containers. Provide full sun and well-draining, loam, alkaline soil. No need to deadhead.

Pests/Diseases—If chewing insect damage is extensive, spray with Spinosad. Wait until the late afternoon when the bees have returned to their hive before spraying.

Landscaping Tips & Ideas—Ptilotus is native to Australia and is heat and drought tolerant. 'Platinum Wallaby' bears lavender feathery blooms practically year-round in mild-winter regions, but where winter freezes are common, treat it as an annual. Use in the middle of mixed containers or water-thrifty flower beds. 'Joey' bears smaller flowers and needs acid soil.

RED CLUSTERBERRY COTONEASTER

Cotoneaster lacteus

Hardiness—Zones 7-10

Color(s)—White flowers, red berries

Bloom Period—Summer blooms, fall-winter berries

Mature Size (H & W)—6 to 8 ft. x 8 ft.

Water Needs—Water every 7-10 days until established, thereafter water once every 2-3 weeks, depending on weather and growth conditions. Withhold water during seasonal rains.

Planting/Care—Plant in fall or spring from containers spacing them 10-12 ft. on center. Provide full sun or partial shade in porous, well-draining, neutral pH soil. Prune only for shape or to remove deadwood.

Pests/Diseases—Few disease or insect problems affect Cotoneasters.

Landscaping Tips & Ideas—Red Clusterberry Cotoneaster is larger and less dense compared to other Cotoneasters. The deep-red clusters of berries contrast dramatically with the dull, gray-green foliage from fall-winter. Use as a screen and plant with other water-thrifty plants such as Silverberry and Butterfly Bush.

RED HOT POKER

Kniphofia hybrids

Hardiness—Zones 5-9

Color(s)—Red, orange, peach, yellow, white, pale green

Bloom Period—Summer, spring or winter depending on hybrid

Mature Size (H & W)—1½ to 8 ft. x clumping

Water Needs—Water every 7 days until established, thereafter wait until soil dries slightly before watering again. During the rainy season, withhold watering.

Planting/Care—Plant in fall or spring from containers spacing 2-8 ft. on center. Provide full sun or part shade and well-draining soil. Where winter freezes are common, tie leaves over their clumps in fall.

Pests/Diseases—Few disease, insect problems and is deer resistant

Landscaping Tips & Ideas—Plant Red Hot Pokers close to the house for colorful vertical accents as well as fire-resistance. 'Christmas Cheer' flowers from fall-late spring, but needs space for its 6-8 ft. height. 'Flamenco' is 2-3 ft. with spikes of red, orange and yellow.

RICE FLOWER

Ozothamnus diosmifolis

Hardiness—Zones 9-10

Color(s)—Rose, white

Bloom Period—Spring-summer

Mature Size (H & W)—24 to 40 in. x as wide

Water Needs—Water every 7 days until established, thereafter wait until soil dries slightly before watering again. During the rainy season, withhold watering.

Planting/Care—Plant in fall or spring from containers spacing 2-3 ft. on center. Provide full sun and well-draining, slightly acidic soil. Prune back after bloom cycle to keep it compact. Use only organic fertilizers, because high phosphorous fertilizers will kill it.

Pests/Diseases—Few disease, insect problems, but susceptible to root rot if planted in poor-draining soil.

Landscaping Tips & Ideas—Perfect flowering landscape shrub for mixed beds in a waterwise garden or containers. As a cut flower, it is an excellent filler with each stem bearing up to 100 buds and lasts about two weeks.

ROCK AND ROCKSPRAY COTONEASTER

Cotoneaster horizontalis, C. microphyllus

Hardiness—Zones 5-10

Color(s)—Pink flowers, red berries

Bloom Period—Spring flowers, fall berries

Mature Size (H & W)—2 to 3 ft. x 4 to 6 ft.

Water Needs—Water every 7 days until established, then wait until soil dries slightly before watering again, once every 2-3 weeks. During the rainy season, do not water.

Planting/Care—Plant in fall or spring from containers spacing 4-6 ft. on center. Provide full sun or part shade and well-draining soil.

Pests/Diseases—If aphid damage is extensive, spray with a stream of water or use a canola-based horticultural oil.

Landscaping Tips & Ideas—Rockspray Cotoneaster grows in mounds and can be pruned into formalized shapes and Rock Cotoneaster has a fan-like spreading habit. Both are ideal for waterwise groundcovers and cascading over rocks. Also a fire-resistant plant to use in the 30-ft. zone around a home.

ROCK ROSE

Cistus x purpureus

Hardiness—Zones 8-10

Color(s)—Pink, white, purple

Bloom Period—Spring

Mature Size (H & W)—4 ft. x 4 ft.

Water Needs—Water every 7-10 days until established, thereafter water infrequently about once every 2-3 weeks and withhold during fall-winter rains.

Planting/Care—Plant in fall or spring from containers spacing 6-8 ft. on center.

Pests/Diseases—Deer resistant with few disease or insect problems.

Landscaping Tips & Ideas—Rock Rose is a Mediterranean native where annual rainfall is minimal. The flowers resemble wild roses with distinctive reddish-maroon brush marks at the base of each petal. Excellent shrub for waterwise gardens and a good companion for California Lilac and Pride of Madeira. 'Brilliancy' bears clear pink flowers and 'Betty Taudevin' produces deep, reddish-pink blossoms. 'Alan Fradd' has papery-white flowers.

SEDUM (STONECROP)

Sedum rupestre

Hardiness—Zones 4-9

Color(s)—Yellow flowers

Bloom Period—Summer

Mature Size (H & W)—4 in. x 2 ft.

Water Needs—Keep moist, not soggy until established, thereafter water when soil dries and withhold during winter dormancy.

Planting/Care—Plant from containers in spring-fall spacing them 2 ft. apart. Provide full sun or part shade and excellent-draining, sandy soil.

Pests/Diseases—Deer resistant. Control mealybugs and scale with a canola-based horticultural oil and use an iron phosphate bait to get rid of snails and slugs.

Landscaping Tips & Ideas—The 3-6 in. tall 'Angelina' has golden-yellow, needle like foliage with a trailing habit and 'Lemon Coral' is taller at 6-8 in. and has a brighter yellow color with a more upright habit. Use these evergreen succulents in rock gardens, in front of borders, water-thrifty containers or contrast with dark-foliaged, drought-tolerant plants. 'Angelina' is also attractive draping over stone walls or rocks.

SENECIO
(BLUE CHALK FINGERS)
Senecio vitalis 'Serpents'

Hardiness—Zones 10-11 or treat as an annual

Color(s)—Green-blue leaves

Bloom Period—Not applicable

Mature Size (H & W)—18 in. x as wide

Water Needs—Keep moist but not soggy until established, thereafter allow to dry out slightly before watering again (about once every 2-3 weeks).

Planting/Care—Plant from containers in spring-fall spacing 8-10 in apart. Provide full sun or part shade and excellent-draining, sandy soil.

Pests/Diseases—Few pests or disease problems, except overwatering and poorly draining soils often leads to root rot.

Landscaping Tips & Ideas—Senecios vary from Dusty Miller to Cineraria, but 'Serpents' is a unique succulent with densely-packed, needle-like, blue-green foliage that tolerates full sun and partial shade. It is stunning in mixed cactus or succulent containers, waterwise planting beds and can even be acclimated to indoor conditions as a houseplant provided there is sufficient bright, indirect light.

SILVERBERRY
Elaeagnus pungens

Hardiness—Zones 8-11

Color(s)—Creamy-white

Bloom Period—Fall

Mature Size (H & W)—6 to 8 ft. x as wide

Water Needs—Water every 7-10 days until established, thereafter water when soil dries slightly about once every 2-3 weeks depending on weather and growth conditions.

Planting/Care—Plant in fall or spring from containers spacing 6-8 ft. on center. Provide full sun or part shade and well-draining, neutral pH soil. Prune for shape.

Pests/Diseases—Deer resistant. Control rust with a canola-based horticultural oil.

Landscaping Tips & Ideas—Silverberry is a large shrub with a natural, loose-growing form. Use for a background plant, barrier planting or visual screen. Grayish-green foliage with fragrant flowers in spring resembling tiny, elongated bells followed by red berries fall-winter. Seashore, drought- and wind-tolerant once established. 'Fruitlandii' has large, silver- colored foliage, 'Variegata' leaves are edged in yellow and 'Marginata' is edged in silvery-white.

YEW PINE
Podocarpus macrophyllus

Hardiness—Zones 8-11

Color(s)—Dark-green foliage

Bloom Period—Not applicable

Mature Size (H & W)—8 to 15 ft. x 2 to 4 ft.

Water Needs—Water every 7-10 days until established, thereafter water every 2 weeks depending on weather and growth conditions.

Planting/Care—Plant in fall or spring from containers spacing them 4 ft. on center or 3 ft. on center if using as a hedge. Provide full or part sun and porous, well-drained, neutral pH soil. Can prune into a hedge.

Pests/Diseases—Control aphids or scale with a canola-based horticultural oil and periodically wash out accumulated debris.

Landscaping Tips & Ideas—The Yew Pine's dense, evergreen, columnar form is popular in formal landscapes, as narrow hedges or between windows. An excellent choice for foundation plantings, visual screens or boundary definitions. 'Maki' grows a shorter 8-10 ft. and is also popular with bonsai enthusiasts.

MORE WATERWISE RECOMMENDATIONS

DROUGHT-TOLERANT NATIVE PLANT RECOMMENDATIONS

- California Laurel, *Umbellularia californica* (tree)
- California Fan Palm, *Washingtonia filifera* (tree)
- California Fuchsia, *Zauschneria californica*, (perennial)
- California Lilac, *Ceanothus* spp., (shrub)
- California Poppy, *Eschscholzia californica* (perennial; often grown as annual)
- Coast Live Oak, *Quercus agrifolia* (tree)
- Coast Redwood, *Sequoia sempervirens* (tree)
- California Sycamore, *Platanus racemosa* (tree)
- California Toyon, *Heteromeles arbutifolia* (shrub)
- Dwarf Coyote Bush, *Baccharis pilularis* (shrub)

- Flannel bush, *Fremontodendron californicum* (shrub)
- Manzanita, *Arctostaphylos* spp. (shrub)
- Matilija Poppy, *Romneya coulteri* (perennial)
- Monkeyflower, *Mimulus* spp. (perennial)
- Oregon Grape, *Mahonia aquifolium* (shrub)
- Penstemon, *Penstemon* spp. (perennial)
- Pine, *Pinus* spp. (tree) (also non-native spp.)
- Siskiyou Lewisia, *Lewisia cotyledon* (perennial)
- Western Columbine, *Aquilegia formosa* (perennial)
- Western Redbud, *Cercis occidentalis* (shrub or tree)
- Yarrow, *Achillea* (perennial)

DROUGHT-TOLERANT NON-NATIVE PLANT RECOMMENDATIONS

- Acacia, *Acacia* spp. (shrub or tree)
- *Banksia* spp. (shrub)
- Bottlebrush, *Callistemon citrinus* (shrub)
- Butterfly Bush, *Buddleja* spp. (shrub)
- California Pepper, *Schinus molle* (tree)
- Cape Plumbago, *Plumbago auriculata* (shrub)
- Carob Tree, *Ceratonia siliqu* (tree)
- Chinese Pistache, *Pistacia chinensis* (tree)
- Coast Rosemary, *Westringia fruticosa* (shrub)
- Cotoneaster, *Cotoneaster* spp. (shrub)
- Crape Myrtle, *Lagerstroemia indica* (shrub/tree)
- Deodar Cedar, *Cedrus deodara* (tree)
- Dusty Miller, *Senecio cineraria* (perennial)
- Elephant Bush or Elephant Food, *Portulacaria afra* (succulent)
- Eucalyptus, *Eucalyptus* spp. (tree/shrub) (perennial)
- Firewheel Tree, *Stenocarpus sinuatus* (tree)
- Geraldton, *Chamelaucium uncinatum*
- Grevillea, *Grevillea* spp. (shrub/tree)
- Hopseed Bush, *Dodonaea viscosa* (shrub)
- Juniper, *Juniperus* spp. (shrub/tree)

- Lantana *Lantana* spp. (perennial)
- Lavender, *Lavendula* spp. (perennial)
- Leucadendron, *Leucadendron* spp., (shrub)
- New Zealand flax, *Phormium* spp. (shrub)
- Oak, *Quercus* spp. (tree)
- Olive, *Olea europaea* (tree)
- Pincushion, *Leucospermum* spp. (shrub)
- Pine Trees, *Pinus* spp. (tree) (also Native spp.)
- Pomegranate, *Punica granatum* (tree/ shrub)
- Pride of Madeira, *Echium candicans* (shrub)
- Protea, *Protea* spp. (shrub)
- Red-Hot Poker, *Kniphofia uvaria* (perennial)
- Rock Purslane, *Calandrinia grandiflora*
- Rosemary, *Rosmarinus* spp. (herb)
- Strawberry Tree, *Arbutus unedo* (shrub
- Tea Tree, *Leptospermum* spp. (shrub/tree)
- Tower of Jewels, *Echium wildpretii* (shrub)
- Trumpet Vine, *Campsis radicans* (vine)
- Waratah, *Telopea* spp. (shrub)
- Wisteria, *Wisteria* spp. (vine)
- Xylosma, *Xylosma congestum* (shrub)

DEER-RESISTANT PLANTS

"Deer resistant" is a relative term depending on the plant's toxicity as well as the individual deer's culinary palate and level of hunger. The following are some suggestions:
- Beard-Tongue (*Penstemon* spp.)
- Bush Anemone (*Carpenteria californica*)
- Butterfly Bush (*Buddleia davidii*)
- California Lilac (*Ceanothus* spp., primarily small-leaved spp. or hybrids)
- California Poppy (*Eschscholzia californica*)
- Century plant (*Agave americana*)

- Coyote Bush (*Baccharis pilularis*)
- Manzanita (*Arctostaphylos* spp.)
- Matilija Poppy (*Romneya coulteri*)
- Monkeyflower (*Mimulus* spp.)
- Oregon Grape (*Mahonia* spp.)
- Rock Rose (*Cistus* spp.)
- Spanish Bayonet (*Yucca* spp.)
- Stone Crop (*Sedum* spp.)
- Tower of Jewels (*Echium wildpretii*)

JANUARY

- Learn what natives grow nearby. Write down their growth habits and under what conditions—sun, shade, rock outcroppings, or stream beds.

- Cultural compatibility is of primary importance in determining if specific drought-tolerant plants will thrive. Select the largest plants first because they set the stage for the space and place smaller water-thrifty varieties in mass plantings, clustered in groups or drifts separate from water-thirsty plants.

- If your property has a wilderness view, take advantage of the "borrowed scenery" and select the same plants that are thriving at the edges of your landscape.

- Check for faulty sprinklers, emitters and irrigation lines and repair them so that they are in working order for the upcoming spring months.

- Winter rains encourage weeds to germinate. If you are not planting from seed, apply a pre-emergent to suppress weeds before they appear.

- Protect plants from browsing deer with physical barriers such as wire enclosures, olfactory repellants and deer-resistant plants.

FEBRUARY

- Winter is a good time to start drought-tolerant native and exotic annuals and perennials from seed indoors. Use a sterile, porous commercial cactus or seed-starting mix.

- For cacti and succulents, sow seeds in small 2- to 4-in. pots and cover with ¼ inch of fine potting mix or grit. Spray thoroughly without dislodging the seeds. Also provide a plant heat mat and keep at 70-75 degrees.

- Once seedlings have emerged, place in bright indirect light or under grow lights. Begin feeding after second set of true leaves emerge with an organic liquid fertilizer diluted to ¼ strength every time they are watered.

- Transplant when seedlings are one-inch or larger in 2-in. pots. Handle seedlings carefully and repot at the same depth and in the same type of potting medium.

- Withhold watering newly transplanted seedlings for a few days and return them to a place with bright, indirect light. Allow to dry out slightly between watering intervals.

MARCH

- Visit Mother Nature's wildflower displays at Anza Borrego, Bear Valley, Carrizo Plain and Antelope Valley.

- While hiking in the backcountry, snap photos of interesting plants and take them to your nursery or public garden for proper identification.

- If you do decide to "go native" buy from a retailer specializing in native seeds. Native plants and their seeds need to be left alone in the wild if they are to survive.

- Spring is the time to plant California natives and other water-thrifty varieties, especially where winter freezes are common.

- If transplanting a waterwise plant from a container, dig a rectilinear-shaped pit to discourage roots from circling themselves.

- Match the texture of the excavated soil to the texture of the soil in the rootball. If the excavated soil is denser than the rootball soil, blend in organic humus material into the excavated soil. The final backfill should be about 30-40% of organic material.

APRIL

- Spring is one of the best times to plant, re-pot or take cuttings from most cacti and succulents while they are in their growth cycle.

- Build watering basins around large shrubs twice the diameter of their canopies and form 4-in. berms.

- At planting apply a product rich in humic acid and use a root stimulator with naphthalene acetic or indolebutyric acid, three times, two weeks apart.

- For plants with crowns like Aeonium and Lewisia, mulch around their crowns with 1-2 inches of pea gravel to keep moisture away from their crowns.

- Prune most blooming shrubs after their flowers are spent.

- Large, rangy plants like Flannel Bush and Butterfly Bush benefit from hard pruning once they are established.

- Dark discolorations and soft spots on drought-resistant plants such as cacti and succulents are signs of rotting tissue usually caused by poor drainage or too much water. Cut back on watering and improve drainage.

MAY

- Feed native and waterwise plants with a complete organic fertilizer every 45-60 days during the growing season or use a controlled release fertilizer.

- Drought-tolerance refers to an established plant's ability to survive drought, but all native and waterwise plants require regular water the first year or two, about once a week.

- Once waterwise plants develop deep roots, most can survive 2-3 weeks between watering intervals.

- Most cacti and succulents have shallow root systems because in their native habitats, rainfall occurs in sudden downpours. Soak established cacti and succulents thoroughly and wait until the soil dries before watering again.

- Pull weeds before they go to seed and use a pre-emergent weed control to prevent future weeds from germinating.

- Allow seedpods to ripen on the plant before harvesting. Clean off any chaff or pulp from fruits or pods, dry the seeds, store in a clean jar or envelope and place in a cool, dry place.

JUNE

- Summer is still a good time to plant or transplant cacti and succulents because most are still in their growth cycle.

- Spray transplanted selections with an anti-transpirant and apply a root stimulator three times, once every two weeks.

- Although most succulent and cactus plants have shallow root systems, they conserve moisture by a process called Crassulacean Acid Metabolism (CAM) where the stomata close during hot, dry days and open during cool, humid nights.

- Even though established drought-resistant plants survive heat and dry conditions, they will look better with watering whenever summer temperatures rise to the 90s and above.

- To plant succulents in containers, select pots that are wide and shallow for a showy display.

- Clay pots are perfect for waterwise plants, but they dry out faster than those planted in the ground. Stick your finger into the top inch of the soil and water if it feels dry to the touch.

JULY

- The more you include and establish waterwise plants, the less you need to irrigate.

- Water early in the morning or early evening for the most efficient time to irrigate.

- From mid-to late summer start preparing the ground for fall planting. Till in 4-6 inches of organic soil amendment, humus, compost or worm castings down to a depth of 18 inches for trees, shrubs and perennial flowerbeds.

- Break up the ground and pulverize dirt clods thoroughly to prepare an area for annual wildflower seeds. Hoe out weeds and water the area for several weeks prior to fall planting.

- If foliage shows green veins and yellow interveins it may indicate chlorosis. Spray with a chelated iron product.

- Maintain 2 inches of humus or compost over the surface around plants to conserve water, keep the weeds down and stabilize soil temperature, but keep 2-4 inches away from the trunk or main stem.

AUGUST

- Compost piles work faster in hot weather. Keep them turned and moist.

- To control rampant or leggy growth, reduce the size of the plant by 20-40% and lace dense interiors to let in more sunlight.

- Deadhead spent flowers to encourage more blooms unless you are saving seeds.

- Whiteflies may collect on the undersides of leaves especially Butterfly Bush, Matilija Poppy and Flannel Bush. Giant whitefly leave white, cotton candy-like streamers. Spray with a canola-based horticultural oil or a systemic insecticide with imidacloprid.

- Water-thrifty plants are susceptible to phytophthora, a fungal root rot that attacks plants when they have been overwatered in heavy clay soils. Treat with compost tea, a product with humic acid and apply a 1-in. layer of worm castings. All help increase the beneficial microbes and oxygen supply in the soil.

- Avoid spraying water directly on top of plants that are susceptible to crown rot such as Lewisia and Calandrinia.

SEPTEMBER

- Nurseries have a good selection of native and waterwise plants in fall and will provide helpful cultural information.

- Fall is not only an excellent time to plant drought-tolerant specimen where winters are mild, but also for cold-winter regions if there are at least six weeks before the ground freezes. If not, wait until spring.

- As daylight hours decrease, reduce watering to about once a month even if there is no rain. During normal rainfall, most can survive without supplemental irrigation.

- Site tall, water-thrifty plants such as Ceanothus, Matilija Poppy, Butterfly Bush and Flannel Bush on the outer perimeters of your landscape and fleshier, lower-growing varieties such as Sedum, Aloe and Agaves closer to the house as a fire-resistant zone.

- In clay soils, plant drought-tolerant specimen on slopes, raised beds or containers.

- Deer may visit gardens to browse in autumn. Plant deer-resistant plants like Ceanothus 'Blue Sapphire'. For more deer-resistant plants, see pg. 258.

OCTOBER

- Plant most drought-tolerant selections about 1 inch above the surrounding soil to account for settling.

- Maintain a 2-in. layer of mulch around plants, but keep 2-4 inches away from plant stems or trunks. Mulch with pea gravel around plants susceptible to crown rot.

- Plant California native seeds now and broadcast by hand or spreader and lightly rake in about $1/16$ to $1/3$ inch deep. For large areas, scatter a thin covering of organic mulch over the sown seeds.

- For a natural drift of wildflowers, plant in swaths 50-100 ft. long and 20 ft. wide. Spread 50 pounds per acre or 1 quart of seeds for 200-500 square feet for a high rate of coverage.

- Sow California Poppy seeds directly where you want them because they do not transplant well.

- Seedlings may be mistaken for weeds in their early development. Plant some in containers with labels to properly identify them in the landscape.

NOVEMBER

- The best time to divide many succulent and cacti plants is when they are dormant in fall or winter. After divisions callus over, plant them in a cactus mix and water sparingly until new growth is evident.

- Seedlings and transplants need time and adequate water to establish their root systems.

- For the first year or two, water every other week along the coast, once a week inland and adjust for weather, soil and growth conditions. Once established, most survive on winter rains and an occasional summer watering.

- During heavy rainfall, if there are basins built around waterwise trees and shrubs, open a section of each basin to drain off excess water.

- Withhold fertilizing when water-thrifty plants go dormant. Exceptions are certain species of *Aeonium, Crassula* and *Epiphyllum* that continue to grow from fall-winter.

- After Matilija Poppy leaves turn yellow and brown, cut down to 4-6 inches or all the way to the ground.

DECEMBER

- Take advantage of a lull in gardening by reviewing catalogues and searching websites for information about waterwise and fire-resistant garden designs as well as plant selections.

- Whether starting a brand-new drought-tolerant landscape or partially replacing a water-thirsty garden, learn more about your local climate and unique microclimates in your yard.

- Visit water conservation gardens, sign up for workshops at local schools and nurseries and join local garden clubs and societies.

- Make a rough sketch noting the existing trees, shrubs, beds and current structures to determine appropriate sites for waterwise plants and fire-resistant zones.

- Set out rain gauges and high-low thermometers to record in your garden journal.

- If you forgot to plant California wildflowers in fall, there is still time to sow seeds. Plant in full sun and water until they germinate if no winter rains arrive. California Poppies and Lupines do particularly well in our Golden State.

ROCK ROSE

BOTANICAL NAME INDEX

COMMON NAME INDEX

NOTES